YES! *WELL* ...

THE HISTORICAL SERIES OF THE REFORMED CHURCH IN AMERICA
NO. 87

YES! *WELL*...

Exploring the Past, Present, and Future of the

Church: Essays in Honor of John W. Coakley

James Hart Brumm, Editor

WILLIAM B. EERDMANS PUBLISHING COMPANY
Grand Rapids, Michigan / Cambridge, UK

Wm. B. Eerdmans Publishing Co.
2140 Oak Industrial Drive SE, Grand Rapids, Michigan 49503
PO Box 163, Cambridge CB3 9PU UK
www.eerdmans.com

Printed in the United States of America

Library of Congress Cataloging-in-Publication Data

Cataloguing data applied for and in process.

For Margaret, Mary, Philip, and John,

who came to NBTS

and enriched the life of our community

as well as the Reformed Church in America

The Historical Series of the Reformed Church in America

The series was inaugurated in 1968 by the General Synod of the Reformed Church in America acting through the Commission on History to communicate the church's heritage and collective memory and to reflect on our identity and mission, encouraging historical scholarship which informs both church and academy.

www.rca.org/series

General Editor
>   Rev. Donald J. Bruggink, PhD, DD
>   Western Theological Seminary
>   Van Raalte Institute, Hope College

Associate Editor
>   James Hart Brumm, MDiv
>   Blooming Grove, New York
>   New Brunswick Theological Seminary

Production Editor
>   Russell L. Gasero
>   Archives, Reformed Church in America

Commission on History
>   James Hart Brumm, MDiv, Blooming Grove, New York
>   David M. Tripold, PhD, Monmouth University
>   Douglas Van Aartsen, MDiv, Ireton, IA
>   Matthew Van Maastricht, MDiv, Milwaukee, Wisconsin
>   Linda Walvoord, PhD, University of Cincinnati

Contents

...

Preface

In September of 1984, I had my first day of classes at New Brunswick Theological Seminary. So did John Coakley. We met in Classroom Two of Zwemer Hall; he wore a suit and tie and sneakers—I believe the sneakers accommodated his walk to campus from his home in Highland Park—but didn't yet have his beard, and he wrote careful outlines on the chalkboard, then lectured according to the outline. I was left believing that this was how all church historians presented their lectures—John W. Beardslee, III, would disabuse me of that—and that John Coakley was slightly rumpled, very wise, and very polite—none of that would change in thirty-two years.

As a polite, thoughtful person, John never wanted to be rude to anybody. As a gifted scholar, John never wanted to actually affirm us in ideas or opinions that were anything less than well-informed and cogent. This, I think, led to a phrase John has been heard to use often (by this author, at least): "Yes! Well . . ."

"Yes! Well . . ." is a marvelously vague phrase that seems to be applicable in a number of contexts. There is the "Yes, well" that allows the speaker a bit of time to contemplate an appropriate response—helpful for scholars who have no pipe to light. There is also the "Yes! Well . . ." that can politely replace expressions of utter disbelief at absurd statements, allowing one time to change the subject or excuse yourself from the situation.

But the "Yes! Well . . ." that all of John's students probably hoped he used the most with us, the one that is meant by the title of this festschrift, is one of affirmation and challenge. "Yes," the listener is on the right track, and has gotten things right as far as things went; "well," there is more to be said, further to go.

John would affirm all of us, but always challenge us to go further, to say more, to dig a bit deeper. At least with my generation of students, he would challenge us to develop our "So What? Bone"—this was another contender for a title for this book. He told us it wasn't enough to find some new facet to the thought of some saint who had gone before us or some interesting aspect to some long-ago event; we also had to think about what difference it made to the contemporary church and the congregations we served. This is a "Bone" I have tried to develop in my own students.

The essays in this volume involve areas of thought and practice to which John has devoted his mind and teaching. And his thinking and teaching have informed all of us who have written here. My thanks to everyone who has contributed to this book: the authors who have set aside time to share their talents here; the members of the RCA Commission on History, who allowed for an express process for this volume in the *Historical Series*; Ramona Larsen and Steve Mann, who helped surreptitiously collect photos of John which Willem Mineur has capably used in the cover; and Gregg Mast, who provided crucial help in funding, and the Reformed Church Center Committee at NBTS, who supported this grand scheme. Most special thanks go to Donald Bruggink, General Editor of the *Historical Series* since its inception, who has taught me so much about working with authors and putting books like this together, and to Russell Gasero, Archivist of the RCA and Production Editor for the *Historical Series*, who has had my back every inch of the way through this project. My name gets to be on the cover, but all of them have done great honor to John.

The occasion of John Coakley's retirement is, I am sure, another "Yes! Well . . ." moment: yes, he is putting a period on an illustrious teaching career that has been a gift to the whole Church in ways we can only begin to imagine. Well, now that this is done, there is more for him to say, deeper digging to be done, and more questions to answer, which I am sure his scholarship and writing will be answering, providing challenges to all of our thinking for many years to come.

Soli Deo Gloria!
James Hart Brumm
The third Sunday of Easter, 2016

Contributors

Thomas A. Boogart is Dennis and Betty Voskuil Professor of Old Testament at Western Theological Seminary in Holland, Michigan.

James Hart Brumm is pastor and teacher of Blooming Grove Reformed Church, DeFreestville, New York, director of the Reformed Church Center at New Brunswick Theological Seminary in New Brunswick, New Jersey, and author of approximately 200 published hymns.

Kathleen Hart Brumm is a minister of Columbia-Greene Classis, Reformed Church in America, and an author, composer, and children's choir clinician.

Jaeseung Cha is an associate professor at New Brunswick Theological Seminary whose specialty is Doctrine of Atonement. He extends his theological interests to Christ's Nature and Person from diverse contexts and Theological Methodology.

James F. Coakley taught Early Christianity at Lancaster University (in England); then Syriac at Harvard and finally Cambridge Universities. Since his retirement in 2014, he has continued his research in Syriac studies.

Sarah Coakley is the Norris-Hulse Professor of Divinity at Cambridge University and Professorial Fellow of Murray Edwards College, Cambridge.

Matthew Gasero is an archives assistant at the Archives of the Reformed Church in America and is working on the digitization and transcription of the Zwemer diaries.

Russell Gasero is Archivist of the Reformed Church in America and has served in that capacity since 1978. He is co-editor of Servant Gladly, and editor of the *Historical Directory of the Reformed Church in America, 1628-1992* and the *Historical Directory of the Reformed Church in America, 1628-2000,* all in the *Historical Series of the Reformed Church in America.*

Allan Janssen served as a pastor in the Reformed Church in America for forty years, and is an Affiliate Associate Professor of Theological Studies at New Brunswick Theological Seminary as well as a Professor of the General Synod.

Lynn Japinga is Professor of Religion at Hope College in Holland, Michigan.

Mary L. Kansfield is an independent scholar and the author of *Letters to Hazel: Ministry within the Woman's Board of Foreign Missions of the Reformed Church in America*, volume 46 in the *Historical Series of the Reformed Church in America*. She also serves as archivist and historian for Room for All, the organization advocating for LGBTQ inclusion within the RCA.

Norman J. Kansfield is delighted to be the husband of Mary Klein Kansfield, the father of the Rev. Ann M. Kansfield and John Livingston Kansfield, the father-in-law of the Rev. Jennifer Aull, and the grandfather of John Aull Kansfield and Grace Carol Aull Kansfield. For more than forty-five years he has served the RCA as pastor, seminary librarian, and seminary president.

James Jinhong Kim has taught at New Brunswick Theological Seminary since 1993 and serves as the Director of the Horace G. Underwood Center for Global Christianity at NBTS.

Gregg Mast has served as president of New Brunswick Theological Seminary for the past ten years.

Dirk Mouw is a Fellow of the Reformed Church Center at New Brunswick Theological Seminary, a historian, and a translator.

Ondrea Murphy is Librarian for Technical Services at Gardner A. Sage Library, New Brunswick Theological Seminary.

Mark V.C. Taylor is pastor of The Church of the Open Door, Brooklyn, New York.

David W. Waanders is an Emeritus Professor of the General Synod of the Reformed Church in America and Professor Emeritus of Pastoral Care and Counseling at New Brunswick Theological Seminary.

An Appreciation for John W. Coakley

David W. Waanders

It was in 1984 that I first met John Coakley when he came to be interviewed for the Church History position at New Brunswick Seminary. Those of us on the search committee could see readily that Dr. Coakley was exceptionally well suited for this position. His academic training had been superb and thorough. He had a passion for scholarship. He was articulate and engaging with people and had been a pastor in two congregations over the span of ten years and spoke about his pastoral experience with deep appreciation.

We could envision this pastoral experience transferring into effective teaching in the class room and in caring relationships with students. It also did not escape my attention when John happened to mention at dinner with the search committee that he played the clarinet and had done some recital work in various settings.

Over the years that I was a colleague of John Coakley, each of these early impressions proved to be accurate and more so as he assumed his position on the faculty teaching courses in the Church History field.

In the classroom, Dr. Coakley is a very dynamic presence, making Church History and its complexities come alive for students. His passion for the material or issues under consideration is infectious and helps students enter into the questions, the conflicts, and the dilemmas of history with enthusiasms of their own and helps students see their own theological traditions represented in the discussions. One could sense high levels of energy in the class discussions as one passed by in the hall outside Dr. Coakley's classroom.

Dr. Coakley's scholarship has been impressive, ranging from significant work in advancing the knowledge of "the Academy" in his book *Women, Men and Spiritual Power: Female Saints and Their Male Collaborators* and in a number of essays and articles dealing with related themes to books and articles specific to the Reformed Church in America, advancing the church's understanding of its history. Most recently, Dr. Coakley has published a wonderful history of New Brunswick Theological Seminary with many photographs, which has been enthusiastically received by a wide audience.

Dr. Coakley holds himself to very high standards in his scholarship and this could be seen in his role as a colleague on the faculty as well as in his committee work, in his participation in debate on issues of policy or curriculum or planning. He was always very thorough and insightful in his reports, very solid in his reasoning skills when arguing a point of view and his high expectations of himself influenced others of us on the faculty to seek similar high standards.

Another significant contribution which Dr. Coakley made to the faculty and the seminary was to serve as Faculty Secretary for many years. He took great care in writing the minutes of faculty meetings, and had the rare gift of capturing sometimes long and complicated discussions in concise and well written descriptions. His minutes and record keeping were much appreciated by his colleagues.

As someone raised in the Baptist tradition and then having served two congregations in the New England Congregational (United Church of Christ) tradition, Dr. Coakley came to value and embrace the traditions of the Reformed Church in America and its roots in the Netherlands. His scholarship reflects this, but also his interest in frequent travels to the Netherlands with the seminary's Summer School program and in his participation, since 1995, in the Reformed Church's General Synod Professorate (The Fourth Office), serving on several denominational committees and participating regularly with colleagues from Western Theological Seminary in providing guidance to the denomination.

Another of Dr. Coakley's contributions to New Brunswick Seminary has been his research on the St. Nicholas legend, writing a dramatic script that has been used with great fun and hilarity at the annual Christmas party at the seminary. Various members of the faculty and staff would play the roles of St. Nicholas and his daughters with costumes to identify their roles. This dramatization was always a highlight for the children at the Christmas party.

Finally, I want to comment on John's love of music and his playing of the clarinet. For a number of years John and I played in a woodwind quintet which met at a friend's house on average once per month. John was the most accomplished player in the group, yet he was very gracious with the rest of us. I was always impressed with his capacity to play complex musical passages with accuracy even when he was unfamiliar with the music. I saw a different side of John when he was making music. He would be completely relaxed and thoroughly enjoying himself as he immersed himself in the music. He could also bring his critical/analytical skills to that setting as he would comment on interpretations of the music or share some anecdotes about the composer.

John Coakley has been a valued colleague of mine for many years, and my wife, Janet, and I have enjoyed our friendship with John and his wife, Margaret, through our various interactions at First Reformed Church in New Brunswick, where we are all members, and in sharing many social times together.

My congratulations to you, John, on a long and significant teaching career at New Brunswick Theological Seminary, and many good wishes for a well-deserved retirement.

Part 1

"Yes! Well . . ." and the Exploration of Scripture and Theology

John Coakley, historian, is first and foremost John Coakley, pastor and teacher. He has a heart for wrestling with God's Word and sharing the results with God's people. For John, to say, "This is the Word of God" is the "Yes," then we get to "Well," how can we follow God's Word even further?

In these first four essays, we follow God's Word and the implications of the Word further. Tom Boogart begins in Genesis, exploring a story and a method for seeing it with fresh eyes. Jaeseung Cha wrestles with the humanity of Christ. John's brother James looks at an ancient middle eastern mystic nd his spirituality in a way that should also appeal to John's poetic sense. And Sarah Coakley, John's sister-in-law, applies her own pastoral sense and philosophical mind, as well as ideas suggested in John's own work, to take a deeper exploration into Thomas Aquinas' *Summa Theologica*.

CHAPTER 1

The Arduous Journey of Abraham: Genesis 22:1-19

Thomas A. Boogaart

Introduction

Over the past few decades, students of the Scriptures have come to the realization that the narratives of the Hebrew Bible were originally dramas. Each narrative comprises a series of scenes that unfold according to a pattern that is characteristic of dramas across cultures both ancient and modern: conflict, rising action, and resolution. Each of these scenes features the speech and actions of the main characters—in biblical scenes there are either two or three. This scenic structure is readily apparent when we slow down in our reading and take a closer look. Here is an example of a scene from one of the narratives in the Elisha cycle. It comes at the beginning and introduces the conflict; note especially the dialogue (2 Kings 4: 1-2a):

> And a woman, a wife of one of the followers of the prophets, cried out to Elisha:
>
> *"Your servant, my husband, is dead. And you know that your servant was one who feared the Lord. And the debt collector has come to take my two children to be his slaves."*

And Elisha said to her:

"What can I do for you?
Tell me, what do you have in the house?"

The presence of dramatic structure in the biblical narratives implies that they were originally performed. They do not stand on their own. They require someone to give voice to the main characters and to embody their actions so that an audience can both hear and see the drama unfold. We cannot fully experience a narrative without such a performance. Take the scene just cited above: to fully experience this narrative, the audience would need to hear the tone of the widow's voice and to see her facial expression and her gestures. All these things carry meaning in a biblical narrative.

That the structure of the biblical narratives implies performance should not be surprising to us. Performance is exactly what we would expect from a culture like that of the ancient Israelites. The vast majority of the Israelite people could not read or write, and they would have absorbed their traditions through their participation in the various rituals that constituted public worship at their sanctuaries—not only seeing the performances of the narratives, but also singing the songs of faith, reciting the law, eating meals together at the Lord's table, uttering prayers of lament and praise, etc.

Furthermore, a performance of scenes from the lives of their ancestors is exactly what we would expect from the people of Israel who, like all ancient peoples, placed a high value on honoring their fathers and mothers. The people of Israel believed that God had been present in the lives of their ancestors and had been forming them for God's mission in the world. Therefore, their lives bore meaning, and the events of their lives were potentially sacramental. The performance of a narrative probed this deeper meaning in the lives of the ancestors and made it accessible to their descendants. In the moment of a narrative performance, the barriers of time and space were overcome, and the people were caught up in the drama—in the same way people today are caught up in the performance of a drama . The people of Israel heard again the words of their fathers and mothers, and they saw again their deeds. In this way, they honored their ancestors as a source of wisdom and guidance in the ways of the Lord.

We do not perform the biblical narratives anymore. Unlike the Israelites, we do read and write, and our ancient traditions have come down to us in the form of a book. We tend, therefore, to assume that the Bible is a document, and that the narratives were composed to document the history of Israel. Such assumptions lead us to particular ways of reading the narratives both in private and in public. As a private document, we tend to read the narratives silently on our own with the goal of appropriating the historical information contained therein. As a public document around which we gather in worship, we tend to read the narratives in a flat tone of voice with the goal of presenting the historical information objectively.

Missing a public performance of the narratives, we also miss their theological achievement. Modern Christians often assume that the people of Israel were somewhat unsophisticated theologically, and they assume it is their task to systematize the raw material of Israel's religious experience. The reality is that we have failed to appreciate the particular way that the ancient Israelites engaged in theological discourse, the way in which these narratives probe the depths of God's character and the nature of God's presence in the world.

In what follows, I want to take what is perhaps the best-know narrative in the Hebrew Bible—the Binding of Isaac, Genesis 22: 1-19—analyze its dramatic structure, and probe its theological depths. It is important to say at the outset that this essay is dependent on the work of many others. For a number of years now, I and my students and colleagues have been memorizing Hebrew narratives and performing them in both Hebrew and English to audiences in the seminary and the surrounding churches. Moving from the "page" to the "stage" has forced us to ask questions of the text that we would never have otherwise asked and has alerted us to a richness of meaning that we would never have otherwise seen. In performing the narratives, we have together experienced the power of the Bible to shape us in ways that we had not experienced in our more traditional forms of exegesis and in ways that gave us a new understanding of what it means to affirm that the Bible is inspired.

Dramatic Structure of the Binding of Isaac (Genesis 22: 1-19)

Conflict

And after these events, time passed. And God tested Abraham, and he said to him:

"Abraham."

And he said,

"Here am I."

And he said,

"Take your son, your only son, whom you love, Isaac, and go to the land of Moriah, and offer him up there as a burnt offering on one of the mountains that I will describe to you."

Rising Action

Scene 1

And Abraham rose early the next morning, and he saddled his donkey. And he took two of his young servants with him, and Isaac, his son. And he chopped wood for an offering. Then he got up, and he went to the place that God had described to him. On the third day, Abraham lifted up his eyes, and he saw the place from afar. And Abraham said to his young servants,

"Sit down here with the donkey. I and the young boy, we will walk over there, and we will worship. And we will return to you."

Scene 2

And Abraham took the wood for the burnt offering and placed it upon Isaac, his son. And he took in his hand the fire and the knife. And the two of them walked on together.

And Isaac said to Abraham, his father . . . (voice falters ?)

And he said,
"My father."

And he said,
"Here am I, my son."

And he said,
"Behold, the fire and the wood, but where is the lamb for the burnt offering?"

And Abraham said,
"God will provide for himself the lamb for the burnt offering, . . . my son."

And the two of them walked on together.

Resolution

Scene 1

And they came to the place that God had described to him. And Abraham built an altar there. And he arranged the wood. And he bound

Isaac, his son. And he placed him on the altar on top of the wood. And Abraham reached out his hand and took the knife to slay his son. And the angel of the Lord called out to him from heaven, and he said,

"Abraham! Abraham!"

And he said,
"Here am I."

And he said,
"Do not reach out your hand toward the boy, and do not do anything to him. Indeed now I know. Indeed you are a God-fearer, and you have not withheld your son, your only son, from me."

And Abraham lifted his eyes, and he saw. . . . And behold, a ram, behind, caught in a bush by his horns. And Abraham went, and he took the ram. And he offered it as a burnt offering instead of his son. And Abraham called that place,
"The Lord will provide."

As it is said even today,
"On the mountain of the Lord, it shall be provided."

Scene 2

And the angel of the Lord called to Abraham a second time from heaven, and he said,
"By myself I have sworn, says the Lord: Because you have done this deed, and you have not withheld your son, your only son, indeed, I will surely bless you. And I will made your descendants as numerous as the stars of the heavens and the sands on the seashore. And your descendants shall possess the gates of their enemies, and all the nations of the earth shall bless themselves by your descendants because you have listened to my voice."

And Abraham returned to his young servants. And they got up, and they walked on together to Beersheba. And Abraham stayed in Beersheba.

Dramatic and Theological Analysis

Thin Places

The people of Israel sang with the seraphim, "Holy, holy, holy is the Lord of hosts; the whole earth is full of his glory" (Isaiah 6:3). This doxology expressed succinctly their view of the world. They believed in two realms: one a place where God dwelled, often called heaven, and the other a place where humans dwelled, called earth. Heaven was a place of inexhaustible power, often called glory, and earth was a place of exhaustible power. The people of Israel believed that the boundary between heaven and earth was thin and that in certain places glory—the radiant, life-giving power of God—broke through. The Scriptures often refer to this breakthrough as the "heavens opening." These were places where people experienced visions and rejuvenation. Should someone happen upon such a thin-place, he or she would mark it by setting up a stone or building an altar there. Over time, people would add to the stone or the altar and build a temple. They would make pilgrimages to these places hoping to have a vision of their own and to experience the rejuvenating power of God's glory.

A number of the biblical dramas show someone on an arduous journey and happening upon a thin place. Hagar is one example. Banished by Abraham, she wanders with her son Ishmael through the wilderness of Beersheba with only bread and one skin of water. Near death, Ishmael cries out from under a bush, and God hears him. The heavens open, and an angel calls out to Hagar and promises her that God is with her son and that he will live to become the father of a great nation. God then opens her eyes, and she sees a well of water, a well that she apparently could not see before. She approaches this well and gives her son a life-saving drink of water (Genesis 21:14-19). At this thin-place, Hagar's eyes are opened, and she sees that the world is full of God's glory, God's radiant life-giving power.

Jacob is another example. He flees his home and land, fearing for his life because he has stolen his brother's birthright and his blessing. A fugitive, he has lost his place in the world, and he journeys alone through alien land. Night falls, and he has nowhere to lay his head. He takes a stone for a pillow and makes his bed in a place seemingly without any significance. Yet at this place, the heavens open, and Jacob has a dream. He sees the angels of God ascending and descending on a stairway, and he hears the Lord promising him children and companionship. When Jacob awakens, he knows that this place is no ordinary place. He says: "Surely the Lord is in this place. . . . How awesome is this place! This is none other than the house of God, and this is the gate of heaven" (Genesis 28:10-17). Before he leaves, he sets up a stone to mark this thin-place.

"Go to the Land of Moriah"

The Binding of Isaac is yet another drama about someone on an arduous journey who happens upon a thin place. God sends Abraham to a remote place known only to God and commands him to sacrifice his son there for reasons known only to God. This command can best be termed grotesque in the sense that it departs markedly from the natural, the expected, or the typical.

With this grotesque command, God strips Abraham of his identity and his place in the world. He moves into what cultural anthropologists today would call the liminal zone. As he takes steps to carry out this command, we witness Abraham's increasing separation and isolation. First, Abraham separates himself from his home and family in Beersheba, presumably from his wife, Sarah, who is never mentioned in the drama, and he travels for three days with his two young servants and with Isaac. Then Abraham separates himself from his two young servants, and he travels on with Isaac, his son. Finally, arriving at the place that God had pointed out to him, he builds an altar, lays the wood in order, and binds Isaac. He reaches out his hand, takes the knife, and faces the final separation, that of father and son.

With the grotesque command to sacrifice his son, God sets the two most intimate relationships of which human beings are capable against each other, two relationships that, under normal circumstances, are supposed to reinforce each other: love of family and love of God. Abraham must now do what no parent should ever be asked to do: choose between his child and his God. God sends Abraham into uncharted territory, both geographically and morally. There is no map to guide him to this place, and there is no moral code to instruct him once he gets there. He will have to depend completely on God to guide him and provide what he needs.

The few words that Abraham speaks suggest that he is in uncharted territory and straining to understand the meaning of this journey. Abraham says to the two young men: "Sit down here with the donkey. I and the young boy, we will walk over there, and we will worship. And we will return to you" (verse five). Abraham uses first-person, plural pronouns. What could he have meant by saying "We will return to you?" If he sacrifices Isaac, his son obviously will not be returning with him. Some people suggest that he is saying this to keep the young servants in the dark about what he has been commanded to do. He fears what they will think about him, even that they may try to stop him. Others suggest that he is so distraught that he does not know what he is saying. There is yet another way to interpret his words. I am inclined to interpret them in the light of what he said just previously to his young servants: "We will worship."

Abraham frames what he is doing as an act of worship. He sees his arduous journey as a pilgrimage; he sees himself as coming into the presence of God. Is he hoping that communion with God will be so intimate and the feeling of belonging so intense that it will not matter whether Isaac lives or dies, as the apostle Paul would later put it? Is he hoping to experience a bond of love so powerful that nothing can ever separate it, neither death, nor life, nor angels, nor rulers, nor things present, nor things to come, nor powers, nor height, nor depth, nor anything else in all creation? Is Abraham on a journey and moving toward an understanding of the power of God's love that will at sometime in the future, long after he has died, be expressed in the notion of the resurrection of the dead? The author of the Book of Hebrews connects his faith and the belief in the resurrection:

> By faith Abraham, when put to the test, offered up Isaac. He who had received the promises was ready to offer up his only son, of whom he had been told, 'It is thorough Isaac that descendants shall be named for you.' He considered the fact that God is able even to raise someone from the dead. . . . (11:17-19).

If Abraham did not have a fully articulated belief in the resurrection, did he not have the beginnings of it?

We see more evidence of Abraham straining to understand the meaning of this journey to a mountain in the land of Moriah. When he is confronted by his son, who poignantly asks, "Where is the lamb for the burnt offering," he responds: "God will provide for himself a lamb for a burnt offering, my son." What could Abraham have meant by saying this? Some suggest that he was keeping his son in the dark as he had earlier kept his young servants in the dark. Others suggest that he may have been contemplating the possibility that God had provided him miraculously with a son in his old age and that God was now demanding that son. Again, if we read these words in the light of Abraham's earlier words to the young servants, "We will worship," he may have been hoping that this place of worship would be a place where the rejuvenating power of God would break through, a place of miraculous provision where the line between life and death would be erased. He and those who followed after him believed in thin-places where a few loaves of bread and fish could feed multitudes, bushes could burn and not be consumed, water could run from a rock, and a jar of oil could keep pouring. We latter-day worshippers still gather at a table and pray: "Send your Holy Spirit upon us, we pray, that the bread which we break and the cup which we bless may be to us the communion of the body and blood of Christ."[1] We believe that Jesus' body and blood

---

[1]   "Communion Prayer" in *Worship the Lord: the Liturgy of the Reformed Church in America* (New York: Reformed Church Press, 2005), 13.

can be infinitely multiplied and that rejuvenating power is ours when we eat the bread and drink the cup.

The strain on Abraham can be seen in his interaction with his son. The audience hears immediately that Abraham loves his son, Isaac, and they are reminded of that love throughout the drama. The words "father" and "son" are used repeatedly, and each time the audience feels the love implied in that relationship and the horror of the command to severe it. Twice the narrator tells the audience that the "two of them walked together," and this picture of their togetherness heightens the tension and keeps the audience's attention focused on Abraham's anguish. Yet in his anguish there is a hint that he is distancing himself from his son. When Abraham and his entourage come to the place that God had pointed out to him, Abraham tells his young servants to stay where they are and that he and the young boy *("hana'ar),"* will carry on. He does not refer to Isaac by name or by his familial status, my son; he uses a generic term. Then Abraham leaves the donkey, that was presumably carrying the wood, behind, and he puts the wood on Isaac. This action hints that Isaac is being reduced to the level of an animal, a fact that is already implicit in the command to sacrifice him. There is always a danger of reading too much into the action in a drama, but there is a hint here that this test might be easier for Abraham to bear if he can see Isaac as an animal and not a son.

"Take your son, your only son...Go...Offer up"

When the people of Israel thought of God, they frequently pictured God as a sovereign who sat on a throne and issued decrees. God's word both created and sustained the world. In the beginning, the Lord God said, "Let there be," and the world came into existence by his spoken word. The psalmist expressed it this way: "By the word of the Lord the heavens were made, and all their host by the breath of his mouth" (Psalm 33:6). The word of the Sovereign One created the world, and it also sustained it. The prophet Isaiah expressed it this way:

> For as the rain and snow come down from heaven,
>   and do not return there until they have watered the earth,
>   making it bring forth and sprout,
>   giving seed to the sower and bread to the eater,
> so shall my word be that goes out from my mouth;
>   it shall not return to me empty,
>   but it shall accomplish that which I purpose,
>   and succeed in the thing for which I sent it (55:10-11).

Many of the biblical dramas also picture God as a sovereign who issued decrees. In The Binding of Isaac, God gives three commands to Abraham: *take* your son; *go* to the land of Moriah; and *offer him up* as a burnt offering. These three commands: take, go, and offer up, determine the course of action in the drama. Abraham obeys the first two commands almost immediately. The narrator tells the audience that Abraham "took" two of his young servants with him and his son Isaac (verse three). The fact that he takes the two young servants along with his son Isaac has spawned much speculation as to Abraham's reason for doing this. He may have wanted them only to carry the supplies on this journey, but he may have been seeing them as possible substitutes for his son. Many who have treasured this drama and pondered its meaning over the years see a hint here of Abraham's inner turmoil in the light of God's grotesque command to offer up his son.

After fulfilling the first command to take his son, the narrator tells us that he fulfilled the second one; he "went" to the place that God had pointed out to him (verse three). Abraham makes preparations to obey the third command, but the angel of the Lord intervenes to stop him: "Do not reach out your hand toward the boy, and do not do anything to him." Abraham lifts up his eyes and sees a ram caught in a bush by its horns. At this point in the drama, the narrator returns to all three commands and tells us that Abraham fulfilled each one of them, although not in the same order. He "went," "took" the ram; "offered" it as a burnt offering instead of his son (22:13). These three commands of God determine the course of action in this drama. They are the framework in which Abraham lives and moves and has his being.

Many people assume that disciplined reflection on the nature of God only came only with the modern era. But the dramas in the Scriptures offer disciplined reflection. In this and other dramas, the people of Israel are reflecting on the nature of their God who has revealed himself to them as the Sovereign who creates and sustains the world by his word. This drama shows that the word of God does not return empty but accomplishes that which God intends. The word of God determines the movements of Abraham in the same way that it determines the movements of all of creation. Believers in Israel did not make a sharp distinction between nature and history the way Western believers do today, where nature is a closed system of matter and motion and history is an open system in which God is personally active. For the people of Israel, the word of God set the course for both nature and history, indeed, the world and the fullness thereof. God commands the clouds, the wind, the rain, the snow, and the ice (Job: 37:1ff.). God sets the pathways for the birds: the storks, the turtledoves, the swallows, and the cranes (Jeremiah 8:7), and God sets the courses for the stars (Job: 38:31-33). God also sets the pathway for all the people of the world. For much of history, they stray from this pathway, but in the end they will follow it in the same way that the birds and the stars do. All the people of the world will eventually say:

> Come, let us go up to the mountain of the Lord,
> To the house of the God of Jacob;
> That he may teach us his ways
> And that we may walk in his paths.
> For out of Zion shall go forth instruction,
> And the word of the Lord from Jerusalem (Isaiah 2:3).

"Here I am"

In this drama Abraham has a series of personal encounters. At the beginning, God calls his name, and he responds, "*Hineni*/ Here I am" (22:1); in the middle, Isaac addresses him, and he responds again, "*Hineni*" (22:7); and at the end, the angel of the Lord calls his name twice, and he responds, "*Hineni*" (22:11). The full meaning of this phrase, "here I am," is hard for the American audience to understand.

All personal encounters in ancient Israel carried great significance and were governed by a set of conventions that were appropriate for each person's place in the social order. People used different forms of address when speaking to an older person, a friend, an acquaintance, a stranger, or God. Many European cultures have similar sets of conventions, whereas they are disappearing in cultures west of the Atlantic. The Dutch, for example, use different titles to address people with different degrees of authority, and they use different second person pronouns to address people outside of their circle of friends and family. In addition, encounters were never just casual in ancient Israel— never two people exchanging the greeting: "Hi, how ya' doing?" "Fine," and passing by each other on their way to somewhere else. Encounters followed patterns, or "liturgies," and they bound two parties together in a relationship with varying degrees of privileges and responsibilities, similar to covenant-making.

In the first encounter between God and Abraham, God addresses Abraham by name. This fact itself is significant. It implies that the two parties have exchanged names and thus are intimate with each other. They are friends. They have given each other the right to address them personally and have assumed the obligation to respond to such an address. For example, in the story of Jacob wrestling with the mysterious man at the river bank, we read: "Then Jacob asked him, 'Please tell me your name.' But he said, 'Why is it that you ask my name?' And there he blessed him" (Genesis 32:29). And with that the man disappears from Jacob's life. The man does not want to give his name and thus, apparently, does not want to be addressed in the future and therefore obligated to Jacob.

When two parties exchanged names, they obligated themselves to respond when called. The nature of their response indicated how far they desired to go in the conversation and therefore in the relationship. People had certain standard responses that could limit the conversation and therefore the obligations of the relationship, and they had responses that could make themselves more available to the other.

Those of us raised in North America seldom consider the conventions that govern our encounters, but we have them, too— all cultures do. For example, if I should find myself in the hallway at Western Theological Seminary and call out someone's name, and that person ignores my call and walks past me, we would find this to be rude, a breach of the rules that govern relationships. In a similar scenario, if I should call out to someone, "Hey you," and that person ignores me, we would not find this to be rude. We would find the call, "Hey you," to be non-binding, even inappropriate, and not demanding a response.

The word "*hineni*" has to be understood in the light of the set of conventions that governed encounters in ancient Israel. According to many Jewish and Christian students of the Scriptures, it means something like, "I am here for you" or "at your service." It indicates a commitment to conversation and to the relationship. Yet Abraham says it three times in this drama: once to God; once to Isaac; and once to the angel. These three responses highlight the conflict, rising action, and resolution of the drama. The first two highlight the conflict and the rising action because Abraham cannot be available to both God who commanded him to sacrifice his beloved son and to Isaac who is seeking his father's assurance that nothing is amiss in this strange pilgrimage to the mountain. The last "*hineni*" highlights the resolution of the conflict because now Abraham can fulfill both his obligations to God and to his son.

And Isaac said to Abraham, his father. . .

When you set out to perform the biblical narratives, when you try to move from the page to the stage, you discover many "gaps" in the narrative flow that need to be filled. These gaps are not mistakes by the composer or the result of words that have been lost in the transmission of the text. These gaps are intentional. They are, in essence, the composer's invitation to participation. They invite the performers to move more deeply into the drama and to come up with interpretations that enhance the performance. We have found as performers that filling in these gaps has been one of most theological enriching parts of the whole experience.

In the narrative of the Binding of Isaac there are two such gaps that we had to fill. We find the first gap in verse seven. The text literally says this: "And he said, Isaac, to Abraham, his father . . . and he said, 'My father.'" In biblical dramas, direct speech is introduced by the phrase, "and he said" (*yaiyomer*). In this verse, the composer uses the word *yaiyomer* twice, but, after the first one, there is a gap; there is no recorded speech. Most translation ignore this gap, and smooth it over this way: "And Isaac said to his father Abraham, 'Father.'" (NRSV) As performers, we struggled with what to do with the text before us. Should we ignore the gap, as do the various translations, or should we assume that it meant something? We entertained the possibility that the composer may have been suggesting that Isaac wanted to say something to his father but was initially too distraught to mouth the words. After all, Isaac is beginning to realize that something is amiss at this point in the drama.

We ended up taking the gap seriously. We had the person playing the role of the narrator say, "And Isaac said to Abraham, his father . . .", whereupon the person playing the role of Isaac tries to speak but cannot, overcome with emotion. Then we had the narrator say a second time, "And Isaac said . . ." whereupon Isaac gets out the words, "My father." Was this the composer's intention? How would we ever know? Yet this interpretation was consistent with the rest of the drama, lent significance to Isaac's dilemma, and was faithful to the text as we have received it.

We find the second gap when Abraham has Isaac on the altar and sees the ram. At this point the narrator says: "And Abraham went, and he took the ram. And he offered it as a burnt offering instead of his son." When we began enacting this scene, we had a problem. There is no mention of how Isaac got off the altar. Did Abraham untie him? Did the angel who stayed Abraham's hand untie him? This is the moment of Isaac's salvation. You would expect that the composer would have supplied every detail. Why would he or she leave it to us to fill a gap at this pivotal moment in the drama?

We ended up filling the gap in a way that led us into a conversation about the nature of salvation that we had not expected. This scene puts

Isaac bound above the wood of the altar. It puts Abraham above his son with the knife in his hand. The composer makes it absolutely clear that the knife is in his hand: "And Abraham reached out his hand and took the knife to slay his son." Knife in hand, Abraham sees the ram caught in the thicket by its horns. The most natural action at this point is for Abraham to look down upon Isaac and to cut his bindings with the knife in hand. This, then, is how we filled the gap, and, as soon as we enacted it, we all stood in wonderment as to its meaning.

The knife that was to be the instrument of Isaac's annihilation had become instead the instrument of his salvation; a dramatic reversal indeed. The Scriptures tell versions of this truth again and again. All things work together for good. . . . You meant it for evil, but God meant it for good. . . . C. S. Lewis calls it the "deep magic" of God at work in the world.[2] The drama of the Binding of Isaac is closely related to the drama of the Fiery Furnace. Nebuchadnezzar meant the fire of the furnace to incinerate Shadrach, Meshach, and Abednego, but in the end it served to liberate them, burned not their bodies but the ropes that bound them so that they were free in the fire; again, a dramatic reversal. How would we ever know what the composer of the Binding of Isaac meant to convey by this gap? It led our group into a deep and profound conversation about the meaning of salvation.

"On the mountain of the Lord, it will be provided"

By sending Abraham on an arduous journey with an impossible command, God strips him of his identity and place in the world. God does not command him to leave Beersheba, we trust, to destroy him as a person, but to make him into a new one. The whole experience is a rite of passage—more specifically, a rite of initiation. In language familiar to Christians, Abraham is dying to his old self and rising to a new one; he is losing his life in order to find it again. In the language of the narrator, the whole experience is a test—"After these things, God tested Abraham."

On a mountain in the land of Moriah, the heavens open, and Abraham's eyes are opened. He sees the world in a new way. The narrator tells us: "And Abraham lifted his eyes, and he saw. And behold, a ram, behind, caught in a bush by his horns." In the same way that God opened the eyes of Hagar, and she saw a well nearby that she had not seen before; in the same way that God opened the eyes of Elisha's

---

[2]   *The Lion, the Witch, and the Wardrobe* (New York: HarperCollins, 1994), 163.

servant, and he sees horses and chariots of fire surrounding Elisha, God opens Abraham's eyes, and he sees a ram.

Abraham sees that, in the most barren places and under the most unlikely circumstances, God is present and provides what is necessary for life. What could only have been a hope when he said to his son, "God will provide a lamb for a burnt offering," he now has sees as a reality. Abraham celebrates his vision and his new insight by naming this place on a mountain in the land of Moriah: "The Lord will provide." And that was not the end of it. Abraham's descendants followed in his footstep and made their own journeys to the mountain of the Lord. They saw their own versions of the ram and the provision of the Lord. They coined a proverb: "On the mountain of the Lord, it shall be provided."

To return to what has already been briefly discussed, the people of Israel believed in the existence of two realms, earth and heaven. Earth was the visible world that was passing away, a world of exhaustion, rot, rust, decay, flesh, and death. And heaven was an invisible world that was eternal, a world of provision, radiance, energy, spirit, and life. Yet, despite their differences, earth and heaven were not two separate worlds. The invisible world of spirit sustained the visible world of the created order in the same way that breathing sustains the body, a spring sustains an oasis in the wilderness, and the sun warms the earth and energizes the plants. For the people of Israel, all these visible structures of the created order pointed to a deeper, invisible structure: life-giving power came from God and filled the earth. The people of Israel called it glory. Paul shared this world view and spoke of the life-giving power of God filling human beings as an extraordinary power in "clay vessels." He went on to expand on this image with these words:

> Even though our outer nature is wasting away, our inner nature is being renewed day by day. For this slight momentary affliction is preparing us for an eternal weight of glory beyond all measure, because we look not at what can be seen but at what cannot be seen; for what can be seen is temporary, but what cannot be seen is eternal (2 Corinthians 4:16-18).

Many people today find this Israelite view of the world to be primitive and problematic. They emphasize the radical otherness of God and tend to see the created order as an autonomous, self-regulating mechanism. In their estimation, any attempt to connect God to the world puts one on the road to pantheism. Yet the Israelite world view is hardly primitive and hardly problematic. Scientists today are making daily advances in our understanding of the structures of the world around us, and they are telling us that the world is made up of things seen that are passing away and things unseen that are eternal.

The latest advance is the verification of the existence of the Higgs boson. It is just the latest elemental particle to be discovered, joining a long list of others, sixty-one in all, with equally intriguing names: quarks, leptons, gluons, and photons. For most of us, the instruments, the calibrations, and the mathematics that led to the discovery of these particles and explain their relationships are beyond our understanding, but the emerging picture of the cosmos is not.

The elemental particles are miniscule bundles of energy that were concentrated in a super-heated "space," (sometimes called a singularity) and then released in a momentous expansion of that space. As space expanded, these bundles of energy cooled and have combined and recombined over billions of years to form the evermore complex structures of the world around us, structures ranging from those as small as atoms to those as large as galaxies. Some of these structures we can see and others we cannot see. For example, I can see the oak table now in front of me. I am writing on it. It is fine-grained and brown, and it is solid and inert. What I cannot see, but know to be true, is that oak is made up of carbohydrate and lignin molecules—which in turn are made up of various combinations of carbon, hydrogen, and oxygen atoms—which in turn are made up of various combinations of electrons, protons, and neutrons—which are made up of various combinations of elementary particles—which are manifestations of energy that was released in a momentous, expansion sometimes called the "big bang" and sometimes the "flaring forth." The table that I can see will eventually decompose, and the molecules, atoms, and elementary particles that I cannot see will recombine to form still other structures.

The people of Israel and people today in many ways share a view of world. The fundamental difference between them is that the people of Israel saw the energy in the world as a manifestation of the life-giving power of God and the world's emerging structures as expressions of God's love. They saw the structures of the world as God's provision, what my physicist friend calls the "hands of God." When they felt the touch of the hands of God in their daily lives, they were not inclined to pantheism; they were inclined to love God more dearly.

"God tested Abraham"

The question on everyone's mind when experiencing this drama is: why did God test Abraham? Was God supposed to learn something about Abraham in this test? Or was Abraham supposed to learn something about God? I am inclined to think it was the latter. But what learning could have been so important that it justified such an ordeal? All of us are challenged by this drama and try to make some sense of it. There are many interpretations. Let me add another.

I remember browsing in a gift shop in the Jewish quarter of Jerusalem. The proprietor was selling an attractive print of the Old City. I was inspecting it, when I suddenly noticed that the Dome of the Rock was gone and had been replaced by a temple. "What is this," I asked? "The third temple," the proprietor answered. He told me that the raw materials for building the third temple and all its accouterments have been assembled and stored away. He and others like him were waiting for someone to blow up the Dome. They needed to clear the ground in order to build the new temple, believing that the messiah would return when he finally had a temple to enter.

This proprietor was part of a group that had sprung to life after the June 1967 war, when, in a matter of days, the Israeli army captured the West Bank, the Sinai Peninsula, and the Golan Heights. Many Jews saw in this swift victory the hand of God and believed that the end of time was near. God had restored the ancient borders of the nation of Israel and was ready to send the messiah. The only thing missing was a temple and the Ark of the Covenant, the place and throne from which the messiah would rule.

The proprietor in the gift shop equated God with a particular piece of land and a particular people. We have seen this before in history, and it has led to the slaughter of countless people. People who believe that God is on their side show little capacity for self-reflection and no mercy for those who oppose them. They pursue their ends with genocidal zeal. Words like these in Abraham Lincoln's second inaugural address are rare in history:

> Both [parties] read the same Bible and pray to the same God, and each invokes His aid against the other. It may seem strange that any men should dare to ask a just God's assistance in wringing their bread from the sweat of other men's faces, but let us judge not, that we be not judged. The prayers of both could not be answered. That of neither has been answered fully. The Almighty has His own purposes.[3]

If these radical Jewish groups succeed in blowing up the Dome of the Rock, the third most holy site for Muslims, the ensuing slaughter will engulf us all.

---

[3] Abraham Lincoln, "Second Inaugural Address," as found on "Bartleby.com: Great Books Online," http://www.bartleby.com/124/pres32.html.

The people of the Israel struggled with the meaning of God having chosen them as his people, having chosen the land of Israel as his special portion in the world, and having chosen the city of Jerusalem as the location of his house. They realized that God had created the material world and called it good and that God had created all of humankind to fill this good world. They were neither Gnostics nor spiritualists; they knew that God had not called them to leave their bodies and to live above the ground. They realized that they needed to build their communities around places and things. But they also understood the dangers that came when they located God in a particular place and thing. They could easily limit God and begin to see God as advancing their interests rather than to see themselves as advancing God's interests in the world. They had prophets who reminded them that God's choice of them as a people and the gift of children and land were for the purpose of bringing a blessing to all the families of the earth, a light to the nations. Election was a responsibility not a privilege. They had prophets who warned them that God's choice of the land of Israel and his presence in the temple of Jerusalem were not permanent and that his power was not always on their side. God could withdraw his presence if they as a people failed to build the kind of kingdom that God desired, one where justice rolled down like waters and righteousness like an ever-flowing stream (Amos 5:24).

God called Abraham so that, through him, all the families of the earth would be blessed (Genesis 12:1-3; 18:18). To achieve this state of blessedness, the peaceable kingdom, God gives him family and land. But there is a danger lurking in these gifts. Ties to both can become so strong that they can draw attention away from God and his purpose in giving them in the first place. Blood and land easily become in the hearts of believers objects of devotion and praised as the source of life itself. So elevated, they divide peoples and set them at each other's throats.

One way to interpret the meaning of Genesis 22 is this: God tested Abraham to deepen his understanding of the moral consequences of his heart commitments. He would not be a means of blessing to all the families of the world if his affection was drawn to one family and one land. Abraham needed to learn that life was not in the blood of Isaac and not in the promised land; it was in God. Only God provides. Abraham groped for this understanding when he said to Isaac, "God himself will provide the lamb for the burnt offering . . . my son" (22:8). And he achieved it when he finally gave a name to his place of testing, "The Lord will provide" (22:14).

This radical notion of providence counteracts the power of tribalism and nationalism and reveals to Abraham and all the followers of God their true pedigree. God is the provident one, the giver of life, the parent. All tribes and nations are brothers and sisters in the family of God. The hope of blessing for all the families of the earth rests in this revelation being planted deeply in the heart of Abraham and the hearts of believers.

CHAPTER 2

Is Christ's Humanity on the Cross Complete or Unique in Theodore of Mopsuestia?[1]

Jaeseung Cha

Introduction: The Significance of the Subject, Christ's Humanity and His Crucifixion, and A Theological Location of Theodore of Mopsuestia

Christ's proclamation at the Last Supper, "Take; this is my body (σῶμά)," suggests that his body can be shared with his disciples, particularly through his death.[2] According to Hebrews, Christ's body

---

[1]   The provisional form of some part of this paper was originally presented at the Free University in the Netherlands in May of 2010, sponsored by its *Research in Residence* program.

[2]   Mark 14:22. NRSV is used for the English translation. Mark's and Matthew's accounts focus on Christ's interpretative proclamation of his immanent death rather than on the initiation of the Lord's Supper in that both accounts include Christ's blood, poured for many, but omit the order of 'remembrance' as in Luke's and Paul's accounts. The question of whether the word σῶμά is a Greek translation of the Aramaic word *bisra* 'flesh or skin' or *guph* 'body' has been debated. Edward Schweizer leaves it inconclusive (*The Good News according to Mark*, trans. Donald H. Madvig [Atlanta: John Knox, 1970], 303) whereas William L. Lane prefers *guph* following J. Behm (*The Gospel according to Mark*, The New International Commentary on the New Testament, vol.2 [Grand Rapids: Eerdmans, 1974], 506). Regardless of which word is preferred, the interpreters seem to view the word as a 'holistic person'

was offered once for all.[3] Paul also asserts that man Christ Jesus
(ἄνθρωπος Χριστὸς Ἰησοῦς) gives himself as a ransom for all,[4] that we
have died to the law through the body of Christ (διὰ τοῦ σώματος τοῦ
Χριστοῦ),[5] and that we all die in Christ's death.[6] How can a person's
body be distributed to others, be offered once for all, become a ransom
for all, have others die to the law, and unite all others with it at their
death? If Christ's humanity is involved in these mysterious works—not
in general but precisely in his crucifixion—what is the true reality of
Christ's humanity on the cross? Certainly, Christ's death tells us that
his humanity is *homoousios* with our humanity. Yet a serious question
can arise as to the distinctiveness of Christ's humanity when we read
the biblical texts above: Is Christ's humanity on the cross different
from our humanity? If it is different, do we still regard it as a type of
humanity?[7] Who is Christ on the cross?

---

rather than a physical flesh, on the basis that words like 'flesh' or 'body' describe
the whole human in both Hebrew and Aramaic (Schweizer, *The Good News*, 303). In
addition to the view that *Theological Dictionary of the New Testament* suggests eight
different Hebrew equivalents to the Septuagint σῶμά (ed. Gerhard Friedrich, trans.
Geoffrey W. Bromiley, vol.7 [Grand Rapids: Eerdmans, 1971], 1044-5), however, we
must remember that both *bisra* and *guph* tightly relate to 'corporeality' of humanity,
compared with the Hebrew words, *ruach* and *nephesh*. When *guphah* is used in 1
Chronicles 10:12, it denotes 'corporal bodies' of Saul and his sons to be buried. The
corporality is definitely implied by σῶμά of the Septuagint as the Greek translation
for *basar* in Leviticus (6:10; 14:9; 15:2-27; 16:4-28; 17:16; 19:28). Even the Greek
word σῶμά that is more strongly linked with a holistic aspect of humanity than σάρξ
has the sense of corporeality in pain, sickness, and healing (*Theological Dictionary*,
1048). Moreover, we must consider the context Christ uses it. Christ intends his
body and blood to be distributed to his disciples as he anticipates his coming death.
How his body and blood can be distributed to his disciples is beyond human ability
to comprehend. Even in this mystery, however, Christ's holistic humanity and his
corporal reality is deeply involved because the concrete elements of bread and wine
are connected with his body and blood given to his disciples not as spiritual rituals
in remembrance of the Passover but by the concrete event of the cross on which
Christ hands over his body and sheds his blood. Thus, Christ's humanity in his
declaration of his body in relation to his death must receive its due appreciation,
which is definitely relevant to the present subject.

3   10:10.

4   1 Tim. 2:5-6.

5   Rom. 7:4.

6   Rom. 6:8; 2 Cor. 5:14; Gal. 2:19.

7   The idea that humanity is the criterion by which Christ's humanity is viewed does
not imply that humans are eligible to project their own images unto Jesus. Instead,
it points out that human humanity, if this wording is to be permitted, must be of
a vital relevance to the present discussion as far as Christ's humanity is concerned.
Moreover, by viewing human humanity we may be able to grasp the uniqueness
of Christ's humanity that shines over diverse human cultural contexts (Wolfhart
Pannenberg, *Jesus-God and Man*, trans. Lewis L. Wilkins and Duane A. Priebe
[Philadelphia: The Westminster, 1977], 200).

It is mostly when Christ's incarnation and resurrection are discussed that theologians find the distinctiveness of Christ's humanity. Christ's humanity is crucially involved in the restored image of God as the life-itself (αὐτοζωή) in his incarnation and resurrection.[8] Jesus is not simply a human singled out to exhibit what only God can do,[9] because Jesus' humanity *per se* achieves human perfection in his sinless incarnation and receives gifts of immortality in his resurrection.[10] Unfortunately, Christ's crucifixion has not adequately drawn our attention with regard to his humanity. Presumably, the vital connection between humanity and death is too obvious to provoke serious concerns other than the fact itself that Jesus died.

How to understand the reality of Christ's humanity has been one of critical issues of Reformed Christologies. The debate between Lutheran and Reformed theologians on Christ's presence at the

---

[8] Athanasius, *De Incarnatione*, 20, ed. and trans. Robert W. Thomson, *Athanasius: Contra Gentes and De Incarnatione* (Oxford: Oxford University, 1971), 182-3. There is no doubt that Christ's united *persona* is the very subject to do this mysterious work. Yet an emphasis on the union of Christ's *persona* often overwhelms the distinctive reality of Christ's twofold nature, without the consideration of which theological discussions on the mystery of Christ's person and work would be a simple announcement of the union itself rather than an elaborated explanation of in what ways the union is a genuine mystery and of what the actual contents of the mystery are. Dealing with Christ's humanity distinctively, however, does not imply that we need to begin Christology with two distinctive natures of Christ and then move on to the union between them in person. Instead, this paper has three points of provisional presupposition. (1) The two natures are not competitive with each other because of the ontological difference between Christ's divinity and humanity, i.e., *vere deus et vere homo*. (2) This never means they are separated. Rather, they are mystically (substantially and existentially, statically and dynamically) united in Christ's *persona*. (3) The union is asymmetrical in the sense that the primacy of Christ's divinity must be maintained. Thus, this paper intends not to negate Orthodox Christology but, with these presuppositions, to find adequate *loci* of Christ's humanity in connection with his crucifixion. In addition, theological orientations for the two natures of Christ can be distinguished from each other. Discussions on Christ's divinity on the cross can begin with the biblical reality of Christ; for the concept of the suffering divinity may seldom be found in human cultural and philosophical contexts. Thus, the uniqueness of Christ's divinity and his crucifixion has been placed at the center of Christian confessions. But, when it comes to Christ's humanity on the cross, questions become intensified, because the subject goes beyond a confessional nature on the basis of the historicity of Jesus and is diversified when it is viewed in light of humanity developed in various cultural and philosophical contexts. This paper, as a part of the larger project on Christ's humanity and his crucifixion, limits its scope to Christ's humanity in Theodore of Mopsuestia.

[9] Kathryn Tanner, *Jesus, Humanity and the Trinity: A Brief Systematic Theology* (Minneapolis: Fortress, 2001), 22.

[10] Tanner, *Jesus*, 49-50.

Lord's Supper was indeed caused by their different understandings of Christ's humanity as we can perceive them in the concepts of *genus maiestaticum* and a distinction between *totus* and *totum*. It was, however, Patristic Christology that yielded a variety of different views on Christ's humanity. Whether Christ's humanity has its own hypostasis or not was the issue when the paired concept of *anhypostasis* and *enhypostasis* was discussed as an attempt to compensate what is missing in Chalcedonian Creed. A clue of *divine* or *unique* humanity of Christ can be found in the concepts of *theandrikos* in Pseudo-Dionysius[11] and of *kyriakos anthropos* in Mark the Monk.[12] Maximus the Confessor alluded to three aspects of Christ's humanity, such as our humanity, the Savior's humanity, and the Son's humanity.[13] But no thoughtful discussion on the relationship between Christ's humanity and his crucifixion can be found even in Patristic Christology, except for the idea of the completeness of Christ's humanity on the cross.

As a part of the subject, "Christ's Humanity and his Crucifixion," this paper will narrowly focus on Theodore of Mopsuestia, who develops his view on Christ's humanity as the pre-eminent exponent of the School of Antioch, revealing a full-fledged view on the completeness of Christ's humanity. Frederick G. McLeod argues that Christ's humanity plays a pivotal role in human salvation in Theodore of Mopsuestia in the sense that the Assumed One relates himself to being the head of the body, the Church, to recapitulating the bond of the universe, and to restoring the image of God.[14] *Prima facie*, Theodore exceedingly elevates the role of Christ's humanity to the extent that Christ's complete and cosmic humanity may be an intrinsic foundation for the bond between cosmic humanity and Christ,[15] and that his transitional humanity in

11   Pseudo-Dionysius, *Letter* 4, *Pseudo-Dionysius: The Complete Works*, trans. Colm Luibheid (New York: Paulist, 1987), 63-4, *MPG* 3.1072C.

12   Mark the Monk, *Incarnation* 20.1-15, *Sources Chrétiennes* vol.455 (Paris: Les Éditions du Cerf, 2000), 274, C. Calrk Carlton, "*The* Kyriakos Anthrōpos *in Mark the Monk,*" *Journal of Early Christian Studies* 15/3 (2007), 401.

13   Maximus the Confessor, *Opusculum* 6, *On the Cosmic Mystery of Jesus Christ: Selected Writings from St. Maximus the Confessor*, trans. Paul M Blowers and Robert L. Wilken (Crestwood: St. Vladimir's Seminary, 2003), 173-176, *Opusculum* 3, in Andrew Louth, *Maximus the Confessor* (London and New York: Routledge, 1996), 186.

14   *The Roles of Christ's Humanity in Salvation: Insights from Theodore of Mopsuestia* (Washington: The Catholic University of America, 2005), 11.

15   The ideas and expressions of a cosmic bond of humanity and cosmic restoration of Christ are found in Theodore in his *The Creation of Adam and Eve* (*Theodore of Mopsuestia*, trans. Frederick G. McLeod [London: Routledge, 2009], 92-93. McLeod also pays his keen attention to this cosmic aspect of Christ's humanity in Theodore (*The Roles*, 120-1).

the process of being united with his divinity may reflect a true reality of human changeability. On its deeper level, however, questions remain as to whether or not this complete and transitional humanity of Christ can fully disclose the genuine reality of Christ's humanity, especially when it comes to Christ's crucifixion. In order to understand a theological location of Theodore's Christology, we will first discuss his view of Christ's complete and cosmic humanity in its ontological aspect. Second, we will touch on the concept of the Christ's Sonship as the root of the cosmic bond between Christ and humanity, and further on his notion of the progressive and transitional nature of the prosopic union between Christ's humanity and his divinity. Last, we will critically deals with Theodore's atonement thought to evaluate how Theodore's view of Christ's cosmic humanity and his Sonship remains problematic when the completeness of Christ's humanity on the cross is the single focus of his Christology.

Christ's Humanity in Theodore of Mopsuestia: Complete and Progressive

According to Theodore, Christ's humanity is complete like *prosōpon*: "And the *physis* of the man is complete and likewise his *prosōpon*."[16] The completeness of Christ's humanity is sufficiently discussed in his *In Opposition to Apollinaris* as he objects to Apollinaris' argument that the deity replaced the assumed man's nous. While Gregory of Nazianzus, among many points of counter-arguments against Apollinaris, unfolds a soteriological reason that"The unassumed is the unhealed,"[17] Theodore enumerates the reasons for Christ's complete humanity in the ontological reality of Jesus' humanity: (1) Jesus has a soul as he experiences fear of his impending passion, (2) the Spirit helps Jesus, which implies that the Logos does not take the place of his nous, (3) neither body and soul by itself is ever absolutely and properly said to be a human being, and (4) Jesus grows in age, wisdom, and grace, which signifies that Jesus assumed a rational soul.[18]

---

[16]   On the Incarnation 8, Theodore, 135, "τελείαν δὲ καὶ τὴν τοῦ ἀνθρώπου φύσιν, καὶ τὸ πρόσωπον ὁμοίως" (*Theodori Episcopi Mopsuesteni in Epistolas B. Pauli Commentarii*, ed. H.B. Swete, vol. 2 [Cambridge: Cambridge University, 1882], 299).

[17]   "ἀπρόσληπτον ἀθεράπευτον," "*quod assumptum non est, curationis est expers*" (*Letter on the Apollinarian Controversy* 101.5, *On God and Christ*, Popular Patristics Series 23 [Crestwood: St. Vladimir's Seminary, 2002], 158, *MPG* 37.181C10, 182C10-183A1).

[18]   *In Opposition to Apollinaris* (McLeod, *Theodore*, 151-7). Grillmeier finds a soteriological interpretation of Christ's nature in the early church: "In its original context, however, the question of Jesus' nature was precisely the question of his soteriological function and meaning" (*Christ in Christian Tradition: From the Apostolic Age to Chalcedon (451)*,

This complete humanity of Christ builds the cosmic bond between Christ and all other humans. Both Christ's humanity and our humanity are cosmic in their natures according to Theodore. God created the whole of creation as one cosmic body,[19] human beings are all united as one body by the bond of nature,[20] and God fashioned a human being to be God's pledge of friendship of all of creation.[21] Theodore sees Christ's humanity as cosmic humanity as well. God bestowed on Christ's humanity universal domination over all,[22] and all things are bonded and reintegrated in Christ according to the flesh (*secundum carnem Christus*).[23] Jesus is a human being like all human beings, differing in no way.[24] Theodore states,

> We all are one human being by reason of our nature. For each one of us holds a membership role for the common good [in common]. So also Christ is the one who has begun the future life, with all sharing in a common way in his resurrection and, after his ascension, in his immortality, seeing as we have become one with him. For each one of us has a communal membership role with him due to our actual resemblance [by nature to him].[25]

Although the actualization of our sharing of Christ's immortality is seen as futuristic in Theodore, the commonality between Christ and us is grounded on the very nature itself—i.e., our one humanity and its resemblance with Christ's nature. Thus, it seems that sharing the same nature itself in Theodore warrants its bond. *Analogia entis* works out here in that, precisely because we have become sharers in the first state of Adam, we will necessarily realize a sharing in the future state of the second Adam, according to the flesh, who possesses this same nature as ours.[26]

---

trans. John Bowden [Atlanta: John Knox, 1975], 7). But this correlation between Christology and soteriology unveils two problematic confusions: (1) the reality of Christ's nature is confused with a soteriological function and (2) the necessity of our salvation is confused with the reality of Christ's nature.

[19]   *The Creation of Adam and Eve,* McLeod, *Theodore,* 92.
[20]   *Commentary on John's Gospel,* McLeod, *Theodore,* 101.
[21]   *Commentary on Ephesians* 1:10, McLeod, *Theodore,* 121.
[22]   *Commentary on John's Gospel,* McLeod, *Theodore,* 102.
[23]   *Commentary on Colossians* 1:16, McLeod, *Theodore,* 124-5, *Theodori Episcopi Mopsuesteni in Epistolas B. Pauli Commentarii,* ed. H.B. Swete, vol. 1 (Cambridge: Cambridge University, 1880), 269.
[24]   *On the Incarnation* 1, McLeod, *Theodore,* 127.
[25]   *Commentary on Galatians* 3:27-8, McLeod, *Theodore,* 119.
[26]   *The Creation,* McLeod, *Theodore,* 89.

Secondly, the simple fact itself that Christ shares with our humanity may not be all the immanent force for Christ to unite other humans since, according to Theodore, birth in the mortal Adam needs to be changed into rebirth in the immortal Christ.[27] After death was introduced, the cosmic bond of humanity in creation was dissolved; for the soul was separated from the body and the body underwent a total disintegration.[28] This dissolved humanity is restored in Christ's humanity that receives honor, rule, and grace from God.[29] For this reason, the cosmic humanity both in Adam and Christ goes beyond its intrinsic value. They are united in a cosmic way because Christ's humanity has acquired an extraordinary gift of his Sonship that exceeds that of all other humans through his union with God.[30]

How does Christ's humanity receive a gift of the Sonship of Christ? Here, Theodore's view of the twofold nature of Christ is critical. It is unambiguous that Theodore has a concrete idea of the union between two natures. He asserts, in his *Commentary on Philippians* 2: 8: "So, wherever there is a dispute about Christ, [Paul] generally says everything as [being asserted] of one *persona*."[31] Since the two natures are united as one in "body and soul," in "the inner and the outer,"[32] and in "man and woman," it is absolutely impossible for the assumed one to be apart from the one who dwells in him.[33] It is even argued, in his *On the Incarnation*, that God the Word and the assumed one are simultaneously the same person whose two natures are not to be confused (*inconfusa*) nor the person to be perversely divided (*indiuisa*).[34] Moreover, Theodore points out the difference between God's relationships with human beings and with Christ in order to explain the union between Christ's two natures: The former is based on God's good pleasure, whereas the latter is founded by the Sonship.[35] Not ignoring difficulties caused by terminological uses in different translations, we may appreciate that the *prosopic* union of Christ's two natures in Theodore is more than a simple connection (συνάφεια).[36] Because of this concept of *prosopic*

[27]   *Commentary on John's Gospel*, McLeod, *Theodore*, 102.
[28]   *Commentary on Ephesians* 1:10, McLeod, *Theodore*, 121.
[29]   *On the Incarnation* 13-4, McLeod, *Theodore*, 140.
[30]   *On the Incarnation* 12, McLeod, *Theodore*, 138.
[31]   McLeod, *Theodore*, 111.
[32]   *On the Incarnation* 8, McLeod, *Theodore*, 136.
[33]   *Catechetical Homilies* 8.14, McLeod, *Theodore*, 163.
[34]   5, McLeod, *Theodore*, 128, Swete, vol.2, 292.
[35]   *On the Incarnation* 7, McLeod, *Theodore*, 129-130.
[36]   On the one hand, Theodore seems to distinguish in his Syriac fragment between a *prṣwpā* (*prosōpon*) and a *qnōmā* (*hypostasis*) that is identical with nature *(kyānā)*:

union in Theodore, McLeod claims that it would be a misinterpretation of Theodore if we find in him a moral connection only between Christ's humanity and human humanity and between Christ's humanity and his divinity.[37] Aloys Grillmeier also appreciates Theodore in his searching for a new interpretation of the participation of humans in God.[38]

It is, however, not clear in Theodore how substantially Christ's two natures are united in *prosopic* union. What he constantly emphasizes is that there is an ontological difference between Christ's divinity and humanity. In his *Commentary on Philippians* 2, Theodore maintains,

> What is meant here then, that the one being raised is the one raising? Did the assumed one assume the form of God or that of the slave? Is he the Creator of the universe or did he rise and receive worship because [he was] graced? Let every tongue stop such blaspheming! For the blessed apostle clearly teaches how the natures differ; what is the glory belonging to the assuming nature and who is this one who has been assumed. The former is the form of God, and the latter is the form of the slave. . . . For it is because they both have a role to play in the assumption that we distinguish the natures: between the One who assumes and the one who is assumed, and between the One who is the form of God and the other the form of a slave. We recognize the prosopic (*prçwpa*) union by the glory that the latter imparts to God the Word by his death on the cross.[39]

So critical is the ontological difference between God the Word and the assumed one that glory may belong to the assuming one and death to

---

We say that the nature of the soul is one and that of the body another, understanding that each of them has a *hypostasis* (*qnōmā*) and a nature *(kyānā)* and granting that, while the soul is distinguished from its body, it remains in its nature and in its *hypostasis*. Each of them has its own nature and *hypostasis*, as we have learnt from the apostle that there is an inner and outer man. We state their unity by combining both the "inner and the outer" in a common way [as one *prosōpon]*, so as not to call [the two] by a single term as if they were united in the same *hypostasis*. Rather we respond to [our critics] that there is one *prçwpā* (*prosōpon*) and say that, these two are [united] in one [*prosōpon*] (*On the Incarnation* 8, McLeod, *Theodore* 136).

On the other hand, the distinction between hypostasis and *prosōpon* seems to disappear as Theodore states in his Greek fragment, "So too, whenever we attempt to distinguish the natures here, we say that the man's *prosōpon* is complete and that the divinity's is also complete (*teleion*). But whenever we look to the union, then we assert that both natures are one *prosōpon*..." (*On the Incarnation* 8, McLeod, *Theodore*, 135).

37   *Theodore* 40, 57.
38   *Christ in Christian Tradition* , 424.
39   McLeod, *Theodore*, 115-6.

the assumed one *exclusively* and that the union may be realized when the assumed one receives the grace from the assuming one and imparts the glory to God the Word by his death. Doubt about the integral nature of *prosopic* union between Christ's two natures remains more critical when Theodore views works by the indwelling of God the Word in the assumed one as 'providing him with a considerable cooperation (συνεργείαν),'[40] and Mary is the mother of God the Word not by nature but by a relation (ἀναφορᾶ).[41]

Thus, the prosopic union between the assuming and the assumed is *transitional and progressive* as God aids Christ. Although Theodore accepts that Christ's humanity was united to the Word right from the beginning of its fashioning within the womb, the union seems to have been actualized gradually as Jesus grew in his human nature. God the Word was guiding Jesus *step by step* to his destiny[42] and the divinity was *mediating and aiding* him to succeed in overcoming his struggles.[43] As a result, a substantial union between the two natures is jeopardized, whereas a universal similarity between Christ's humanity and our humanity is achieved: "What stands out in [Christ's] relationship, in comparison to all others, is that his [growth] occurred more swiftly for him than it is customary for others of [his] age, yet in a way fully appropriate [to his state]."[44] The distinction between Christ's two natures seems to be qualitative while Jesus remains in a quantitative distinction from humanity, and Jesus' cosmic and universal bond with humanity in the first Adam is strengthened while Jesus' participation in the Sonship as the second Adam is weakened.

With these points in mind, thirdly, we may explore Theodore's view of Christ's humanity in his crucifixion. Up to the cross, Christ excels in his virtue by God's aid: "Up to the time of his crucifixion he was allowed to excel in virtue for our sake, by relying on his own resolve, but with God urging him on in these efforts and aiding him to completely fulfill what was at hand."[45] The reality of Christ's humanity on the cross, however, remains nothing other than the completeness and perfection of humanity. Indeed, Theodore once mentions forgiveness of our sins and abolishment of mortality by

---

40 *On the Incarnation* 14, McLeod, *Theodore*, 141, Swete, vol. 2, 309.
41 *On the Incarnation* 15, McLeod, *Theodore*, 142, Swete, vol. 2, 310.
42 *In Opposition to Apollinaris*, McLeod, *Theodore*, 151.
43 *On the Incarnation* 15, McLeod, *Theodore*, 142.
44 *On the Incarnation* 7, McLeod, *Theodore*, 132.
45 *On the Incarnation* 7, McLeod, *Theodore*, 132.

Christ's death.[46] But he frequently avers in his *Commentary on Philippians* that death strictly belongs to Christ's humanity: "So [Paul] adds that he humbled Himself and surrendered to death, a death upon a cross— which indicates his human condition."[47] A simplistic distinction made by Theodore is that Christ's death is the role of his humanity whereas his resurrection to that of his divinity.[48] This functional distinction results in a stronger stress, related to the union between Christ and us, on Christ's resurrection than on his crucifixion: "So also Christ is the one who has begun the future life, with all sharing in a common way in his resurrection and, after his ascension, in his immortality, seeing as we have become one with him."[49] Christ's humanity on the cross is either *completely* human in its death or *perfectly* human in its showing an example. Jesus as our big brother who completes a virtuous life in a more perfect way than all other humans[50] submits his life as an example (τύπον) for us.[51] Theodore claims, "See how clearly he says that God the Word has made the assumed man perfect through sufferings and has called the leader of salvation. . . ."[52] Christ's humanity on the cross continues his passion for our salvation[53] and imparts glory to God the Word.[54] Clearly, we can see here a danger of reductionism caused by a moralized view of the atonement.[55] If we follow Theodore's view to its extreme, the cosmic bond of Christ's humanity with our humanity

---

[46]   "Therefore, [John] calls 'grace' by the name of 'truth' (that is, true grace) because Christ has pardoned former transgressions and has provided salvation for the remission of sins. Moreover He has also destroyed death, which has ruled because of our sin, and given us a firm hope of resurrection as his adopted children" (*Commentary on John's Gospel*, McLeod, *Theodore*, 101).

[47]   McLeod, *Theodore*, 115-6, cf. 110, 114.

[48]   "For one is dissolved [by death], and the other is the One who raises him up. The former is the temple who is subject to dissolution, whereas the One who raises him up is God the Word, who has promised to raise up the temple that has been dissolved" (*On the Incarnation*, McLeod, *Theodore*, 146).

[49]   *Commentary on Galatians* 3:27-28, McLeod, *Theodore*, 119.

[50]   *On the Incarnation* 7, McLeod, *Theodore*, 134.

[51]   *On the Incarnation* 7, McLeod, *Theodore*, 133, Swete, vol.2, 297.

[52]   *On the Incarnation* 12, McLeod, *Theodore*, 138.

[53]   *Commentary on Philippines*, McLeod, *Theodore*, 113-4.

[54]   *Commentary on Philippines*, McLeod, *Theodore*, 116.

[55]   The idea that Christ shows an example on the cross must be included as one of the atonement views. But an exclusive argument that Christ on the cross shows an example only remains problematic in three ways: (1) if Christ's death represents moral values *alone*, we do not have to imitate it because we all die, (2) if it represents a value of *obedience* and endurance, we can find so many cases of sacrificial and voluntary death in history which are superior to obedient death, and (3) if it represents a *divine* obedience, it cannot be a moral value because we cannot imitate the *divine* obedience.

would hardly be achievable on the cross unless we endure our own suffering as much as Jesus did. What Theodore fails to see is a logical problem that death without any further value, e.g. sacrifice, cannot be an example of perfection because we all perfectly die. Death *as such* is not a moral value but a human reality for the sake of which we do not have to make any efforts. Ironically, if Christ's death has a moral value only, it cannot have any moral value. Theodore's concept of moral perfection, even though moral exemplary motif must be included as one of many motifs of the Christ's crucifixion in Scripture when it is based on other motifs, falls short of revealing the biblical proclamation that Christ's humanity participates in the mysterious and unique work of Christ, not only in general but precisely on the cross as his body is shared by all and the man Jesus Christ is our ransom.

Conclusion

Theodore's Christology—that Christ shares his humanity with our humanity ontologically in his nature and transitionally in his progress—must be fully appreciated. Christ's incarnation is the very cosmic mark that Christ is ontologically united with humanity and that Christ's humanity in its gradual progress accurately reveals the accidental and transitional reality of humanity. This genuine completeness of Christ's humanity must not be overshadowed by Christ's divinity since Christ's divinity does not compete with his humanity.[56] The problem in Theodore is, however, that Christ's humanity is too *complete* to represent its genuine uniqueness for its mysterious union with his divinity and with our humanity. The union with this unique humanity qualitatively surpasses any type of human unions between man and woman, soul and body, and the inner and the outer beings. Furthermore, the second Adam is different from the first Adam as concretely in his crucifixion as in his incarnation and resurrection. What is absent in Theodore is that Christ's humanity *on the cross* is cosmic not only because Christ has a complete and universal human nature in his death or that he shows a perfect human nature in his gradual progress, but because Christ also uniquely and cosmically shares his body and blood with humanity, including *omnia* into his death. Only in this *total* and *unique* sense does Christ's humanity participate in Christ's cosmic work of recapitulating all things in heaven and on earth.[57] Only in this *Christus totus et unicus*

---

[56] A competitive understanding of the relation between God and the world creates the dangers that the more the humanity of Jesus is emphasized in modern Christologies the more the divinity of Jesus is downplayed, and vice versa (Tanner, *Jesus*, 8).

[57] Eph. 1:10.

(the total and unique Christ) can the church as his σῶμα be πλήρωμα to fill all in all,[58] and all the divine πλήρωμα dwell *bodily* (σωματικῶς).[59] Christ's humanity is *completely* human and *uniquely* cosmic because of his death.

The completeness and changeability of Christ's humanity is not all about the true reality of Christ's humanity. The major conundrum affecting modern Christianity is not so much prompted by over-respecting Jesus' humanity but provoked by the inappropriate way Jesus' humanity is appraised: Jesus' humanity on the cross is either minimized to the oneness with human humanity or moralized for a quantitative distinction from our humanity. Ironically, this paves an easy way for us to ascend to Jesus but a difficult road for Jesus to take us all even to his own perfection. Elevating Jesus' humanity in this way is, in reality, downplaying his humanity.

From the biblical passages suggested in the beginning of this paper, where we can find divine and unique aspect of Jesus's humanity, we may reach a provisional conclusion that the following two points of views need to be fully developed in a balance: (1) Christ's humanity is *genuinely* and *completely* united with our humanity on the cross as Christ is abandoned into human suffering, pain, sin, death, and limitations, and (2) at the same time Christ *uniquely* and *cosmically* shares his body and blood with us on the cross as we are crucified with him. The former, the oneness of Christ's humanity with our humanity on the cross, has been sufficiently developed throughout the theological history. The latter, the uniqueness of Christ's humanity on the cross, needs to be further specified in future Christology.

[58]   Eph. 1:23.
[59]   Col. 2:9.

CHAPTER 3

A Forgotten Syriac Saint:
A Metrical Discourse on the Spiritual Way of
Life of Mar Shamli

James F. Coakley

My brother John and I were brought up as Baptists and are, perhaps, unlikely scholars to be found working in the field of hagiology, the study of the saints. For him, to be sure, it has been a considered and career-long home, while I am only an occasional visitor. Still, I am glad to have the chance to make this small offering to him on his retirement, with affection and admiration.

Mar[1] Shamli, the subject of the Syriac text that I present in translation here, is "forgotten" in the sense that he is unknown to members of the Assyrian Church of the East today. He has no *dukrana* (saint's day in the calendar), nor is he mentioned in any of the liturgical books of the church, either printed or (as far as I know) manuscript.[2] In scholarly literature, too, he was until recently almost unknown, with only a passing mention in J. M. Fiey's geographical survey *Assyrie*

---

[1]   *Lit.*, my lord: a title given to senior ecclesiastics and to male saints.

[2]   We have however to mention one of the manuscripts of charms edited by V. Gollancz under the title *The Book of Protection* (London, 1912). Here (p. 54) "Shamli the just" appears at the end of a rabelaisian list of obscure saints invoked to repel demons.

chrétienne (1965) and no entry at all in his dictionary *Saints syriaques* (2004).[3]

A recent and admirable study by S. Chialà has brought the saint out of obscurity as far as is ever likely to be possible, by collecting his literary remains and references to him in other Syriac sources. These are: (1) a letter of Mar Shamli himself to a disciple; (2) a metrical discourse on Shamli attributed to his disciple, Mar Brikisho; and (3) the writings of a certain Behisho which mention Shamli as the author's teacher.[4] To summarize Chialà's discussion of these sources and result: Shamli was a solitary ascetic saint who lived in about the eighth century in the region of Qardu (across the Tigris to the east from modern Cizre in Turkey)[5] and whose cult was centered in the local monastery of Kamula.[6]

It is source (2), the metrical discourse, or *memra*,[7] on Mar Shamli that is the subject of the present article. This naturally contributes the most toward such a picture of the saint as we have. But the reader of the translation below will notice at once that it is poetry, and not intended, evidently, to satisfy the wants of a biographer. Addai Scher, who read the *memra* sometime before 1907, said "Ce discours ne contient aucune notice historique."[8] That is not exactly true, but the harvest of information is indeed slight. We gather that Shamli was an ascetical

---

[3]   J. M. Fiey, *Assyrie chrétienne*, vol. 1 (Beirut, 1965), 155. Fiey evidently considered him to be of doubtful historicity.

[4]   "La *Lettre* de Mar Šamli à un de ces disciples: écrit inédit d"un auteur méconnu," *Le Muséon* 125 (2012): 35-54. The letter in the title, which he publishes with a translation, is source (1). The discourses on the monastic life by Behisho (source (3)), which he discusses on pp. 40-5, are not published. A partial translation (although not including the references to Shamli) is M. Blanchard, "The discourses of Beh Isho' Kamulaya" in *To Train His Soul in Books: Syriac Asceticism in Early Christianity*, ed. R. Darling Young and M. Blanchard (Washington, DC, 2011), 176-88. On Behisho (or Beh Isho, "In him is Jesus") see further G. Kessel and K. Pinggéra, *A Bibliography of Syriac Ascetic and Mystical Literature* (Leuven, 2011), 52-3.

[5]   Anciently in the Church of the East, Qardu was a diocese in the province of Nisibis to the west. The name is cognate with "Kurd."

[6]   For this monastery, about 20 km. east of Cizre, see Fiey, *Nisibe: métropole syriaque orientale et ses suffragants des origines à nos jours* (CSCO 388; Leuven, 1977), 199-201. The connection with Shamli is *via* his disciple Behisho "Kamulaya" (source (3)) who will have been a monk there.

[7]   *Memre* are compositions, some longer than this one, consisting of lines in pairs all having the same number of syllables. In our text that number is twelve, generally divisible within the line into 4+4+4. The masters of this meter in the fifth and sixth centuries were Jacob of Serug among the West Syrians, and Narsai among the East.

[8]   "Notice sur les manuscrits syriaques conservés dans la bibliothèque du Patriarcat chaldéen de Mossoul," *Revue des bibliothèques* 17 (1907): 227-60, specif. 246. Cf. Fiey, *Assyrie chrétienne*, i. 155.

hero and mystic (*passim*); had a teacher, Joseph[9] (line 103); lived for at least part of his career in a cell that was known as "Water of plane-trees" (253) and "Mount Sinai" (259) in the mountains of Qardu (277) where he had two particular visions of Christ (263, 354); was also itinerant (294 etc.); was a priest (323, very incidentally mentioned); attracted a large following for whom he effected healings (472), and specifically monks to whom he gave ascetical guidance (479ff.). He was one of the saints of the author's monastic "congregation" (613).

Whether our *memra* actually preserves a lively memory of Shamli is a somewhat different question. The caption title (but not the text itself) seems to name the author as "Mar Brikisho, a disciple of Mar Shamli." This attribution is accepted by Chialà, mainly on the grounds that Behisho, who was himself certainly a disciple of Shamli, mentions a Mar Brikisho, "one of our brothers."[10] But this has to be set against the internal evidence of the *memra*. Just perhaps a claim to have known Shamli lies in the words "A complete man *I* saw on earth in a hard generation" (line 93); but the previous lines (89-90) "The great sea of his glorious deeds I shall enter, though I do not know the hard labors of his victorious life" suggest the opposite. Other internal evidence points in the same direction. While the *memra* agrees at obvious points with the letter–that Shamli was insistent upon fasting, for example,[11] and that he had a particular vision of Christ[12]–the letter depicts a more severely reclusive person than the *memra* in which Shamli moves easily between solitude and society.[13] The idea of the "guarding of the mind" or "guarding of the heart," evidently a watchword of his, occurs just once in the *memra*.[14] The *memra* is also notably devoid of anything anecdotal

---

[9]   Not impossibly, the spiritual writer Joseph Hazzaya: Chialà, 46-7.

[10] Chialà, 43 and n. 33.

[11] The letter (§6) complains that having visitors involves eating cooked food. Cf. *memra* lines 481-2: "The beginning of the way of God is fasting and abstinence from foods."

[12] The letter (§11) mentions a vision of Christ in the "doubleness of his united *prosopa*"(!). Cf. *memra* lines 263, 354.

[13] In the letter, Shamli resolves not to entertain visitors at all (§13). Cf. *memra* lines 459 and 463ff. which do not suggest any reluctance on Shamli's part to minister to others.

[14] The letter makes ܪܥܝܢܐ ܢܛܘܪܬܐ and ܢܛܘܪܬܐ ܕܠܒܐ to be characteristics of the true monastic life (§§16-18). Likewise, according to Behisho, Shamli said "continually" to those who consulted him to "watch over the guarding of the heart" (quoted by Chialà, 40). This term is found in earlier spiritual writers: see S. P. Brock, *Isaac of Nineveh (Isaac the Syrian), 'The Second Part', Chapters IV-XLI* (CSCO 555; Leuven, 1995), 131 n. 7[1]. Here see only *memra* lines 537-9, specifically (539) ܢܛܘܪܬܐ ܕܠܒܐ. "Heart" is not used as a mystical term in the *memra* except in phrases to do with "purity of heart."

that we might expect in the reminiscences of a disciple. In particular, could someone who knew the saint have written "Let me come to our virtuous father's leaving and day of departure" (line 577), and then said nothing about the manner, or day, of his death? It is more likely that we should see the *memra* as a composition by a later–perhaps much later–monk of a literary bent (whose name was, of course, not necessarily Brikisho[15]). He used the occasion to range widely and poetically over biblical history and various other matters of theology in the course of praising the local saint of whom there was only a vague and general memory.

My introduction to the present text came in the course of preparing a catalog of manuscripts in the Cambridge University Library acquired since 1901. A miscellaneous group of manuscripts donated to the library in 1928 by Huw Ifor Lloyd included this one, now ms. Or. 1132. It is a nineteenth- or twentieth-century manuscript in a clear hand, of just 14 leaves consisting only of this text and without any date or other provenance information. Two other manuscripts, one of them old, were seen by Chialà but are not accessible to me.[16] A few textual uncertainties in the Cambridge manuscript might be resolved by reference to these other manuscripts, in particular whether some words in the margin (e.g., line 83) are original to the text. These and some other difficulties are pointed out in footnotes. Some other inconsequential errors are tacitly corrected in the translation.

Our text has, no doubt, some interest as a document of East Syriac mysticism in its own right. The author's idea of a spiritual "land" or "place" associated with biblical figures and with Shamli, elaborated in two long passages (183-232, 369-426), is striking.[17] But

---

[15] A. Baumstark, looking for another Brikisho, attributed our *memra* to Brikisho bar Shqape, a probably later abbot of the monastery of Beth Qoqa (*Geschichte der syrischen Literatur,* Bonn 1922, 323 n. 10; cf. Fiey, *Assyrie chrétienne,* i. 155). But there is no good reason to do this.

[16] These are Baghdad (Dawra) Syriac 329 (14th cent.?) and 580 (1894), previously NDSem 149 and 200 respectively (J. Vosté, *Catalogue de la Bibliothèque syro-chaldéenne du Couvent de Notre-Dame des Semences,* Rome, 1929, 55 and 75). See Chialà, 37 (but these mss. are no longer in Baghdad). Another ms. also not locatable at the moment of writing is Chaldean Patriarchate 74 (1520/1), catalogued in 1907 by A. Scher, "Mossoul" (n. 8 above), 246. Ms. Seert 115 (14th cent.), catalogued by A. Scher, *Catalogue des manuscrits syriaques et arabes, conservés dans la Bibliothèque épiscopale de Séert (Kurdistan) avec notes bibliographiques* (Mosul, 1905), 83-4, is presumed to have perished in 1915.

[17] It builds, no doubt, on the use of phrases with "place of" (e.g. ܐܬܪܐ ܕܫܠܝܐ "place of silence", ܐܬܪܐ ܕܫܘܚܐ "place of clarity," etc.) that are common in East Syriac monastic writings (Brock, 6 n. 1[7]). So for example Behisho's fourth discourse is

a commentary on the mystical and ascetical vocabulary of the *memra*, even if I were competent to provide it, would be inhibited by the way the demands of poetry so often override the technical definitions found in prose literature. Different words for "love," for example, are used synonymously and not distinguished as by other mystical authors;[18] likewise the various words for "mind," "thought" and "intellect."[19] The way these synonymous words are collocated makes it impossible even to keep the same English word for each Syriac one. Giving up the attempt to do so, I have aimed generally at a readable rather than word-for-word translation. Lines are indented simply where there seems to be a change of subject in the narrative.

◆ ◆ ◆

Next, with divine support I write a *memra* on the spiritual way of life of Mar Shamli, useful also for the way of life of monks. And Mar Brikisho, disciple of Mar Shamli, interpreted this *theorem*.[20] May his prayers be upon the whole world, and especially upon the present copyist, a sinner. Lord, help me in your mercies. Amen.

1 The good Lord, who in his unspeakable love
created creation from nothing, by a great wonder,
In the wisdom of his power, drew up the fixture of height and depth
and ordained rational beings to contemplate his great glory.
And when he began to create people and spiritual beings
to become heirs of his great riches hidden on high,
In the beginning he created our father Adam and placed him in Eden
and honored his name by calling him "his own image."[21]
But because he sinned and did wrong and despised the commandment his Lord laid on him,
10 his departure from paradise took place nakedly.
And because he obeyed the counsel of the Enemy and ate the fruit,

---

"about the entrance of the intellect to that pure place the name for which is 'the Promised Land'" (Blanchard, 180-1).

18 In particular, ܪܚܡ /ܪܚܡܬܐ over against ܚܘܒܐ/ܚܒ. See R. Beulay, *La lumière sans forme: introduction à l''étude de la mystique chrétienne syro-orientale* (Chevetogne, 1987), 60-4, 128-30.

19 In particular, ܗܘܢܐ, ܡܕܥܐ,ܪܥܝܢ: Beulay, 24-29.

20 Reading ܬܐܘܪܝܐ with Chialà, 37. Our ms. has ܬܐܪܝܐ. It is still an unclear expression.

21 Gen. 1:26.

he became heir to the earth of thorns and of curses.
As a child he received the sentence of the verdict
and became a slave to the Evil one and death, and to sin.
And having stripped off his glory and great comeliness
he took the yoke of death on him and on his descendants.
The spiritual ones put on great mourning at his fall
and were grieved at the corruption of the son of dust.
All his dusty race labored in slavery,
20   in error and the worship of images and foul sacrifices.
And because the Good one saw that the demons derided the image of his image
he sent and purified it and delivered it in mercy and made it his.
His will settled on a temple of a body from the house of David:
he took from it the leaven of peace for the renewal of all.
He made him a dwelling and an adorable temple for his deity
and gave authority into his hands: riches above and dominion below.
He made him king over beings spiritual and bodily
and in him was repaid the debt of mankind in paradise.
He betrothed to him first the holy church and dwelt in it
30   and he put in it treasures full of the riches of his deity.
Through John the herald of the Spirit he wedded her in his love
and called her his own and made her the bride of glory of his name.
He poured into her mysteries and depicted in her spiritual types
for the upbringing of her babes and pardon for the sins of the multitude of her children.
And he granted to it the mysteries of baptism for the purification of the defiled,
and placed in it his body, a living food for the childhood of its offspring.
In a chamber he made a spiritual banquet
and there spiritual and bodily ones have come together and borne him up.
He invited prophets, summoned Apostles and teachers,
40   excellent martyrs, and just men who have laboured, and righteous ones.

Companies of them, rank on rank, he placed in his church
that they should bear it up in name and glory, in every
generation.
O queenly one, comely in beauties and mistress of treasure,
how many voices you have to praise the bridegroom who has
taken you to wife!
At the summit of Golgotha he repaid the debt of your father
Adam
and set his children free from the slavery of the Evil one and
death.
He has trod out ahead the way of the kingdom on high
and ascended, and sat down at the right hand of the one who
sent him.
O the gracious act that was done for you, race of Adam:
50 how many voices you have to praise the love that had mercy
on you!
O how far has the name of "dust,"[22] the dust of Adam, become
great
and how exalted the arm that reached down to you in
supremacy!
Who gave you a rank on high and authority below
and made you lord over beings spiritual and bodily?
Who made you "lord," which you are not by nature,
so that angels on high and people below worship you?[23]
His living voice rang out in his gospel to the earthly one:
"Everyone who loves me, let him bear his cross and come after
me.
Whoever wishes to be an heir in the kingdom,
60 let him free himself from the slavery of this world.
Let him leave his race and the house of his parents and deny
himself
and cleave to me in faith and seemly love."[24]
Just people who heard that life-filled saying
left the world and went speedily after him.
They hated the world and its passing delights
and naked entered the spiritual stadium.
On earth they possessed no cities, no parents,

---

[22] Gen. 3:19.
[23] Phil. 2:9-11.
[24] Cf. Matt. 16:24.

no money, nor treasury nor treasures.

They left behind brothers; they renounced parents and children

70 and loved the love of the Son of God above everything.

They hated their temporal life, and entered the contest

and handed themselves over to the cruel demons of all kinds of distresses.

Some of them were in tortures and the repeated torments of fire and sword

and before kings and rulers were crowned with victory.

Others by fasting and laborious vigil-keeping and prayers

finished their lives and snatched back their captivity from the Strong one.[25]

Others dwelt in crevices and dens in the earth, alone

and by dwelling with wild animals lived excellently.

O how laborious and hard is the way of the Son of God

80 and very narrow the gate leading into that kingdom.[26]

Strait is the gate and narrow the path to the kingdom above,

and is not easy for everyone to enter its narrowness.

............[27]

one who bears his cross every day on his shoulder.

And because I shall be unable to recount the story of all the just,

so – I take an example in one member of their body.[28]

One of the children of the holy church I delight to approach,

though I am unequal to recounting the labors of his athletic contest.

The great sea of his glorious deeds I shall enter

90 though I do not know the hard labors of his victorious life.

One of the just, children of the kingdom, I will praise:

his name, Mar Shamli, a valiant soldier of righteousness.

A complete man I saw on earth in a hard generation,

a remnant[29] of the Spirit, rarer in our time than in all others.

From the archives of books of the Spirit he took riches for himself,

---

[25] Satan, alluding to Matt. 12:29.

[26] Matt. 7:14.

[27] A line has apparently dropped out here. The margin contains a replacement line: "Few are they who go into its narrowness," but this cannot be original.

[28] *Lit.,* bodies.

[29] Alluding to Rom. 9:29, Isa. 1:9 and Gen. 18.

became rich and great, and went up and ascended on high.
From his childhood he began his labors in righteousness,
and travelled straight on to the mansions of the kingdom on
high.
He went out from the world that racks its children with all
kinds of miseries
100 and bore the yoke of the Son of God on his shoulders.
He left his parents in the flesh, his race and family
and delighted greatly to become a fellow to the just who
labored.
He discipled himself to a just man named Joseph,
a son of the kingdom, best attested among the saints.
He showed him the path, directed him the way of the kingdom
on high,
and from him he received the good seed of the word of life.
He put into his hand a mighty staff–his prayer for him–
and he poured out on his head the power of the Spirit by his
blessings.
He put on him the armor for the contest–good labors–
110 to make light work of the ranks of rebellious demons.
And being armed, this just worker in the ways of the just,
he sent himself out to the contest of every kind of strife.
He set his foundation on the rock of faith,
and no storms or restless waves shook it.
Meekness is ground bearing all good things:
in him it was shown: delightful beauties in the likeness of his
Lord.
He kept his mouth from the enjoyments of pleasures:
it was songs of the Holy Spirit that were sung.
With poverty of spirit he secretly clothed himself,
120 to be worthy of the blessing that was spoken[30] by our Savior.
He put modesty with chastity at the forefront of his affections,
for he had made his soul a lovely bride to the Lord who chose
him.
Good spirits and tranquillity did the just man possess,
and his speech conveyed always peace and calm.
His eyes he commanded not to look arrogantly,
lest he be condemned by our Savior with the lewd.
His ears he kept far from vain chatter

---

[30] Matt. 5:3. For ܐܬܡܠܠ "spoken" perhaps read ܐܬܡܠܟ "promised."

and strained to hear spiritual whispers.
His nose he stopped from bodily smells
130 and took delight in the pure incense of righteousness.
In reverent fasting and prayers was he always occupied,
and laborious vigils and study of spiritual books.
He fastened himself to spiritual virtues
and while mortal, showed in himself a likeness to the angels.
O fleshly mortal, dust of Adam,
Who made you become like the angels on high?
O bodily one, corruptible, home of passions,
who made you worthy to live a life that was not in your nature?
In the beginning when the Maker created our lowly dust,
140 he placed in it a spiritual soul, a treasury.
And because we became hostages to the Evil one and to death, in slavery,
we were too much impoverished to do anything good.
And when the Good one saw that our soul's beauty had been corrupted,
it did not please him that the Evil one should mock the image of his image.
At the end of times when his mercies on our fallen state were stirred
he sent his Son and saved us by his blood and made us his.
He placed the first fruit of his living Spirit in our hearts,[31]
that we might yield fruit .....[32] of our soul, like spiritual beings.
In a cell smaller than anyone's did the victorious one live,
150 in silence and quiet – a similar and like state to the angels on high.
By hunger and thirst, with meditation, night and day
he subdued the beasts of passion in his members.
Piteous weeping and repeated mourning he made for his soul
and night and day he wept for it as for one that was dead.
His cell was made a house of lamentation, in sorrow and mourning;
by piteous chants and by songs of the Holy Spirit.
Satan saw it, he who from the beginning was the killer of men:

[31]   Rom. 8:23.
[32]   Ms. ܐܚܡܘܗ 'rotten condition'? The scribe has not written a vowel on *mem*, perhaps indicating that he did not understand the word here.

it did not please him to see a likeness of the angels on earth.
He raved and burned with rage, and began to draw the bow of his anger,
160 and fired off sufferings and redoubled tortures upon the victorious one.
He marshalled despair, sloth, depression,
covetous desire, with boasting and vainglory.
With these he attacks the saints in every generation
to separate them from their Lord and to become his.
The Holy Spirit strengthened the affections of the just man
and cut the cunning meshes of his nets.
The claw of the Evil one did not snare him anyhow
nor did the cruel blasts of his wicked anger shake him.
Like an anchor he held on in himself to the love of his Lord.
170 and every desire that came to him he tore up and cast away.
By self-emptying he trod down the desire of avarice
and crushed it and banished it away from his soul.
By piteous weeping and lamentation day and night
he quenched the desire of vainglory and boasting.
Like iron in his constant might,
he defeated despair and sloth and depression.
By hunger and thirst and self-denial
he rooted out from his members the passion of hateful desire.
By his good spirits and his perfect love, the love of his Lord,
180 he quenched the passion of anger and wrath, along with envy.
By these labors and spiritual virtues
he purified his body and cleansed his soul from spots.
He passed on from the land of the unnatural to that of the natural
in which he saw the image of his soul, as in a mirror.
As on a bridge he passed over from the tears of remorse
to that pure land full of milk and honey.
He passed from the land of lamentation in hard labors
and entered the chamber of the Holy of Holies, of the purity of his heart.
In a little time, and by his diligence in good works
190 he received the treasure[33] of the pearl of comely beauty.
This is the kingdom on high, which our Lord named,

---

[33] A two-syllable word evidently dropped out of this line. The word ܣܝܡܬܐ "treasure" is in the margin apparently in the first hand. A second hand has curiously written ܟܟܪܐ "talent" (a less good reading) above the line.

and he plundered what was hidden, and the door of passions
was shut.
This is the treasure of which Paul, the preacher of the Spirit,
says
it is placed within us[34] and by labors its beauty shines out.
This is the land of peace and promise
and it was named "place of the Lord"[35] by Israel.
This is purity of heart and the land of peace
where all light is blurred in the light that is unspeakable.
This is the place,[36] purer than any day and full of beauty,
200 all resplendent with the delightful beauties of contemplation.
In this place, the just of the House of Israel settled
and were borne up in its wide places by the light in them.
In it stood the Moses, a great one in Israel, son of the Hebrews
writing on the formation of all creatures.
In it he was enclouded in great glory on the mountain of
Sinai[37]
and face to face he saw God, in a secret sense.
Isaiah too, son of Amoz, one renowned among the prophets,
in this place saw the spiritual ones crying out praise.
In the greatness of the wonder of their holiness he was
terrified
210 and was sorry and lamented over his sins and the faults of his
soul.[38]
Here Daniel too, prophet of the Spirit, saw
wheels of fire and ranks of the Spirit before the Creator.[39]
Ezekiel too, seer of secret things,
here told about the revival and quickening of the dead.[40]
And Elijah, venerable for his zeal for God,
here brought living fire against the unbelievers.[41]
Here he prayed in the purity of his heart and his fieriness
and bound the air and held back the rain for a length of
time.[42]

[34] 2 Cor. 4:7.
[35] Syriac ܪܟܬܐ ܡܕܗܘܐ, not quite the same as Gen 28.16 where Jacob says ܪܟܬܐ ܐܬܪ ܐܬܪܠܝܬ ܪܝܗ ܪܝܐܬܪܐ.
[36] From this point I generally translate ܐܪܬܐ as "place" rather than "land" as in previous lines.
[37] Exod. 20:23.
[38] Isa. 6:1-5.
[39] Dan. 7:9-10.
[40] Ezek. 37:1-14.
[41] 1 Kings 18.17-40.
[42] 1 Kings 17:1-2.

And Elisha son of Shapat, heir of the just one
220 here performed all kinds of signs by the Spirit he received.
He parted the Jordan and brought to life the Shilomite woman's son,
and purified and cleansed the leprosy of Naaman the Aramean.[43]
In this place the just Jacob saw a ladder
and he was called by the name of "Israel":[44] he saw God.[45]
In this place the prophet Samuel took delight:
he was ordained prophet and priest and anointer of kings.[46]
Here the prophet of the Spirit cries out with sweet voice,
"How fair are the dwellings and habitations of the house of Israel!"[47]
At this place the saints kept vigil in all their generations
230 and poured out tears night and day.
At this gate they stripped off their old man
and put on the new one, called the "image of God."
At this gate the blessed Shamli the just kept vigil
with hard labors and with prayers night and day,
Until he stripped off the coat of desires from his mind
and entered and took possession of the places of the purity of his heart.
O man, how wondrous is your story and great your might:
among creatures there is none who can recount the triumph of your labors!
And because the just one perceived that the mercies of his Lord pitied him freely
240 he was fervent with zeal in his desire for quiet and a wilderness dwelling.
What was said by the son of Amoz he desired:
"on the top of mountains and in high places"[48] to praise the Lord.
"Who has given me the wings of a dove,"[49] he cried and said,

---

[43] 2 Kings 2:14, 4:32-7, 5:1-27. In the story in 2 Kings 4 the Syriac version has ܫܝܠܐ "Shiloh" instead of "Shunem"; but the woman is called ܫܝܠܘܡܝܬܐ "Shilomite" with an *m* (vv. 12, 36).
[44] Gen 28:12, 32:28.
[45] An etymology of *Israel* from Hebrew *'iš ra'a 'el* "man saw God".
[46] 1 Sam. 3:20, 7:9, 8:22.
[47] Cf. Num. 24:5 (words spoken by Balaam).
[48] Cf. Isa. 2:14. The words "top of mountains," making up the meter, are in the margin.
[49] Ps. 55:6 (Peshitta).

to fly and alight in the wilderness, without the society of man.
The blessed one went out in courage and faith
to the outer wilderness and to dwell with wild animals.
In the steps of Mar John the herald of the Spirit
he walked and went on in virtue all his days.
On mountains and waste places he made his dwelling at all hours:
250 at the tops of crags and on islands and lowlands.
Walking barefoot he trod over mountains and sharp rocks
until the blood ran from his holy footsteps.
The just man's cave was called "Water of the plane-trees"[50]
and it became a stronghold on the high mountains and islands.
And it became lush with a host and great number of all kinds of trees,
and it became beautiful like Elim[51] among the Israelites.
He called it "Eden of paradise" figuratively
and lived there like Elijah in the garden of Eden.[52]
Again, he sometimes named it "Mount Sinai,"
260 for it was delightful, glorious, and rich in divine visions.
"Let us go up again to Mount Sinai," he called to everyone,
for there Moses face to face saw God.
Twice he received our Lord Jesus there
and for this reason he called it by this name.
Beautiful and lovely was Mount Sinai, on account of its visions,
but more so our Sinai, the "Water of plane-trees."
Delightful and lovely was Eden of paradise, full of good things,
but more so the vacant wilderness of Shamli the just.
O how lovely and very beautiful was the mountain of our father
270 and like a king was he borne in state in his palaces.
O how lovely was he, his staff in his hand and his thoughts on high,

50 Syriac ܡܝܐ ܕܕܘܠܒܐ. Fiey proposes to identify this place with Ayn Dulba ܥܝܢ ܕܘܠܒܐ ("well of the plane-tree"), now the village of Deleb, near Dohuk in northwest Iraq (*Assyrie chrétienne*, i. 155 n. 5). But the name here is not that of a village, nor is Deleb in Qardu.
51 Exod. 15:27.
52 Elijah was taken into heaven (2 Kings 2.11), but here it is inferred that he was translated to the garden of Eden.

on foot and barefoot going around on the sharp rocks,
His body was in the material world of miseries
and his mind resplendent above in heaven with the angels.
On Mount Sinai was Moses the just enveloped in cloud,
in a lofty vision of natural contemplation.
Our excellent father on the mountains of Qardu saw Christ
in the delightful light and lovely glory of his deity.
In lovely light, that of nature, Moses took delight,
280 the just new prophet of the house of Israel.
And our excellent father – in new light that nature does not possess
his virtuous soul was illuminated continually.
There, likenesses and foreshadowings were effected:
here, it was the truth, plain and brighter far than the sun.
The just one received the Holy Spirit, which nature does not possess,
that which was called by our Lord the Paraclete.[53]
"Behold, I go up to my Father and my God, to the height above,"
his living voice cries out and proclaims to his disciples,[54]
And "I send the Holy Spirit to be with you
290 and in him you will take delight always."[55]
This power the just Shamli received and inherited
and in it he trod over height and depth and everything in them.
In it he pulled down high walls and fortified strongholds
and in it he went round on the mountaintops and high places.
In it he subdued the longings of desire in his own members
and in it he defeated hunger and thirst and fearsome deaths.
In it he defeated the world and its passing pleasures
and in it he was strong in the outer wilderness all his days.
In it he became high and grew above the just men of his day
300 and in it he saw the ends of the earth and everything there.
In it he did all kinds of signs and wonderful works
that witnessed to his blessedness among the saints.
By it he saw off the threats of rebellious demons
and by it he silenced the fearsome clamors of their blasphemies.

[53] John 14:26.
[54] Cf. John 20:17.
[55] Cf. John 14:16-17, 16:7.

By it he made their armies quiver in fear and trembling
and by it he defeated the great power of the Enemy.
Dread gripped the Prince of the air, and fear and trembling,
for he saw the just one who defied and made light of his
evildoing.
He became indignant and strong in his evil intention and
cruel bile
310 and raised a revolt and fearsome warfare against the victorious
one.
He gathered his hosts, the sons of error,
to hold a contest with the saint in great clamor.
Some of them with swords, some with lances, and much
weaponry,
and the Archon at their head, prancing like a king.
"Who is this?–a mortal, sunk in corruption,
and he will lose his life and no more be found in the land of
the living."
So he encouraged his armies–but they were not encouraged,
because he had been defeated in past contests by our Savior.
He had already brought down the power of the Enemy,
320 broken his sting, torn off his crown, and made sport of him.
From that day his dominion over mortals had ended.
He took back our captivity and gave victory to our whole race.
The virtuous just priest Shamli, with courage,
raised his voice against the ranks of rebellious demons.
He made the sign of the cross of the Son against them in faith
and they turned tail away from the just one in defeat.
They were shaken and stunned by the power of the Spirit
hidden in the just one
and returned to the light-less place of their defeat.
O man, how you have become splendid with what is not
yours,
330 and how you have become great with riches you have taken by
grace and freely!
Who made you, a bodily person, a base nature, so that
spiritual beings are routed so speedily by you?
Who made you, a son of the powdery dust of Adam, so that
you see off in power the evil of the Prince of the air?
Who put the leaven of life in the recess of your soul
and inflamed you with the Spirit and made you an
indestructible vessel?

Who made the beauty of your mind to be radiant with
delightful visions
and let you know all worlds and their chiefs?
The Envious one saw that the soldier of truth was not moved
340 nor shaken by his swift attack or the number of his soldiers.
He came once more and set up a snare and clever schemes,
an image of error and burning lights.
The clever one conjured hallucinations of fire and light
to captivate the just one and, as he thought, make sport of
him.
He assembled his troops, all fiery,
himself borne up among them like a lamp.
A throne of fire and crown of light the foul one placed before
him,
and like a king he was bowed to by the soldiers.
The just man, who perceived the schemes of the evil Archon,
350 aroused himself, put on strength and put on the armor of
humility.
The Holy Spirit strengthened his affections with faith
and he was victorious and came out in gladness of heart and
cheer.
And because in everything the just Shamli came out
victorious,
he received the crown of the triumph of his labors: the vision
of the Son.
He saw Christ in the great glory of his deity,
being carried along the broad way of the purity of his heart.
By a great wonder he received the beauty of the Son of God
in a hidden mystery, making himself known in essence.
The Trinity was conveyed in an image of his mind:
360 Father, Son, and Holy Spirit, one in nature.
Three Persons, one Essence, one will,
whose beauty shines out in the embodiment of our Lord
Jesus.
He is the dwelling and adorable temple of deity
and in him the Trinity is worshipped by rational creatures.
One is the power, one the will, one the glory,
one the lordship, not ever to be divided.
He is the effulgence, he the light, he the beauty
and he it is who is revealed in the pure minds of those who
befriend his love.
This is the place of spiritual life, perfect in everything

370 in which is no dread, nor any robbers nor plunderers.
   This is Zion, mother of the sons of light,
   in whom the just take their rest, who were wearied in many
   struggles.
   This is the city of light of which Paul said
   that in it dwell all the spiritual assemblies.[56]
   This is the place in which our Lord said there is no worm
   nor thieves, nor weevil nor locust.[57]
   This is the word that our Lord said to the One who sent him:
   "Let them, Father, be one in us in union."[58]
   These unspeakable blessings the saints have seen,
380 and have endured labors and strange deaths in many contests.
   In this place the just Simon received authority
   and accepted the keys that bind and loose in height and
   depth.
   "A rock" he was called, who was not shaken by storms,
   upon which should be set the building of the holy church.[59]
   To this place the chosen Paul came up and ascended
   and heard fearsome sounds and utterances that are
   indescribable.
   Here he reveals secret mysteries of things to come
   and of the gladness there will be at the end for the race of
   Adam.
   To this place the just Shamli came up and ascended,
390 entered, and was protected from harm in the king's palace.
   He came up with Paul and ascended to the third heaven
   and heard and perceived utterances indescribable.
   Day and night he remained in the beauty of the new world,
   whether in the body or without the body he did not know.[60]
   This is the place wholly proof against fears,
   and with no dread, no Adversary and no misadventure.
   There is no depression and no despair in this place,
   nor envy nor sloth or passion of desire.
   Nor yet is there anger, nor wrath in this place,
400 and no boasting or vainglory, and no pride.
   In it there are no kings and rulers and no judges,

[56]   Heb. 11:22.
[57]   Cf. Matt. 6:19-20 (but without "locust").
[58]   Cf. John 17:21.
[59]   Cf. Matt 16:18-19.
[60]   Cf. for this whole passage 2 Cor. 12:2-4.

for one is the king who reigns there over all creatures.
There are no rich or poor in this place,
for one is the rich thing that the just inherit: the vision of the Son.
Nor are there sicknesses or diseases in this place,
for it is exalted far above ills and adversity.
There is no hunger and no thirst in this place,[61]
for one is the food and drink of the just: the love of our Lord.
There is no freedom or slavery in this place,
410 for one is the rank of all the just: that of sons.
There is no dominion in this place for the Prince of the air
and here the dominion of death, and of sin, is at an end.
Here Paul the chosen one, Apostle of the nations, cries out,
"Where is your sting, o death[62] that devoured the children of Adam?"
Here has been fulfilled that which was said in figures;
now be glad, o mortals. Death has come to an end.
All love and pleasures is this place,
and it is all light and gladness and cheer.
This place did the just of the house of Israel expect,
420 priests and kings and just prophets in their generations.
But the evening of death overtook them in the expectation of hope
and they went and took their rest without having seen or entered it.
Its gate was closed in the face of all
and no one came to open it until the appearance of our Lord Jesus.
He himself is the gate, he is the place, he is the light
and he is the haven and hope of life for those who befriend his love.
"I," he said, "am the great gate of the kingdom on high
and anyone who enters by this gate will live for ever."[63]
"For I am the light of the world," he said too,
430 "and anyone who shall believe in me has passed from darkness
and found light."[64]

---

[61] Lines 407-12 are in the margin.
[62] 1 Cor. 15:55.
[63] Cf. John 10:9.
[64] John 9:5 and cf. 5:24.

By this gate the saints entered the kingdom on high,
found rest, and settled in the haven of hope of the beauty of Jesus.
Like a mirror our Lord was depicted before their eyes
and they rejoiced in him day and night, far more than treasure.
For he is the pearl of the kingdom on high
whose beauty is revealed in the pure minds of the just who have labored.
Our father found this treasure in his mind's eye
and he rejoiced in it day and night, insatiably.
This became the pearl of the just Shamli
440 and he guarded it night and day from plunderers.
For its sake he sent himself out to the mountains and waste places
and guarded it lest it be taken forcefully by thieves.
For its sake—hunger, thirst and repeated dangers of death,
lest its surpassing beauty should be sullied by worldly pleasures.
For its sake—laborious fastings and prayers
lest the hateful filth of some passion or other should take control of it.
For its sake he fled and secreted himself in mountains and desolate places[65]
that its beauty might more and more shine in his thought.
For its sake—his cross on his shoulder every day
450 and for its sake he acquired no house or money.
For its sake he was put constantly in danger
by journeyings and moving from place to place.
Sometimes it was to the wilderness, sometimes to monasteries,[66] sometimes to habited places,
and to the east and to the west, to every quarter.
Happy the champion who so guarded the rich thing that he received,
diminished not at all in its magnitude.
Happy the victorious one who hid his pearl so
and enjoyed its delightful beauty constantly.
In the desert it was with him, in a desolate place it was with him; in society it was with him;

[65] Reading ܟܘܪ̈ܐ for ܟܘܪ̈ܐ in the ms.
[66] Syriac ܡܥܡܪܐ , *lit.* dwellings; but here the meaning "monasteries" seems to fit in between uninhabited and inhabited places. Cf. the same word in line 586.

460 everywhere he rejoiced in it more than any treasure.
It became his food; it became his drink; it became his pleasure.
and on it he was nourished all his temporal life.
And because his Lord saw that he guarded his riches and increased his talents
he put into his hand his great house to govern.
The tidings of his victorious life spread to the four quarters
and kings and lowly people alike came together at the hearing of his name.
The light of his virtuous deeds shone at the ends of the earth
and hearers flooded in to enjoy benefit in his prayers –
Just ones, laborers and masters of labors from monasteries,
470 and laymen, everyone distressed by diseases and illnesses.
Who was distressed and not comforted by the sight of him.
and who was sick and not healed by his prayer?
Who wished to go on the way of the kingdom on high
and did not receive counsel from his mouth for his way of life?
He was set as a watchman for all the just, the workers,
and they, the workers of the truth, looked to him in friendship.
The sick he made well, illnesses he cured, and lepers he cleansed,
demons he cast out by the living word of our Lord Jesus.
His children and disciples multiplied in every place:
480 he gave them to hear the word of the light of his teaching.
He said, "The beginning of the way of God
is fasting and abstinence from foods.
Restrain your mouths from the luxuries of pleasures
and put on the armor of good labors and enter the contest.[67]
Put on the helmet of faith on the head of your minds
and bear the yoke of humility, in imitation of your Lord.
Put on your feet the truth of the preparation of righteousness
and gird up the loins of your members with chastity.
Apply modesty to your affections and to your eyes,
490 for such is seemly for freemen and good slaves.
Put to death the passions of your members by hunger and thirst
and put away from you anger, wrath and vainglory.
Do not lay up for yourselves a treasure on earth,[68] or property

---

[67] Cf. Eph. 6:10-17 but the items of armor are differently named.
[68] Matt. 6:19.

and keep in mind always the remembrance of death, which is
near.
Flee from pomp and elegance and the ornament of fine
clothes:
dress in worn-out and dirty rags to cover the body.
Put away from you fatness of the belly, a wicked wolf
that how ever full is not ever satisfied.
Put away from you wicked envy and calumny
500 and acquire love, which is full of the fruits of the Spirit.
Love one another, as befits heirs of the Son,
for it is written that one who hates his brother is a second
Devil.[69]
Put away from you the drinking of wine, and drunkenness,
lest it defile your members with debauchery.
See that you do not become dissolute, or thieves
lest you be driven out with the wicked to outer darkness.
Guard the truth and put away from you lying
lest you imitate Satan, the enemy of mankind.
Make your nourishment bread and water, to sustain the body
510 that you may be pure, like the angels of[70] the children of the
kingdom.
Love the poor and visit the sick and the distressed
that you may be found worthy of the blessedness spoken of
by our Savior.[71]
And much more than all these things, love the service of the
Psalms
by reverent standing and wakeful vigil all night.
And more than all, love the reading and study of the Scriptures
that you may inherit from them the kingdom on high and
the treasure of life.
See that you do not become itinerants in cities
lest you estrange yourselves from the benefit of the monastic
life.
Flee from idle words and vain speech
520 and love silence, which is all full of the fruits of the Spirit.
Keep yourselves awake at all times in penitence
that with those who mourn, you may acquire the hope of the
kingdom on high.

---

[69] An inference from 1 John 4.20 and John 8.44.
[70] But perhaps read ܟܝܢ for,ܝܢ : "angels, the children."
[71] Cf. Matt. 25:34, 39.

And more than all, acquire purity and clarity of heart
that you may see in your minds the blessing: the beauty of the
Son.
With diligence make peace between angry parties
for our Lord Jesus has great joy at peace among people.
Put away from you enmity and malice
and become good like your Father in heaven.
Love silence and have great affection for poverty
530 For such befits the pure life of monasticism.
Flee from the world that everywhere chokes its children
and bear on you the living yoke of the Son of God.
Grasp in your hands the rod of might, the living cross
with which you may drive the rebellious demons from before
you.
At the head of your words, acquire the humility of faith
and engage with might the notional[72] Philistines.
And by bodily guardings and intense labors
acquire with prudence a mind wakeful at all times.
Guarding of the mind, with spiritual song
540 well makes for purity of the soul and prudence.
And more than all, diligently acquire self-denial,
the mother which nurtures the pure fruits of righteousness.
Concentrate closely at all times in your minds
to see the blessing, the glorious vision of our Lord Jesus.
He dwells within us in the holy of holies of the purity of our
heart
and the door of passion is closed against us and it is invisible
to us.
For he is the kingdom on high, in which is hidden
the pearl of comeliest beauties within us.
Flee from the sight of the vain things of this world
550 that you may see the beauty of the new world within your
hearts.
Estrange yourselves from reports and news of earthly things
that you may be worthy to hear the delightful sounds of the
hosts on high.
Stop up your nostrils from the odors of this world
that you may enjoy the living breath of the Holy Spirit.

---

[72]   Or "metaphorical"; Syriac ܐܪܙܢܝܬܐ.

Restrain your mouths from the cookery[73] of rich foods
that you may take delight at the table of love of our Lord.
Strip off from you the coat of passions, a hateful garment,
that you may put on the spiritual robe of the power of the
Spirit.
Strip off your old man of worldly pleasures
560 that you may put on the new one, full of light and holiness."
By this spiritual light-filled teaching
the just man gave benefit to the multitudes of his children.
With these spiritual life-filled words
he launched them as on wings up to heaven.
Like babes, children of the world, he nursed them
with the pure milk of his spiritual teaching.
By this food and delightful drink of the word of life
our virtuous father nourished them for obedience.
In him was fulfilled what was spoken by our Lord Jesus,
570 that rivers of living water flowed from his belly.[74]
O man, how perfect is the food of your teaching
and sweet the drink of the words of your mouth, far more
than honey.
O mortal, child of the powdery dust of Adam,
who made you the one to provide spiritual things?
O man of flesh, lowly dust, son of mortals,
who gave you authority over treasures and treasure of the
Spirit?
With sadness of spirit and a broken heart let me now come
to our virtuous father's leaving and day of departure.
Having finished the course of his labor in righteousness,
580 he was pleasing to Christ, who removed him from here to the
place above.
From his youth he did work in the vineyard of the Son
and did not rest or let up until he reached the evening of
death.
In the morning his labors were in the field of righteousness,
and at eventide he took the first fruits, the coin of life.
What mountain did the just one's foot not traverse?
Into what monastery did he not walk barefoot? [75]

---

73   ܛܘܿܝ ܐܠ, a rare word; more narrowly "frying" or "grilling." For this meaning see T.
Audo, *Dictionnaire de la langue chaldéenne* (Mosul, 1907) *s.v.* ܛܘܿܝ. The word appears
in a similar negative context in Shamli's letter (§6).
74   Cf. John 7:38.
75   Fiey, *Assyrie chrétienne*, i.155, quotes this line.

In what desert did he not dwell and make it inhabited,
  and what wilderness did he not make a dwelling-place?
  His cross was borne on his shoulders night and day
590 like the band of the twelve apostles of the Son.
  If I liken you to an apostle, o our virtuous father,
  You are alike, in no way less, in all your doings.
  And if I should compare you to John the Baptist,
  you are very comparable: your dwelling was with the wild
  animals.
  If I should liken you to those with Pachomius or with
  Anthony,
  you are very like them in the hard labors of your contest.
  Our excellent father went out from the misery-filled world
  bearing a crown as his chief ornament: his vision of the Son.
  And because the Good one saw that the man of the Spirit had
  well achieved greatness,
600 he said of him the saying applying to good servants:
  "Because you have left the world and its treasures and
  possession of its riches,
  come, be heir of the new world full of all blessings.
  Because you hated brothers and parents, race and family,
  come, be one of the delightful ranks of the hosts on high.
  Because you have kept your mouth from the luxuries of
  worldly pleasures,
  come, enjoy the wedding-feast[76] of the kingdom on high."
  The blessed just one Shamli, goodly in his way of life, set out
  and parted from his children, the image of his way of life a
  good example.
  He set out and left for the place above, free from all dreads
610 and left here his body, all beneficent.
  Blessed are you, our father and blessed your soul, full of
  treasures:
  I cannot describe your blessing as it is.
  Blessed is our congregation which has a father among the
  saints,
  by whose prayers our ranks are preserved from ills.
  Blessed is the place in which the contest of his labors was
  accomplished,
  on whose inhabitants peace may reign by his prayers.

---

[76] A conjectural translation: the Syriac is ܪܠܝܠܐ ܪܥܐܝ .

Blessed is our congregation in which his virtuous body is borne up,
that with him we may be heirs on high with the spiritual ones.
Blessed are the faithful who take refuge in him in faith,
620 who from him take all benefits and all healings.
Let the prayer of the just one be a protecting wall for the whole world
and most especially this our congregation for ever.
And the Lord, who gave him victory in all contests and accomplished his calling –
to him be praise from every mouth for ever. Amen.

Praise to you from every mouth, who give victory to those who love you and who keep your commandments; to you who magnify them here on earth and above in heaven. Finished is the story of Mar Shamli, and to God praise ever.

CHAPTER 4

Transubstantiation and its Contemporary Renditions: Returning Eucharistic Presence to the Body, Gender, and Affect

Sarah Coakley

Introduction

My brother-in-law, John W. Coakley, has devoted a lengthy span of his scholarly career to the critical retrieval of medieval themes of sanctity, gender, and spiritual authority. Much of the material he traces in his already-classic monograph on this topic[1] relates to the fascinating nexus of affect, gender projection, and bodily symbolism that attended the Christian piety of female saints and their confessors (or "promoters") throughout the long middle ages. A particularly significant context of such a constellation of themes was that of the Eucharist, which could—by turns—produce ecstatic and empowering visions of Christ's direct and intimate presence to women saints, or else engender disturbing female ambitions of inedia and self-annihilation for the sake of Christ's body. In either scenario, the role played by a holy woman could potentially out-maneuver her male interlocutor, even

---

[1] John W. Coakley, *Women, Men and Spiritual Power: Female Saints and Their Male Collaborators* (New York, Columbia University Press, 2006).

though his status as a monk or priest remained superior in terms of ecclesiastical standing.[2]

The purpose of this paper is to provide an ancillary *theological* investigation to John Coakley's subtle analysis of gender and embodiment in relation to medieval eucharistic practice. The technical doctrine of "transubstantiation" that was to be promoted by Thomas Aquinas in the thirteenth century (amidst a host of earlier and alternative explanatory renditions of eucharistic presence) was, of course, later to become normative for the Roman church at the Council of Trent; but this was not before a veritable cacophony of lampooning critiques from the Protestant Reformers had made themselves heard and demanded response. In the course of these highly polemicized debates it is perhaps unsurprising that the doctrine became, by degrees, significantly de-contextualized from its original locus in Thomas's thinking as a whole; and this de-contextualization has also tended to be true of contemporary attempts to revitalize and reparse the Thomistic account.

How to construe Thomas's rendition of transubstantiation coherently in *philosophical* terms, first, and in the matrix of his own particular contextualized reception of Aristotle, is a highly technical issue which this particular essay can only discuss in a preliminary and somewhat glancing manner. What I am more interested in exploring here lies suitably closer to John Coakley's own instincts as a medieval historian of *embodiment*: It is the incarnational theology that underlyingly sustains Thomas's exposition of transubstantiation in the third and final part of his *Summa Theologiae*, and his consistent accompanying interest in the physical, moral and affective aspects of eucharistic *efficacy*. In short, my central thesis will be that to extract the "doctrine of transubstantiation," so called, from these crucial insights into embodied, sacramentally-infused Christian life, is to demean its subtlety from the outset, and to disconnect it from the whole sweep of the *Summa* which precedes it.

My attempt, then, will be to provide a brief but (I trust) sensitive new rendition of Thomas's account, especially as it relates to implicit

---

[2]   See esp., ibid, 21-22, 62, 113, 145, 205, for Coakley's treatment of relevant eucharistic themes. A comparison of the ecstatic eucharistic visions of the nuns of Helfta and the (later) punitive fastings of Catherine of Sienna and Catherine of Genoa is especially instructive in this regard: see Caroline Walker Bynum, *Jesus as Mother: Studies in the Spirituality of the High Middle Ages* (Berkeley, CA, University of California Press, 1982), ch. V; and eadem, *Holy Feast and Holy Fast: The Religious Significance of Food to Medieval Women* (Berkeley, CA, University of California Press, 1987), ch. 5.

questions of the body, desire and gender. Only rarely are these points of connection noted in the secondary literature on transubstantiation;[3] and—as we shall show—the most sophisticated recent attempts to give Thomas's theory new coinage in the categories of post-modern philosophy have also tended to occlude these important accompanying concerns.

In what follows I shall thus limit myself to three distinct tasks, each of which will bring my own reading of Thomas's doctrine of transubstantiation into relation with an emerging central systematic thesis about the eucharist as the locus of transformed and transforming "desire".

First, I shall turn back to the medieval discussion of transubstantiation—that despised "second captivity" of the church, as Luther later saw it[4]—and argue briefly, following a train of complex recent scholarship on the matter, that no *consistent* explication of this doctrine could be achieved in the medieval period following the supposed mandating of it by the fourth Lateran council (1215). Much was at stake, as different renditions of Aristotelian categories of "substance", "accident", "form" and "matter" were construed and re-construed through a variety of imported lenses; but perhaps the most important contemporary lesson overall, and however this contextualized reception of Aristotle is understood, is that his understanding of transubstantiation needs also to be staked out *apophatically*, and in explicit correlation with his equally-mysterious christological account of the "hypostatic union" in the *Tertia Pars* of the *Summa*.

Having made this proposal, I shall then (and secondly) throw into contrast two intriguing and creative contemporary re-interpretations of the Thomistic doctrine of transubstantiation in the work of Jean-Luc Marion and Catherine Pickstock. I shall go on to argue that, for all their own apophatic insights, Marion and Pickstock have so far failed to give a fully-convincing account of the accompanying embodied transformations that eucharistic presence, *if efficacious*, should bring about. Here I shall expose, in a way inspired by Thomas himself, the relation of sacramental theology to questions of bodiliness and desire,

---

[3]   One careful recent account of Aquinas's rendition of transubstantiation does however trace the link (albeit briefly) between transubstantiation and the affective and moral efficacy of the eucharist, as it draws the believer into unity with Christ's own sacrifice: see Matthew Levering, *Sacrifice and Community: Jewish Offering and Christian Eucharist* (London, Routledge, 2005) 115-167.

[4]   Martin Luther, "The Babylonian Captivity of the Church" (1520), tr. A. T. W. Steinhaüser, *Three Treatise* (Philadelphia, Fortress Press, 1959).

and also bring the issues of sacramental *validity* and *efficacy* much more closely together than is customary, thereby suggesting simultaneously a possible route of *rapprochement* for ecumenical divides on eucharistic theology that go back to the Reformation.

Finally, I shall draw some systematic conclusions. As John Coakley's work well illustrates today, the more subliminal associations of ritual and eucharistic practice are often the ones where we see bodily and affective transformation most powerfully in play; and Aquinas's insights into progressive personal eucharistic assimilation along these lines are part and parcel of what he sought to defend in his deeply *incarnational* theory of transubstantiation. The contemporary systematic theologian or philosopher of religion therefore does well to attend to the fullness of Thomas's text, as well as to contemporary historians like John Coakley who have traced the earthed manifestations of medieval and early modern eucharistic devotion with such acute attention to embodied practice.

Medieval Diversity and the Thomistic "Theory" of Transubstantiation

Any attempt to understand the goals of Thomas's "theory of transubstantiation" must take some account of Thomas's own context, and of his particular motivations for proposing the account as theoretically normative. Three preparatory points should, perhaps, be stressed here initially, for these may startle those brought up on an earlier historiography of doctrinal development.

First, it is certainly not the case that the specific, technical doctrine of transubstantiation (the theory that the "substance" of bread and wine is *turned into* the body and blood of Christ) was regarded as a necessary "article of faith" after the condemnation of Berengar of Tours at the Synod of Rome (1059), when a mere "symbolic" reading of eucharistic transformation was firmly ruled out; nor even—more surprisingly—after the anti-Albigensian decrees of the Fourth Lateran Council (1215), in which the very word "transsubstantiatio" was first used with official favor. Well after 1215, as James McCue showed in a justly-famous article,[5] a variety of theories of eucharistic presence were for a while well-tolerated in the West (most especially so-called "consubstantiation", the theory that the true body and blood are

---

[5]   James F. McCue, "The Doctrine of Transubstantiation from Berengar through Trent: The Point at Issue", *Harvard Theological Review* 61 (1968): 385-430.

present *along with* the unchanged substance of bread and wine).[6] It is only *with* Thomas, then, that an insistence on transubstantiation as the sole acceptable explanation was pressed; only *after* him that alternative theories were retroactively rejected as "heretical" by appeal to the Fourth Lateran Council; and only from the later time of Duns Scotus that the Council was (re-)interpreted as "a *formal definition* of transubstantiation over against cons[substantiation]."[7] So there is more looseness and fluidity in the history of development of this doctrine than is still sometimes supposed. And especially in the earlier period before the Lateran Council began to exercise repressive influence, there was an extremely rich diversity of eucharistic theologies, which do not, as Gary Macy's work reminds us,[8] "represent a ... harmonious development,"[9] and should not be constrained, falsely and teleologically, towards the disjunctive eucharistic alternatives of "the great prism of the Reformation."[10]

Secondly, even when the theory of transubstantiation did become normative, it remained hotly contested and debated because of the inevitable philosophical *aporiai* it appeared to involve, especially where the problem of the application of the Aristotelian notion of "substance" was concerned. Since, in Aristotle's philosophy, "substance" is that which *endures* through change, the idea—at the heart of the various renditions of transubstantiation—that it is the "substance" of the bread/wine that *turns into* that of Christ's body/blood, whilst leaving the "accidents" (the visible features) of the bread and wine unchanged, is seemingly entirely counter-intuitive in Aristotelian terms.

Yet this problem has itself spawned different trajectories of historical explanation in contemporary scholarship. On the one hand, as an important monograph by David Burr[11] and an elegant article by

---

[6]   And this despite the fact that influential thinkers other than Thomas also implied or stated their rejection of it as contrary to the Catholic faith, e.g., Alexander of Hales, Albert the Great, and Bonaventure. "Consubstantiation" was, of course, to become Luther's preferred eucharistic theory.

[7]   McCue, " The Doctrine of Transubstantiation", 392, my emphasis.

[8]   Gary Macy, *Theologies of the Eucharist in the Early Scholastic Period: A Study of the Salvific Function of the Sacrament according to the Theologians c. 1080-c.1220* (Oxford, Clarendon Press, 1984).

[9]   Ibid, 137.

[10] Ibid, 4.

[11] David Burr, *Eucharistic Presence and Conversion in Late Thirteenth-Century Franciscan Thought: Transactions of the American Philosophical Society,* V. 74, Pt. 3 (Philadelphia, 1984).

Marilyn Adams[12] have argued in detail, there is the critical view that the philosophical desperation—or ingenuity—thereby induced in theologians devoted to "Aristotelian" metaphysics and physics in the later medieval period necessarily involved questionable special pleading of various sorts; and Thomas's particular ploys here—shortly to be discussed—thus have to be seen against this wider backcloth of other, and subsequent, alternatives. On Adams's rendition, then, the Aristotelian "bind" led authors as diverse as Thomas himself, Bonaventure, Giles of Rome, Henry of Ghent, Scotus, and Ockham, to have to make *different* sorts of final appeal (to *sui generis* infusions of divine grace, to multiple miracles, or finally to the mere institutional authority of Lateran IV), to attempt to get over the explanatory problem. In short, a diversity of interpretations of transubstantiation is not a thing of the past after Thomas. On the contrary, Adams would argue that it led to multifarious and somewhat desperate re-thinkings of Aristotelian notions of space and change, especially, to accommodate even "miraculous" possibilities for the doctrine's philosophical coherence.[13] The troubling *uniqueness* of the eucharistic presence demanded this re-thinking.

A somewhat different contemporary scholarly rendition of Thomas's contextualized approach, however, would not question this acknowledgement of eucharistic uniqueness, nor would it deny the difference of varieties of rendition of "Aristotelianism" on offer in Thomas's life-time and after. But what it would stress (in *riposte both* to the standard skeptical modern charge of a classic "Aristotelianism" meeting its inevitable *dénouement* in transubstantiation, *and* to Adams's account of a multifaceted philosophical desperation over this doctrine in particular), is the narrative of a consistent re-appropriation by Thomas, even from the time of his *Sentence Commentary*, of crucial influences from the variant "Aristotelian" metaphysics of the great Islamic philosopher, Avicenna.[14] According to this alternative narrative, Thomas's assimi-

---

12   Marilyn McCord Adams, "Aristotle and the Sacrament of the Altar: A Crisis in Medieval Aristoteliansim", in eds. Richard Bosley and Martin Tweedale, *Aristotle And His Medieval Interpreters, Canadian Journal of Philosophy*, supplementary vol. 17 (1991): 195-249.

13   See Adams, ibid, esp. 249 for this last point. Note that more recently Adams has returned to this topic in greater historical detail in her monograph, *Some Later Medieval Theories of the Eucharist* (Oxford, OUP, 2010); and that in her Gifford Lectures, *Christ and Horrors: The Coherence of Christology* (Cambridge, CUP, 2006), ch. 10, she declares in more systematic mode her own preference is for a theory of "impanation" over Thomistic "transubstantiation".

14   The classic article by Étienne Gilson on this exegetical point is "Quasi Definitio Substantiae'" in Armand Maurer, ed., *St. Thomas Aquinas 1274-1974: Commemorative Studies* vol. 1 (Toronto, Pontifical Institute of Medieval Studies, 1974), 111-129.

lation of Avicennan metaphysics caused him significantly to *modify* the historical "Aristotelian" accounts of "substance" and "accidents", "form" and "matter", and from there to do creative and coherent new business with some of the most paradoxical features of classic Christian doctrine, including that of transubstantiation.[15] This latter line of approach, then, is much more sanguine than Adams's about Thomas's own metaphysical consistency and coherence—and across a range of doctrinal issues to which Avicenna's metaphysical adjustments were apposite, especially the linked doctrines of "hypostatic union" and transubstantiation. Whilst this particular exegetical debate about different forms of "Aristotelianism" and their reception cannot be settled in the brief context of this essay, the important lesson is that Thomas's account of transubstantiation is necessarily a subtle and indexed one, and was never intended as a straightforward exposition of "Aristotelian" principles in their original form. Nonetheless, as we shall see, the importance for Aquinas of some account of "substantial" *continuity* in the process of transubstantiation remained crucial. This principle will remain at the heart of our analysis.

Thirdly, then—and here we approach the systematic nub for our own purposes—we need to admit that whereas modern analytic exponents of Aristotle often regard Thomas's theory of transubstantiation as arrant nonsense, others more sensitive to his context may read it as a sign of his "apophatic" *subtlety*. But there is a difference between nonsense and mystery here, which we must carefully chart. Despite the undeniable difficulties in expounding Thomas's "positive" philosophical account of transubstantiation, as already indicated, it may be that its greater wisdom lies finally not so much in what it does say but in what it does *not*.[16] In short, in Thomas's own understanding, *"explanation" in this area has to be a highly chastened form of explanation*—or rather, the delimiting of a space of mystery that mainly focuses on ruling out *errant* explanations rather than providing a complete and definitive positive analysis. This is a classic apophatic strategy, note,[17]

---

[15] For a detailed extension of Gilson's insights on Thomas's critical assimilation of Avicennan views on "substance" (and the application to transubstantiation amongst other topics) I am indebted to Daniel De Haan's unpublished MS, "*Ens Per Se Non Est Definitio Substantiae*: Avicenna, Aquinas, and the Aristotelian Doctrine of Substance".

[16] We might say that this instinct also permeates Thomas's justly-famous eucharistic hymn, *te adoro*: "O thou whom now beneath a veil we see" . . . etc.: it is only in heaven that we shall know and understand Christ's presence fully.

[17] Right from the start of his *Summa* Aquinas regularly reminds his readers that strictly speaking we cannot know what God is, but only what he is *not* (see *Summa Theologiae* I. q3, Prologue).

that is by no means a *giving up* on theological explication (rather as *The Anglican-Roman Catholic Agreement* disappointingly shrugs off "transubstantiation" and relegates it to a mere footnote),[18] let alone a collapse into simple incoherence; instead it is a manifestation of precisely the form of chastened "desire" (desire to control, to predict, to define "divine things") that surely should attend any account of the eucharist and its meaning. This is a very important point for my current purposes; because I want to posit here that Thomas, precisely because of his metaphysical subtleties in neo-"Aristotelian" terms, gives us also certain *resistant markers* of how to proceed rightly with the question of eucharistic "presence"; and if these are ignored we are led on to graver doctrinal and pastoral difficulties. I say this moreover in the spirit of ecumenical *rapprochement*, because I think these features of his account are important for anyone who wishes to defend a doctrine of "real presence" (and that would of course include Anglicans, Lutherans, and Orthodox, as well as Roman Catholics), whether or not they wish to encumber themselves with the traditional Catholic bag and baggage of the language of "transubstantiation". Let me explain further.

"Resistant Markers" in Thomas's Account: A "Discerning Apophaticism"

My suggestion is that we posit the following "resistant markers", so-called, in Thomas's own discussion of transubstantiation in *Summa Theologiae* III. qq. *73-8*.[19] First, there is this matter of choosing a *discerning* apophaticism, as I have just called it. Secondly, there is the principle that the operation of this apophaticism must be congruent with the metaphysics of *incarnation* that ultimately sustains it, including the relation of the divine Word and "fleshliness" that is thereby implied. And, thirdly, there is the question of attendant sacramental *efficacy*, in particular the transformation of what Thomas calls the "affections", an issue which I shall argue is an intrinsically significant accompaniment to what he discusses under the rubric of "transubstantiation". I shall essay a reflection about each of these strands of thought in turn.

---

[18] *The Anglican-Roman Catholic Agreement on the Eucharist*, orig. 1971, ed. Julian W. Charley (Bramcote, Nottingham, Grove Books, 1972), 11, n.2: "The term [transubstantiation] should be seen as affirming the *fact* of Christ's presence and of the mysterious and radical change which takes place. In contemporary Roman Catholic theology it is not understood as explaining *how* the change takes place".
[19] All citations are from the Blackfriars edition of the *Summa Theologiae* (vol. 58, ed. William Barden O.P., Cambridge, CUP reprint, orig. 1964).

It is in the first area, of course—that of the extent of Thomas's capacity to *explain* presence—that all the blood is spilt in assessing the "success" or otherwise of his theory. As we have already acknowledged at some length, is not difficult to demonstrate that Thomas's purported attempt to "explain" Christ's "transubstantiated" presence in the bread and wine of the Eucharist *positively* runs into insuperable difficulties if one simply applies the normal assumptions of classic Aristotelian physics and metaphysics. P. J. Fitzpatrick, for instance, is one commentator who drives this critique home with ferocity when he claims that "transubstantiation is a eucharistic application of Aristotelian terms which *abuses them to the point of nonsense*".[20] But a close reading of *ST* III, q. 75, shows Thomas insistently and carefully explaining why it cannot be that *this* change—in transubstantiation—is like any other sort of "natural" change: Christ's body cannot be in the sacrament in the same way as any other body is in place (*art.* 1); for this body "begins simultaneously to be in different places" (*art.* 2); the bread cannot be annihilated, according to Thomas, or reduced to "prime matter" (leaving it with no form at all), so it must be transformed in some divinely *unique* and *sui generis* way (*art.* 3); and hence—the apophatic *coup de grâce*—"This conversion is *not like any natural change*, but is entirely beyond the powers of nature and is brought about *purely by God's power* . . . Hence this change is not a formal change, but a substantial one. *It does not belong to the natural kinds of change (Nec continetur inter species motus naturalis)*" (*art.* 4). The result is that we cannot be guided by our senses in assessing *this* particular kind of change; we are required to respond in *faith* (*art.* 5), or—as Thomas puts it later (q. 76, art. 7)—with the intellect in its capacity as a "*spiritual* eye".[21]

Although Thomas's ruling out of the "annihilation" option was to remain contentious,[22] it is obvious that Thomas is playing his "mystery cards" here with great care and caution; and this is what I mean by a "*chastened* or *discerning* apophaticism". He is perfectly aware

---

[20] P. J. Fitzpatrick, *In Breaking of Bread: The Eucharist and Ritual* (Cambridge, CUP, 1993), 11, my emphasis.

[21] The "spiritual senses" doctrine does therefore seem to inhere significantly in *some* way in Thomas's eucharistic thought, *pace* Richard Cross's insistence that Aquinas has no consistent epistemological need for a formal account of such: see Richard Cross, "Thomas Aquinas", in eds. Paul L. Gavrilyuk and Sarah Coakley, *The Spiritual Senses: Perceiving God in Western Christianity* (Cambridge, CUP, 2012), 174-189.

[22] As Marilyn McCord Adams puts it, defending Scotus's later alternative: if you are going to have a *sui generis* divine intervention anyway, why not one involving Christic presence *without* conversion, as such, but simply a new *relation* of presence? (Adams, "Aristotle and the Sacrament of the Altar", 224).

that he can only apply the Aristotelian distinctions in a particular—though not *random*, note, or *irrational*—sense; but he equally does not wish to multiply discrete appeals to the miraculous. His insistence on the substantial change of bread *into* Christ's body, moreover (instead of an extrinsic miracle of annihilation and replacement) seems to me entirely consistent with his general sacramental principle (*ST* III. q. 60, art. 6) that the Eucharist must be seen as an *extension* of "the mystery of the Incarnation", in which "Word is united to the flesh", and thus our bodies given "medicine" just as our souls receive the word in "faith". Eucharistic change is an unfolding of that fundamental, incarnational transformation of fleshly life, and in continuity with it: were there "annihilation" rather than *change* something basic to this incarnational understanding of "sacrament" would be abrogated.[23] The result, at one climax moment of the discussion of transubstantiation, is a passage with important implications for desire and gender as understood by Thomas: citing Ambrose, Thomas argues that transubstantiation *must* be "unlike any natural change" since it is the outcome of the original divine impregnation of the Virgin (*ST* III. q. 75, art. 4). It is seemingly therefore a primal, and unique, erotic act crossing the boundary between divine and human that both guarantees and parallels the unique "change" involved in eucharistic presence.

Once we read the section of the *Tertia Pars* on transubstantiation in close relation to the earlier section on the "hypostatic union" (*ST* III. qq. 1-6. esp. q. 2), then the playing of "mystery cards" that we have already noted in Thomas's discussion of eucharistic presence assumes a structural parallel to the treatment of the equally mysterious *particularity* of Christ's human nature (*ST* III. q. 2, art. 5) in which soul and body are *uniquely* joined together "in such a way as to be conjoined to another and higher principle [the divine Word]." *Pace* Richard Cross, who sees this ploy as dubious and tending to monophysitism,[24] I am more inclined—as I have argued in detail elsewhere[25]—to read it as a firm stress on the non-negotiable, albeit hypostatically unique, *reality* of Christ's incarnate humanity, a *guarding* of the full integrity of the humanity. It is this marked care over the transfigured capacity of human nature that surely explains Thomas's repeated insistence on

---

[23] On this point see also Herbert McCabe, O.P., *God Matters* (London, Geoffrey Chapman, 1987), 154, to whose own account of transubstantiation we shall shortly return.

[24] See Richard Cross, *The Metaphysics of the Incarnation* (Oxford, OUP, 2002), 51-64.

[25] "The Person of Christ", in *The Cambridge Companion to the* Summa, eds. Denys Turner and Philip McCosker (Cambridge, CUP, 2016), 222-239

the resistant incarnational *fleshliness* of the sacrament of the Eucharist and its significance no less as transformative "food" than as spiritual reality (e.g., q. 73, art 6). Participation in God precisely involves *eating*, ingesting, even though—as Augustine had already said in the *Confessions*—its spiritual nature makes it more like being turned into what one eats (Christ) than turning Him into you (q. 73, art. 3).

One final feature of Thomas's account demands our attention, as I have already hinted. There are several places in Thomas's discussion of the Eucharist where he expatiates on the necessarily transformative effects of the rite (if efficacious) on our "affections", or what we might call the apparatus of our desire.[26] In a moving passage in *ST* III, q. 73, art 5, Thomas first reiterates his point about the incarnational foundation of the eucharist, and explains that Jesus had to give us a "sacrament of his body and blood" so that the " body which he had hypostatically united to himself" could still be salvifically available to us. He goes on— in language that is now rendered particularly evocative for descendents of Newman and the Oxford movement[27]—that "the parting of friends is the affection of love most sensitive" (*inflammatur affectus ad amicos*), and thus, in Jesus' institution of the eucharist, he transformatively invested his own human affective intensity and sense of impending loss; thus, as Thomas goes on, "the more our affections are involved, the more things are deeply impressed upon our souls" (q. 73, art. 5). In fact, the Last Supper was Jesus' ritualized way of gathering into *integrity* the affections, memories, and bodily dispositions of his disciples so as to rightly relate them to their souls – an authentic "incarnational" propulsion in ritualized form. However, conversely, if this uniquely integrated form of transformation *fails* to occur, Thomas warns later (q. 79, art. 8), desire is *not* purged and venial sin "hamper[s] this sacrament's effect". In that case the crucial affective dimension of eucharistic presence is blocked. What should be happening, however, he says, quoting John Damascene, is that *"The fire of that desire within us which is kindled by the burning coal, namely the sacrament, will consume our sins and enlighten our hearts, so that we shall be enflamed and made godlike"* (ibid, citing *de Fide Orthodoxa*, VI).

---

[26] The theme of "desire" in Aquinas is of far-reaching significance, and performs both a metaphysical and an epistemological role. For one recent study of this topic in Aquinas which focuses especially on what (in contemporary parlance) is now called "emotion", see Nicholas E. Lombardi, O.P., *The Logic Of Desire: Aquinas and Emotion* (Washington, DC, CUA Press, 2010).

[27] See John Henry Newman, "The Parting of Friends", in ed. Francis J. McGrath, F.M.S., *The Letters and Diaries of John Henry Newman*, vol. IX: *Littlemore and the Parting of Friends, May 1842-October 1843* (Oxford, OUP, 2006), 733-740.

I have taken this much time here on neglected strands in the text of Thomas himself on the theme of transubstantiation in order to emphasize his peculiar significance, even ecumenically, for *any* attempted discussion of "eucharistic presence". Whilst it is tempting, with *ARCIC* and other eirenic ecumenical endeavors,[28] to bracket Thomas on transubstantiation as a theological mine-field that can lead only to harmful explosions in the ecumenical realm, I have here been suggesting exactly the opposite case. One should not hastily "retire hurt" from this crucial ecumenical debate, and either step back away from a metaphysical account to a "symbolic" theory, or disappear into an *undiscriminating* apophaticism in which "mystery" is invoked as a blanket that could cover anything. For there is an important alternative, as we have now seen. Thomas has a resistant "subtext" that is deeply theologically fruitful and regrettably overlooked: first, he has an intense interest in philosophical coherence, but an equally sophisticated way of indicating the *limits* of his own positive, explicative powers; secondly, he plays the "mystery card" in eucharistic presence in precisely the same way as he does christologically (admitting what is non-identifiable with natural changes, and thus to be expressed apophatically, and insisting simultaneously on the transformative, if transgressive, *continuity* between two states of affairs, x following y);[29] thirdly, he sees what happens in the eucharist precisely as an *extension* of the mystery of the annunciation/incarnation, and thus as a bodily matter of insemination/birth; and finally he is correlatively insistent on the significance for the eucharist of bodily ingestion, integrative ritual enactment, and the importance of "affective" transformation.

Transition to Contemporary Expositions of Transubstantiation

Having presented this textual thesis in succinct detail, I want now to contrast these "resistant markers" of Thomas's account with some ingenious re-workings of his theory of transubstantiation that are currently on offer in the post-modern philosophical milieu. I shall shortly focus on a brief comparison of the work of Jean-Luc Marion and Catherine Pickstock in this regard, because both are consciously operating in the train of the post-Derridean discussion of "gift" that has dominated continental philosophy of religion of late,[30] and with

---

[28]   Ibid., n. 18. [Anglican-Roman Catholic International Commission-ed.]
[29]   See esp. *ST* III, q. 75, art. 8, resp.
[30]   For an introductory account of this complex debate in post-Kantian continental philosophy of religion, see my article "Why Gift? Gift, Gender, and Trinitarian Relations in Milbank and Tanner", *Scottish Journal of Theology* 16 (2008): 224–35.

results that are—in my view—both revealing and concerning, especially where gender and "bodies" are concerned. However, let me bridge into this comparison with a transitional comment on an influential, but slightly earlier, re-reading of Thomas on transubstantiation by Herbert McCabe, O.P.,[31] since McCabe's approach may already reveal a trend which the other exponents intensify.

On the face of it, McCabe would appear precisely to exemplify the "discerningly *apophatic*" approach to transubstantiation I have already proposed, and that is certainly his intention. Yet on closer inspection we see that he performs this task in a Wittgensteinian mode that troublingly seems to subsume ontology—and even bodies, too—into mere "language". Thus, McCabe will write, intriguingly, that "Our language has *become* his [Christ's] body";[32] or that "language itself is transformed [in the Eucharist] and becomes the medium of the future, *the language itself becomes the presence*, the *bodily* presence of Christ";[33] . . . "his body is present in the mode of language—rather as meaning is present to a word."[34] The underlying intuition is, once more, the need to protect a mystery: that we cannot "explain" transubstantiation in terms of a *secular* set of presumptions about "stuff" and change. We have to learn a *new* "language"—one which only the body of Christ can disclose to us. So far, so good. McCabe admits that his approach is "enigmatic", but then tries to clarify it by saying that, "What makes a human body *human* is that it is involved in linguistic communication."[35]

But at this point I baulk, precisely as one informed by the insights of Thomas's example, outlined above. For if bodies are "really" words, then what we have is a theoretical subsumption of flesh into Word, an incipient gnosticism that also threatens to render "inhuman" the pre-linguistic baby at the breast, the brain-damaged mute, or the inarticulate groaning of the dying. And this is odd and unexpected from McCabe, who equally wants to stress the necessity of bodiliness for all communication, and—at one point in the same discussion - the special communicative significance of the intimacy of lovers' gestures.[36] Yet at

---

[31] McCabe, *God Matters*, 116-129.
[32] Ibid, 118, my emphasis.
[33] Ibid, 128, my emphasis.
[34] Ibid, 118.
[35] Ibid, 118, my emphasis.
[36] See ibid, 117. Of course, McCabe might well riposte that, from the Wittgensteinian perspective from which he writes here, there *are* no words without bodies. Yet it remains puzzling that he does not focus more explicitly on the sustaining importance of "fleshliness" or "materiality" for any account of eucharistic presence.

the same time he is willing rhetorically to reduce bodies to "language", albeit the new language learnt almost uncomprehendingly in the Mass.

Here is one theological danger, then, that threatens when we try to escape what I have identified as the cumulative lessons of Thomas's "resistant markers": the possibility of a subsumption of body *into* Word. This lesson may be remainingly important. But for now we turn briefly to two others, equally revealing and instructive. If McCabe attempts, in his re-thinking of transubstantiation, to re-parse ontology as *language*, with undergirding Wittgensteinian assumptions, then Marion—as Gerard Loughlin has recently put it—more truly "transcribe[s] . . . ontology into . . . *temporality*";[37] to which we might add: and Pickstock realigns "Aristotelian" ontology into neo-Platonic *ecstasy*. With Marion and Pickstock, however, the philosophical conversation-partners are more Heidegger and Derrida than Wittgenstein, as we shall now see. In each of their cases, a new response to "Aristotle" goes well beyond even the options outlined in our earlier discussion of contextualized, late-medieval alternatives.

Marion's "Gift" and the Occlusion of Gender; Pickstock's "Ecstasy" and the Problem of Enfleshment

I am obliged in this context to treat Marion's and Pickstock's intriguing renditions of transubstantiation more briefly—and more cavalierly—than I should like. Yet some broad brush-strokes will at least indicate their main points of unity and difference, and also the reasons why I find certain *different* strands of their arguments both positive and problematic, especially in the light of what we have learnt from Thomas himself.

The novelty of Marion's approach to transubstantiation in his renowned monograph *God Without Being*[38] first lies in his insistence that, here in the Eucharist, if anywhere, is what Derrida sought in his notion of a "*pure* gift",[39] and at the same time supposedly the only means of escape from the problem of "metaphysics" in Heidegger's sense—that is, the problem of the false reification of Being.[40] Coming straight from Thomas, we have to remind ourselves that, for Marion, the true

---

37   See Gerard Loughlin, "Transubstantiation: Eucharist as Pure Gift", in eds. David Brown and Ann Loades, *Christ: The Sacramental Word* (London, SPCK, 1996), 123-41, at 136.

38   Jean-Luc Marion, *God Without Being: Hors-Texte* (Chicago, University of Chicago Press, 1991).

39   See Jacques Derrida, *Given Time: 1. Counterfeit Money* (Chicago, University of Chicago Press, 1992); idem, *The Gift of Death* (Chicago, University of Chicago Press, 1995).

40   See Marion, *God Without Being*, 161-182.

God can only be *"without*—or beyond—Being"—an idea that would, of course, have been completely senseless to Aquinas himself (for whom God *is*, by definition, *esse subsistens*).[41] But, for Marion, this extrication from Being (in his Heideggerian sense) is crucial if we are to avoid the taint of *idolatry*. How, then, is such a God available to us at all, if He is *beyond* Being? According to Marion, we do not have to wait for death (as in Derrida) to receive this "pure gift", since Jesus Christ, who "exceeds every metaphysic,"[42] gives himself to us in the Eucharist in a way that transcends, or trumps, the normal way we think about *time*; and precisely this allows us to receive the "pure gift" now. Instead of time being seen as something controlled by *our* consciousnesses from moment to moment, this eucharistic time is *given* afresh every moment in a way that both gathers up the past and opens us to the future: "The eucharistic presence comes to us, at each instant, as the gift of that very instant, and, in it, of the body of the Christ in whom one must be incorporated".[43] Only thus can it be an *icon*—a true window into God— rather than an *idol*[44] (this is a distinction crucial in Marion's thought as part of his response to Heidegger, though in it we see him reaching—not for the first or last time—into the resources of Greek patristic thought, with echoes of the classic defense of icons at Nicaea II).

Now, given Marion's antipathy to classical metaphysics in general, and Aristotle in particular, it would seem highly unlikely that he would want to hang onto the language of "transubstantiation" at all, since—as Loughlin has rightly commented—it is a new dimension of *temporality* that here seems to be doing the work that was previously done by ontology, almost by a kind of *fiat*. However, there is here a surprising twist: Marion does want to rescue Thomas's account of transubstantiation by reading it in a way that is not just *"discerningly* apophatic" (as I have outlined above, in my own exposition of Thomas' view), but what we might call *thoroughgoingly* or even *obliteratingly* apophatic. For Marion claims that Thomas is here using the language of *substantia* in a way *utterly* divorced from Aristotle;[45] and that only the Council of Trent, later, misconstrued Thomas's views in a way that

---

41 Note that since writing *God Without Being*, Marion has acknowledged that he there falsely implicated Aquinas in the Heideggerian problem of Being: see his "In the Name: How to Avoid Speaking of 'Negative Theology'", in eds. John D. Caputo and Michael J. Scanlon, *God, the Gift and Postmodernism* (Bloomington and Indianapolis, Indiana UP, 1999),20-41.

42 *God Without Being*, 163.

43 Ibid, 175.

44 See ibid, 7-24.

45 See ibid, 163-4.

reconstrained the theory of transubstantiation back into a flat-footedly Aristotelian way of thinking about substance, and thus fetishized the host into a controllable object of *our* gaze.[46] For eucharistic presence to continue to take us "beyond Being", and beyond normal time, says Marion, we must be aware of our *complete lack* of intellectual control of its explanation (such that even the "resistant markers" I have noted in Thomas apparently evaporate): the presence of the Gift should be reduced neither to an idolatrous object that we can manipulate, nor to a code for a social program of reform that we approve. The host is raised before us as a reminder of that *lack* of grasp, of complete unknowing; hence we must talk as truly of Christ's absence or "distance" as his presence, until—eschatologically—all is fulfilled in Christ.[47] Meanwhile, "only [this] distance . . . renders communion possible",[48] and we must prepare for this communion with the silence of contemplative prayer, so that it will be really Christ that is given to us, and not some counterfeit we have made in our own image.

If Marion stresses the transformation of *time* in the eucharist, and the necessity of silence in welcoming that time non-idolatrously, Pickstock is, in contrast, surprisingly resistant to Marion's insistence on silence as a counterpart to Word. Like McCabe in this regard, she wants the Eucharist, and Christ's transubstantiated presence, to signal a *new* language so different from our current one that it subsumes all previous haltering attempts at sign and language, rather than throwing us into a realm of silence supposedly *beyond* language.[49] This indeed is a significant part of *her* latter-day riposte to Derrida (and she shares this ambition with Marion): the endlessly deferred meaning of Derrida's "deathly" (as she sees it) program of deconstruction is, she insists, not just brought to completion in the eucharist, but *founded* in it. Hence her striking claim, at the climax of *After Writing*, that transubstantiation is the "condition of the possibility for *all* meaning".[50]

What is meant by this? Pickstock's contention is that, rather than the Eucharist somehow requiring us to go *beyond* language (so Marion), it "situates us more inside language than ever";[51] yet it is a completely new language with seemingly no obvious transition of

---

[46] See ibid, 164.
[47] Ibid, 169.
[48] Ibid.
[49] Catherine Pickstock, *After Writing: On the Liturgical Consummation of Philosophy* (Oxford, Blackwell, 1998), 262, for this contrast with Marion.
[50] Ibid, 261.
[51] Ibid, 262.

continuity with our current one. And at this point Pickstock starts to sound more like McCabe: "For the resurrected body is a completely *imparted* body, *transmuted into a series of signs*".[52] Again, then, we note that "body" in Pickstock's eucharistic theology has a tendency, as in McCabe and Marion, to turn into *something else*, and in Pickstock's case something intrinsically sign- and word-related. Yet there is another side to her argument, and this differentiates her rhetoric significantly from Marion's (which she criticizes): she does insist in the final paragraphs of her book that she would wish to distinguish her position from any form of Platonism or neo-Platonism in which the body must ultimately be *transcended*;[53] her claim, then, is that the ecstasy of "desire" in the eucharist (and Pickstock, as an exponent of the Platonist tradition in this regard, significantly does *not* repress the language of desire) in some sense makes us *more* bodily (in Christ) rather than less.[54]

The trouble for many commentators with this claim is that Pickstock seeks to explain transubstantiation (again, with an intensified apophaticism somewhat reminiscent of Marion) as a veritable neo-Platonic *sublation* of "Aristotelian" categories in Thomas. Indeed, her stated view is that Thomas himself has given up on any rendition of "substance" *qua* "Aristotelian", not only in his section in the *Tertia Pars* on transubstantiation, but by extension everywhere else in his *Summa* as well.[55] He has, she claims, "disturbed" the ontology of "substance" and "accidents" with the neo-Platonic distinction between "being" and "essence" (*esse* and *essentia*): "Hence", she writes, "every creature is 'pulled' by its participation in *esse* beyond its own peculiar essence—it exceeds itself by receiving existence—and no created "substance" is truly substantial, truly self-sufficient, absolutely stable or self-sustaining".[56] This represents an intriguing but controversial rendition of Thomas's ontology, *tout court*, which has received much critical attention;[57] and

---

52 Ibid, 266, my emphasis (in the latter part of the sentence).

53 See ibid, 273.

54 Ibid, 231.

55 To provide a complete picture of this metaphysical vision one would need to consult and discuss John Milbank and Catherine Pickstock, *Truth in Aquinas* (London, Routledge, 2001), especially given the fact that Pickstock scarcely cites Thomas himself in *After Writing*.

56 *After Writing*, 261. Pickstock does not discuss the historical complications of the *various* renditions of "Aristotelianism" in Thomas's own lifetime (see our earlier discussion, above). Some of her rhetoric might initially suggest a potential parallel with the "Avicennan" rendition of "substance", but in her case the solution is found in a neo-Platonic "ecstasy" which cancels classic "Aristotelianism".

57 Some of this is merely dismissive: e.g., Anthony Kenny, "Aquinas and the Appearance of Bread", *Times Literary Supplement*, 5th October, 2001. But see also the penetrating

the exegetical questions it raises necessarily go beyond the scope of this particular essay. All I want to stress here again, however, is the insights of our earlier account of the "resistant markers" in Thomas's text; for these are precisely intended to respect the mysterious divinely-ordered *continuity* between ordinary resistant fleshliness and incarnational transformation.

This brief comparative sketch of Marion and Pickstock is, of course, unsatisfactorily over-simplified; their suggestive brilliance and originality is undeniable, and I have by no means been able to do justice to the full complexity of their positions in this account. But what I think my brief outline shows us is two outcomes to take forward into our conclusions, one negative, one positive.

My critical response to Marion and Pickstock, first, may be apparent from the way that I earlier set up my "resistant markers" in Thomas. In both Marion and Pickstock (and despite their mutual disagreements), we confront an apophatic maneuver so profound that it threatens any resistant *continuity* between material existence as we now know it and Christic presence as delivered in the host. Indeed, this difference between here and there, or now and then, is profoundly interruptive, established either by an eschatological *fiat* (Marion), or an ecstatic invasion (Pickstock), launching us into a completely new realm and *against all appearances*. The result of this intensified apophaticism is that in both Marion and Pickstock the *ordinary* fleshliness of the incarnation seems threatened,[58] as does the implicit emphasis on physical feeding and bodiliness in the rite itself. One is eerily reminded of the *destructive* inedia of the medieval saints described by Caroline Walker Bynum in *Holy Feast, Holy Fast*,[59] for whom eating *only* the host became an obsession, to the point of women's self-destruction and complete disregard for the ordinary physical body—ecstatic and erotic to be sure, but ultimately "sacrificial" in the falsely *annihilative* sense. Further, although "desire" is a Platonic notion greatly accentuated in Pickstock (*qua* "ecstatic"), it is utilized in a register very different from Thomas's patient insistence on the full integration of bodily affect, memory and understanding in the eucharistic rite over time.

---

assessment in Bruce D. Marshall, review of *Truth in Aquinas, The Thomist* 66 (2002); 632-637. The most patient, sympathetic, but nonetheless exegetically critical account of Milbank and Pickstock on Aquinas is to be found in Paul J. DeHart, *Aquinas and Radical Orthodoxy: A Critical Inquiry* (London, Routledge, 2012).

[58]   And this despite Pickstock's insistence (already noted) that eucharistic presence "repeats" the incarnation, and renders us *more* bodily, not less.

[59]   See n. 2, above.

Finally, it is somewhat eerie, in Marion, to have the distinction between icon and idol that is so crucial for his theory of eucharistic presence worked out *specifically* in the language of the co-called "mirror phase" of Lacan (the point in Jacques Lacan's psychology at which the child begins to repress the memory of pure identification with the mother and to move into the male realm of language and signs[60]). For Marion, this self-regard in the mirror is the *essence* of what he calls "idolatry", whereas the "icon" avails itself to us as excess and gift, *without* our capacity for control. It cannot be that Marion is unaware of the way that Lacan himself "genders" this particular binary—as "masculine" over against "feminine"—and equally impossible to believe that Marion has no awareness, in the cultured Parisian circles in which he moves, of the theological and feminist reflection on this binary of the "mirror phase" developed by Luce Irigaray and Julia Kristeva.[61] Yet not the faintest flicker of acknowledgement of the Lacanian source, nor of its accompaniments, is made: gendered bodiliness is indeed completely occluded in Marion's account of eucharistic longing, a feature that perhaps coheres with what I deem the gnostic-veering tendency of his extreme apophaticism. Yet, as we have seen above, Thomas' own correlation of virginal conception, incarnational transformation of physical flesh, and transubstantiated host, is in contrast shot through with implicit gender evocations from the outset: it is precisely through the "yes" of the Virgin that Christ takes ordinary human flesh and transforms it.

The positive conclusion that I draw from these authors, on the other hand, is that the illuminating emphasis on the eschatological implication of time in the eucharist helps to drive home afresh something also differently hinted at in Thomas: that eucharistic presence in the host is constricted, incomplete, without *efficacious* fulfillment; and therefore that "presence" and "absence" are seemingly two sides of the same eucharistic coin as long as historical time endures. This reflection helps us to draw attention away from the danger of the host as a *fetishized* object (as both Marion and Pickstock remark), and instead look to the transformative presence of Christ disposed into the "body" of believers *and* in those they seek to serve, as well as densely in the bread and wine themselves, and reflectedly in the person of the

---

[60]   For this now-classic short essay, see Jacques Lacan, "The mirror stage as formative of the function of the I", in idem, *Écrits: A Selection*, (London, Tavistock, 1977), 1-7.

[61]   For their reception and feminist critique of Lacan, see Luce Irigaray, *Speculum of the Other Woman* (Ithaca, NY, Cornell University Press, 1974), and Julia Kristeva, *Powers of Horror: An Essay on Abjection*, (New York, Columbia University Press, 1980).

priest who celebrates. This conclusion need not, I believe, undermine the continuing significance for many Christians of adoration or exposition of the host itself; but it does chasten it into a continued reflection on the necessary ethical and spiritual *outcomes* of Christ's efficacious presence. This greater *distribution* of the sense of Christic presence, indeed, opens the possibility of a certain renewal of ecumenical understanding, since it was in the tortured controversies of the Reformation *Abendmahlstreit* that false alternatives were set up on eucharistic presence that threw, for instance, presence in the host and presence in the people into a disjunctive ideological choice which split the Church.[62]

Conclusions: Flesh and Blood – The Eucharist, Desire and Affective Transformation

Let me now try to sum up the systematic conclusions to this essay.

Inspired in part by John W. Coakley's rich work on gender, affect, and bodily transformations in medieval saints' lives, I have attempted in this essay to re-read Aquinas's account of eucharistic presence as "transubstantiation" with new attention to his accompanying sub-texts of virginal impregnation, incarnational transformation of the possibilities of human flesh, and eucharistic efficacy as affective, bodily and desire-oriented. What these accompanying features drive home afresh is his absolute insistence on the transformative continuity and congruence of ordinary physicality and divine presence in the eucharistic host, the instinct that lies at the heart of his understanding of transubstantiation, whatever the particular rendition or reception of "Arisitotle" that sustains it. At the same time, and in *riposte* to outright scoffers at that "Aristotelian" rendition, I have drawn attention to the careful "apophatic" markers in Aquinas's text, his insistence as to the limits of philosophical explanation in this matter, limits which again link to the insistent bodily emphasis of his account. Finally, I have commented briefly, both critically and appreciatively (and by way of contrast to my own rendition), to some important contemporary post-modern accounts of transubstantiation that attempt to modify or dissolve the seemingly-problematic links with "Aristotelianism", and replace those with inspiration from other, more recent, philosophical

---

[62]   For a brilliant recent résumé of the eucharistic divergences of the early Reformers, see David C. Steinmetz, "The Eucharist and the Identity of Jesus in the Early Reformation", in Beverly Roberts Gaventa and Richard B. Hays, *Seeking the Identity of Jesus: A Pilgiimage* (Grand Rapids, MI, William B. Eerdmans Publishing Company, 2008), 270-284.

conversation-partners, or with an appeal to neo-Platonic "ecstasy". Their efforts, I have argued, have been only partially successful to the extent that they tend to abstract disarmingly from ordinary physicality or fleshliness, and so to intensify their apophatic strategy as to render the meaning of transformed, efficacious bodiliness puzzling or "ecstatically" arcane.

Returning finally to Thomas's own accompanying account of sacramental efficacy, then, is a fit focus for any attempt to assess his views on transubstantiation, *tout court*. In short, what medieval women and men thought was happening to their bodies, desires, and affects in and through the practice of the Eucharist (a matter on which John W. Coakley has taught us so much) is of deep relevance to any theological account of eucharistic "presence", then and now, and in any branch of the Church. Perhaps it is time to put "affective" and "bodily" efficacy under the spot-light in any future ecumenical attempts at eucharistic *rapprochement*.

Part 2

"Yes! Well . . ." and the Exploration of Education and Historiography

"Yes," John Coakley has spent the last few decades of his life as a historian, educator, and General Synod professor, and that means that how the educating happens and how the history gets written is very important to him. "Well," it is worth thinking about these processes in new ways, exploring new frontiers in things that have formed the basis of teaching at New Brunswick Theological Seminary and reflecting on how we might look at them in new ways in the future.

We begin with the future, as Mark Tayler looks at aspects of the life of the church's history that have traditionally been overlooked, especially around issues of race—something else John has been involved with at NBTS—and discusses how we might, and must, see them differently. Norman Kansfield expands on his earlier research into Philip Milledoler, John Henry Livingston's successor at NBTS, the unfortunate way in which his tenure at the Seminary ended, and what that has meant for the school and the church. Finally, this editor looks at the life and work of Edward Tanjore Corwin, a pivotal historian of the RCA, and how his work was influenced by the scholarly standards of his time—something which John helped me understand, even when he didn't know this project existed—as well as how he set standards for future scholars.

CHAPTER 5

Western Clouds, Southern Winds, and a Post Modern Interpretation of Church History

Mark V.C. Taylor

Introduction

John Coakley began his work during a time when there was a major consensus among historians in American Church History. He leaves New Brunswick during a very different time, when there was such overarching consensus which has given way to much fragmentation. Some scholars, in trying to summarize the intellectual and social challenges of this era, have called it the "postmodern period." What this period is and why I agree with this description of our times is something that I will explain and argue for in this paper. As an adjunct professor under Coakley's supervision and a colleague and a co-worker, I feel as though Coakley, like so many of the ablest historians of his generation that I have met, has passed on, not a baton, but a burning torch—the torch of the legacy of the history of Christianity in the West and in the world.

In our brief but profound association, he often demonstrated his deep Christian faith and broad understanding of that faith, as well as great personal kindness and professionalism. The faithful would call such demonstrations "blessings." It has indeed been a blessing to receive this torch from such a great teacher and student of the history of the Church of Jesus Christ. May all who have been blessed by the light of Professor John Coakley carry it as brightly and as boldly as he.

Tulsa, May 21, 1921

As they stumbled to scattered positions, smoke filled the air, scorching their lungs and blinding their eyes. Amid the shouts and sounds, they could barely see one another as their pitiful band took up sniper positions against the surging mob down below. Some of them hated the fact that they were in the belfry of a church, and a new church at that. But their being there was as crazy as the night itself. They had faced a crowd of over 1,000 at the courthouse where they marched twenty-five men strong to stop a looming lynching.

"Stupid fool," one of them muttered, "to stumble into a white girl in an elevator. What else was she going to do but cry rape?" "Well, I know that, boy", said another. "He might be a fool but he ain't no rapist." So a number of the Negro men in the community gathered together because they heard that white men were gathering at the courthouse, and all the Negro people of Tulsa knew how quickly a crowd of white men could become a lynch mob.

Twice the Negroes came down to the courthouse and the sheriff assured them that there would be no lynching. By the second visit, the Negro group numbered 75 men. Some of the whites thought this was the beginning of a Negro rebellion. Many also resented the success and coveted the wealth of the "uppity" Negroes from what they contemptuously called "Little Africa."

The second time the Negro men came to the courthouse, the larger crowd of over 2,000 white men turned on them. The mob of white men went from attacking them to beating, burning, and then looting Negro homes. The most militant among the Negroes had fought back, but their struggle was a losing one. The Tulsa police were even passing out guns to the white mob. The local National Guard helped the mob find and beat Negroes. The mob of 2,000 whites swelled during the night to between 5,000 and 10,000.

The police also used a machine gun mounted on a flatbed truck against the Negro defenders. White attackers shot at Negroes from airplanes in the sky, one of the first aerial attacks in the United States. White mobs threatened white firemen who wanted to extinguish fires in colored neighborhoods. When the state National Guard finally arrived, they herded Negro Tulsans into a sports arena, ostensibly for their protection. They were actually under police arrest. The arena became a concentration camp.

The Negro men in the belfry of the Mt. Zion Baptist church fought on valiantly, hoping to stop the white mob before they could descend further into the prosperous Negro section of Tulsa known as Greenwood. But the numbers and the firepower of their attackers were too much. As more and more of them were shot dead, the rest had to retreat. Mt. Zion, the pride of Negro Tulsa, was defaced, besotted with holes, and finally set ablaze with the fires of hatred and mob violence.[1]

The history of this incident, usually called The Tulsa Race Riot of 1921, is important, and illuminating. In *Tulsa Race Riot: A Report by The Oklahoma Commission to Study the Tulsa Race Riot of 1921*, the commissioners talk about the disappearance of the incident in Tulsa memorials, newspaper articles, and civic histories. State textbooks omit any reference to it. The incident has been rendered historically invisible by both the intentional and unintentional mechanisms of historical amnesia. I never encountered this event in twenty years of college and post-graduate theological studies.

The incident, its historical obliteration, and the interpretation of it poses unique problems for the discipline of church history. Eight of twelve Negro churches in Greenwood were totally destroyed along with thirty-five city blocks and an estimated 300 people killed (estimated, because many were thrown in unmarked graves).

There were heroic stories of white Christians who hid Negroes in their homes until the mob passed, or who even challenged the mob itself. Other examples of white Christians were less praiseworthy. One clergyman, Richard Lloyd Jones, the editor of one of Tulsa's three main newspapers—the *Tribune*—printed an inflammatory headline, "Nab Negro for Attacking Girl in Elevator," in the same edition where he printed an editorial which helped spur the mob, titled, "To Lynch a Negro Tonight?"[2]

---

[1]   James S. Hirsch, *Riot and Remembrance: America's Worst Race Riot and It's Legacy* (Boston: Houghton Mifflin Co, 2002), 77-113: Tim Madigan, *The Burning: Massacre, Destruction and The Tulsa Race Riot of 1921* (New York: St. Martin's Press, 2001), 104-175: Scott Ellsworth, *Death in A Promised Land: The Tulsa Race Riot of 1921* (Baton Rouge: Louisiana State University Press, 1982), 42-70: Oklahoma Commission To Study The Tulsa Race Riot of 1921, *Tulsa Race Riot: A Report by The Oklahoma Commission to Study the Tulsa Race Riot of 1921* (Oklahoma Historical Society: http:www.okhistory.org/research/form/freport.pdf, 2001, 37-100. The recounting here is written in the same narrative form used by the above historians and others. This form conveys the tragedy, pathos, and power of this incident much more than strict historical reporting.

[2]   Hirsch, *Riot and Remembrance*, 79-83: Peter Hughes, "Richard Lloyd Jones," Dictionary of Unitarian and Universalist Biography, (December 13, 2007), http// uudb.org/articles/richardloydjones.html.

The problem that the Tulsa Race Riot, or as some have called it, the Tulsa Race Massacre, poses for Church history is this: why have such events been omitted from the most prominent narratives of American Church History? What kinds of histories are produced if events like these are omitted? Are they histories that do justice to the diversity of the population of the USA? Or, by omitting detailed accounts like this, where violence and hatred cause murder and theft, are we unintentionally serving vested interests which do the same things today?

Not that we should turn church history into a mere focus on historical crimes and tragedies. But if we just study the high points of Christian history without telling the stories of the historical failures of faith and love, then we fail a faith which has a focus upon justice and the poor, and which has as its high point the bloody murder of its innocent founder. A church historian should ask, "How can these events be investigated and shared as major events in Church History?"

Issues like these came to my attention forcefully as I was preparing to teach classes in the category of what is called, "Modern Church History" in a few seminaries between 1990 and 2015. In many northern seminaries, this period usually is taught as extending from the Reformation in 1517 through the end of World War II in 1945, and for some, up to the 1960's in the United States. Changes in the field of history in general and in Church history in particular, made rethinking the periodization, content and even the teaching of this subject a critical necessity.

Historical Omissions and the Origins of American Church History: The Case of Philip Schaff.

As a focal point in analyzing the link between historiography, collective crimes, and reconceptualizing western church history, I want to focus on Philip Schaff. Schaff's role in developing and advancing the discipline of church history is undisputed. Because of his prominence in defining, refining, and promulgating the discipline of American Church History, an analysis of Schaff is an analysis of the origins of the discipline itself and a good starting place in any effort to rethink what the discipline is and how the discipline should be presented. This analysis is suggestive rather than exhaustive. It is written in the postmodern spirit of play, fragmentation, and disruption, but with the Christian ideals of respect, revelation, and recreating.

Schaff taught at Union Theological Seminary in New York City, from 1844 to 1893. He was a professor of philology, Hebrew, New

Testament, Biblical Literature, and Church History. I first encountered the legacy of Schaff when I was a graduate student at Union in 1986. In that year I landed a job as the Phillip Schaff Tutor of American Church History. I never thought about Schaff or his work too much; I was just grateful to have a job as a paid teaching assistant! Over the years I have taught Church history in many places. As the discipline and the society have changed, I have had to rethink my teaching paradigm. As I began to look back at the formation of the discipline, I found there the name I had overlooked, that giant of old, Phillip Schaff.

Schaff was the driving force behind the creation of the American Society of Church History (ASCH) in 1888. The group first met at Schaff's home with 17 scholars and churchmen in attendance. Another 40 men had expressed their intentions to join the group through correspondence. Besides the ASCH, Schaff was a member of several para-church groups including: the American Bible Society and the Ecumenical Union. [3]

Over a period of almost fifty years, he was a most prolific scholar and activist. His writings include 55 books, twenty-seven major articles, and many sermons, tracts and a voluminous correspondence. His twenty-six-volume *History of the Christian Church* was the standard work of its kind. Schaff's work cannot be effectively summarized in this essay. By way of a partial analysis, then, I want to highlight his ecclesiology and his consequent understanding of church unity.

Schaff argued that the church was the body of Christ, suffering and working in the world for the redemption of humanity and the whole creation. That church was both visible and invisible, mixed and perfect. The former was the combination of Christian persons and institutions evident in society. The latter was the invisible Church, the number of the truly regenerate in the former, which went beyond the ability of the eye to see.

The church then was not just the earthly church; the church was also the actual Church that existed in the mind of God before creation, that Church which was represented in the person of Jesus Christ. Existing within His person, it was the Church in potentiality, perfect and never failing. Existing as the visible—or, as Schaff called it, the mixed church—it was subject to failure and error. Although God

---

[3]   David W. Lotz, "Philip Schaff and the Idea of Church History" in *A Century of Church History: The Legacy of Philip Schaff,* ed. Henry W. Bowden. (Carbondale: Southern Illinois University Press, 1988). Questia Online Research Library: http//www.questia.com/read/35468192/a-century-of-church-history-the legacy-of-philip, 6.

would separate the visible church from the invisible church at the end of time, the earthly church still had power to transform society, culture, and all creation, because it was suffused by the Spirit with the person of Christ, who held within His person, the perfect church, as it existed in the mind of God.

According to church historian David Lotz, Schaff's idea of the Church emphasized the concept of its organic development. This idea was the fruit of German Romanticism's impact upon German philosophy, evident in Georg Hegel, and in German theology, evident in Fredrich Schleiermacher's disciples and Schaff's own teachers, Anthony Neander and Ferdinand Bauer. Schaff's idea of the organic development of the church held two foci: First of all, the church was itself an organic entity developing like a plant from seed to bush to a mighty oak. Or, like a child who grows from infancy to puberty, then through adolescent to mature adulthood. Such organic entities exhibited the laws of genesis, growth, and development.[4]

The church—according to Schaff, existing "potentially" in God's mind and plan, and "actually" in Christ's person—leads humanity to become more and more like Christ. But since Christ is the Second Adam, this progressive realization is also a movement towards true and perfect humanity. So, through the church, humanity is both progressively divinized and progressively humanized.

The second focus of Schaff's idea of organic church development was the notion of dialectical development appropriated from Hegel and Bauer.[5] In this view, Schaff saw the early church as the model church represented by the Apostle Peter. This church was characterized by the conservative principles of law, authority, and objectivity. For Schaff this was Catholic Christianity at its best. As the church progressed, it came under the leadership of the Apostle Paul, the Apostle of gentile Christianity. Paul stamped the church in this period with the progressive principles of gospel, freedom, and subjectivity. As the church moved from its Jewish roots into the Gentile world, the principles of law, authority, and objectivity became rigid and static, causing and giving way to the emphases on gospel, freedom, and subjectivity.

The tension between the Petrine and the Pauline types of churches is resolved under the leadership of Apostle John, whom Schaff deemed as the apostle of unitive love, the type of love which characterizes the church of the future, the church of evangelical catholicity. For Schaff,

[4]   Ibid., 23f.
[5]   Ibid., 32.

the Church goes through growth and opposition typified by Hegel's ideas of thesis, antithesis, and synthesis, or preservation, negation, and transformation. The end-time church has already been typified in the early church so that the end is but a return to the beginning. The conflict between the Petrine church and the Pauline church is an integral part of the necessary unfolding of Christianity on its way to the church of the future, which is actually the ideal church of the apostolic past represented by Apostle John—the church of evangelical Catholicism. [6]

The practical implication of Schaff's ecclesiology was a lifetime of ecumenical work in efforts to promote Christian unity between different Protestant denominations but more importantly between Protestantism and the Catholic Church. The latter was stricken from its true essence by Romanism, i.e., the spirit of empire and the emperors of old Rome. This spirit of Romanism brought Caesarism and despotism into the Catholic Church.

This Romanism resulted in the coercive conversions of the Inquisition and the Crusades and the degeneration of catholic principles of law and authority into legalism and authoritarianism. Catholic universalism had been diverted into a time and place bound particularism; hence the necessity of the principle of Protestantism— evangelical freedom from authoritarianism and legalism.

But if medieval Catholicism had given way to a rigid Romanism, then post-reformation Christianity had also given way to a loose subjectivism, as seen in the destructiveness of a historical-critical rationalism run amuck (especially in the home of the Reformation, Germany) and the sectarianism of the "Reformed" churches in England and America.[7]

This subjectivism leads to the separations not only of church and state but of Christianity from life. America reels from a subjectivity manifest in revivalism, which separates the subjective from the objective: puts the Bible over church tradition, preaching over sacraments and denominationalism over a sense of the unity of the church. The cure to this disease, Schaff argued, was the completion of the Reformation—a reconciliation of the subjective with the objective, a uniting of Protestantism with Catholicism.

Schaff argued that the goal of Church History was twofold: first, the progressive transformation of human culture and the natural order by Christ. Second, that the actual church becomes the ideal Church

[6]   Lotz., 30-35.
[7]   Ibid., 36-41.

manifest in the Person of Christ as seen by the Johannine church of the end time. History ends with God's third creation: the dialectical union of the first "natural" creation, the earth, with the second "moral" creation, the Incarnation, resulting in the third creation, the Kingdom of God.

The function of the church is to bring this about through persuasion, in the spirit and power of God alone. The church must penetrate all of culture until the state is transformed into the church, i.e. into a grand theocracy. Lotz argues that Schaff saw the proper study of church history as the only way to unite Protestant subjectivity with Catholic objectivity.

> The proper study of church history is itself the proper way to conquer the maladies of church history. History must overcome history! Evangelical catholicity in the church is a fruit of understanding the church in an evangelical-catholic manner. Organic union is a fruit of understanding the church organically. The church's organic growth and dialectical advance occur not beyond but within the church s own self-understanding . . .[8]

This was not just a beautiful intellectual edifice to be admired by the intellectually advanced. This was also a theological matrix that was a program of action. This theological matrix provided the motive power behind Schaff's work in the Evangelical Alliance, the World Parliament of Religions, the Sabbath Committee, the American Historical Society, and the numerous other groups to which he belonged.[9]

Schaff's writings featured his notion and insistence on truth. Schaff's university and seminary training had made him well aware of the rationalistic tendencies of German historical scholarship. Although he was familiar with such skeptics and non-Christians as Ernst Renan and Edward Gibbon, he seemed to have no problem with his belief that an evangelical understanding of the Christian faith reveals absolute truth.

This belief undergirds his repeated calls in the early chapters of the *History of the Christian Church,* (which was a reproduction of an earlier work called, *What is Church History?*) for the historian to write "the truth" [quotations mine]. Schaff assumes that the truth is accessible through the scientific, artistic, and religious efforts of the committed church

---

[8]   Ibid., 43-45.
[9]   George H. Shriver, *Philip Schaff: Christian Scholar and Ecumenical Prophet* (Macon: Mercer University Press, 1987), 47-60.

historian.[10] Such confidence is accompanied by frequent reminders for the historian to be committed to finding "truth" through their work:

> Finally, the Reformation, by liberating the mind from the yoke of a despotic ecclesiastical authority, gave an entirely new impulse, directly or indirectly to free investigation in every department, and produced that historical criticism which claims to clear fact from the accretions of fiction, and to bring out the truth, the whole truth, and nothing but the truth, of history. [11]

Postmodern analysts would argue that Schaff's confidence in the historians' ability to grasp absolute truth or "the whole truth" was problematic. This becomes evident when one considers his efforts at church unity in the aforementioned Alliances, Parliaments, Committees, and Societies, after his arrival in the ante-bellum America of 1844.

Although he was deeply concerned with church unity, Schaff's writings don't discuss the Great Schisms within the American Church in the mid- to later-1840s. On May 1, 1845, the Southern Delegates of the Methodist Church split from their northern counterparts and formed the Southern Episcopal Church South. Then on May 8, 1845, the southern delegates of the Baptist church, after a similar split, formed the Southern Baptist Convention. Then, in 1857, the Presbyterian Church divided over the issue of slavery. The Lutheran and Roman Catholic churches did not suffer schism, but all had constituents who were on either sides of the issue. [12]

Schaff was not oblivious to these issues given his concern and passion for unity. But despite his desire for and efforts towards unity, such schisms were not major issues in his writings.[13] This absence is partly due to the fact that Schaff became immersed in theological controversy almost immediately upon his arrival at Mercersburg; he was accused of advocating anti-Protestant, pro-Catholic doctrines along with his colleague, John Nevin.

Unfolding events, however, would force Schaff to confront the issue that was dividing the nation and the church. Shortly before the

---

[10] Philip Schaff, *History of the Christian Church* (USA: Delmarva Publications, 2013), Kindle edition, Preface, Section 6, location 2372.

[11] Ibid., section 7, location 2641-2644.

[12] Sydney Ahlstrom, *A Religious History of the American People* (New Haven and London: Yale University Press, 1972), 650–669.

[13] Stephen R. Graham, *Cosmos in the Chaos: Philip Schaff's Interpretation of Nineteenth Century American Religion* (Grand Rapids: William B. Eerdmans Publishing Co, 1995), 195.

beginning of the Civil War in 1861, Schaff preached a sermon titled "Slavery and the Bible". His listeners liked it so much that he expanded the sermon into an essay, which he published in 1861 with the same title. In this text, Schaff acknowledges that slavery was a post-fall phenomenon, steeped in human sin and evil, which would be abolished in the apocalyptic redemption of all humanity and creation. But he argues that God, through Noah, cursed Ham's eldest son Canaan as a result of his father's sin. Schaff says (without offering any explanation or evidence) that Noah's curse meant Africans would be enslaved. [14]

Schaff argues that the Bible, in neither the Old Testament nor the New Testament, expressly condemns slavery itself, although it does demonstrate, in cases like the Hebrew Jubilee and Paul's pleadings with Philemon, a leavening influence, which ameliorates the institution. This Christian influence upholds the virtue that will be fully manifest in the end time redemption of all creation.

Hence the imprecations of northern abolitionists are presumptuous and cannot be supported by the Scripture. Furthermore, Schaff adds, if these [Northern] antagonists were to leave off their ferocious attacks, then the southern states would be free to be influenced by their consciences and deal with the issue of slavery in a manner righteous and just, without causing calamity and division.

> The less the people in the north meddle with the system in the way of political agitation and uncharitable abuse, the sooner this desirable end so dear to every Christian and patriotic ear [the end of slavery] will be reached. The sooner we take the vexing and perplexing question out of the turmoil of federal politics, and leave it with the several slave states, in the hands of Christian philanthropy, and of an all-wise Providence, the better for the peace of the whole country. [15]

Schaff thought that, if the southern slave states were left alone, they could care for their slaves and establish codes to prevent the abuses of slavery and train the slaves religiously to prepare them for the eventual extinction of slavery. In this "noble effort," he argued that people of the south, deserve the hearty sympathy, friendly counsel, and liberal cooperation of their brethren of the north. Schaff argues

---

[14]   Philip Schaff, *Slavery and the Bible: A Tract for The Times*, (Chambersburg, PA: W. Kieffer and Co's Caloric Printing Press, 1861), Internet Archive, Library of Congress, Kindle edition, location 71.

[15]   Ibid., Kindle, location 563.

that only this interpretation can be called "the Bible view and the Bible remedy of slavery".[16]

Schaff also argues that the Africans are heathen and barbarous and that God uses slavery as a harsh but helpful school to train them in the ways of civilization. This will redound to great good, for their tutelage in this school will produce fruit in a miraculous and mysterious way for the dark continent itself—Africa.[17]

Schaff's sermon was very popular in Pennsylvania. He frequently was invited to preach it in churches all over Mercersburg and even—ironically—in Gettysburg. He never contradicts or attacks any of the specific claims of the despised abolitionists. On the contrary, he actually defends slavery in an ideal fashion.

For him Roman slavery was evil and unjust, while American slavery, under the influence of a benevolent Christian faith was, vastly different:

> The former [Roman slavery] treated the slaves as mere property, the latter [American slavery] distinctly recognize and protect them as men; the former cared nothing for the souls of the poor slaves, while the latter can never deny altogether the restraining, humanizing and ennobling influence of the Christian relation upon the master, nor refuse its benefits and privileges to the slave.[18]

The "whole truth" for Schaff was that Christianity secreted a spiritual change in American slavery which was making it helpful, (although harsh) for the "poor negroes". Although freedom was acknowledged as a positive good, men and women were not to strive and agitate for it in the present, because: a) the end of slavery was a progressive work of the Holy Spirit within time, b) inferior races like American Negroes need a harsh but helpful school to overcome their natural deficiencies and c) American slavery was just not that bad, because of the ameliorating influence of the Christian faith.

The press of events pushed Schaff to different positions. As he watched Confederate guerillas raid the town of Mercersburg and plunder the goods of the townspeople, as his own housekeeper was forced to hide in the woods to keep from being kidnapped and forced into the servitude of these southern militarists, as homes were ransacked and violated in the search for slaves to conscript, Schaff began to

---

16   Ibid., Kindle, location 572.
17   Ibid., Kindle, location 559-560.
18   Ibid., Kindle, location 298.

change his gradualist views. He became appalled by the idea of rebellion because it threatened the world historical mission of America to bring a dynamically unified Christianity to the world. Schaff gradually became a reverent supporter of the Union. Although he never totally repudiated his views of Negro inferiority, he did become a supporter of the mission of Negro colleges like Hampton Institute.[19]

Schaff biographer Stephen R. Graham argues that, by 1879, Schaff felt that the abolition of slavery brought justice to the Negro. The problems of Reconstruction and the issues of the Negro community were no longer major themes in Schaff's writings.[20] But the problems of the freedmen and women were coming into a new depth—the depth of legal segregation supported by white civic terrorism.

Many, if not most, of Schaff's contemporaries held similar views. In Schaff's case, his views on slavery and Negro inferiority caused him to neglect analyzing an issue important to his project of church unity— the division of churches around the issue of slavery. Included in this omission is an omission of the many facets of the arguments on both sides of the slavery debate. For instance, Schaff does not discuss the issues that the abolitionists dramatically raised, e.g., the rape, beatings, the separation of families and of the sheer cruelty of a system built on coercion, brutality and fear. That he refers to these arguments as "meddling" and "uncharitable abuse" in the quote mentioned earlier, shows that he knew of such arguments. But these issues were not elaborated in his post-bellum writings.

Schaff's omission of issues surrounding slavery is part of a larger set of omissions. His division of church history into three periods— ancient, medieval and modern—includes no analysis of the European colonialism and imperialism which had been going on for over 350 years, by Portuguese, Dutch, Spanish, and British enslavers. This is not surprising, especially since Schaff stated that the Modern History of the Church (1517-1880) was what happened in Europe and North America.[21]

Leopold von Ranke, one of Schaff's models and mentors, had called for "world history"—which was a history of "men" everywhere in the world. It seemed that Africans were not included in this vision. Especially for Schaff, for who enslaved Africans were a problem for his view of America as God's chosen nation. Schaff urged a peaceful,

---

[19]   Graham, *Cosmos*, 193.
[20]   Ibid., 194.
[21]   Schaff, *History of Christian Church*, location 2265.

benevolent acceptance of slavery which eschewed agitation and conflict in his pursuit of the unification of the evangelical Protestantism with true Catholicism.

This brief analysis of Schaff's writings and works suggest that, from the very beginning, the discipline of American Church history featured important omissions and a notion of truth that assumed it was universal and absolute. Actually, due to its omissions, it was particular and partial. Schaff's notion of truth produced a profound ecclesiology, but it also produced history that, by today's standards, seems to omit much of the tragic and dehumanizing side of the reality of the system of slavery.

His investment in the grand project of the Church returning to its pristine effectivity in its Johannine/primitive state, was accompanied by his blindness to the great social crimes of slavery, imperialism and colonialism—and Christianity's complicity in, and challenge to, all three. In Schaff—one of the most prolific, profound, and sincere church historians of his time—we see a tendency characteristic of the entire Euro-American intellectual tradition: the highlighting of ideational/theological constructions over actual human events and actual human suffering.

There were other forms of history being written during his lifetime which could have challenged these omissions. Formerly enslaved persons had begun to write in America. They wrote their life stories and tracts against slavery. And much of their writing was about Christians, Christian churches, and the Christian religion. Many of the writings of this genre were autobiographical. One of the greatest of these new writers was Maria W. Stewart, who wrote in 1831:

> I was born in Hartford, Connecticut, in 1803: was left an orphan at five years of age: was bound in a clergyman's family; had the seeds of piety and virtue early sown in my mind, but was deprived of the advantages of education, . . . was as I humbly hope and trust, brought to a knowledge of the truth, as it is in Jesus, in 1830; in 1831 made a public profession of my faith in Christ... From the moment I experienced the change, I felt a strong desire, with the help and assistance of God, to devote the remainder of my days to piety and virtue, and poses that spirit of independence that, were I called upon, I would willingly sacrifice my life for the cause of God and my brethren. [22]

[22]   Henry Louis Gates, Jr., and Valerie A. Smith, eds., *The Norton Anthology of African American Literature 3rd ed., Vol. 2* (New York: W.W. Norton & Co, 2014), 182.

Another major figure in this emerging genre was Harriet Jacobs, the first woman writer of a slave narrative in the United States. In her book, *Incidents in the Life of A Slave Girl* (1861), she recounts how she hid from her master by faking a runaway and living in a crawl space of a slave quarters for seven years. After leaving there she spent ten years on the run.

Another less well-known document of this different type of church history was *The Fugitive Blacksmith or Events in The History of James W.C. Pennington, Pastor of A Presbyterian Church, New York, Formerly a Slave in the State of Maryland, United States.* (1849). The Rev. Pennington's narrative is full of details about American slavery and highlights Christians, and Christianity's role in the institution.

Pennington tells the story of how a colleague in a southern state sent two young Negro girls to him, telling him that, if he could raise $2,250 dollars, the two girls, one fourteen and one sixteen, could go free. If not, he would have to have them brought back and sent into a life of prostitution. Pennington and six Methodist ministers raised the money and purchased the girls' freedom.[23] Many names of Negro authors could be added to this list: Olaudah Equiano, Solomon Northrop, Elizabeth Hobbs Keckley, Frederick Douglass, and Francis Harper, to name a few.

Schaff's work seems not to include any detailed focus on the existence of the Negro/colored Christian community. This precluded an analysis and discussion of the question of white and Negro unity within Christendom. A major cause of this omission was the fact that the German/American tradition of history, which shaped historians of Schaff's era, was focused upon the beliefs and actions of Christians in Christian institutions. This focus omitted any analysis of specific social traumas and tragedies and the human suffering they produced.

The discussion of some of the omissions and distortions in Schaff's launching of American Church History, alongside this analysis of his ecclesiology and life's work, sheds light on, and raises questions about, the origins of the discipline. This is important because, if Schaff is not re-appropriated for contemporary historiography, he and his work will become both an omission and a distortion in the work of future historians.

One of the cures for historical omissions and distortions is the very dialectical appropriation Schaff himself utilized, borrowing from

---

[23]   James W.C. Pennington, *The Fugitive Blacksmith or, Events in the History of James W. C. Pennington, Pastor of a Presbyterian Church, New York, Formerly A Slave in the State of Maryland, United States* (London: Charles Gilpin, 1849), Kindle edition, Preface, location 56-71.

Hegel and Bauer: negation, preservation, and transformation; thesis, antithesis, synthesis. In this case, Schaff's work constitutes a thesis, these criticisms of his work an antithesis, and an attempt to reconceptualize church/religious history constitutes a (hopefully better) synthesis.

The Post Modern Intellectual Context

The social struggles of the post-World War II era have produced a unique context in the western intellectual world. Even church historians who try to write history oblivious of these changes end up reacting to them. In order to describe this context I turn to a brief analysis of three representative theorists whose work has shaped the intellectual arena of the current time, which some call the postmodern period.

First among these is Jacques Derrida. Derrida sees in western philosophy a use of language as an overarching attempt to encompass everything and provide a foundation for all thought. He argues that this is due to a metaphysics of presence, rooted in religious notions of the transcendent. Following Saussure, he identifies the nature of language as sign and signification of meaning. Derrida argues that all of western thought was plagued by the notion of the transcendent signified—the God-like referent that was the center and foundation of all language. But Derrida argued that the function of all centers was to create an inside and an outside, a privileged entity and a marginalized entity.

All centers, by definition, exclude, ignore, and repress. Hence all of western thought was plagued by the existence of centers, centers which created an inside or an outside, what Derrida called binary oppositions. Binary oppositions were clashes of the inside of the center verses the outside of the center—clashes of privileged versus marginalized entities. Binary oppositions created a violent hierarchy of domination.

Various power constellations of the West utilize binary oppositions within language, where, between two terms, the first term is seen as superior and the second term inferior. For example: "white/black," "male/female," "owner/worker". In western societies, the word play between the two, makes the superiority of the first term and the inferiority of the second term, seem natural. Authorities attempt to freeze the interplay of these oppositions guaranteeing the power and authority of privileged terms and privileged social actors. Such freezing highlights singular dominant meanings of privilege that shape worldviews, institutions, practices, and all manner of social relations, especially economic, political, and cultural relations.

Derrida argued that it was the work of deconstructionism to unmask the binary opposition, and decenter the privileged term from its position and thereby destroy its relation of domination to the second term. The second term itself could become a new center. But because meanings in language are not stable due to an all pervasive dissemination of meaning, both terns could be equalized, as both existed after deconstruction in an erased status which could accent the use of either as part of the inescapable play of differences within language. Deconstructionism has had a major effect on contemporary philosophy and history, and also, ultimately, on religious history, and finally, to a lesser degree, on church history.[24]

Another French intellectual, Michal Foucault, also revolutionized the field of history. Analysts of Foucault usually divide his work into three stages. In the first stage, he specializes in what he calls archeology, which is an attempt to trace the emergence of the social sciences. In this stage he is primarily concerned with how these disciplines were created, what needs they fulfilled, and who was affected by their new function, status and practice. In this phase of his work his archaeologies reveal that such institutions produce a body of knowledge and a concomitant set of practices, the combination of which he calls discourse.[25]

In the second stage, Foucault is concerned with power, knowledge, and truth. In this stage he utilizes a historical approach he calls the genealogical approach, which traces the emergence and development of specific institutions in the society like prisons, hospitals, and schools. His genealogies unearths the ways in which each of these type of institutions employs a discourse which creates "truth" as a function of their power. Truth for Foucault then is never an objective thing that people can find as the result of some search. No, truth is the product of specific institutions which create and affirm their "truth" in their attempt to expand their own power. So power creates truth, not vice versa.

Foucault sees power everywhere in human relations and in human society. Societies and cultures produce "regimes of truth" which clash and contest other such "regimes" and "truths" in society. This analysis also leads him to posit the idea of "subversive genealogies", the interrupting and disjunctional histories of those crushed and defeated by dominant institutions and their "regimes of truth" Subversive

---

[24] Jacques Derrida, "Introduction, From *Speech and Phenomena, Of Grammatology*, From Difference, Signature Event Context," in *A Derrida Reader: Between the Blinds*, ed., Peggy Kamuf (New York: Columbia University Press, 1991), iix-11: Jim Powell, *Derrida for Beginners* (Danbury, CT: For Beginners LLC, 1997).

[25] Steven Best and Douglas Kellner, *Postmodern Theory: Critical Interrogations* (New York: The Guilford Press, 1991), 34-45.

genealogies record the submerged and forgotten histories of those who resist the dominant powers.[26]

A third stage of his work sees Foucault concerned with the "technologies of the self," that is the methods, tools, and practices of thought, art, language, science, and religion used to transform one's own mind and body. His model here is the free citizen of the Greek and Roman societies who attains fulfillment by the taking the socially structured steps laid out by those societies to attain aesthetic proficiency and the stylized life. Although his prior stages found Foucault decentering and making the conscious, free-thinking subject disappear, in this stage he posits a subject who can fight the overwhelming power of institutions and dominant discourses by adopting certain technologies of the self.[27]

Both Foucault and Derrida saw themselves as historians. Historians like these, who challenge conventional western histories, are important because they are trying to unmask and unearth the tendency of western history to hide-by-omission its brutal episodes and its forgotten crimes. Although both Derrida and Foucault refused to identify themselves as postmodernists, most social analysts see them as representing that trend. Although their work has many credible critics their efforts are useful to anyone concerned with including events like the Tulsa Race Massacre of 1921 in the stories of American Church History.

Even more than these two, the work of one avowed postmodern theorist seems to me to demonstrate the usefulness of the category of the postmodern for contemporary church historians. That theorist is an American, Fredric Jameson.

Jameson's book is titled *Postmodernism or The Cultural Logic of Late Capitalism*. Jameson's concept of late capitalism is derived from Ernest Mandel's 1975 book of the same title. For Mandel, the term late capitalism meant a purer stage of the development of capitalism, which went from: 1) market capitalism, 2) monopoly capitalism, and then into 3) late (or multinational or consumer) capitalism. Jameson argues that the critical break, the distinctive rupture between the modern and the postmodern period, occurred sometime between 1955 and 1963. The distinguishing feature of this period is that the transformation

---

26   Michel Foucault, "Introduction, What is Enlightenment, Truth and Power, Nietzsche, Genealogy, History, What is an Author?" in *The Foucault Reader*, ed. Paul Rabinow (New York: Pantheon Books, 1984), 3-120: Stewart R. Clegg, David Courpasson, and Nelson Phillips, *Power and Organizations* (London: Sage Publications, 2006), 228-265.

27   Best and Kellner, *Postmodern Theory*, 59-75.

of the advanced stage of development of the economic system occurs simultaneously with the transformation of the cultural sphere. [28]

The period of late capitalism features the advanced development of technology, for Jameson, following Mandel, sees technology as a type of development of capital. Another feature of late capitalism is that this advance of capitalized technology propels capitalism to penetrate into every social sphere and every cultural zone. Products, people, places, and even principles all become trussed up and truncated in order to be bought and sold as commodities. As the commodification of products grows unchecked, even human beings and human relations become commodified. The strength of the process of commodification in the postmodern period further accelerates the transformation of culture, which in turn produces "postmodern people."

Such persons are consumed by other constituent features of the postmodern period, such as a) the prevalence of a new type of depthlessness or superficiality, b) a weakening of historicity, c) a whole new type of emotional ground tone, or what Jameson calls "intensities," which are grounded in euphoria. The multitude of stylistic expressions and modes of discourse confront the postmodern person with what Jameson call "pastiche," a patchwork grid of information, intensities, ideas, and experiences. Even the masters of the economy cannot override the sheer volume and heterogeneity of these messages. A byproduct of this heterogeneity is the loss of any collective project and even the national language.[29]

Jameson argues that what is necessary for transforming society in the postmodern period is a new form of political art-as-pedagogy called "cognitive mapping." Cognitive mapping is based on the development of the science and art of cartography, the making of maps. Just as the earliest cartographer had to make observations and projections of geographical space based on her (largely unknown) location vise-à-vis the surrounding uncharted terrain, so too must the contemporary cognitive mapper chart his existential position in relation to the larger unexperienced and abstract totality.

Postmodern cognitive mapping, then, is the attempt of individuals to chart their lives in relation to the overall space shaped and dominated by multinational capitalism. The breakthroughs in representation that can come through such mapping allow people to

---

[28]   Fredric Jameson, *Postmodernism or The Cultural Logic of Late Capitalism* (Durham: Duke University Press, 1991), 35-43.

[29]   Ibid., 17.

grasp their own position as individual and collective subjects who now have regained a capacity to act and struggle.

These three historians, in one way or another, are grappling with the reality of absences and omissions in the western intellectual tradition. Elements and aspects of their work are invaluable to the church or religious historian seeking to reinterpret and reintroduce the crimes and crises of history. After Derrida, previous narratives of church history can benefit from a decentering of the exclusive focus on whites, men, and even churches. The hitherto left unquestioned, unnamed, and uninvestigated can now be re-centered in a historiographical play of differences. The prior privileged actors, organizations, and institutions are not eliminated, however; they are held "in erasure" in suspension, as new, more inclusive, more complex, richer analyses are developed.

After Foucault, subversive genealogies are now able to come to light. These genealogies unmask the truths of previous church historians produced in exclusive institutions, with their biased "regimes of truth." Foucaultian analyses help us understand the different "truths" of different Christian formations and helps explain the variety of discourses (combinations of knowledge and action) in the Christian community. A Foucaultian analysis allows church historians to search out the subversive genealogies of devalued, denigrated and destroyed communities and unearth their "truths" of resistance and "technologies of the self and of change."

After Jameson, church historians can begin to trace the historical development of the features of post modernity and how this affects Christian actors, institutions, and organizations. The penetration of overarching corporate capitalism into all cultural spheres and into consciousness itself; the commodification of products, principles and persons; the intensities of "postmodern people" caught up in a technology-based "pastiche" of information and images; and the loss of most, if not all, collective projects, even the reading and writing of church history, all are examples of new avenues and opportunities for church history.

Writing Postmodern Church/Religious History

Historical and theoretical resources like these help us to answer the question, "how should church history be written in the second decade of the twenty-first century and beyond?" James M. Washington, a student of Ahlstrom's, who came to occupy Schaff's chair at Union Theological Seminary, answered this question by focusing on what he called, "the black Church movement." One of the chief institutions of this movement was the National Baptist Convention.[30]

Washington's first book, *Frustrated Fellowship: The Black Baptist Quest for Social Power,* was an analysis of the origins of that convention. He went on to edit a collection of Dr. Martin Luther King's writings, a further analysis of the institutional activity of the Black Church Movement, *A Testament of Hope.* His final major work was a compilation of African American prayers, titled *Conversations with God.* It was a study of practices of African/colored/Negro/Afro American, and African American Christians throughout American history. The practice of prayer transformed self, surroundings, and society. It can be argued that it was similar to Foucault's "technologies of the self".

Cornel West answered the question of how church history should be written in the twenty-first century American context most powerfully in his book *Prophesy Deliverance: An Afro American Revolutionary Christianity.* From start to finish, West's book is largely a history text which decenters the Black Christian church movement, black church leaders, Christian concepts, and, indeed, Christianity, all in an attempt to put forth a revolutionary Afro American Christianity. His historical interpretation of the anti-black impetus of European modernity and African American historical responses to that tradition constitutes a subversive genealogy of an Afro American "regime of truth." [31] The sweep of this work is so broad and the depth of this work is so profound that its challenges often go unnoticed within a church history community struggling to include black history itself.

Post World War II anti-colonial struggles in Africa, the Caribbean, South America, and Asia and the Civil Rights, Black Power, and College Student struggles in the USA had already revealed the power pretensions and the ideological nature of the Western intellectual and academic discourse by the time the Women's Movement arose in the 1970's in North America.

But North American church history departments were slow to integrate the concerns of women in their curriculum. So, as late as 1997, Ann Braude, in a book titled *Retelling Religious History,* had to argue that "Women's History *Is* American Religious History." Braude pointed out that histories centered on the ideas and activities of males omitted the majority of members of American Christian churches—women. She

---

[30] James M. Washington, *Frustrated Fellowship: The Black Baptist Quest for Social Power,* (Macon, GA: Mercer University Press, 1986), xiif.

[31] Cornel West, *Prophesy Deliverance! An Afro American Revolutionary Christianity* (Philadelphia: Westminster Press, 1982), 47-65, 101-104, 126.

demonstrates in this article how a focus on women as the center of American religious history helps to change the entire discipline. More particularly, she argues that focusing on women helps to show that many of the earlier celebrated themes of American religious history were in error, primarily because they omitted women.

For example, a focus on women in religious history leads us to understand that the well-known themes of declension, feminization, and secularization in American Church History never really occurred. They were but the interpretations of [male] historians whose views were skewed by their mistaken focus on men and their neglect of women. Braude argues that American religious history can never stand on surer historical ground until the narrative is reshaped by focusing on the numerical majority of people in the church—women.[32]

If these sociopolitical struggles had showed that American history had to be re-centered because of its omissions, it also showed that sometimes the new, more inclusive center itself also had itself to be deconstructed and re-centered. This was the case when Black women began to argue that white feminists and feminist scholarship had often omitted their experiences and that there was a great chasm of race and class between the two groups.

Darlene Clarke Hine, a product of the call for black history and black historians which came out of the struggles of the 1960s, realized that she herself, in writing black history, had not focused on the specific realities of Black women. It was not until she was challenged by a black woman who was a non-professional community historian that she realized her error and began a long and fruitful journey to produce Black women's history.[33]

In 1994 she published, *Hine Sight: Black Women and the Reconstruction of American History*. In this text, she argues that, if Black women are put at the center of American history, the entire narrative of that history must necessarily change. In one of her articles in this text she divides black historians into three ideal types. First there are the Traditionalists, who accept western methods and produce monographs designed to include the histories of black people into the dominant western discourse.

Next there are the Authentists, who are guided by the goal of liberation from European categories of thought and analysis. They often propose new methodologies that allow African people to produce

---

[32]   Thomas A. Tweed, ed., *Retelling U. S. Religious History*, (Berkeley and Los Angeles: University of California Press, 1997), 87f.

[33]   Darlene Clark Hine, *Hine Sight: Black Women and The Reconstruction of American History* (Bloomington & Indianapolis: Indiana University Press, 1994), xx.

and control knowledge about themselves. Within this group are a subset of people Hine calls the Orginists, who seek to rewrite the origins of civilization basing it in a Black Egypt and Black people's place in ancient history.

Hine's third ideal type category is that of Black feminists who raise questions about the androcentric nature of most black histories. These Black feminists historians probe the subtle and not-so-subtle linkages between gender, race, and class. They seek to highlight the specificity of Black women past reality. All three types challenge American, Black, and church history.

The work of Washington and West, Hine and Braude, Derrida, Foucault, and Jameson all suggest bold new directions for American Church History. Their work and examples suggest that the Eurocentric male paradigm of American Church History be modified so that an approach can be adopted which envisions multicenters in the study of church history.

Decentering and recentering is not just inclusion, however. We must be willing to confront all types of tensions in these narratives, particularly what we might call crimes—crimes of subjugation, genocide, terrorism, torture. The historian must try to figure out who has been left out of the narratives of history and why. Then she or he must construct a new, more inclusive, multi-centered narrative. This narrative does not totally exclude the European giants which have dominated the story thus far. But it seeks to broaden the narrative by placing Luther in relation to Las Cases, Schleiermacher with Sojourner Truth, Jonathan Edwards with David Walker, Charles G. Finney with Charles H. Mason, D. L Moody with Amie Simple McPherson, and Nannie Helen Burroughs with Walter Rauschenbusch.

But what about Lotz's challenge: what do we do if we have taken the "church" out of Church History? As both a church historian and a pastor, I still want to talk about the "church" in Church History. I realize that, given the dominance of the "religious history" model in academia, this desire is highly problematic.

The discussion around post modernism, however, poses a unique opportunity for the church itself. Postmodernism does not have to be accepted as a doctrine or as itself an absolute, since it critiques absolutism. Indeed, as historians like Ferdinand Braudel and Immanuel Wallerstein teach us, postmodern historiography helps us understand how different people in different places can have different epistemologies. This means that people in African American communities (and other ethnic and class communities) can have epistemologies that both embrace the supernatural, traditional authorities and the efficacy of Western intellectual analysis all at the same time.[34]

Seeing that faith and communities of faith are enduring human phenomena, we must continue to talk about the church. But we also realize that the faith that the church embodies entangles those churches in a web of social relations that begs for the best possible analysis. So we ought to continue to speak about the church, critically and affirmatively.

Historical investigations like Ahlstrom's show us, however, that a narrow focus on churches would impoverish our historical work. We must talk about Christian churches, yes, but we also must talk about Christian ideas, institutions and individuals in the context of the larger society and larger social forces.

And we must not be afraid that we, like Schaff, will leave someone or something out. Hopefully we will make more modest claims about our ability to grasp the absolute truth. That should not make us cowards who advance no truth, however.

Conclusions: Church History, and The Tulsa Race Massacre of 1921.

So, then, let us speak about the church and more. We can speak about the church from Foucault's perspective, as an institution that produces its own form of knowledge and action, i.e., its own truth, and its own discourse. We can speak about the church in relation to Derrida, as a center that decenters the hegemonic, texts, troupes, and teachings of various human evils like white supremacy, militarism, sexism, and economic exploitation. Or as a center that itself becomes captive to those powers. We can also speak of churches radically challenged and changed by the inescapable currents of postmodernism pointed out by Fredric Jameson.

Before closing, let's go back to the Tulsa Race Massacre of 1921. New technologies are effecting the telling and the resolution of this history. In true postmodern fashion, my attention was drawn to this historical incident by a post on Facebook, by the Atlanta Blackstar website (http://atlantablackstar.com/2013/12/04/8-successful-aspiring-black-communities-destroyed-white-neighbors/).

The role of Christian ideas, individuals, and institutions in the Tulsa Race Massacre of 1921 are increasingly coming to light. Mt. Zion

---

[34] Fernand Braudel, *The Perspective of the World: Civilization & Capitalism 15th-18th Century Vol. III* (New York: Harper & Row, 1979), 64f: Immanuel Wallerstein, *The Essential Wallerstein* (New York: The New Press, 2000), 160-169.

Baptist Church was rebuilt, although it took the congregation twenty-one years to pay off the $50,000 mortgage note. The charges against the young man accused of rape, Dick Roland, were later dropped.[35] Some of the survivors of the Massacre are still alive, although at the time of the beginning of this writing (August, 2015), many are passing on. Some of the impetus to address and redress this history has come from the Christian community. The issue of reparations, which has been raised for many years by the survivors and their children, and, as of 2001, even by the Oklahoma Commission to Study The Tulsa Race Riot, is starting to gain momentum. But yet the story of the involvement of the churches and the Christian community has yet to be fully told.

But an analysis embodying the concepts, questions, and sensitivities listed above can aid the church historian in developing a postmodern narrative of church history which has the depth and breadth of religious history and the theological precision and grandeur of a thoroughgoing church history. That would be a postmodern history which can pierce the clouds of historical amnesia and social bias, and illuminate reality by recognizing past crimes, as it blows a wind of deliverance, suggesting restitution and redemption worthy of the best of the Christian faith.

---

[35]   Hirsch., *Riot*, 113:Tulsa Preservation Commission, "Tulsa History: Religion (1884-1945)," http://tulsapreservationcomission.org/tulsa-history/religion: Ellsworth, *Death*, 108-114.

CHAPTER 6

Philip Milledoler, Reluctant Inheritor

Norman J. Kansfield

Introduction — New Brunswick Seminary, 1825-1841

When the Theological Seminary of the Reformed Protestant Dutch Church, located in New Brunswick, New Jersey, went to bed on Wednesday, January 19, 1825, everything seemed to be going right. It had a total of twenty students. Their education was under the care of two professors—the 79-year old John Henry Livingston, who had been Professor of Sacred Theology in the seminary since its founding forty-one years earlier, and John DeWitt, who was thirty-six years of age and had served as Professor of Biblical Criticism, Church History, and Pastoral Theology since 1823. These two were assisted by John Mabon, who served as Instructor in Hebrew and Greek, and as Rector of the Grammar or Preparatory School.

The Seminary was housed in the large, stone, neo-classical structure now known as Old Queens Hall. The construction of this building had been begun in 1809, and, in 1825, large portions of it were still unfinished. The chapel, the library, the lecture rooms and two faculty apartments were completed. Scaffolding and debris filled other rooms. But students did not live in the building. They rented rooms and boarded in homes adjacent to the campus.

For several years, the Seminary and the College (then called Queens College) had shared the use of the building's facilities. But, since 1816, all college-level teaching had been suspended because of the financial embarrassment of the college. Classes of the so-called "Grammar School"—later known as Rutgers Preparatory School—did continue to be held in Queens Hall.

Professor John DeWitt, with his family, and Instructor John Mabon, with his family, lived in the faculty apartments in the East and West wings of Queens Hall. The senior professor, Dr. Livingston, lived about a half-mile away, in his own home, on the south side of Livingston Avenue between Townsend and Suydam Streets. He owned and operated a prosperous farm in that area (bordered by Remsen Street and Livingston Avenue, between Townsend Street and the Creek).[1]

It was in this condition that the Seminary went to bed on Wednesday night. But when it awoke on Thursday morning, January 20, 1825, its world had been forever altered. The great Livingston was dead. On Sunday, January 23, 1825, in the middle of a raging blizzard, the venerable professor was laid to rest in the cemetery of the First Reformed Church, and the stunned seminary community began the struggle to reorganize its institutional life.

A special session of the General Synod, to elect a successor to Dr. Livingston, was held in Albany on Wednesday and Thursday, *February* 16 and 17 (NOT January 16, 1825, as both the Title page and the formal heading of the minutes indicate).[2] During this meeting, one man seemed to be everywhere and do everything. In the first two pages of minutes for this special session of Synod, we meet the name of Philip Milledoler no fewer than five times. Milledoler was Chairman of the Board of Superintendents of the Seminary, so it was he who officially announced Dr. Livingston's death and officially called upon the Rev. Thomas DeWitt, President of the General Synod, to proceed with the election of a new Professor of Sacred Theology. It was Milledoler who wrote the memorial resolution honoring Livingston. Milledoler was appointed chairman of a committee to "take into consideration the

---

[1] On Livingston's New Brunswick homes see William H. S. Demarest, History of Rutgers College, 1766-1924 (New Brunswick, NJ: Rutgers College, 1924), p. 217.

[2] The mistake could have been either January 26, 1825 or *February* 16, 1825—both were on Wednesdays. To have met on January 26 seems rather a tight schedule since JHL hadn't died until Thursday, January 20, 1825. His funeral was held on Sunday, January 23. Gunn, p. 475, is explicit; the meeting was in February.

propriety of preparing a monumental stone, with suitable inscription, to be erected over the grave of the Rev. Dr. Livingston . . ." And, just prior to Synod's taking up the process of the election itself, it was Milledoler again, who served as one of three pastors called upon to lead the Reverend Body in prayer.[3]

Ava Neal later privately revealed to Milledoler the exact nature of the vote at synod.[4] According to Neal, the vote proceeded as follows:

	1st ballot	2nd ballot	3rd ballot
[Philip] Milledoler	13	15	23
[John] Ludlow	7	12	13
Tho[ma]s. DeWitt	10	7	
Jesse Fonda	2	2	
James Cannon	2		
P[hilip] Duryea	1	1	
Dr.[Andrew] Yates	1		
	36	37	36[5]

For more than sixteen years, from the seventeenth of February, 1825, until the ninth of September, 1841, Philip Milledoler served the Reformed Church as Professor of Didactic and Polemic Theology in its Seminary at New Brunswick. On the latter date, Milledoler resigned, a broken and frustrated man. This essay will seek to establish an understanding of this man—Philip Milledoler, and of the events which led to his resignation—events which I call the "Battle of 1841".

The Battle of 1841

During the evening of February 13, 1841, the students of the Middle and Senior Classes of New Brunswick Seminary gathered, somewhat secretly, to determine what they might do to change the teaching methodology of the Rev. Dr. Philip Milledoler, their Professor of Didactic and Polemic Theology (Didactic and Polemic Theology was the early nineteenth century equivalent of what we now call Systematic

---

[3]   *Acts and Proceedings of the General Synod* (hereinafter *MGS*), January 16 [actually February 16], 1825, pp. 6-7.

[4]   Neal was quite clearly a trusted confidant. That fact is interesting in the light of several other facts: 1) it was Neal who was finally able to publish Livingston's lecture notes; 2) it was Neal who was suspended from the Ministry by Classis Bergen in 1829 and restored in 1833; *Historical Directory of the Reformed Church in America,* 2001, p. 284.

[5]   Philip Milledoler Papers, New York Historical Society Library, Box 1, Letters, 1825.

Theology.). The students elected Gardner Jones as their chairperson, and Peter Randall as their secretary. Both were seniors. By the end of the evening, the students had carefully identified what they understood to be the issues and the possibilities of the situation. Two Middlers (as second-year students were called), John DeWitt and John Sutphen Himrod, and one Senior, Gilbert Myer, were selected "to prepare a plan of action" to protest against Milledoler's method of teaching. The students met again on February fifteenth and seventeenth.[6] By the conclusion of the meeting on the seventeenth, twenty-six students had signed a seven-page letter addressed to the Board of Superintendents— the equivalent of today's Board of Trustees. The letter, which came to be called "the Memorial," began:

> The undersigned members of the Senior and Middle Classes of the Theological Seminary of the Reformed Dutch Church beg leave, most respectfully to present to your Reverend body, the following Statement of Facts in relation to the Rev. Professor and the study of Didactic Theology.[7]

The Students' case

The students asserted that the only reason they were bringing this matter to the attention of the Superintendents was that their future in ministry depended "under God, upon our being well qualified to expound and defend the doctrines of the word of God."[8] They elaborately stated that they revered Professor Milledoler and intended to do nothing which would in any way harm him or his reputation. But they did, after all, need to be competently prepared for ministry if they were going to be useful within the church. And they were quite convinced that the methodology which Milledoler employed was not competent for such a preparation.

It is quite clear, from the rest of the students' letter, that Professor Milledoler had been carrying on their instruction in a most conservative and formal fashion. Sixteen years earlier, just as Milledoler was beginning his responsibilities as Professor, the General Synod of 1825 had prescribed the use of a specific text book in the area of Didactic and Polemic Theology. Milledoler reported that he began each

6   Ibid.
7   NBTS Archives, Faculty Files, Milledoler Papers -- 7 pages, manuscript copy. Hereinafter referred to as Letter A.
8   Letter A, p.1.

year's course work with seven lectures which he called "Prolegomena," or introductory remarks.[9] After these lectures were completed, students were expected, for each class session, to master five to ten pages of the text book with such thoroughness that they could recite the material in class. In that era, to "recite" something did not mean, necessarily, to speak it from memory, although memorization was to become an issue in this confrontation. It is more likely that "recite" meant "to give an account, in detail, of the material assigned."

It will also be important to take note of the textbook, because it really becomes the single most important focus of the dispute. The text book had been written in 1695 by Johannes à Marck in Leyden, the Netherlands. As its title, *Christianae Theologiae Medulla Didactico-Elenctica,* suggests, it was written in the very clumsy seventeenth-century academic Latin of scholastic Reformed theology.

The students raised two complaints against Milledoler's classroom teaching: 1) he allowed no questions to be asked orally during class; and 2) he expected students to cover more of the textbook at each class session than they were able adequately to prepare.[10] The students found themselves in a most frustrating place. They were forced to work with a textbook which they had to struggle to understand. They felt overwhelmed by the amount of the book they were expected to cover between classes. At the same time, they were allowed no opportunity for asking questions in class. This led to their assertion: that they were "receiving no instruction at all adequate to a preparation for the ministry, in this department of study."[11]

The students conclude their case by stating that:

> After the most vigorous and oft repeated efforts to try to gain something of value, we have fallen back in despair, and relinquished all attempt. There is no interest in the Lecture Room. We do not expect the excitement and interest of romance to attend the grave subject of Theology; but we do expect the interest of truth developed and apprehended. But we are disappointed.[12]

In what one suspects was an attempt to make their case as unassailable as possible, the students wrote: "There is not a dissenting voice."[13] In point of fact, there were at least four dissenting voices,

[9]   Minutes of the Board of Superintendents, 1812-1840, pp.193-194.
[10]   Letter A, p.3.
[11]   Ibid, p.5.
[12]   Ibid, p.6
[13]   Ibid, p.5.

or persons who abstained from signing the Students' letter: William John Thompson (1812-1867), from the Class of 1841, and Barnabas V. Collins (1814-1877), Eben S. Hammond (1815-1873), and Jacob A. Lansing (1792-1856) of the Class of 1842. The students ended their letter as they had begun it, by observing again, underlined this time for emphasis:

We cannot be profited by the present system of instruction.[14]

The Efforts at Compromise

The first response to the students' letter came from a member of the Board of Superintendents—the Rev. Dr. John Knox. Knox was fifty-one years old, and for twenty-five years had been a pastor in the Collegiate Church of the City of New York. During the first nine of those years, Dr. Milledoler had been Dr. Knox's senior colleague within the Collegiate pastorate. Throughout the Battle of 1841, Knox was to prove Milledoler's most faithful friend and advocate. But he was eminently just. The purpose of his letter of February 22, 1841, was to beg the students to withdraw their letter of February 17 before the Superintendents had to deal with it. The character of his letter, and of his hope for peace, is evident in his response to the students' charge that Milledoler required "recitations in Mark, of extreme length."[15] To this he wrote: "I cannot doubt but, that if the Professor is made aware that his exactions are oppressive, he will diminish them and thus abate the grievance."[16]

Above all else, Knox perceived the students' letter as "an impeachment of the competency of the Professor, and a call for his removal."[17]

> This is a very grave affair [wrote Knox]. The principle involved, displacing a prof. at the direct instance of his pupils, is a dangerous one, and if allowed to operate would unsettle discipline and introduce confusion into every institution of learning in the land. . . . Pardon me young gentlemen. I think your movement bold and perillous [sic] in the extreme. Suffer me to beseech you to

---

[14] Ibid, p.7.
[15] Manuscript letter, Knox to Theological Students, February 22, 1841, NBTS Archives.
[16] Ibid, pp. 1-2.
[17] Ibid, p.2.

reconsider what has been done and to recall your communication, and to pause—at least until your friends and the friends of the professor, of the church and her institutions shall have time to consider the case, and ascertain whether the matters of your complaint cannot be met by remedies less violent and perillous [sic] than it seems to me are involved in your movement.[18]

On February 27, the students composed and sent off a letter of response to Knox. It is very clear that they appreciated the fact that Knox had carefully read their case and had heard what it was they wanted heard. It is also clear that the students were impressed by Knox's argument. But, in the end, they told Knox that they "regret to state that our conviction of the entire propriety of the measures we have adopted remains yet unshaken."[19]

In addition to letter writing, a lot of other activity was going on in and around Old Queens Hall. On February 20, Barnabas Collins, a member of the Middle Class, informed Professor Milledoler of the students' actions. On February 21 and 22, Milledoler tried to get the other faculty members, Professors McClelland and Cannon, to take action "against this insubordination."[20] On February 23, Milledoler formally asked Professor Cannon to get whatever information he could on the affair, and particularly to obtain a copy of the students' letter to the Board. Cannon complied, and on February 25, presented Milledoler with a copy of the letter. Late in March, the Rev. Dr. Wilhelmus Eltinge, President of the Board of Superintendents, attempted to mediate between the students and Milledoler. Without any kind of authorization from Milledoler, Eltinge told the students that Milledoler would publish his personal translation of Marck's *Medulla*. The students assured Eltinge that if Milledoler would indeed publish his English text of the *Medulla*, they would withdraw their letter to the Board. When Eltinge informed him of this, Milledoler refused to negotiate or compromise, insisting that the matter be carried through to its juridical conclusion.[21]

---

18 Ibid p.3-4.
19 Ibid.
20 Milledoler Papers II, Letters, 1841.
21 Milledoler Papers II; Letters, 1841. On March 27, Milledoler called another faculty meeting and sought to have his colleagues make some response to the controversy. They refused to do so, because the matter was "slated to come before the Board of Superintendents." Milledoler thought this action was "injudicious and unkind" even though he, on the basis of the same rationale, refused to compromise with the students.

The month of April, 1841, must have provided a strained and fragile interlude to students and faculty within the small community of the Seminary. Milledoler observed that

> During the time that intervened between the outbreak of these stud's [sic] to the close of the session, being desirous (of course) that they might, in some measure at least, be prepared for their approaching examination, I continued to meet with them at the usual hours. It was an irksome task, however—and I often felt that I was casting Pearls where they ought not go.[22]

The student perception of Milledoler's commitment to completing the course, was a bit different. In a copy of Marck's *Medulla* which is now in the John Walter Beardslee Library of Western Theological Seminary, there is a pencil-written, partially obliterated note, in the handwriting of James A. H. Cornell of the Class of 1841. The portions of the note which are legible suggest that the students perceived Milledoler as NOT wanting to complete Marck so that he would be able to suggest to Synod that it was clear that his assignments had not been long enough. Where the note becomes totally clear it reads: "Don't you see how he pokes. We might have finished had he not gone to [New] York."[23] The mention of New York is probably in reference to a March 6, 1841 trip that Milledoler took to New York to consult with the Rev. Dr. John Knox. One additional marginal note in the Western Seminary copy of the *Medulla* is almost certainly also from this time of uneasy calm. Again in the handwriting of James A.H. Cornell, the note reads: "Dr. M. requests students of [the] T[heological] Sem[inar]y to examine Matt.5:23-26 & I Cor. 5:7-8 before next Sabbath which is communion."[24]

Professor Milledoler's Response

On May 11, 1841, in response to the Students' letter, the Board of Superintendents of the Seminary met in special session in New Brunswick. Dr. Milledoler, who up to this point had in no way replied to the students, "came before the Board" and read two documents: 1) a review of and remarks concerning the students' letter to the Board; and 2) "a paper containing a list of charges, with specifications, against the members of the Senior and Middle Classes who have signed the

---

[22]   Ms. note in Milledoler's hand, attached to Milledoler memoir, Milledoler Papers V.
[23]   Western Seminary copy of Marck's *Medulla*, p.v.
[24]   Ibid, p. 244.

communication in the hands of the Board."[25] It is most unfortunate that only the first of these documents remains. It is dated May 10, 1841.

Milledoler understood the students' principal criticism to be that the textbook for his class was not in "the pure Latin of the Classic Authors." While the students did complain about the quality of the Latin with which they had to struggle, that was NOT the focus of any of their charges. Milledoler nevertheless responded as if it were, and then stated that he could not do much about that because "that Book has been put into my hands as well as theirs by the competent authority of the church." Milledoler's letter does give clear indication that he was aware that the textbook was a major part of the problem. He went on to observe that "The real difficulty [with the textbook may be] that it requires more thought than many are willing to bestow upon it—and inculcates Doctrines which it is to be feared are not always suited to their taste."[26]

Regarding the students' charge of being denied the privilege of asking questions in class, Milledoler responded that he had often in the past offered opportunities for questions within the classroom. The result, he said, had always been so problematic that he had decided against further use of the process.

His response to the students' complaint about "the amount or number of pages they were required to prepare" was emphatic. "Your professor is obliged here to declare, and he does it with regret, that the statement [of the number of pages required] is absolutely untrue."[27]

With obviously increasing anger, Milledoler continued: "On two things which are here insinuated it is difficult to suppress an honest indignation." Milledoler read the first of these concerns "which occasionally runs through all their memorial" to be the students' claim that they were "called upon to recite from memory, and if I mistake not, in the very words of the author, things which they do not understand." This, Milledoler asserted, was categorically untrue. He insisted that he had never demanded answers in the words of the author and that students had always been permitted freely to give their own definitions and to develop their arguments in their own words.[28]

There is ample evidence that Milledoler would not even *allow* students to answer "in the words of the author."[29] This response by

---

[25]   Ibid, p. 17.
[26]   Ibid, p.1.
[27]   Ibid, p.5.
[28]   Ibid, p.7.
[29]   Milledoler Papers V; Memoirs, 1827, p.7.

Milledoler appears totally to negate at least this one student charge. There is a problem, however. It is very difficult to find anything in the students' letter which speaks about this kind of memorization. So, as in the first case, Milledoler appears to have misread the students' letter.

Finally, Milledoler responded to the students' claim that if they spent the required amount of time on Didactic theology they would have to pay less attention to their other course requirements. He stated that it was his experience of these students that they seemed always to find time for those things which they really wanted to do.

Having, in his mind, carefully and rationally responded to the content of the specific charges included in the students' letter, Milledoler then allowed himself to conclude his remarks with three pages of emotional reaction. A brief quotation will provide some measure of his feeling:

> How sublime is the spectacle here presented to our view? Twenty-six young men in the vigor of their manly strength, after due deliberation, as they say, and offered Prayer, assaulting an aged minister of Christ of 47 years standing in the ministry—duly placed over them as their Instructor in the Lord, and whom they profess to most highly venerate, and most dearly love—secretly and recklessly attempting to assassinate his character—to fix a deep brand upon his memory—endeavoring first of all to put him on the Rack [sic]—and then for the remainder of his days to cast him out of God's heritage, as the mire of the street to be trodden under the foot of men.[30]

The Roles of the Board of Superintendents and of the General Synod.

The Board of Superintendents carefully listened to their professor and asked him to provide them with copies of his response to the students' letter, as well as his charges against the students. Milledoler provided them with a copy of his response, but refused to give them a written copy of the charges against the students which he had read to them. This left the Board in an awkward position. They were sure that they had the authority to proceed to try students on charges presented by a faculty member. They could not, however, proceed against the students without Milledoler's charges. They were also quite sure

---

[30]   Ibid, p.10.

that they could not proceed against a Faculty member. Professors of Theology were answerable only to the General Synod. In the end, the Board of Superintendents bundled up all of the papers with which they had been presented, and forwarded the entire business to the General Synod for adjudication.

The General Synod met in regular session from June 2 through June 16, in one of the longest meetings of Synod ever held. All of the materials from the May 11 meeting of the Board of Superintendents were referred to a special committee of Synod. The Committee acknowledged "that difficulties exist in the Theological Seminary, in connexion with the Didactic Professorship of such a character as to require the attention of this body."[31] The Committee therefore recommended and the Synod voted:

1. Not to "decide against the abstract right of memorial by the theological students." In other words, the Synod refused to rule that the students had no right to petition the Board of Superintendents or the General Synod, itself. The Synod did, however, return the students' letter to the Board "with the request that the students withdraw said memorial."[32]

2. To establish a committee of five ministers and two elders to meet in New Brunswick and "to inquire into the facts necessary to a competent understanding of the case. If this new committee found anything suggestive of the need to revise the method of teaching in the area of Didactic and Polemic Theology, the Committee had the power to draft a new plan for instruction, to be submitted to the Superintendents for their "concurrence." As soon as the Board agreed with the Committee, any such new plan was to be presented to the Didactic Professor and shall be the law regulating the course of instruction in said department until the next meeting of General Synod.

This Committee met in Old Queens Hall on July 7. The very first thing they did was to hear all that Professor Milledoler had to say to them. They then interviewed a deputation of students from the group which had signed the letter. Understanding that some students had refused to sign the letter, the committee interviewed two of them. Finally, they interviewed the other professors. Then they set to work to prepare a plan for the study of didactic theology. One week later, on July 14, 1841, the plan was presented to the Board of Superintendents.

[31]   *MGS*, June, 1841, p. 521.
[32]   *MGS*, June 1841, p. 522.

The Board slightly amended and then approved the proposed plan. The General Synod, which had met for two weeks in June, had to be called back for a special session in New York City, from September 8 through 11, 1841. The new plan, as presented to Synod, had five principal points:

1. The text book would continue to be used, as a resource for students and as a guide for the professor.
2. The professor was to deliver "original, full, connected, continuous, and well-digested written lectures" following the order of subjects in the text book but related to the standards of the church and all modern controversies in Theology.
3. Theological study was to begin with an elementary course for first year students, the regular course of didactic theology in the second year, and polemic theology in the third year.
4. The professor was to regularly recommend additional reading throughout the course of lectures.
5. The professor was required to prepare a full set of questions which students were to answer in their rooms and at their leisure, and which would form the basis of their examination before the board.[33]

The Synod approved the plan on the evening of September 8. A committee was appointed "to place a copy of the [plan] in the hands of the Rev. Professor Milledoler, by tomorrow morning." The Professor appeared in Synod the following morning. His response was brief:

> On action now had by this General Synod, there is but one course left for the undersigned to pursue.
>
> After expressing his entire dissatisfaction with all the proceedings which have led to this result, from the reception of the memorial to the present hour, and especially to the precedent thereby sustained, and which in his apprehension goes to destroy the good order of every literary institution in the country, he feels himself constrained to declare, that he must, and hereby does resign his Professorship . . .[34]

Thus ended the Battle of 1841. But how had this event come to happen?

---

[33] *MGS*, June 1841, pp.521-522.
[34] *MGS*, September 1841, pp. 23-24.

How Could This Come to Be?

The "Text Book"

The textbook, *Christianae Theologiae Medulla Didactico-Elenctica,* very quickly became the principal focus of the confrontation. The year 1841 was not the first time that the book had been the center of theological argument. It had its origin in a seventeenth-century Dutch theological controversy between two warring parties within the Reformed Church in the Netherlands—the Voetians (who were followers of Gijsbert Voet or Voetius:1588-1676) and the Cocceians (who were followers of Johannes Koch, Cock, or Kok: 1603-1669). The book's author, Johannes à Marck (1655-1731),of the University of Leyden, was the leader of a faction within the Voetian party known as the "Dead," or far-right Voetians.[35] The book, in the format used here, was first published in Leyden in 1695.

One major virtue of the book may have been its size. In an era of monumental summaries of theology, such as Francis Burmann's two-volume *Synopsis Theologiae* (Utrecht: Cornelius Jacobi Noenaert, 1687), Marck had limited himself to only 470 little pages. In order to achieve such compactness, Marck chose a style that was half catechetical and half propositional. He described the work as *elenctico,* that is an "abstract, outline, or synopsis," and *Medulla,* that is "marrow or essence." How could such a book become the central focus of a North American conversation in 1841? It was, by then, almost 150 years old, and it was written in the arcane Latin of the seventeenth century. While these two factors may seem to be detriments to us, they may, indeed, have been the very virtues for which the book was selected for use in the Americas.

On December 30, 1772, when the Rev. John Rutsen Hardenbergh, the Rev. John Leydt, and the Rev. John M. VanHarlingen, Trustees of Queens College, wrote to the Reverend Classis of Amsterdam requesting a recommendation for a professor of theology to teach in their school, they listed ten qualifications which their ideal candidate should possess. Tenth among those qualifications was: "Finally, he should be pleased to dictate on Mark's *Medulla.*"[36] Subsequent history has made us aware that the Classis of Amsterdam wrote back to these good men and told them that their request was not consistent with the "Articles of Union"

---

[35] It should be here noted, however, that when Hermanus Witsius (1636-1718), third generation leader of the Cocceians, was dying, it was Marck who sat with him, and who preached his funeral oration.)

[36] *Ecclesiastical Records of the State of New York,* p. 4257.

(1771), which had specified that the theological professorate should stand in relationship to no established college, and that the Classis had already recommended a young man named John Henry Livingston for such an appointment.

After 1784, when he was finally elected to the Professorate, Livingston did not use Marck's *Medulla* in any obvious form during the forty-one years of his teaching. Instead, Livingston developed his own systematic theology and delivered it in formal lectures, which the students carefully wrote down in copybooks. In this way, Livingston's systematic theology became the "orthodoxy" of the Reformed Church in America. Any pastor trained by Livingston had, sitting on his library shelf, his own copy of Livingston's lectures, to be consulted any time questions of correct doctrine or correct practice arose.

But in 1825, the venerable Livingston died. And he died just as the Reformed Church in America was struggling with its first significant secession. On October 28, 1822, five pastors formally withdrew from the Reformed Dutch Church in North America.[37] They were led by Solomon Froeligh (1750-1827), who had been ordained in 1774, served as pastor and patriot during the Revolution, and whom the General Synod had elected Professor of Theology (1797 to 1822). Their indictment against the Reformed Church included practicing lax discipline, consorting with other theological traditions (most notably, the Methodists), and teaching "Hopkinsianism"—that is, the theology of Samuel Hopkins (1721-1803), a student of Jonathan Edwards. Hopkins took some mildly different views on the theology of Original Sin and, therefore, on Atonement. Froeligh and his followers called themselves "The True Reformed Dutch Church," saw themselves as the proper inheritors of the Reformed tradition of the Netherlands, and were quick to use the theology of Wilhelmus van Brakel (1637-1711), especially as expressed in his *Redelyck Godtesdienst* (various editions throughout the eighteenth and nineteenth centuries in the Netherlands), as the theological foundation upon which truth was to be understood.[38]

Brakel and Marck came from the same theological party in the Netherlands. Each represented a faction within the Voetians. Brakel was the leader of the "green" or "Live" Voetians. Marck, you will recall, led

---

[37]   In addition to Froeligh, these pastors were Abram Brokaw (1772-1846), Henry V. Wyckoff (1771-1835), Sylvanus Palmer (1770-1846), and John C. Tol (1799-1848). See *Manual of the Reformed Protestant Dutch Church* (New York: Board of Publication, 1859), pp. 134-135.

[38]   Jacob Brinkerhoff, *History of the True Reformed Dutch Church in the United States of America* (New York: E. B. Tripp Printer and Stationer, 1873), pp. 84ff.

the "Dead" Voetians. So, if the Secession chose to base its case on Brakel, the Reformed Church could hardly do better than to claim Marck as the framework for its counter-case. This may be why, on September 13, 1825, following Livingston's death and Milledoler's election to the professorate, the Board of Superintendents first approved a new curriculum and then, in a separate action, voted:

> Resolved that the board of Superintendents deem it expedient that a text book be adopted in this institution, which shall be used in the course of instruction in Didactic & Polemic theology, and that Mark's *Medulla* be said text-book.[39]

As a badge of Orthodoxy, the book may have been great. But as a means by which to educate Americans for ministry in the nineteenth century, Marck's *Medulla* was almost immediately problematic. Please remember that it replaced Livingston's theology within the training of ministerial candidates. There is no way to characterize Livingston's theology other than to call it "conservative." And yet, Livingston took Dutch Reformed orthodoxy and made it work in America. Just as his contribution to our church order was called and functioned as "explanatory articles"— explaining or adapting the early seventeenth-century Church Order of the Synod of Dordt to the new American situation almost two hundred years later—so too his theology was adaptive. He moved Reformed Orthodoxy solidly into the post-Enlightenment era and into the pluralistic context of American culture. There was no way that Marck, firmly rooted in the Dutch ethos of 1695, could naturally enter either one of those worlds. As early as 1829, seminary students were protesting the continued use of the *Medulla*.[40] In 1833, the Board of Superintendents concluded their report to the General Synod by presenting the following resolution:

> resolved, that it be referred to the Gen. synod to consider whether it is expedient to continue Mark's *Medulla* as a text Book in our Theological Seminary.[41]

The Synod voted:

> that Mark's *Medulla* be continued as the Text Book in Didactic Theology in the Seminary, and if there exist any objections to

---

[39] Minutes of the Board of Superintendents, 1812-1840, p.191. The *Medulla*, as edited by Willem van Irhoven van Dam had been published in Philadelphia in 1824 and 1825 by J. Anderson.

[40] Milledoler Papers V; Memoirs, 1815-1833, pp.68-90.

[41] Minutes of the Board of Superintendents, 1812-1840; 1833, p.4.

the manner in which it is used, the Board of Superintendents examine the same.[42]

This sort of uneasiness continued through the Battle of 1841. As late as 1888, after the Synod had approved another revision of the curriculum for New Brunswick Seminary, it could not resist attaching the following recommendation:

> The use of some Latin compend in Doctrinal Theology, such as Marckii, *Medulla* or Amesii *Theologia,* as tending to make students familiar with scholastic Latin, as well as giving an exact Syllabus of Definitions and Proofs. The book and the manner of using it to be at the discretion of the Professor.[43]

The Students

The first thing to be noticed about the members of the Classes of 1841 and 1842 is their sameness. They were, as we would have expected for that era, all white males. Of the thirty members of the Seminary Classes of 1841 and 1842, twenty-one (or 70%) had graduated from Rutgers College in 1838 or 1839. One of the remaining three had also graduated from Rutgers, but in the Class of 1834.

Once one takes a closer look at the students, their diversity begins to make them sound more like New Brunswick's present student body than might have been imagined. Three of them came to seminary without a college education as preparation. At least two of the students in the Class of 1842 were married and had families. The age of the students in 1841, at the time of the confrontation, ranged from 20 years (John DeWitt) to 49 years (Jacob A. Lansing). Of the twenty-eight students whose birth dates are known, only ten (36%) were twenty-five or younger in 1841. Sixteen were between twenty-six and thirty-five years old (57%). Two members of these classes were more than thirty-five years old (7%).[44]

Several students had careers prior to entering college. Some of these and several others had had some sort of career between college and seminary. The majority of the students had grown up in New York state, outside New York City. Northern New Jersey was home to

---

[42] *MGS*, 1833, p.220.

[43] *MGS,* 1888, p.544.

[44] Most of the student demographics were assembled from Edward Tanjore Corwin, *A Manual of the Reformed Church in America*, Fourth Edition Revised and Enlarged (New York, Board of Publication, 1902).

the next largest group. Two students had been born in Britain. One student came from Massachusetts and one from Pennsylvania. Only one student (Elbert Porter) came from the area immediately adjacent to New Brunswick. He was from Millstone.

Six of these students had grown up in parsonages. One of them, Gardner Jones, was the son of a minister who had been suspended and who had then seceded from the Reformed Church. He ultimately became a Baptist. The son, Gardner, ultimately became Roman Catholic.

Let us return to the characteristic shared by most members of these classes—that they had graduated from Rutgers College in 1838 or 1839. This means that twenty-one of these students had been at Rutgers College during the tremendous revival of religion among the students between May 16 and May 22, 1837. A number of the students in the Seminary Classes of 1841 and 1842 were in seminary principally having heard a call to ministry in the context of that revival.

These factors may provide us with a reasonable sketch of the personal character of the student participants in the confrontation which has been examined here. But these characteristics fail to provide even a suggestion of catalyst for the spirit and determination which we have seen in them. For that catalyst, we can consider the annual reports which Professor Alexander McClelland sent to the Board of Superintendents in 1836, 1837, and 1838.

McClelland had joined the seminary faculty as Professor of Oriental Literature and Biblical Criticism in 1832, following the death of John DeWitt. He was thirty-eight years old at the time, and had already taught for seven years at Dickinson College, Carlisle, Pennsylvania, and for three years at Rutgers. His ecclesiastical background had been the Associate Reformed Presbytery of New York—a Scottish secessionist body which merged into the Presbyterian Church in 1822.[45] This background meant that McClelland, who was unusually perceptive anyhow, came to the Seminary with a fresh outlook. He soon began to notice patterns within the cultural and educational experiences with which students entered New Brunswick Seminary.

In his 1836 report, he suggested to the Superintendents that the students were coming to Seminary with limited academic preparation. He reminded them that in his own field, particularly in the study of biblical languages, "the road along which I am to guide them is not strewed with flowers." These studies were exceptionally difficult for the students of the era because "the majority of young men are imperfectly

---

[45] Corwin, *Manual*, 591.

prepared, in consequence of the lack of habit of studying languages required in our preparatory institutions."[46] In McClelland's 1837 report, he pointed out that there was within the Reformed Church

> a strong tradition which actually encouraged young men to put off actual communion with the church till marriage, and settlement in the world. The consequence is that they who are really and deeply serious *conceal* their feeling, and the pastor is unacquainted with the spiritual condition of the most interesting part of his flock. Thus hundreds grow up unknowing and unknown, not even suspecting to what high and noble uses they might be put. Bye and bye they marry and make a profession of love to the Redeemer, which they might have made with sincerity perhaps six years before. *Now* the Pastor has discovered them, but too late to secure their services to the church.[47]

In 1838, McClelland added one more facet of understanding to the Board's knowledge of its students. He observed that "One thing is to be exceedingly lamented, the entire unpreparedness of many of [the students] commencing a course of theology in consequence of their want of *elementary Christian knowledge*."[48] McClelland continued:

> I do not in the least exaggerate that there are individuals among us who cannot repeat the ten commandments. As to the creed, or catechism I doubt whether they have ever seen them except by accident.... This is not the fault of the young men, but the dismal consequence of the want of early religious education. ...[49]

Having analyzed the situation from the student's perspective for three years in a row, McClelland cannot resist offering a suggestion for curricular revision aimed at bridging the gap between where the students were, as a result of their church and academic experience, and where the seminary curriculum expected them to be. Clearly stepping out of his own field, and surely, to some extent, stepping on his colleague Milledoler's toes, he proposed the creation of:

> an elementary course in doctrinal instruction during the Junior year, based either on the confession of Faith, or the Heidelberg

---

46   Minutes of the Board of Superintendents, 1812-1840, July 14, 1836, 4.
47   Ibid, July 13, 1837, 5.
48   Ibid., July 11, 1838, 4.
49   Ibid.

Catechism. In this way general ideas would be acquired which would materially assist their progress in every branch of study; especially that of exposition of the scriptures, and prepare them for the systematic course of the Middle, and Senior years.[50]

All of this, then, helps us to understand the students as being very highly motivated for ministry, and extremely desirous of a theological education which would be "useful" to their future in ministry. At the same time, they were frustrated by the weaknesses of their own academic preparation, by their limited experience within the church, and by their very limited knowledge of the basic shape of the church's theology. Their frustration must have been transformed into pure anguish, when their first exposure to Didactic and Polemic Theology—which they understood to be the most important subject in all of their ministerial preparation—*began* with a tightly reasoned, condensed, Latin theological text, and a professor who allowed no questions to be asked in the classroom.

The Professor

"A Brief Biographical Outline" is appended to this study. The reader may want to consult that outline at various points in what follows.

Milledoler as Churchman

While Milledoler moved easily between the German Reformed, the Dutch Reformed, and the Presbyterian denominations, in each of these communions he was recognized as a "traditionalist" and a "conservative" voice. His own theological teachers had been conservative, as were his early associations. But his conservatism could not be moved to radicalism. His sense of the unity of the church was sufficiently strong to keep him from sectarianism or secession.

This last point is very important, and a little surprising, given his basic character. He seems, by nature, to have had no close friends and to have been suspicious of persons—always looking out for intrigues against him or against the institutions he held dear. In a real sense his life was the embodiment of the old 1960's slogan: "Just because you're paranoid, doesn't mean they aren't really out to get you." He had the tremendous capacity to create an enemy out of a person whom he was very much going to need about ten minutes later. For example, as

---

[50] Ibid, 4-5.

President of Rutgers College, he expelled a student—Theodore Thomas Romeyn—in 1828. Concurrently, Theodore's father was President of the Board of Superintendents of the Seminary. In 1841, when all of the issues relating to the students' letter arrived on the doorstep of the General Synod, Theodore Romeyn's brother James was elected President of the Synod.

Milledoler as Theological Educator

The record here can be read in only one way. Philip Milledoler was clearly recognized as an able teacher of theology. In 1812, the Presbyterians founded their first seminary—the Seminary now called Princeton. When they installed the Rev. Dr. Archibald Alexander as their first professor of theology, it was Milledoler who was asked to give the charge to the new Professor (and, incidently, to the "Young students in divinity"). As the German Reformed Church began to plan for the establishment of their seminary, they unanimously elected Milledoler to be their first professor. (The salary he was offered by the Germans—$2,000 per year—was far more than he ever received in the Reformed Church.) It was only when the Germans began to haggle about whether classes were to be in German or in English that Milledoler declined the position. And it was Milledoler who was chosen by the Reformed Protestant Dutch Church as their spokesperson and preacher, to respond, in 1824, to the members of the True Reformed Dutch Church who seceded in 1822.

With all of this trust and all of this talent, what led Milledoler to be so intransigent about his teaching methods? Some of the problem may have been a product of one of his life's greatest successes—the re-establishment of Queens College and its reincarnation as Rutgers College. It must be recalled that when Milledoler was elected to the office of Professor of Theology, he was concurrently elected to the office of President of Queens College. The college was clearly very important to Milledoler, and his work for the College may have become the principal focus of his daily activities. Teaching Didactic and Polemic theology may not have been his first love. He had begun the teaching of theology with high energy and determination. In 1825, as he took up his responsibilities, he wrote:

> The Gen'l Synod at their meeting at N.Bruns. Sept, 1825 adopt'd Marcks Medulla, as their Text Book. — The exam'n of the School was to take place in Ap'l follow'g. In the Interim, I translated Marck. making a fair Copy, and a Compend to be used

at Examination. This labor was severe, Espec'ly as I had never previously read Marck. Through the goodness of God, I was enabled to accomplish it, and the exam'n was well rec'd by the Superint's.[51]

But he had also seen very clearly that the restoration of the college was pivotal to the success of the seminary and the long-term health of the church. In attempting to serve two masters—college and seminary—he may have come to "love the one and hate the other."

One other clue to his personality may be provided by H.M.J. Klein, in his description of the attempt to establish a seminary for the German Reformed Church. "Dr. Milledoler," Klein said, "was a brilliant preacher but he was not a man of enterprise."[52] "Enterprise" meant, in this sense, the capacity to embrace the new—to take risks. It may have been a fortunate thing, for Milledoler, that the Board and the Synod voted in 1825 to establish Marck's *Medulla* as the textbook for the Seminary. That meant that Milledoler did not have to risk much in the teaching of theology. There certainly was high risk in following a legend like Livingston. After the decision about the textbook, Milledoler had some protection in this regard. He was controlled, just as were the students, by the textbook with which they both had to work. Why he never published his translation of Marck may be a function of this same phenomenon.

What Was Lost and What Was Gained?

Lost?

1. Perhaps most important, among what was lost to the Seminary and to the church in this skirmish was Philip Milledoler himself! He left New Brunswick a quite broken man, to live with his daughter, Abian, and her husband James W. Beekman in Manhattan, summering on Staten Island. His participation in the life of the denomination was very limited. After 1841, Milledoler published only two brief biographical articles and his little volume on *Incestuous Marriages*, in 1843.
2. Single-voiced theological education within the RCA was also lost in the Battle of 1841. From 1784 to 1825, the Reformed

---

[51] Milledoler Papers V.
[52] H.M.J. Klein, *A Century of Education at Mercersburg* (Lancaster: Mercersburg Academy, 1936), p.4.

Church had relied on the magisterial character of John Henry Livingston to define the character and limits of its theology. From 1825 to 1841, it assigned that task to Marck's *Medulla* as interpreted by Milledoler. After 1841, the Reformed Church surrendered the prospect of continuing so unitary a voice for its theology.

3. Theology also lost its classic format. With the loss of "A Textbook"—either Livingston's or Marck's—the shape of theology became much more malleable. A textbook of the sort represented by Livingston or Marck, represented both a *structure*, for the shaping and study of theology, and a *box* within which orthodoxy would be found. One did not "color outside the lines" or "think outside the box."

4. In addition, Theology lost its "superior" role. As long as Livingston was alive, there was no doubt who was the professor in charge. His person *and his subject area* made him the pre-eminent professor in the seminary and the denomination. When Milledoler began his tenure, John DeWitt had already been on the faculty for two years. Very quickly, Milledoler seized the pre-eminence of the position of Didactic and Polemic Theology, and began to operate as if he were the "Professor-in-Charge." This was clearly difficult for Cannon and McClelland to live with. After 1841, this sense of priority was gone.

Gained?

1. Students were recognized as full participants in the processes of theological education. It ought not to be assumed that students were immediately given the privilege of collegial participation in the shaping and direction of their theological education. That was not the case. But, for the first time, attention was paid to the specific character of their needs and their perspective was taken seriously in institutional planning.

2. "Usefulness within the church" came to be understood as an important driver of the theological curriculum. In the classic sense of St. Paul's questions, the church in 1841 asked: "what does it profit a man if he can recite Marck's *Medulla* but hasn't the foggiest idea of how to respond to the pressing needs of a parishioner or congregation in the middle of the nineteenth century?"

3. The *Church* itself assumed a responsibility for defining the

Seminary's task. Since the discussions of 1771 and 1784, which had given rise to the concept of a seminary, the church had not had a really good discussion about what it wanted its seminary to be doing or how it expected the Seminary to do it.

4. The Seminary faculty came to a full sense of mutuality and collegiality. Following the "Battle of 1841" Systematic theology—previously the "Queen of the Sciences"—became a sister among equals, with biblical studies, historical studies, and pastoral studies.

5. All of this allowed a full sense of "theological seminary"—a curriculum of studies, all intended to fit together, for the sensitive preparation of a person for effective ministry within the church—to come, at last, to New Brunswick Theological Seminary.

◆ ◆ ◆

PHILIP MILLEDOLER
A Biographical Introduction

Born: Rhinebeck, NY, September 22, 1775

Baptized: George Philip Milledoler

Parents: Father, John Milledoler (Muhlithaler) Kleinstock, Hertzenbochsee, Canton of Berne, Switzerland; Mother, Maria Mitchell, Canton of Zurich, Switzerland

Education: Columbia College, graduated May, 1793
According to a document in Milledoler Papers, Box 1, file 1785-1801, he entered Columbia College ranked fifteenth in his class and graduated ranked fourth. In the same place is a record that indicates that, in 1793, the whole faculty of Columbia recommended him to "the Rev'd Wm (?) Cutting, "Principal of the college at Brunswick in New Jersey" to serve as "teacher in mathematics and lecturer in Natural History." He noted "the above was frustrated by my application to my favorite study of theology... and by the death of Dr. Cutting." He makes no mention in this context of the tangled state of Queens College at that time. In 1793, the Trustees appointed a committee to confer with a similar committee from Princeton. These met and in September proposed a plan which consolidated the

boards of trustees, which under a new charter would maintain a preparatory school in New Brunswick and a college in Princeton. This plan was rejected by a vote of nine to eight at the October 1793 meeting of the Queens College Board (McCormick, 21).

Following his graduation from Columbia and until May 21, 1794, when he was and ordained by the German Reformed Synod: Milledoler
- Studied theology with John Daniel Gros (1737-1812), pastor of the German Reformed Church on Nassau Street (between Maiden Lane and John Street) and Professor of Moral Philosophy at Columbia College.
- Studied Hebrew with John Christopher Kunze, pastor of the Lutheran Church and Professor of Oriental Languages at Columbia College.

D.D., University of Pennsylvania, 1805

Licensure and Ordination:

Examined and approved for ordination by the Synod of the German Reformed Church in North America on May 18, 1794 in Reading, PA. Ordained there on May 21, 1794 (Milledoler papers, Box 1, file 1785-1801)
- "Dr. Gross, my respected Teacher in Theology, with his Lady and myself were politely and hospitably car'd for at the house of the Hon. Gen. Heistler at Reading, and on our return to New York we visited Bethlehem and were most kindly received by the Moravian Brethren."

Ministry:
- Nassau Street German Reformed Church, New York, 1795-1800
- Preached both in German and English
- Third (or Old Pine Street) Presbyterian Church, Philadelphia, 1800-1805
- Stated Clerk of the General Assembly and Secretary of its Board of Trustees
- Rutgers Street Presbyterian Church, New York, 1805-1813
- Moderator of the General Assembly, 1808
- "Charge to Professor Alexander and the Students of Divinity at Princeton," 1812

- Collegiate Church, New York, 1813-1825
- Founding participant in the American Bible Society, 1816.
- September, 1820, elected theological professor in the German Reformed Seminary to be located at Frederick, MD. (Salary of $2,000)
- President of General Synod, 1823.
- Chairman of the Board of Superintendents, New Brunswick Theological Seminary, 1824-1825.
- Professor of Didactic and Polemic Theology, 1825-1841
- President of Rutgers College, 1826-1840

Family: Married Susan Benson, daughter of Lawrence and Maria Benson, in March, 1796. They had six children: Maria, Susan Ann, Philip Edward, Cornelia, Benson, and Lawrence. Susan Benson Milledoler died in July, 1815.

Married Margaret M. Steele in 1817. They had four children: Abian Steele (1820-1897), Aletta Beekman, William Steele, and Margaret. Margaret Steele Milledoler died September 23, 1852.

Retired: September 9, 1841

Died: September 22, 1852.

CHAPTER 7

Searching for Edward Tanjore Corwin

Throughout the twentieth century, if not throughout the modern and post-modern history of the Reformed Church in America (RCA), one name that every minister learned besides John Calvin, Jonas Michaelius, John Henry Livingston, and Albertus Van Raalte—though Livingston and Van Raalte might receive differing emphases depending on where a minister went to seminary—was Edward Tanjore Corwin. This was because Corwin was necessary to the study of RCA history. His name graces the *Manual of the Reformed Church in America*,[1] the first and largest *Digest of Constitutional and Synodical Legislation of the Reformed*

---

[1] The first edition was actually the *Manual of the Reformed Protestant Dutch Church* (New York: Board of Publication of the Reformed Protestant Dutch Church, 1859). The subsequent editions were titled *Manual of the Reformed Church in America, Second Edition, Revised and Enlarged* (New York: Board of Publication of the Reformed Church in America, 1869), same title, *Third Edition, Revised and Enlarged* (same publisher, 1879), same title, *Fourth Edition, Revised and Enlarged* (same publisher, 1902), and, finally, Charles E. Corwin, *A Manual of the Reformed Church in America, 1628-1922* (New York: Board of Publication and Bible-School Work of the Reformed Church in America, 1922). These will be referred to hereafter as *Manual* 1, *Manual* 2, *Manual* 3, *Manual* 4, and *Manual* 5, respectively.

Church in America,[2] and the *Ecclesiastical Records of the State of New York.*[3] For many ministers, this was *the* published history of the RCA prior to the premiere of the *Historical Series of the Reformed Church in America* in 1968—especially since it has only been in the last generation that the *Historical Series* has reached its present size. Even then, many footnotes in *Historical Series* volumes refer readers back to Corwin. While Corwin wasn't the first RCA historian—David Demarest[4] and Alexander Gunn[5] are the most noteworthy examples, not to mention many historical articles in the *Christian Intelligencer*[6]—he became the most prolific and best known.

So who, exactly, was this Edward Corwin? While his own *Manual* 4 includes stories and commentaries on many of the other ministers listed, he remains fairly coldly clinical in his self-description:

> CORWIN, EDWARD TANJORE, b. in N.Y.C., July 12, 1834; Coll. Of the City of New York, 53, N.B.S., 56, l. Cl. Bergen; Resident Graduate at N.B.S., 56-57, Paramus, 57-63, Hillsborough (Millstone), 63-88; also Instructor in Hebrew and O.T. Exegesis in N.B.S., Nov., 83-May, 84; Rector of Herzog Hall, 88-95; Instructor in Heb. and O.T. Exegesis, Jan.-Mar., 89, Jan. and Feb., 90, Sept., 90-May., 91; Instructor in N.T. Exegesis, Jan.-May, 92; Greenport, Columbia Co., N.Y., 95-97; General Synod's Agent in Holland, for collecting ecclesiastical documents relating to America, Aug. 21, 97-Nov. 13, 98; editing said ecclesiastical documents (as well as others obtained by J. Romeyn Brodhead in 1841-4), for the State of New York, July, 1899— D.D. by R.C. 1872; President of General Synod, 1891.[7]

The entry for him in *Manual* 5 includes the facts that he died on June 22, 1914 and that he received a Litt.D. from Rutgers in 1911,

---

2   (New York: The Board of Publication of the Reformed Church in America, 1906). Hereafter referred to as *Digest.*

3   In seven volumes, (Albany, NY: James B. Lyon, State Printer, 1901-1907). Hereafter referred to as *ERNY.*

4   *History and Characteristics of the Reformed Protestant Dutch Church* (New York: Board of Publiation of the Reformed Protestant Dutch Church, 1856).

5   *Memoir of the Rev. Dr. John Henry Livingston* (New York: Board of Publication of the Reformed Protestant Dutch Church, 1829).

6   Periodical of the RCA which began publication in 1830 in New York, succeeded by the *Intelligencer and Mission Field,* the *Intelligencer-Leader,* and, finally, the *Church Herald.*

7   *Manual* 4, 394-5. This includes several standard abbreviations standard to the *Manual*: "b." for "born," "l." for "licensed" by a classis ("Cl.") for ordination, and "N.B.S." for New Brunswick Theological Seminary (usually referred to in modern abbreviations as NBTS). Other entries also include "d." for died.

though it drastically curtails the publication list—probably out of necessity, since *Manual* 5 was 300 pages shorter than *Manual* 4. His son, Charles, also included a brief description:

> Dr. Corwin was a genial, conscientious man, a faithful and a Scriptural preacher. He was a genius for hard work and he became the most eminent historian of the Ref. Ch. [*sic*][8]

This was hardly the longest biography even in this shortened *Manual*, and it seems to have been lifted from the obituary in the *Christian Intelligencer* for May 3, 1915, written by "C.E.C." Since Charles E. Corwin was a writer for the *Intelligencer*, it is easy to assume that this wasn't a dispassionate account, but was his son's personal recollection.

This leaves us still wondering just who Edward Corwin actually was. Lacking other available evidence, we need to search for this RCA historian using Charles' obituary to map the terrain, with an examination of some of Edward's best-known published work to lead us through the twists and turns.

Corwin's Life

Corwin was born in New York City on July 12, 1834. On his father's side he was descended from the Puritans of New England, while through his mother he was related to the Dutch founders of New Netherland.

Dr. Corwin's youth was passed in the metropolis whose history he knew so well and in whose affairs he was so much interested. He graduated in 1853 in the first class sent out by the College of the City of New York. In 1856 he graduated from the Seminary of the Reformed Church at New Brunswick, N.J. After a year spent in special linguistic studies, he was ordained and became for six years, 1857-1863, the pastor of the Reformed Church of Paramus, N.J. His chief pastorate, of twenty-five years, was spent at Millstone, N.J. In 1888 he became Rector of Herzog Hall of the Reformed Church Seminary at New Brunswick, N.J. Seven years later he accepted a call from the Reformed Church of Greenport, N.Y. He served in this, his last pastorate, from

---

[8]   *Manual* 5, 290. Russell L. Gasero, in the *Historical Directory of the Reformed Church in America* (William B. Eerdmans Publishing Company, 2001), 79, also notes that Corwin was interim pastor at Highland Park 1890-91, a position overlooked in all of the Corwin Manuals.

1895 to 1897. In the latter year he was sent by the General Synod of the Reformed Church to Holland on a mission of historical exploration. The results of his discoveries in the archives of the Classis of Amsterdam and elsewhere are embodied in the Ecclesiastical Records of the State of New York. After his return to America he devoted himself entirely to literary work. He resided first at New Brunswick, and after the death of his wife, in 1905, with his son at North Branch, N.J. He died there, very suddenly, on June 22, 1914.[9]

We don't have a record of which church Corwin might have attended while growing up in New York; in those days, "New York City" would refer only to what is now known as the borough of Manhattan, and probably, primarily, the lower portion of that island—what is still known as "The City" by residents of the five boroughs today. In The City, during Corwin's childhood, there would have been three Collegiate congregations—North, Ninth Street, and Middle (Nassau Street would have become a post office building by the time he was ten)—and the churches called East 68th Street, Greenwich, Bloomingdale, Madison Avenue, South, Market Street, Seventh Avenue, Thirty-fourth Street (also known as Broome Street), Manhattan (called "Manhattanville" by Corwin)[10], St. Paul's, Washington Square (also known as New South Dutch), and Washington Heights.[11] In *Manual* 4, there are affectionate and lengthy biographical sketches of the three Collegiate ministers who would have been present during Corwin's childhood—William C. Brownlee, Thomas DeWitt, and Thomas E. Vermilye—as well as Isaac Ferris from Market Street and James M. Mathews and Mancius S. Hutton, who were both at Washington Square. All of them borrow material from other authors (more about that below).

Based upon that, we might guess that Edward Corwin's family might have attended a Collegiate church, or perhaps Market Street, or maybe Washington Square. There doesn't seem to be much to narrow it down any further. Interestingly, only two of the potential pastors—DeWitt and Ferris—went to New Brunswick, and both studied with Livingston; DeWitt would have moved to New Brunswick with Livingston in 1810. But all of them had connections to the Hudson Valley, from Ulster County up through Schenectady—Mathews was the

9   Charles E. Corwin, "The Rev. E.T. Corwin, D.D., Litt.D.," the *Christian Intelligencer,* May 3, 1915.
10   *Manual* 4, 391.
11   Gasero, 595-99.

only one not to pastor upstate, but he graduated from Union College.[12] All of them are noted by Corwin, in *Manual* 4, as gifted, biblical preachers of deep learning, which they applied to the lives of their congregations.

We can be somewhat more certain of Corwin's influences in theological education. John Ludlow was serving for the second time as a Synod professor, having been professor of Biblical Literature from 1819 to 1823, and returning to New Brunswick to teach Church History and Government a year before Corwin arrived, while at the same time teaching Metaphysics and Philosophy at Rutgers; he died a year after Corwin's graduation. In the years between his professorates he was pastor of First Church in Albany and provost of the University of Pennsylvania.[13] Samuel Alexander Van Vranken was Professor of Didactic Theology and taught Religion and Logic at Rutgers; he had been there for a dozen years when Corwin arrived.[14] William Henry Campbell arrived at New Brunswick two years before Corwin as Professor of Oriental Literature; he had not come directly out of the parish, but had been principal of the Albany Academy.[15] Van Vranken and Ludlow had booth been students of Livingston and contemporaries at New Brunswick, but Campbell had graduated from Princeton Seminary.

Corwin would have been one of the last Seminary students to study in Old Queens Hall, a building which the College and Seminary had shared since a year after the Covenant of 1810 had moved the theological professorate to New Brunswick.[16] By the time he arrived, the college was a more going concern, and the Covenant of 1825, which had supplanted the 1810 covenant, was coming unraveled. Corwin would have most likely been one of the students who had complained to the Seminary's superintendents that, since the Seminary didn't provide on-campus housing for its students—there was no room in Old Queens—board cost them significantly more than that of students at Princeton or Union seminaries. But the new Peter Herzog Theological Hall on the then-distant "Holy Hill" would not be completed until the year Edward graduated[17]—unless he stayed there while completing his "special linguistic studies."

---

12   Ibid., 259.

13   *Manual* 4, 583.

14   Ibid., 862. Van Vranken, who was Milledoler's successor (see Norman Kansfield's essay in this volume), was the first Theology Professor since 1810 to not also serve as President of Rutgers College.

15   Gasero, 63.

16   John Coakley, *New Brunswick Theological Seminary: An Illustrated History, 1784-2014* (Grand Rapids, MI: William B. Eerdmans Publishing Company, 2014), 6-7.

17   Ibid., 27-28.

New Brunswick in Corwin's student days was a hub of transportation, much as it is now. While it is now a nexus of highways, it was then a point of intersection for several railroads:

When I entered the Seminary in 1853, having come from the College of the City of New York, New Brunswick was a city of about half its present size in actual built up area and in population. . . . It was then yet a city at the junction, or rather terminus of two different railroads, the Camden and Amboy Railroad and the New Jersey Railroad. . . . For the first railroad across New Jersey was from Camden to Amboy, and this road ultimately extended a branch from Trenton to New Brunswick, which belonged to the Camden and Amboy system . . . A little subsequently another Company, called the New Jersey Railroad, obtained a charter for a road from Jersey City to New Brunswick, with certain special concessions to prevent competition . . . these two railroads were yet distinct corporations. Through tickets could indeed, be bought from New York to Philadelphia, and a few parts beyond, at a different rate; but the cost was a dollar more than if tickets were bought on each individual road. . . . These roads had then but a single track, which was, indeed the case with most railroads at that time, with double tracks only at stations for trains to pass each other. This condition continues on these roads until 1861, at the breaking out of the war . . . The single track, up as far as the Mile Run Brook, was a favorite promenade for the students on pleasant afternoons. They almost always passed up Bayard Street, which was the finest street in the City, a sort of Fifth Avenue, and then took to the track.[18]

Evidently, there were many ways for the students to entertain themselves:

Another favorite walk of the students in those days was along the canal under the bluff, and up to the Landing; and sometimes home again on the other side of the river. As the terms of both Institutions then extended until to the last of July, the students often availed themselves of that secluded walk along the canal to take a swim. We eagerly awaited the 20th of May, after which we

---

[18]   Edward Tanjore Corwin, "New Brunswick Fifty Years Ago: Reminiscences by Rev. Edward T. Corwin, D.D.," an unpublished paper read to the New Brunswick Historical Society, April, 1905, in the Archives of the Reformed Church in America.

regarded it safe to go in the water, whether the temperature was just right or not. We often crossed the canal at these times, and also swam or waded across the river . . .[19]

Exercise, however, wasn't limited to swimming in the as-yet-undeveloped city:

Some distance beyond the Livingston residence was the Van Nuys house, where students fond of compulsory exercise sometimes boarded. In those days these students were Edward Livingston and John S. Jeralmon [Joralmon-ed.], belonging to the Seminary class of '55. They came daily to the class rooms with rosy faces, covered with perspiration, and in the Winter with mud painted boots, having waded their way to the City.[20]

While Corwin spoke of the integration of New Brunswick primarily in terms of the Dutch Reformed, Presbyterians, and Methodists, along with a small contingent of Roman Catholics, he noted that the city wasn't entirely Caucasian. His description of First Reformed Church on a Sunday morning mentioned "the eight or ten long pews, back of the Elders' seat in the southwest corner of the church . . . were literally crowded with colored members. I can yet distinctly see that large square bloc of African faces. . . . at least forty or fifty of them."[21]

Paramus seems to have been a good and fruitful first charge for Corwin, but it was Hillsborough that was, in many ways, the church of Corwin's heart. His children were born there—his son, Charles, in 1868, his daughter somewhat after, but in time to date Samuel Zwemer in 1888[22]—and he was so beloved by the congregation that they erected a plaque in the church in his memory in 1916, twenty-eight years after he had moved away.[23] Preaching on the twentieth anniversary of his installation there, Corwin referred to Hillsborough as the place he hit his stride:

To-day [*sic*] completes twenty years of my ministry among you. Such a period is a large part of a man's active life. It takes many years to get ready for a ministerial career, and an additional decade to get fairly initiated in the work. The priests of olden

---

[19]   Ibid.
[20]   Ibid.
[21]   Ibid.
[22]   See Matthew and Russell Gasero's essay in this volume.
[23]   *Christian Intelligencer*, March 22, 1916.

time did not begin their labors in the sanctuary until they had reached the age of thirty. With seven years of service elsewhere, I had almost reached that once prescribed age, when I came among you to preach the Word of Life.[24]

In 1888, he went back to New Brunswick Seminary, though not to the Seminary that he knew. Herzog Hall hadn't yet been built when he was a student, and only Samuel Woodbridge remained from the faculty in those years. Corwin brought his wife and daughter with him as he served as rector of Herzog Hall and occasional language instructor. There was a piece of Corwin that seemed to have been most happy with this different life, as his return to a pastorate at Greenport (currently known as Mt. Pleasant in Hudson, New York[25]) was brief and not terribly notable, save that he was succeeded by his own son.[26] But what came next, even though it was but a one-year contract, seems to have been a pivotal experience of his late life.

The story of documenting the relationship between colonial Reformed Protestant Dutch congregations and the Classis of Amsterdam begins in 1841. Thomas DeWitt, a minister of the Collegiate Church in New York, informed the General Synod, convened in October, of his communication with J. Romeyn Brodhead[27] that the Archives of Classis Amsterdam contained extensive correspondence regarding the colonial origins of the American church. DeWitt was given authority to have these records translated into English at the Synod's expense. This

---

[24] Edward T. Corwin, *Sermon on the Occasion of the twentieth Anniversary of the Settlement of Edward T. Corwin as Pastor of the Reformed Church of Hillsborough at Millstone, N.J., Preached December 30, 1883* (Somerville, NJ: The Unionist-Gazette Printing House, 1884), 3.

[25] Gasero, 560.

[26] The relationship between Dr. & Mrs. Edward Corwin and their son, Charles, seems to have been quite close: when Charles moved to Rutgers College in New Brunswick—a distance that wasn't necessarily easily commuted in that day—Edward and the rest of the family went to live at the Seminary. The year Charles was ordained and installed in Cuddebackville, in western Orange County, New York, Edward and his wife—it is unclear whether his daughter was still at home at that point—moved to Greenport; not exactly in the backyard, but 70 miles away rather than, by the travel of that day, nearly 150. It is easy to imagine that the elder Corwin also arranged for his son to succeed him. Charles moved back to New Brunswick, working briefly for the Presbyterians in 1905, when his mother died—close to his father—and then Edward moved in with his son in North Branch, New Jersey. On top of this, Charles showed early interest in and aptitude for visual art, evidenced by sketches he did as a youth, now found in the archives of the Hillsborough Reformed Church, and yet he went into ministry, writing, and research, like his father.

[27] J. Romeyn Brodhead was a well-known historian and the son of Jacob Brodhead who was then pastor of Central Reformed Church in Brooklyn. *Manual* 4, 341-42.

never happened; instead, Brodhead had some of the correspondence transcribed, and secured a four-year loan of the letters from America to Amsterdam. By 1845, DeWitt was sent to try to secure ownership of those letters. He was given a bound set of the transcribed letters, which remained in his and Brodhead's custody, Brodhead using them in his research and DeWitt translating select letters for the *Christian Intelligencer*. Interest in the letters waxed and waned until, in 1875, the entire collection ended up in the Archives at Sage Library of NBTS.

Intermittent interest continued. By 1887, Randall Hoes, a navy chaplain, reported that there were more items in the Amsterdam archives. Corwin enters the picture here; about to travel to the Netherlands, he is recruited by the Synod of 1887 to secure copies of what he could, have all of them translated, working with Hoes, and ultimately published. Collegiate pastor Talbot Chambers and Stated Clerk of the General Synod David D. Demarest are appointed to be a committee with Corwin and Hoes to see to all of this. Amsterdam declines to sell or lend the documents, but would provide facilities for someone to transcribe them on-site. Finally, the Synod of 1896 decides to appoint a "competent agent" to do this work, appoints E.B. Coe to replace Chambers on the Committee, and assigns the committee the task of raising the necessary funds for someone to do this research. In 1897, Corwin was appointed as official historiographer for this plan, and he departed for Amsterdam in August, returning in November of the following year.[28] This seems to mark the only period where Corwin was being paid by the RCA to study RCA history.

Upon his return in November, 1898, Corwin wrote a report for the General Synod—which, presumably, was presented to the Synod of 1899—talking about the scope of the work.[29] After addressing what was done, he looked forward to the remaining work: "This is by no means small."[30] He was thorough and fairly specific.

> To complete . . . this revision would require several months. Then all the new material awaits translation along with a small portion of the old, say about 3,500 pages in all, Then comes the classification of the whole mass, old and new, with the general editing of the whole work. Need it be said that the classification,

---

[28] Corwin, *Digest*, 34-35.
[29] Edward Tanjore Corwin, "Report of the General Synod's Agent on His Searches in the Ecclesiastical Archives of Holland, 1897-8," pamphlet, dated November 21st, 1898, in the Archives of the Reformed Church in America.
[30] Ibid., 7.

with the editing of this work, is a very large undertaking by itself, even when all the translations are ready at hand. One individual cannot do both. But with sufficient means placed at his disposal, both for the editorial work (including the classification), and for a sufficient clerical force for the work of translation, he thinks the enterprise could be carried so far forward as to be ready for the press in about a year or fifteen months.[31]

Somehow, the New York State Legislature was persuaded to take on the cost of this work.[32] They made an initial appropriation of $5,000.00,[33] along with subsequent appropriations as the work ballooned to seven volumes including the index. Corwin was engaged by New York to do most of the work, along with Daniel Van Pelt, pastor of First Reformed Church in Astoria, who died as the first volume was published in 1901.[34] This work dominated Corwin's professional life until 1907, by which time his wife had died and he had moved to North Branch, New Jersey, to live with Charles. He continued speaking and writing smaller papers, working with congregations in the RCA, local groups in New Jersey, and the American Society of Church History. At the time of his death in 1914, he was working on his most ambitious project yet: "The Ministry and Churches of All Denominations in the Middle Colonies [including Maryland and Virginia east of the Chesapeake Bay] from the First Settlement Until the Year 1800."[35]

Corwin as Pastor

In each of his pastorates he became immediately interested in local church and town history. The results of these studies were preserved in published discourses. All these discourses became standards for their class.

For ten years, during his pastorate at Millstone, he received into his home and educated for college, [*sic*] Japanese students. These young men were sent by their government to receive a western education. Several of them have risen to positions of power and honor in the Sunrise Kingdom. . . .

To those who knew him personally, the historical scholar was merged in the conscientious, kindly man. He was absolutely

31   Ibid., 8.
32   Corwin, *Digest*, 35.
33   *ERNY*, vol. 1, ii.
34   Gasero, 431.
35   Unpublished manuscript in the New York State Archives.

upright in his dealings with his fellows, and justice was continually passing into mercy. Each of his pastorates, especially that at Millstone, was solidly successful. He was greatly loved by multitudes whom he served.[36]

It is difficult to tell whether the emphasis placed upon Corwin's affection for the Millstone church is a true reflection of Edward's preference of one congregation over the others, or if Charles' recollections were colored by the fact that this is where he grew up. He wasn't even born when his father lived and worked in Paramus, and he was concerned with his own family and work by the time the elder Corwin was in Highland Park—which was probably a part-time position of primarily supply work while Edward lived and taught in New Brunswick—and Greenport. Edward's surviving writings don't mention Greenport very much, either; his time there was quite brief, leaving one to wonder whether, at 63 years of age, after being out of the pastorate for seven years, he found that he preferred full-time studying and writing.

Much of what we can infer about Corwin's attitude toward the pastoral task comes from his sermon celebrating his twentieth anniversary in the Millstone pulpit. It has already been noted that he felt he had only hit his stride as a minister of the Word in this, his second pastorate; it is likely that every pastor who is honest with herself or himself has felt that same way about that first charge. He was twenty-nine when he answered the call to Millstone. By his own testimony, it was there he fully matured as a pastor, and it was there that he settled down into a family life.

The sermon he delivered on December 30, 1883, was about 12,000 words long, so that we might imagine it took a bit over an hour to deliver.[37] His lection was exactly one-half verse long—Exodus 20:24b: "in all places where I record my name I will come unto thee, and I will bless thee."[38] This becomes, for Corwin, a jumping-off point to explore the Christ's care for the Church universal, offices in the Church, Christ's care of the Millstone congregation, the history of the congregation, revivalism, and the call upon the congregation to be evangelists.

Corwin frames the history of the congregation in terms of revivals: a group of smaller revivals in 1781-82, 1797, 1817-18, 1837-

---

[36]   Charles E. Corwin, *Christian Intelligencer.*
[37]   This is a somewhat arbitrary estimate, based on my experience that I speak at about 120-125 words per minute when preaching.
[38]   Corwin, *Sermon,* cover.

38, 1842-43, 1851-52—a year when 73 families joined the church, but it was still considered to be small—1858, 1861, 1867-68, and 1883; and three larger revivals, in 1831, 1870, and 1876. The revival of 1831, in particular, is described by Corwin in some detail—a four day preaching event that began on August 31 and included ten preachers. It may make sense that Corwin, who grew up during the Second Great Awakening in the United States—1790-1850[39]—and whose primary pastoral years were during the Third Great Awakening—1850-1900[40]—would see revivals as a driving force in the life of a church. But, while he reported periods of phenomenal numerical growth, he did not see them as the be-all and end-all of Christian life.

> In looking at this part of the spiritual history of this church, it is interesting to notice the fact that there seem to be periods of considerable length during which a blessing is enjoyed, and then ensue periods of less ostensible results. Yet in these latter periods the benefit may be no less real. Such times are not necessarily barren. They may not be real declensions in religion, unless evident signs of a worldly spirit take possession of the hearts of the people. They may be considered as periods of instruction and growth in knowledge. The new converts listen with great interest and profit. During revivals sermons take, to a considerable extent, a hortatory character, while at other times this element is less. They then become more didactic, and the people are built up in the principles of religion, its great doctrines and the practical duties. It also appears by examination that the members gathered in the church at the periods of special blessing equal almost exactly in the course of years those gathered in during the intervening periods.[41]

So we have in Corwin someone for whom the sermon was a great oration, who looked for the power of the Holy Spirit to do grand things in the lives of churches where the people were attentive and obedient to God's will, but who was willing to be patient—by his own count, periods of revival only described five of his first twenty years in Millstone. He seems to have brought his historian's interest to his pastoral role. One

---

[39]   Donald G. Matthews, 1969. "The Second Great Awakening as an Organizing Process, 1780-1830: An Hypothesis". *American Quarterly* 21 (1). Johns Hopkins University Press: 23-43.

[40]   Mark A. Noll, *A history of Christianity in the United States and Canada* (Grand Rapids, MI: William B. Eerdmans Publishing Company, 1992), 286-310.

[41]   Corwin, *Sermon*, 10-11.

last thing we can glean from the stories he told in that anniversary address is that he had a genuine fondness for preaching.

> It was on the fourth Sunday of October, 1863, that I first preached in this church. My text was Col. iii:1 [*sic*], "If ye then be risen with Christ, seek those things which are above, where Christ sitteth at the right-hand of God." The theme was, of course, Union with Christ in His Sufferings, Resurrection and Glory. . . . In the afternoon I preached from Dan. xii:3, "And they that be wise shall shine as the brightness of the firmament; and they that turn many to righteousness as the stars for ever [*sic*] and ever." On account of the greatness of the reward we see the importance of this heavenly wisdom. Who are truly wise, and where is wisdom to be found?— these were the points considered. But with the conclusion of that service some of the good people of the church sent up a request that I should lecture in the Bloomingdale district in the evening at six o'clock. It was then nearly five. So we were conducted thither. I talked on the forty-fifth Psalm in its Messianic import: Christ, the glorious king, speaking words of grace, and going forth to victory.[42]

It is striking how Corwin's description of the day when he first visited Millstone as the candidate being considered for a call as pastor matches, in style and tone, his description of the 1831 revival, where ten ministers did the preaching. Still, he makes it clear throughout the sermon that he sees preaching as his central pastoral function and bringing souls to Christ through membership the *raison d'être* for the existence of the church—when he says "your present servant for Jesus' sake has been permitted to break unto you the Bread of Life"[43] he is clearly referring, not to the Lord's Supper, but to preaching, and the fruit of this is that "(d)uring this time four hundred and seventy-eight [*sic*] have united with this church."[44]

Corwin as Historian

> From the beginning of his ministry he took an interest in the history and larger relations of his own denomination. The Manual of the Reformed Church in America was the result. The first edition of this work, published in 1858, was a small book of

---

[42]   Ibid., 19-20. One can see where such a preaching schedule as what we now call a candidating sermon could give a congregation an impressive sense of the breadth of a candidate's preaching skill.

[43]   Ibid., 8.

[44]   Ibid.

166 pages. A second edition, much larger, appeared in 1869. An edition still further enlarged was issued in 1879. In 1902 the last edition of 1,082 pages was published. This work is unique among church manuals. There is no other denomination in the country which has so much information in regard to its ministry and churches in so accessible a form. A Digest of Synodical Legislation of the Reformed Church in America brought out in 1906 was the by-product of many years of toil.

It was, however, in the discovery and editing of the Amsterdam Correspondence, incorporated in the Ecclesiastical Records of the State of New York, that Dr. Corwin's historical instincts were most fully revealed. In Holland his ability to find what existed, and to find out about what had been lost, amounted to a peculiar genius. As the hart pants for the water brooks, so he searched for documents of the Dutch colonial period until he found them. The present index of the Ecclesiastical Records of New York State completed by Dr. Corwin, but not issued before his death, brought to conclusion these valuable historical labors.

Beside these major works he was author of innumerable essays and magazine articles on historical and Biblical subjects, and co-editor in the preparation of several important volumes. He left, unfinished, an elaborate history of the Collegiate Church of New York City upon which he had been engaged for several years. During the last few months of his life he had in preparation for the American Society of Church History a list, with sketches of all the ministers of all denominations, who served in the Middle States before 1800. He was at work upon this list on the day he died.

Dr. Corwin's genius was a genius for hard work. His industry was tireless and he had an infinite capacity for taking pains. Not by sudden inspiration but by patient toil did he accomplish so much.[45]

It is in describing his father's work as historian that Charles Corwin speaks with the most pride and goes on at the most length. Yet he is mistaken in reporting *Manual* 1 as the elder Corwin's first published historical work. In the same year, 1859, Corwin publishes, at the request of the Consistory there, *Manual and Record of the Church of Paramus. 1859. Revised and Enlarged.*[46] In the introduction, Corwin notes that "The previous Manual of the Church was necessarily imperfect."

---

[45]   Charles E. Corwin, *Christian Intelligencer.*
[46]   (New York: Hosford and Company, Stationers and Printers, 1859).

He reports that there were records that had not yet been brought to his attention when the earlier version was created. Therefore, while we have no surviving copy of the first edition of the Paramus *Manual*, we know that it existed, and was probably Edward Corwin's first published historical research work.

Corwin says that the Paramus *Manual* "is intended . . . as a sort of documentary History [*sic*] of the Church, only such connecting paragraphs being thrown in, as were deemed necessary to render the whole intelligible. By it the members of the congregation will understand the true position of the Church."[47] The resulting volume of 109 pages includes a listing of the membership as of 1859 and the Consistory of the church in that year, a "Sketch of the Paramus Church" which is, as Corwin described, a collection of selections from what we would call primary source documents with minimal narrative to provide context and make connections. All of the source documents are acknowledged in rudimentary footnotes. The "Sketch" goes on for 69 pages, followed by a listing of all the installed pastors, a listing of elders and deacons for the years 1748 to present,[48] a listing of all members of the congregation from its founding, arranged alphabetically and sub-sorted by the year when the person joined the congregation, a table of the statistics reported to the General Synod between 1799 and 1859,[49] and an index. It would seem that Corwin began his historical research into the congregation he served shortly after his arrival in 1857, and that he was already convinced of something he would put into words in Millstone twenty-six years later:

> History, if read aright, is a most excellent teacher. The lessons of experience, not of individuals only, but of families and generations, are ever most useful to a man of wisdom. While we should never rest in the past, yet we should use it as a means for making true progress.[50]

In the same year that the revised Paramus *Manual* was published, he brought out what was to be his first volume of denominational

---

47　Corwin, Paramus *Manual*, 3.
48　Corwin notes that the records of Consistory membership prior to 1748, as well as those from 1777-1799, are lost. Paramus *Manual*, 82, 83.
49　Corwin seems to have intentionally avoided reporting on the history of his own pastorate—not a reticence that he has as much in Millstone—as well as leaving out details of the history of the congregation's last thirty years from the "Sketch," "many of the parties being yet alive." Paramus *Manual*, 3.
50　Corwin, *Sermon*, 4.

history. *Manual* 1, which was a modest volume at 167 pages, started out to be something even less ambitious.

> Having been requested by a committee, which had been appointed to issue the Triennial Catalogue of the Alumni of our Seminary, to revise and correct that Catalogue for them, I thought it would be an improvement to add in some way the names of those ministers who had been educated under Livingston and his associates before the removal of the Seminary to New Brunswick. And upon executing this task, it appeared improper, among so many names respected and beloved, to omit those who had gone from our own shores to Europe, to be educated, or those who, with a missionary seal, had left their fatherland to come to the inhospitable shores of the New World. And when all those names were collected, it would have seemed unjust to omit those faithful servants who have entered our ranks from other denominations.
>
> But to give interest to the names, it was necessary to give the respective settlements of each—a task which, if it had been fully realized at the beginning, would hardly have been undertaken. Thus the Triennial Catalogue grew into this Manual, which, therefore, presents a complete list of all the ministers of our Church, with their respective settlements, and the dates of reception to and dismission from each. To give completeness to the work, it was deemed necessary to add a list of the Synods, Classes, and Churches, with their respective dates of organization.[51]

The book is a book of lists, in tables, with no narration, followed by eight appendices—identified as "Notes" A through H—covering the topics "On the Secession" (a listing of ministers who left for the True Dutch Reformed Church); General Synod, its location and presidents, which included the provisional synods dating back to 1771; "Domestic Missions" then "Foreign Missions," noting in narrative form the actions of various synods on each; "Education," treating the matter of theological education in a similar fashion, then listing the professors of theology; "Organization of Boards;" "Tabular View of Accessions to the Ministry;" and a brief entry on "Board of Sabbath School Union." An index closes the book.

One gets a sense of a historian's curiosity here, as the collection of each bit of data revealed another bit of data which, quite logically, must be included. It is possible to imagine that, at some point, the Board of Publication might have dispatched one or more members to

---

[51]   *Manual* 1, 3.

tell Corwin that his project had completely overrun its bounds, and had to be reigned back in.

Ten years later, *Manual* 2 appeared, with over twice as many pages as its predecessor. In the introduction, Corwin reported that "frequent requests have been made for a new and revised edition," which he acknowledged to have taken on a new form—modern readers will recognize the *Manual* which RCA scholars came to know.

> If it were interesting before to have a book of reference, which showed the general changes of the ministry, which gave a slight view of the churches, and a very succinct account of the origin and development of the benevolent Boards; it is believed it will not be less interesting, in this volume, to find brief characterizations of many of the worthy dead; a fuller view of the churches with their pastorates; and a much more detailed account, not only of the origin and progress of the Boards, but also of our Library and Theological Institutions. To all this a General Historical Introduction has been prefixed, and steel plates[52] of several of our ministers have been added.[53]

As he had done with the Paramus *Manual*, Corwin gathered material from a variety of sources and wove it together, rather more deftly than he had in his earlier works. An attentive reader would be quite aware of this going in.

> In collecting the material, not only have the general histories and memorial sermons been consulted, but circulars sent to all the churches and pastors, where printed matter did not already avail. These received very general and kind responses. In the delineations of character, the initials of writers are frequently given. Not a few of the sketches, however, are condensations of articles which have appeared in the Magazine of the Church, in Reviews [*sic*], or in the *Christian Intelligencer*. The language of these articles, or of memorial sermons or of church histories, has been freely used, abridged, or amplified, as was found expedient.[54]

It is the idea of material being "freely used, abridged, or amplified" that becomes problematic for the modern scholar, especially for someone using the *Manual* as a reference book and not reading it from cover to cover. In contemporary academic writing, such free use, without

---

[52] A reference to the engraving process for printed pictures in this era.
[53] Corwin, *Manual* 2, iii.
[54] Ibid.

very careful attribution—notice how many footnotes accompany this one essay—would be called plagiarism. The standards of citation we now consider inviolable, however, were largely up for grabs until the twentieth century, with various philosophies and schools of thought pushing the issue back and forth from the Middle Ages until the early twentieth century.[55] It would be in the 1880s and 90s that university-bred historians began to subject history in the United States to more rigorous analysis, carefully following and citing documents where prior historians were weaving stories.[56] Corwin was clearly part of the pre-1880s camp, weaving together stories in large, single volumes that purported to cover all of a subject in a way that modern and post-modern historians would never attempt.[57]

> In 1879 a third edition was issued, an octavo volume of nearly 700 pages. It was now possible to present the history of the Colonial period much more fully and satisfactorily, as that portion of the Amsterdam Documents secured by the Hon. J. Romeyn Brodhead in 1841-43 had become accessible.[58] Many of the articles in the preceding edition were also rewritten and many new biographical sketches were incorporated and, as in previous editions, everything was brought down to date. A new feature was that the publications of the ministers were added to their names. . . . This third edition was exhausted in a couple of years.[59]

To be precise, *Manual* 3 weighed in at 676 pages, 70 percent larger than its predecessor and over four times the size of *Manual* 1—a vast expanse in the space of just two decades. This volume, in addition to bringing all that had been done before up to date, included a nine-page article on church architecture by T.S. Doolittle of the Seminary faculty.[60] An appendix told the story of the Widow's Fund,[61] a second one listed the ministers chronologically from the date each one's ministry in the

---

[55] For a complete and engaging discussion of this issue, see Anthony Grafton, *The Footnote: A Curious History* (Cambridge, MA: Harvard University Press, 1997).

[56] Ernst Breisach, *Historiography Ancient, Medieval, & Modern* (Chicago: University of Chicago Press, 1983), 310 ff.

[57] See Mark V.C. Taylor's essay in this volume.

[58] The refers to the saga of the Dutch colonial documents, which Corwin finally fully transcribed, as told earlier in this essay.

[59] Corwin, *Manual* 4, iii. He also reports that 2,000 copies of *Manual* 1, 1,000 copies each of *Manual* 2 and *Manual* 3, and 2,000 copies of *Manual* 4 were printed.

[60] Corwin, *Manual* 3, 152-60.

[61] Ibid., 651-56.

RCA began,[62] while a third listed the churches chronologically from the date of their organization.[63]

Twenty-three years passed before *Manual* 4 went to press. In this time, Corwin had left the parish, first for NBTS and then, after his brief tenure in Greenport, for more or less full-time, occasionally paid work as a historian. His continued curiosity had helped this, the largest of the Manuals, swell to 1,082 pages, almost six-and-a-half times the size of the original work he had done in Paramus.

> (T)he work has grown beyond all anticipation. The preliminary history seemed to require expansion in certain lines to show the ever-growing tendency in the Colonial period to a separation of Church and State. The history of the Boards and institutions, also, needed to be partially or wholly rewritten and brought down to date. Then, also, several hundred new names had to be added to the biographical part, while the increasing number of publications of the ministers greatly swelled the book, notwithstanding the omission of many of the former sketches.[64]

Corwin also reported that he found the need to leave out several articles, some commissioned by other writers, including an article by John B. Thompson on hymnody, an article on the German Reformed Church by William J. Hinke, and a piece on the Christian Reformed Church by Henry Beets, then pastor of LaGrave Avenue Christian Reformed Church in Grand Rapids, Michigan[65]—an early example of cooperation between the separated denominations. All in all, Corwin said, these pieces "would have added, probably 200 pages to the Manual, and have made it necessary to issue the work in two volumes."[66]

As the twentieth century dawned, Corwin was beginning to realize that everything that needed to be said on his subject of choice—the RCA—couldn't be said in a single volume. This realization would come to about all historians eventually. But it also points up an apparent aspect of his work as a historian: there seem to be no stories that Corwin doesn't want to tell. Some of this desire exists in all historians, but they discipline themselves to narrow the focus of a given story; historians

---

[62] Ibid., 657-69.

[63] Ibid., 670-76.

[64] Corwin, *Manual* 4, iv.

[65] Richard H. Harms, ed., *Historical Directory of the Christian Reformed Church in North America* (Grand Rapids, MI: Historical Committee of the Christian Reformed Church in North America, 2004), 147.

[66] Corwin, *Manual* 4, iv.

need to have a point of view, so that all facts are not equally important. Corwin seems to have indulged his wish to follow every lead. It comes up in the way he moved from story to story in his Millstone anniversary sermon, which we cited above. In his 1905 address to the New Brunswick Historical Society, also cited above, he spent five pages of a thirty-two page presentation discussing the General Synod of 1855—a fascinating topic, as the Synod was forced to grapple with the issue of slavery, which it generally avoided, but connected to his topic at hand only by the fact that the Synod met in New Brunswick that year.[67] In his essay on "The Character and Development of the Reformed Church in the Colonial Period," part of the book of *Centennial Discourses*,[68] he wanders extensively between the polity implications of the Coetus-Conferentie dispute and the issues surrounding the failed attempt at a theological professorate at King's College. These are deeply interrelated issues, but Corwin's arguments, which show his desire to leave nothing out, become confused and bogged down in their own facts.

On the other hand, it can be said that Corwin's great gift to RCA historiography is his tendency to be a collector of facts, which are most capably presented in lists and excerpts from other sources. His last great work, mentioned by Charles in his *Christian Intelligencer* obituary but largely unseen by the world, is an example of one final expansion in his historical curiosity—having begun with congregational work, then moving to the denominational interests, he moved to the ecumenical— and an insight into just how Corwin the historian worked. *The Ministry and Churches of All Denominations in the Middle Colonies [including Maryland and Virginia east of the Chesapeake Bay] from the First Settlement Until the Year 1800*[69] exists only in two folders in the Archives of the State of New York. The first contains about 138 pages, an alphabetical list of ministers from all churches in those places—a letter from W. Walker Rockwell indicates his belief that Corwin was not quite done with Eastern Virginia and Maryland at the time of his death,[70] but, in a brief examination by this author, they appeared rather complete—and the second folder a roll of churches, also alphabetical, about 140 to 150 manuscript pages long.

---

[67]   Corwin, "New Brunswick Fifty Years Ago," 9-14.
[68]   James Anderson, T.W. Chambers, E.T. Corwin, eds., *Centennial Discourses: A Series of Sermons Delivered in the Year 1876, by order of the General Synod of the Reformed Church in America* (New York: Board of Publication of the Reformed Church in America, 1877).
[69]   Unpublished manuscript in the New York State Archives.
[70]   Letter from W. Walker Rockwell, on behalf of the American Society of Church History to A.J.F. VanLaer, New York State Archives, January 5, 1915, in the collection of the New York State Archives.

While the essays and anecdotes we find in Corwin's *Manual* are absent, it seems to be intended to be more like the modern *Historical Directory of the RCA*. The folders have been resident in the New York Archives and, evidently, largely untouched since January, 1915. The American Society of Church History, of which Corwin was a member and one-time president, had hoped that the State of New York would take up the cost of publishing this, as they had *ERNY*. The State declined, but kept the manuscript.

While it is a shame that the book has never been published, there is a sense in which we are rewarded with an insight into how this pre-word processor historian worked. Almost all of the entries—saved those snipped from *Manual* 4—are handwritten. As Corwin found new entries, he cut his own manuscript pages apart and integrated the entries at the appropriate places in the indices with cellophane tape. Clearly, he was constantly working on this project as he did other writing and researches—the additional entries are written on the backs of other old letters and notebook pages, clipped apart to fit the new-found entries. One can imagine that the work, were it ever seen to fruition, would be a book of about two hundred-fifty pages.

In the Manuals, in the *Digest,* and in the mammoth *Ecclesiastical Records*, Corwin synthesized and digested information from diverse sources and catalogues it in a way that has made it accessible to generations of scholars. Not only did Corwin's *Digest* pave the way for Mildred Schuppert's two subsequent versions,[71] the directories in the Manuals set the template for the *Historical Directories* prepared by Peter VandenBerge and Russell Gasero,[72] taking that work into the present day. The *Historical Series of the Reformed Church in America*, which reaches 87 volumes over forty-eight years with this book, would probably not be possible were it not for the stories that Corwin told, that made so many people want to find out more.

Edward Tanjore Corwin was born less than a decade after John Henry Livingston died, and was brought up in the ministry by Livingston's students and their contemporaries. When he died, airplanes had flown, World War I had begun—even if the United States wasn't in it—and the world was on the verge of the modern era. Corwin's curiosity, storytelling, and desire to make lists and leave

---

[71]   *Digest and Index of the Minutes of the General Synod of the Reformed Church in America, 1906-1957* (Grand Rapids, MI: William B. Eerdman's Publishing Company, 1984) and *Digest and Index of the Minutes of the General Synod of the Reformed Church in America, 1958-1977* (Grand Rapids, MI: William B. Eerdman's Publishing Company, 1979).

[72]   Gasero, ix.

no one out made it possible for the modern RCA to have tools that linked us to our origins. His expansive curiosity linked us to the larger world, maintaining connections to sister churches that has separated from us. Our search has brought us to just a piece of Edward Corwin— sadly, while we can learn about his ancestry through the genealogy he produced,[73] we may never learn about his family life—but it is the piece that gives us a foundation for our history, and, as he said in Millstone in 1883, "While we should never rest in the past, yet we should use it as a means for making true progress."

---

[73] *The Corwin Genealogy (Curwin, Curwen, Corwine) in the United States* (New York: Green, 1872).

Part 3

"Yes! Well . . ." and the Exploration of the Reformed Church in America

David Waanders has already pointed out that John Coakley was adopted into the Reformed Church in America—or perhaps that he adopted the RCA. As a minister of the Word and Sacrament and a General Synod Professor, John has been helping this denomination understand itself even as he has worked to understand us. In that context, we can say "Yes," the RCA has done better than most American churches at studying itself—this is the eighty-seventh volume of the denomination's *Historical Series*—while also saying "well," there is more for us to learn.

Fully half of the essays in this festschrift fall into this category, showing us many of the places where the denomination's study has yet to go. Dirk Mouw examines the controversy over the formation of King's College—now Columbia University—the failed attempt at establishing a Reformed theology chair there, and how that impacted the church's developing identity. Matthew and Russell Gasero look at a bit of a diary from pioneering missionary Samuel Zwemer, a window into our past that also points out the advantages of making primary sources available in new ways. The work of another missionary graduate of NBTS—

Horace Underwood—forms the subject of James Jinhong Kim's essay, while he also helps us imagine new ways of thinking about missions. Lynn Japinga expands on her earlier work in the modern history of the RCA, bringing it forward to issues before the General Synod today. The formation of "Room for All" and the church's evolving understanding of human sexuality and how and who we welcome into our communion is the subject of Mary Kansfield's contribution. Al Janssen looks at how our Reformed polity—which wasn't created with a separation of church and state in mind, expresses that reality of our American context. And Gregg Mast closes our collection of essays by looking at how words matter in the our liturgical life and how a change in emphasis in the liturgy for the Lord's Supper changed how we understand the feast.

CHAPTER 8

"A Matter of So Great Importance": The King's College Controversy and the Dutch of British North America, 1745-1755

Dirk Mouw

When the idea of establishing an institution of higher education in New York was contemplated in 1745, it was not controversial at all. New England had colleges; Virginia too. Some proud New Yorkers thought their province should have one as well. Few took quick action, however. When plans to found the College of New Jersey (later Princeton University) ceased to be a matter of rumor and speculation, upon the issuance of its charter the following year, that seems to have prodded some New Yorkers into action; evidently they felt that if New Jersey was to have a college, New York must as well. Damaged pride may, therefore, have been enough to spur members of the provincial assembly of New York to pass a bill authorizing a lottery to raise funds for a college in New York in 1746. Still, plans and preparations for what would eventually become the King's College (later Columbia University) proceeded with little sense of urgency. While few if any New Yorkers expressed *opposition* to the proposal, there was hardly a grand groundswell of *enthusiasm* for it either. The same held true among those who frequented the pews and pulpits of the Dutch Reformed congregations in the colony; there is no evidence of spirited support for the college—at least not of the sort that

159

loosed the knots on purse strings. Indeed, although instruction was already under way at the New Jersey college by 1747, it was not until late 1751 that even the small step was taken in New York to appoint a board to manage the few thousand pounds that had been raised for founding the college. Matters such as where the college would be located or what the theological affiliations of its faculty were still far from settled. When those issues came to the fore, however, Dutch Reformed were pulled into—and pulled apart by—a fierce dispute.[1]

At first blush, it is not evident why the overwhelming majority of adherents and office bearers of the Dutch Reformed congregations of the region took so little interest in the founding of a college in the years after fundraising began. Others outside the Dutch communion saw the power the Dutch could exert in the planning process. Indeed, in the 1750s, two feuding religio-political groups in New York became convinced that Dutch Reformed laity and clergy had the numbers and strength to play a decisive role in shaping the character of the college, if only the Dutch would take the trouble to flex their political and financial muscles. On the one side were men powerful in the colonial New York political sphere who were members of the Anglican communion; on the other was a group—one might call them an opposition party—who frequently locked horns with and made accusations against the Anglican partisans. The latter were affiliated with the Presbyterian church. These partisans would come to believe that they had common interests with the Dutch and that, together with the Dutch, they were in grave danger of losing a political chess game of profound importance—a match which the Dutch Reformed appeared to be entirely unaware was under way. Parties sympathetic with the Anglican politicians would also woo Dutch Reformed laity and clergy.

Undoubtedly to the surprise of the Presbyterian partisans, the Dutch Reformed entered the fray on both sides; though the first Dutch salvos in the debate could more accurately be described as being directed against both of the Anglophonic parties. Had theology been the sole determinative factor—or form of church governance for that matter—the Presbyterian partisans would seem to have been the obvious ally of the Dutch in the growing controversy. Theology and church governance were not, however, the only considerations.

---

1   David C. Humphrey, *From King's College to Columbia, 1746-1800* (New York: Columbia University Press, 1976), 3-4; Colonial Laws of New York, 25 November 1751, in Edward Tanjore Corwin and Hugh Hastings, eds., *Ecclesiastical Records: State of New York*, 7 vols. (Albany: James B. Lyon, 1901-1916), V:3207-08. Hereafter, *ERNY.*

The Dutch eventually did join the lists—often passionately, but not uniformly in support of one side or the other—because the debate was about much more than alliances based on similarities in doctrine or church order; it was about the institutional foundations, the status and the character of the Dutch Reformed Church in the Old World and in the New, as well. The conclusion of the dispute was poignant and ironic for the Dutch Reformed: all of them lost, no matter which side they had taken. Still, some of the issues raised from 1745 to 1755—most notably the relationship of the colonial Dutch Reformed congregations and its membership to British governmental authorities, as well as the need for a colonial institution to provide theological education for would-be Dutch clergy—remained points of discussion and contention among the Dutch Reformed in New York and New Jersey over the decades that followed. Those conversations and conflicts had arguably much happier outcomes than the King's College controversy for the Dutch Reformed of North America—at least in the long term.

One reason that the colonial Dutch Reformed Church did not weigh in early or with one voice at the outbreak of the King's College controversy is that there really was nothing one could call a colonial "Dutch Reformed Church." In 1745, the Dutch Reformed congregations of British North America were, in most respects, individual outposts of the national church of the Netherlands. Some congregations shared ministers and/or routinely held joint consistory meetings, and wealthier congregations occasionally made gifts to smaller churches and frequently allowed their ministers to visit empty pulpits to preach and administer the sacraments. Still, few Dutch Reformed clergy or laity were thinking of colonial congregations in any collective sense, or about their shared institutional needs. There were *congregational matters* but one cannot fairly speak of any recognition that there were *colonial Church matters*. Thus, when it came to the proposal for an educational institution in New York, since the location of the prospective college had not been determined, and since a college located on Manhattan or in some rural location would at *most* affect the nearest congregation, it is not surprising that none of the Dutch Reformed were outspoken supporters or opponents of the proposal to found an academy, at least in the early stages of the planning and fundraising process.

The same cannot be said for Anglicans in New York; there were numerous partisans among the Anglican communion, some politically powerful, who were firmly committed to the growth and prosperity of the colonial Anglican Church. Indeed, one could say that some among them actively sought to advantage the Church of England and disadvantage all other Protestant competitors. Thus, while the action of the vestry of Trinity Anglican Church in Manhattan in the spring of 1752 was not particularly provocative, it was decidedly in keeping with a desire to give the Anglican Church the advantage in the colonial religious sphere: the vestry donated a piece of land for the use as a campus for the proposed college. While the vestry had attached no strings to the 1752 donation, one of its members did acknowledge later that the vestry expected that the "gift...would be the means of obtaining some privileges to the [Anglican] Church...." When the vestry reissued its offer in 1754, it was less subtle: provisos were added requiring the exclusive use of the Anglican liturgy at worship services at the college and stipulating that the president of the college be an Anglican.[2]

Even before the Trinity vestry began openly insisting that the proposed college be Anglican in character, three men (sometimes referred to as the "triumvirate") who were affiliated with the Presbyterian church but who were, more broadly, a sort of Whiggish opposition party unto themselves, discerned the intentions of Anglican leadership and began sounding the alarm. Led by William Livingston, they took to the press to attack plans for a "sectarian" (i.e. "Anglican") college funded with public monies, advocating instead for a "free" college (one without association with any Protestant communion in particular). The chief problem both the Anglican and Presbyterian parties faced was an inability to carry the day in the legislature without help from another bloc. If either was able to draw large numbers from among the Dutch Reformed to its side, it could thwart the other. Livingston was optimistic about his party's chances:

> Those of the Dutch Church, can alone govern this whole affair; and were they once sufficiently apprized [sic] of sinister views, and impressed with the importance and advantage of a free Academy, and the destructive tendency of its opposite, we should have nothing to fear.

Livingston energetically set himself to the task of apprising and impressing the Dutch. Samuel Johnson, an Anglican cleric (and later first president of King's College), agreed with Livingston's political math, but not much else. The triumvirate, he opined, were radicals, "free thinkers," who would rather have a college in which "no religion

---

[2]   Rector, Church Wardens, and Vestry of Trinity Anglican Church, minutes, 5 May 1752 and 14 May 1754; Trinity Church, New York to the Society of Propagating the Gospel, 3 November 1755 in *ERNY*, V: 3220, 3611, 3478.

at all should be taught" than that the Church of England should "have any precedence" in it. Now the Presbyterians were trying "to disaffect the Dutch towards us," a population, he observed, "who otherwise were peaceably disposed." As one scholar has noted, each party sought to inform the Dutch of events, going so far as to publish in the Dutch language in their efforts to warn the Dutch of the other party's "lust for 'Dominion' and to emphasize the harmony of its own church's doctrine and organization with those of the Dutch Reformed church."[3]

Had there been an odds maker calculating the chances of either Anglicans or Presbyterians successfully making the case to members of the Dutch Reformed Church that their church was doctrinally and organizationally more similar to the Dutch church, she or he would have probably given a large point spread to the Presbyterians; particularly so if she or he had begun with a side-by-side comparison of the Westminster and Belgic Confessions. Yet the triumvirate received fierce criticism from more than one quarter of the Dutch church. Livingston waxed sarcastic (as he was known to do) after a Dutch Reformed minister in New York City launched what must have been a withering attack against Livingston from the pulpit. Livingston mockingly thanked the minister for doing him "the signal Honour, last Sunday" of making him the "Subject of his Sermon," admiring the minister's "Ingenuity in proving [Livingston] to be the Gog and Magog of the Apocalypse, who have, hitherto, puzzled all the Divines in the World."[4] While the content of the New York City minister's criticism is lost to history, we have a much better idea of why Livingston's writings troubled another cleric. David Marinus was a young Dutch Reformed minister in New Jersey of a Dutch Reformed pietist bent. Marinus charged Livingston with anticlericalism, a latitudinarianism that extended beyond civil toleration into a refusal to renounce heresy, and low standards when it came to judging theological orthodoxy and biblical faithfulness.

---

[3]   Preface to *The Independent Reflector; or, Weekly Essays on Sundry Important Subjects More particularly adapted to the Province of New-York*, (New-York: [Henry DeForeest], [1754]), 18; Humphrey, *From King's College to Columbia*, 19, 40-44, 54, 58; Samuel Johnson to Bishop Sherlock, 25 October 1754, in *ERNY*, V:3503-04. See also, William Livingston, essays, 22 March et seq., and 5, 12, 19 and 26 April 1753, *Independent Reflector* in *ERNY*, V:3338-41, 3354-57, 3359-62, 3362-65, 3366-69 as well as Beverly McAnear, "American Imprints Concerning King's College," *The Papers of the Bibliographical Society of America* 44 (1950): 301-39.

[4]   *Independent Reflector*, 11 January 1753, 102. Though unsigned, the note has all the characteristics of something penned by Livingston. Though Livingston was not explicit about which minister had thus attacked him, a bibliographer has stated that it was a Dutch Reformed minister. See McAnear, "King's College Imprints," 308.

Marinus wrote a letter to a periodical published by the triumvirate, at once adopting an apologetic tone—wishing that he could "enter the lists" with Livingston in Dutch or Latin, instead of "the English" which most of Livingston's readers would understand "best"—while he simultaneously lit into Livingston with rhetorical skill Livingston himself might well have grudgingly admired. Marinus wrote, "[F]or ought I can discover in your Papers, in Regard to what you write about *religious Matters*, you drive like *Nimrod* and *Jehu*... and rush on with such Fury and Impetuosity, as if you thought yourself independent even of God, and of his sacred Revelation."[5]

Once it became obvious that there was an Anglican effort afoot to give "precedence" to the Church of England in the proposed academy, any support that the Anglican partisans might have hitherto enjoyed among the Dutch Reformed appears to have evaporated, or at least to have temporarily gone into hiding. The same young Dutch Reformed minister from New Jersey who had so eloquently criticized Presbyterian partisans, David Marinus, wrote for publication two more times, first in 1754 and again in 1755. In the first essay Marinus allowed that Livingston (who had been silenced a year earlier when his opponents pressured his printer to abandon him) was no paradigm of doctrinal correctness but that Livingston had been helpful in certain ways and was, in any event, a far less dangerous voice than some others whose ideas were being published. Marinus took particular note of William Smith, an Anglican priest who had in the previous year published an essay on education. Marinus unleashed a vitriolic denunciation of Smith; Marinus charged Smith with teachings that were not just "false" but "Soul destructive to those who are so unhappy to believe" them. False doctrine in a treatise concerning education was particularly dangerous because "Our Land is at present, in a critical Conjuncture...we are about [to be] erecting a College for the Education of Youth...." Smith's purpose and intended audience is worthy of note. On the title page of his work, he "Address'd" his essay "to the Consideration of the Trustees nominated by the Legislature, to receive Proposals, &c. relating to the Establishment of a College in the Province of New York." Pedagogical plans founded upon and including "false" teachings, particularly of the sort that were "soul destructive" were—to say the least—worrisome, especially in that context and under those circumstances.[6]

---

5   [David Marinus] David Marin Ben Jesse, *A Letter to the Independent Reflector* (New York: Hugh Gaine, 1753), 5.

6   [David Marinus] David Marin Ben Jesse, *A Remonstrance* ([New York]: [Hugh Gaine], 1755), 4, 9; W[illiam] Smith, *A General Idea of the College of Mirania; with A Sketch of the*

At almost the same time as Marinus was penning his invective against Smith, two other important events, both relevant to Dutch involvement in the King's College controversy, were unfolding. The first was that, in September of 1754, Gerardus Haeghoort, a Dutch Reformed minister in Second River (now Belleville), New Jersey, proposed the formation of a broader assembly for the colonial congregations—a North-American classis; his proposal received wide, albeit far from unanimous, support among the clergy and laity of the colonies. This could fairly be considered the beginning date of the Coetus-Conferentie conflict, sometimes referred to as a "schism," which divided the colonial Dutch Reformed against each other, into pro-classis and anti-classis factions, for many years. The second event probably took place in Manhattan, most likely in last few months of 1754; a plan was put forward to move a charter through the provincial legislature for the colonial college. Under the terms of the deal, the Dutch would lend support for the charter—notwithstanding the fact that, in some respects, the college would have an Anglican cast. In return, however, a Dutch Reformed professor of divinity would be appointed to the college faculty. Dutch Reformed students could be instructed by Anglican professors in common subjects, such as the ancient languages, but would have classes of their own for subjects such as theology, doctrine, and church order. Livingston, for one, liked the proposal, believing the presence of "a Dutch Calvinistic professor" on the faculty would "diminish that badge of distinction to which the Episcopalians are so zealously aspiring." And, if Anglican leadership rejected the proposal, Livingston was certain it would "animate the Dutch against" the Anglicans and "convince [the Dutch] that all [Anglican] pretences to sisterhood and identity" with the Dutch "were fallacious and hypocritical."[7]

Method of Teaching Science and Religion, in the several Classes: and Some Account of its Rise, Establishment and Buildings (New York: J. Parker and W. Weyman, 1753). Though the *Remonstrance* was published in 1755, Marinus dated it 4 November 1754.

[7] Twelfth Coetus, minutes, 17-19 September 1754, in "'Records of the Cœtus of the Low Dutch Reformed Preachers and Elders in the Provinces of New York and New Jersey, Subordinate to the Rev. Classis of Amsterdam, Begun at New York, the 8th of September, 1747'; Followed by the Proceedings of the Conferentie 1755-67," in *The Acts and Proceedings of the General Synod of the Reformed Protestant Dutch Church in North America, Vol. I, 1771-1812: Preceded by the Minutes of the Coetus (1738-1754) and the Proceedings of the Conferentie (1755-1767), and followed by the Minutes of the Original Particular Synod (1794-1799)* (New York: Board of Publication of the Reformed Protestant Dutch Church, 1859), lxxxix-xciii; Livingston to Noah Welles, 18 October 1754 in *ERNY,* V:3501. I present a fuller discussion of the Coetus-Conferentie controversy in "*Moederkerk* and *Vaderland*: Religion and Ethnic Identity in the Middle Colonies, 1690-1772" (Ph.D. diss., University of Iowa, 2009) 243-610.

The consistory of the New York City Dutch Reformed Church took the lead in pursuing the proposal but divided over the best way to proceed. The final outcome was not a happy one for members of colonial Dutch Reformed congregations, no matter how they had felt about the plan the New York City consistory had negotiated. To the dismay of the Manhattan consistory, word came that the provincial assembly would soon take up the matter of the college charter and that the draft legislation they would take up would *not* include any provision for a Dutch Reformed professorate. Consistory members received conflicting advice: some thought the consistory should move quickly to get language inserted into the legislation guaranteeing the Dutch professorship before it passed. Others thought that unwise; the consistory should allow the bill to pass without a provision for a Dutch professor and subsequently petition the college board for the professorship (and a majority of the board, the consistory was assured, would approve). The consistory opted for the former approach, sending a petition to the legislature for a provision in the charter for a Dutch chair on the faculty. Less than a week later, the acting governor, angry with the consistory for petitioning the legislature instead of him, decided to issue a royal charter, circumventing the legislature entirely. As issued, the royal charter gave the college a strongly Anglican character, and there was no provision for a Dutch Reformed chair. Anglican advisors nevertheless assured the consistory that the acting governor could be "pacified." With the help of the triumvirate, the legislature acted to table any action on funding the college indefinitely; notwithstanding the fact that the acting governor could not fund the college from the provincial treasury without an act of the legislature, he nevertheless delivered the royal charter to college's trustees anyway.[8]

In Marinus' final publication, written not long after the royal charter had been issued, he was more vitriolic than ever. He also targeted more of his text at Dutch Reformed readers in an effort to inform them of the sins perpetrated against them and persuade them to act accordingly—and quickly. Marinus employed numerous parables of his own devising, to make the case that Anglicans were bent on transferring public wealth, largely from Dutch pockets, to undermine the Dutch Reformed Church, by founding an Anglican college with provincial

---

[8]   Humphrey, *From King's College to Columbia*, 56, 59-62; "Petition of the Collegiate Church, of New York City, to the [Provincial] Assembly, for a Professorship of Divinity in Kings College," "Royal Charter of Kings College, New York," and Henry Barclay to Samuel Johnson, 25 and 31 October, and 4 November 1754, in *ERNY*, V:3505-6, 3506-14, 3517-18.

money. In one parable, Anglicans were French Legions, who used false accusations as pretexts for depriving British subjects of property rightly theirs. In another parable, Anglicans were cast as an evil aunt who demanded that her good sister enroll her own daughters, along with her nieces, in a "dancing school" so that they would learn their evil aunt's "gay and grand Airs." Adding insult to injury, the evil sister demanded that the good mother was so "much obliged" to the evil sister for her "Proposal" that all the children take the lessons dance lessons, that the evil sister expected the good mother to pay, not only for the lessons of her own girls, but for those of her evil sister as well, adding, "Don't look so grave, for do it thou shalt; I have already agreed with the dancing Master...." Thus it was in New York, Marinus argued. The Dutch were the good mother and the Anglicans were the evil sister. The evil sister not only demanded that all the children receive dance lessons (which the good mother did not want them to have), so that the girls would attain the refinement and "airs" (which the good mother despised), but the evil sister (the Anglicans) insisted that the good mother (the Dutch) pay the costs of the refinement (Anglican education) for all of the girls (both Dutch and English). There was no sense wasting time and breath complaining, the agreement with the dance master (the governor) had been signed and sealed. Marinus piled up more such parables; in each, the point was the same; all are summed up in the Mosaic prohibition Marinus chose to feature on his title page: "Thou shalt not seethe a Kid in his Mother's Milk." Anglicans, he felt, were effectively using the resources of the Dutch in an effort to cook (destroy) the colonial Dutch Reformed churches.[9]

Once again, Marinus expressed far less antipathy toward Presbyterians than he did toward Anglicans. He believed that God had used the triumvirate as "a Means to bafle and frustrate an incroaching Party, in their unjust Demands," noting, nevertheless that he, Marinus, was "not of his [Livingston's] Sect as to Principles in Religion...." The College of New Jersey, founded by Presbyterians of a very different theological orientation than that of the triumvirate, received muted praise from Marinus as well. Indeed, Marinus hoped his fellow Dutch Reformed would "wish the Jersey College well" largely "because their Aim at grasping after all our Churches, hath not hitherto been so glaring, as that of the High Church [i.e., Anglican] College in this Province"; besides, Marinus argued, "the religious Principles inculcated"

---

9   [David Marinus] David Marin Ben Jesse, *A Remark on the Disputes and Contentions in this Province* (New York: H. Gaine, 1755). Quotes are from title page, 4, 6.

at the College of New Jersey, "agree better with Holy Scripture, and with the Confession of our Church, nay, even with the doctrinal Part of the Articles of the Church of England, than I expect will be taught" at the new Anglican college in New York.[10]

Two features of Marinus's essay represent significant historical departures worthy of note here. The first is the fact that this essay made—early and forcefully—a case for a colonial Dutch Reformed institution for the education of would-be ministers in the Dutch Reformed Church. Precisely when in 1755 he wrote is not clear, but he did know that negotiations between the New York City consistory for a Dutch chair at the college had gone horribly awry. It seems altogether possible that he may have put pen to paper before May 28. On that day, he was among the signatories to a document produced in a meeting of delegates invited by the Dutch Reformed minister of Albany, Theodorus Frelinghuysen, Jr., a body which endorsed a plan for both a Dutch Reformed classis in the colonies as well as a Dutch Reformed "Academy or Seminarium...in these new far-flung parts of the world," all, they pledged, in keeping with the doctrine and order of the "Synod held at Dor[drech]t *anno* 1618 and 1619." The fact that Marinus credited his colleague Johannes Hendricus Goetschius with the idea of a Dutch classis in the colonies and did not mention either Haeghoort or Theodorus Frelinghuysen Jr. could well be significant. Scholars, myself included, have credited Theodorus Frelinghuysen Jr. with the first public proposal for a Dutch Reformed seminary in North America but the fact that the language Marinus and Theodorus Frelinghuysen, Jr., used in reference to the proposed educational institution is so similar, strongly suggests that one was borrowing from the other and it is at least as likely that Marinus deserves the honor of first publically proposing a Dutch seminary in North America than his colleague does.[11] Whether or not he made his argument for a colonial

---

10   [Marinus], *Remark*. Quotes are from 6, 7, 8.
11   For the meeting called to endorse a classis and seminary, see Theodorus Frelinghuysen Jr. to the Ministers and Consistories of the Dutch Reformed Congregations in North America, 17 April 1755, in *ERNY*, V:3541; "Een Alliantie of Unie door de Predikanten en Ouderlingen op de 28ste dag van Meij 1755 in een Broederlijke Conferentie tesamenvergadered," Special Collections, New Brunswick Theological Seminary Library, New Brunswick, N.J. With it is a translation by Gerrit T. Vanderlugt, June 1761. In the "Alliantie" document, Theodorus Frelinghuysen Jr. and the signatories endorsed the proposition that "*een Academie Seminarium of Queekschool worde opgerecht tot onderwijs der Jeught. . . .*" Marinus varied his wording slightly throughout his pamphlet, but "College or Seminary of Learning for the Education of Youth" is typical of his phrasing; these are remarkably similar to each

Dutch academy before Theodorus Frelinghuysen, Jr., did, Marinus was certainly was the first to make the case in print, that, in his words, the Dutch needed, if it "please God, an academy of our own, for the free Education of our Youth," and—referring to the vows made by parents and members of congregations every time a child was baptized—drove the point home by reminding them all that they "did promise and vow before God and his Saints, [those who had baptized] should be instructed in the Doctrine of our Reformed Church."[12]

The second respect in which Marinus' final pamphlet represents and signals an important change in the colonial Dutch Reformed church concerns the way in which the Dutch Reformed of British North America come to think about themselves and each other. Members, adherents, ministers, and congregations had common interests. Addressing the clergy and laity of the Dutch Reformed congregations in North America, Marinus used pronouns of the first person, plural. He wrote of "our" ancestors and "our" missteps and he argued that "we" must take action.

When Marinus shifted his gazed from "us" to "them," he focused frequently, though not exclusively, on assessing the degrees to which individuals, groups, and communions were (or were not) theologically orthodox. No one in the Anglican or Presbyterian communions fully measured up. Marinus believed that the Presbyterians of the College of New Jersey deserved the good wishes of the colonial Dutch Reformed; they were *better*, theologically than most and less aggressive than the Anglicans. The Presbyterians of the triumvirate, on the other hand, were at a very different part of the Presbyterian theological spectrum from those who founded the College of New Jersey; they were theologically weak but they were, at least in the political sphere, useful and helpful.

It would seem, if it made sense for Marinus to speak relatively well of Presbyterians at the College of New Jersey on theological grounds, and to speak up for the Presbyterians of the triumvirate on political grounds, that it would have made no sense for anyone in the colonial Dutch Reformed congregations to side with, or cooperate with, the Anglicans of the province. Nevertheless, some Dutch did and they had important reasons for doing so. The grounds were not necessarily

---

other but not characteristic of the wording used by others—either proponents or opponents of the proposal for the educational institution. See [Marinus], *Remark*, 5. On Goetschius, see *ibid*, 10. For my earlier argument that Theodorus Jacobus Frelinghuysen Jr. was the first to propose a Dutch Reformed seminary in North America, see *"Moederkerk* and *Vaderland,"* 308-315, 322.

[12] [Marinus], *Remark*. Quotes are from 8.

theological, but that did not diminish their importance. The arguments in favor of siding with or cooperating with Anglican partisans—or, more accurately, the frames of reference within which taking the Anglican side or collaborating with Anglicans make sense—fall into three categories. The first involves the status of Dutch Reformed congregations in both the Netherlands and the British colonies of North America. The second revolves around interpersonal relationships within the context of mid eighteenth-century New York City. The third concerns the needs of the Dutch colonial church—before 1745 that church, or rather those congregations, had been largely individual outposts of the national church of the Netherlands, scattered about New York and New Jersey. As we have observed from the writings of Marinus, however, over the course of the decade of the King's College controversy, a collective identity was growing among the Dutch Reformed; and as that happened it became clear that their colonial Dutch Reformed Church needed a more reliable and more affordable source of well-educated clergy.

First, then, the status of the Dutch Reformed Church, both in the Old World and the New made an educational alliance with the Church of England a natural choice. While the Dutch church was not a state church in the same sense that the Church of England was, they were both denominations whose origins and identities were linked to a nation-state. Both were the official churches of great colonial powers with a global reach. The Dutch church was almost an official church in British North America, as well. Under the Articles of Capitulation, by which New Netherland was surrendered to the British, Dutch colonists were guaranteed certain protections. The eighth article stipulated that "The Dutch here shall enjoy the liberty of their consciences in Divine Worship and church discipline." The Dutch, of course, did not always get the same favor shown by governors to the Church of England (most notably following the Ministry Act of 1693), but the Dutch were nevertheless decidedly of higher rank and enjoyed greater security than all denominations labeled as "dissenters" by the British. Indeed, when governors began issuing charters to congregations in the 1690s, only Dutch Reformed and Anglican petitions were granted. The Presbyterian congregation in New York City requested a charter four times between 1721 and 1767; it was denied four times. Thus, in New York, only Dutch and English congregations could borrow money and manage property.[13]

---

[13]   Articles of Capitulation on the Reduction of New Netherland, 27 August 1664, in *ERNY*, I:588; Michael Kammen, *Colonial New York: A History*, A History of the American Colonies in Thirteen Volumes, eds. Milton M. Klein and Jacob E. Cooke

A second reason that an Anglican-Reformed educational alliance would have made sense had to do with interpersonal relationships. By the 1750s there was a long history of colonial clergy crossing theological and denominational lines in the friendships they forged. In a place like mid-century New York City, there was a relatively small circle of highly educated denizens and these often sought each other out. One of the Dutch ministers is known to have had a warm relationship with the rector of the Anglican congregation; the rector himself had some Dutch ancestors, a Dutch wife, and command of the Dutch language.[14] Other vestry and consistory members were often merchants or lawyers and undoubtedly some developed working and/or personal relationships with each other. That people with similar occupations and similar educational achievements would cooperate in the founding of an educational institution would hardly seem to require explanation, even if that involved crossing ethnic and confessional lines.

A final context within which an educational alliance with Anglicans would have made sense goes to some of the foundational characteristics of the Dutch Reformed Church and a growing understanding among the members and clergy of its North American branch of the state and the needs of that colonial church. A central need for almost any congregation is the services of a qualified minister. Beginning with the arrival of Jonas Michaëlius in New Amsterdam in 1628, the norm for Dutch congregations in North America was that they received their clergy from the Netherlands. The colonies did not have the requisite educational institutions or ecclesiastical assemblies to train men for the ministry or to discern whether would-be ministers were qualified. Ancient cities in the Netherlands had august universities with theological faculties that attracted students from across Europe. Some theology professors even attained celebrity status in Dutch society. The office of professor of theology was arguably the most prestigious of the four church offices enumerated in the church order crafted by a national synod gathered in Dordrecht in 1618 and 1619. Indeed, theology faculties at each university were granted authority that was, in some respects, greater than that of a broader ecclesiastical assembly.[15]

(New York: Scribner, 1975), 289; Ronald W. Howard, "The English Province (1664-1776)," in *The Empire State: A History of New York*, ed. Milton M. Klein (Ithaca: Cornell University Press with the New York State Historical Association, Cooperstown, N.Y., 2001), 166.

[14] Humphrey, *From King's College to Columbia*, 56.

[15] In addition to the authority granted exclusively to professors, university faculties were also permitted to assume on some of the primarily assigned to broader

One of the foundational characteristics of the church of the Netherlands was that its clergy were to be well educated. The framers of the church order did not expect prospective ministers to be tutored in the homes of clergy, as was the case in some other communions (though this would become an acceptable way to *prepare* for university in the Netherlands). For this reason, one of the preconditions for an aspirant to be admitted to the ministry was that he possess a letter or testimonial indicating satisfactory educational attainment from professors at one of the universities. Nevertheless, the framers did leave a small door open to an aspirant lacking proper academic credentials. Because the church order had been written at a time when Reformed clergy were in short supply and there was no surplus of university-trained men ready to fill pulpits, an article was included permitting would-be ministers without satisfactory educational credentials to be examined by a classis—but such men had to give "definite assurance of their being exceptionally gifted, godly, humble, modest, and possessed of good sense and discretion, as well as gifts of public address."[16] The very appellation for ministers promoted under this article suggests invoking the clause brought with it stigma: they were known as "*idiotae*." Further evidence that *idiotae* were second-class clerics is found in regulations of the Dutch West India Company which by 1642 forbade *idiotae* from being sent to churches in the colonies.[17]

---

assemblies. Professors of theology could, for instance approve a minister's manuscript for publication as a classis could. Curiously, university professors could also administer both preliminary and final examinations and even perform ordinations. While this authority to examine and ordain was withdrawn from almost all universities by 1636, in Groningen, professors retained this authority until 1815. See article 55 of the church order of Dordrecht for manuscript approval. For examinations and ordinations, see H. H. Kuyper, *De opleiding tot den dienst des Woords bij de gereformeerden* (The Hague: Nijhoff, 1891), 344-45, 352-54, 369-70, 510-22; David Bos, *Servants of the Kingdom: Professionalization among Ministers of the Nineteenth-Century Netherlands Reformed Church*, trans. David McKay, Brill's Series in Church History, ed. Wim Janse, no. 43; Religious History and Culture Series, ed. Joris van Eijnatten and Fred van Lieburg, no. 3 (Boston: Brill, 2010), 119, 119n.

[16]   Article 8 of the church order of Dordrecht; Fred A. van Lieburg, "Profeten en hun Vaderland: De Geografische Herkomst van de Gereformeerde predikanten in Nederland van 1572 tot 1816" (Ph.D. diss., Vrije Universiteit te Amsterdam, 1995), 75.

[17]   *Idiotae* was the more common term in the eighteenth century, though at times such men have also been called "octavists"—people admitted under the eighth article. See T. Brienen, "Theodorus Gerardi à Brakel (1608-1669)," in *De Nadere Reformatie en het gereformeerd piëtisme*, ed. T. Brienen, et al. ('s-Gravenhage: Boekencentrum, 1989), 124; Willem Frijhoff, "The West India Company and the Reformed Church: Neglect or Concern?," *de Halve Maen* 70, no. Fall 1997, 64; Frans Leonard Schalkwijk, *The Reformed Church in Dutch Brazil (1630-1654)* (Zoetermeer, The Netherlands: Boekencentrum, 1998), 131-32; F. A. van Lieburg, "Preachers Between Inspiration

Dutch Reformed standards for the educational attainment of clergy posed two problems for church-goers in North America: getting a university-educated minister from Europe was expensive, often prohibitively so, and even when colonial congregations could muster the necessary resources, the pool of qualified men in the Republic willing to serve a congregation in a British colony across the sea was small, frequently it was—to borrow mathematical terminology— an "empty set." For a colonial congregation desirous of a minister, standard procedure had been (for about a century, by 1745) to write to the Classis of Amsterdam, asking that assembly to find and call a qualified man. A number of variations on this procedural theme were available to congregations, but none that would bring them a qualified, well-educated minister was cheap and none was uniformly successful. The classis had to search for potential candidates; if and when it found such a person it had to issue a formal call and then either hold a vote to approve that call or—if the colonial pulpit would be the candidate's first—administer two examinations and perform an ordination. Special sessions of the classis had to be called and there were expenses involved with many of these classical meetings and activities, expenses for which the classis expected to be reimbursed by the colonial congregations. Once called by the classis, the minister had to take ship with his family and their effects; the congregation was also responsible for these transportation expenses. In one well-documented case, the costs incurred by the congregation before the minister even ascended their pulpit were greater than his first year's salary. And, of course, once the minister did begin work, the congregation had to pay him; one can easily imagine that a university-educated minister from Europe could command a salary that would make him a one-percenter in some colonial communities.[18]

Even for congregations able to muster the resources, however, qualified, university educated ministers willing to serve in North America could not always be found in the Netherlands. In 1753, Johannes Frelinghuysen, a Dutch Reformed minister in the Raritan Valley of New Jersey, begged the Classis of Amsterdam to send ministers to vacant colonial pulpits; some congregations seldom received visits from ministers and thus rarely "had the privilege of hearing a sermon

---

and Instruction: Dutch Reformed Ministers without Academic Education (Sixteenth-Eighteenth Centuries)," *Dutch Review of Church History* 83 (2003): 166-90.

[18] I discuss the procedures by which colonial congregations recruited ministers and the costs consistories incurred in "*Moederkerk* and *Vaderland,*" 153-242, 367-70.

in their native tongue." He warned the classis that where sermons were not preached and the sacraments not performed, churchgoers would seek them out in other communions, "for the people *will* sacrifice, if not at Jerusalem, then at Dan and Bethel...." Johannes Frelinghuysen, who routinely assisted shepherdless flocks himself, knew whereof he spoke; at the time he wrote that letter, there was barely one minister for three organized Dutch Reformed congregations in the colony, and there were preaching stations that were not organized congregations, as well.[19]

There *was*, however, a population willing to serve in Dutch pulpits in British North America that could be tapped to alleviate the shortage: some of the Dutch colonists themselves aspired to the Reformed ministry. In fact, some who were ministers at the time of the King's College controversy had been born in the colonies themselves. Two of the ministers aforementioned, for example, Theodorus Frelinghuysen, Jr., and his brother Johannes, had been born in North America. Both had been privately tutored by colonial ministers but had completed their educations at the University of Utrecht and had been examined and ordained by the Classis of Amsterdam. But this path to the ministry was not open to all colonial aspirants, in great measure because it was costly for both families (who generally bore the educational expenses) and congregations (who generally paid a share of the transportation expenses and all of the expenses for the examination and ordination).[20]

It was mainly for this reason that still other colonists were ordained to colonial pulpits without ever having set foot in Europe. These men were privately tutored by clergy in the colonies, sometimes augmenting their training with classes at a Presbyterian institution, the College of New Jersey. They were then examined and ordained in North America by gatherings of Dutch Reformed ministers (sometimes accompanied by elders) who, in most cases (at least before 1757) acted under authority delegated to them by the Classis of Amsterdam.[21]

While this route to the pulpit had advantages—notably a financial one—it had several drawbacks, as well. A significant problem was that it led to ordinations of men who did not live up to the ideal of the Dutch Reformed Church of a ministerial corps of university-educated men. By

---

[19]   Johannes Frelinghuysen to Classis of Amsterdam, 4 April 1753, in *ERNY*, V:3354. Emphasis added for clarity. The numbers of ministers and clergy are drawn from Mouw, "*Moederkerk* and *Vaderland*," 70-84.

[20]   I have written more extensively about the recruitment of colonial-born ministers in "*Moederkerk* and *Vaderland*," 225-42.

[21]   For more on the series of assemblies that promoted most ministers in this category, see my discussion in "*Moederkerk* and *Vaderland*," 267-73.

definition, these clergy of entirely colonial mint were *idiotae*. And the products of private tutoring were not universally well prepared by it—at least by the lights of some laity and clergy in colonial Dutch Reformed churches. The consistory of Kingston averred that allowing aspirants to enter pulpits by this path "tend[ed] to tarnish and depreciate the Gospel Ministry." Some, so trained, lacked "suitable knowledge" in theology; some even took "written sermons" into the pulpit and were "not ashamed" to read their sermons to the congregation, rather than delivering them from memory, as was then the norm in the Dutch Reformed Church. As reading to the congregation was the job of a lay employee of the church, such clergy degraded the ministerial office.[22]

Thus, the Dutch Reformed congregations of British North America faced some serious problems on Reformation Day, 1754, when the King's College controversy seemed to have concluded with the issuance of a royal charter including no provision for a Dutch professorship. With the benefit of two and a half centuries of hindsight, however, it is possible to discern two positive outcomes from the controversy for the Dutch Reformed of the colonies. First, the controversy shown a spotlight on the importance of theological education and ministerial training for the Dutch of North America. Obstacles precluding a quick solution to the problems the congregations faced were large and numerous, but in many ways it was the King's College controversy that brought widespread attention to a core issue and fostered conversations—and bitter arguments—that led (eventually) to what is arguably a very positive outcome.

The second silver lining for the Dutch Reformed of North America to the cloud of the King's College controversy was that it cultivated a sense of a collective identity among that population. That is not to say that the controversy's conclusion ushered in an era of mutual love and respect embracing all the clergy and laity who frequented Dutch sanctuaries in their various communities or that it heralded an era of irenic cooperation; far from it. But it did foster a sense that together the colonial congregations had a shared future—be that a bright one or a dark one. It is true that angry arguments would, in important ways, come to dominate church life at every level in the ensuing decades—dividing the colonial church as a whole, individual communities and congregations, and even families. Still, they engaged in these battles

---

[22] Consistory of Kingston to Classis of Amsterdam, 27 June 1755, in *ERNY*, V:3564. A very similar statement was made by the consistory of the New York City church; see their letter to Classis of Amsterdam 17 October 1754, in *ERNY*, V:3499.

against each other according to commonly understood rules and they fought with vigor because their common goal was the future welfare of the colonial Dutch Reformed Church. It is at least as important to observe that they came to understand that they shared common dangers and enemies, as well, that threatened the future of their church. The controversy had been waged by Presbyterians, Anglicans, and Dutch Reformed before a wide audience in the public press. At its apparent conclusion, wherein British authorities short-circuited negotiations and shut the Dutch out entirely in a raw, and seemingly capricious, display of sheer political might, the Dutch—no matter which side they had taken—had lost. And through all of the ink spilled in an effort to persuade the Dutch to enter the fray, they had been warned then of the myriad threats their churches faced.

And the stroke that ultimately befell them in October of 1754 with the issuance of the royal charter was not even the end of the matter nor an end to the embarrassment and acrimony attending it, within the Dutch Reformed community. In the final chapter, after the charter was issued, the consistory in Manhattan, which had been the body negotiating for a chair of Dutch theology at the proposed college, decided to pursue the matter no further. One of their number, however, disagreed: the senior minister. Taking action that may have been part of a plan the minister had hatched well before the royal charter was issued, he made a personal petition for an amendment to the college charter providing for the chair he wanted (and the chair he also probably wanted to occupy). His petition was granted. There were at least two major problems with the outcome, however. The first was that—although the professor was to be chosen by the New York City consistory, said professor was to serve at the pleasure of the college's overwhelmingly Anglican board. Second, while provision was made for the Dutch professor's appointment, no provision was made for his salary. Presumably the Dutch consistory would be expected to underwrite that.[23]

---

[23] "Personal Petition of Domine Ritzema to the Governor and Council for Additional Charger for a Dutch Professor of Divinity in Kings College," Kings College Board of Governors, minute, "Action of the Governor and Council on the Report Recommending an Additional Charter to the Charter of Kings College, to give a Divinity Professorship to the Dutch Church therein," and "Additional Charter; to the Charter of Kings College, Allowing a Professor of Divinity to be Appointed therein by the Dutch Church of New York City; Upon the Personal Application of Rev. John Ritzema, Senior minister of Said Church," 5, 13, 19, and 30 May 1755 in *ERNY*, V:3542-43, 3544, 3544-45, 3555.

The consistory apparently reacted with unanimity—excepting the aforementioned minister—and it expressed displeasure. Noting that the new measure gave the consistory the *opportunity* to appoint a professor of theology to King's College, the consistory also observed that it did not oblige its membership to do so. They decided not to avail themselves of the opportunity. The consistory also issued a strongly-worded rebuke to its senior minister, much of the text written for the eyes and ears of the whole congregation. The consistory accused its minister of acting "without the knowledge, advice or consent" of its membership, "nay against their will and purpose" and of acting in secret collusion with "gentlemen of the English Church." The consistory enumerated several points at which the minister had so strayed, including at the time of the drafting of the royal charter, the subsequent personal petition for a Dutch Reformed chair, and thereafter in helping to convince the legislature to release funds for the operation of the institution. On top of that, he had allowed himself to be appointed as one of the token non-Anglican members of the college's board. The professorship resulting from his actions, the consistory argued, was so vulnerable to the whims of Anglicans that "it in no respect answers to our conception of what would be advantageous for the upbuilding of our church...." The "rights and privileges" that should have been theirs had been given away; the Dutch chair at King's College—"a matter of so great importance"—had been so "dearly bought" that it was not worth filling.[24]

In the final episode of the King's College controversy, the Dutch had been duped, betrayed and defeated. One of their own had been a collaborator. It dispirited the Dutch and, as had been the case with much of the rhetoric unleashed throughout the battles in the press, it brought them together—at least in a common sense of anxiety and alarm. Five days after the royal charter for King's College was issued, Antonius Curtenius, a Dutch Reformed minister on Long Island wrote to the Classis of Amsterdam to tell them of recent events in New York (though he still was uncertain whether there would be a Dutch chair at the college). He was pessimistic about the opportunities for theological education in the colonies and worried that heresies might infiltrate the Dutch church, as the two colleges in the area "belonged to Independent Presbyterians" and Arminian Anglicans. Without a Dutch professor at the new college, Curtenius warned that it would be altogether too dangerous to allow "persons who had studied under such [Anglican] professors...into [the ministry of] our Church." He was

[24]   Consistory of New York City, act, 11 August 1755, in *ERNY,* V:3574-76.

pleased to observe, however, that "The Dutch are beginning to get their eyes open."[25]

Curtenius' younger colleague in New Jersey, David Marinus, expressed greater concern in a pamphlet he published not much later. He expressed amazement at "the astonishing Imposition of the incroaching Party"; the Anglicans sought to "monopolize" the new college. He also castigated his fellow Dutch colonists for their

> Infatuation, Stupidity and Lethargy, in doing so little...to assert and secure the inestimable Blessing of Blessings, by Treaties secured unto us, and now in Danger of being snatched from us all at one fatal Grasp; I mean the Enjoyment of Liberty of Conscience in public Worship, and in Church Discipline.

Vigilance and action were urgently needed: "Come on then,...be aroused out of your Lethargy; Start! O! start from your Enchantment." Failure to do so would result in being "ignominiously...despoiled" of their "Religion."[26]

Many came to believe that one of the most pressing needs was a Dutch Reformed institution for the education of men who aspired to the ministry. Support flowed more freely, however, from the tongue and pen than it did from the purse. As noted above, Marinus and Theodorus Frelinghuysen, Jr., became strong advocates for this proposal just as the King's College received its charter, and the idea drew broad, though not unanimous, support among Dutch colonists in the days, months, and years following the issuance of that charter. Theodorus Frelinghuysen, Jr., saw the fate of the colonial Dutch church hanging in the balance: "everyone in the land" was working diligently to give their own denominations the upper hand: the Anglicans with their college in New York, the Presbyterians in New Jersey. Unless the Dutch could erect their own academy, their church would be destroyed and all of the excesses and heresies of the Anglicans and Presbyterians would proliferate.[27] Not all Dutch Reformed were persuaded, however—on either side of

---

[25] Curtenius to Classis of Amsterdam, 5 November 1754, in *ERNY,* V:3519.

[26] [Marinus], *Remark,* 6, 11.

[27] This information is drawn from what appears to be a draft of the plan written by Theodorus Jr. He was likely circulating this document to promote his plan. The manuscript can be found, without date or signature, in Records of the Reformed Churches of Marbletown, Rochester, and Wawarsing, Special Collections, Rutgers University Library, New Brunswick N.J. My translation. Though there is a note in the folder indicating that it had been written 17 April 1755, it seems more likely it was the document referred to by Curtenius in his letter to the Classis of Amsterdam, 20 February 1755, in *ERNY,* V:3532-34.

the Atlantic. The Classis of Amsterdam responded to the proposed academy with scorn and a sarcastic tone wholly uncharacteristic of the measured tone it otherwise adopted for its correspondence:

> How large an undertaking! What wonderful plans! We are, gentlemen...overwhelmed with amazement.... The idea [of a university] is indeed grand, and if it is as important as it is thought, the best. But the Classis, with all the acuteness it possesses, is not able to imagine in what place, or by what authority, or by what means, or out of what treasury, that University is to be established; neither where the Professor will be found who is to teach in that University. Indeed, the Classis, not having been at all consulted in the matter, is not obliged to weary its brains in seeking to interpret this enigma; especially since the opportunity is given... to wait for the time when this new phenomenon shall appear in the American Ecclesiastical Heavens.[28]

Notable among the North American opponents of a Dutch academy was the senior minister in New York City, the man sternly rebuked by his own consistory for his actions with respect to the proposed Dutch professorate at King's College. He could be found still pressing the proposed King's College Dutch professorship in his correspondence nearly a decade and a half after his consistory had rejected the idea and rebuked him for his behavior in pursuing it.[29]

Despite the calls for an "academy of our own" where would-be Dutch Reformed ministers could "be instructed in the Doctrine of our Reformed Church," an institution was not immediately forthcoming. Yet the fruits of those early proposals, hammered out in lead type on the anvil of the King's College controversy, eventually resulted in two Dutch Reformed institutions of higher learning. The first, the Queen's College, chartered in New Jersey in 1766, was envisioned to be both a training ground for ministers as well as a place where men could be instructed in other "useful" disciplines. Some predicted it would succeed because its founders avoided any reference in its charter to the controversies which had preceded its founding, and because it was to be, "founded on the constitution of the Church of Holland, as established in the national Synod of Dor[tdrecht]"; Rutgers University is this year celebrating the 250th anniversary of that charter.[30]

---

28 Classis of Amsterdam to "those who call themselves a regular Coetus," 9 December 1755, in *ERNY*, V:3637-38.

29 Ritzema to Classis of Amsterdam, 21 March 1769, in *ERNY*, VI: 4143-44.

30 Abraham Lott to John Henry Livingston, September 1767, in Alexander Gunn, *Memoirs of the Rev. John Henry Livingston, D. D.* (New York: Rutgers Press, 1829), 187.

The other institution that eventually arose from those early proposals originated with the 1784 appointment of John Henry Livingston to the office of professor of theology by the synod of what was a relatively new North American denomination, the "Reformed Dutch Churches in the States of New York and New Jersey,"[31] in (as its name suggests) an even newer political context. By 1810, the professorate was relocated to the hometown of the institution now known as Rutgers, but the college was then in truly dire straits. It had ceased to function entirely in 1794, and its trustees hoped they could forge an educational alliance with the Dutch Reformed Churches that would bring about an educational revival in New Brunswick. That alliance prospered and, in subsequent years, that which had simply been known as the "professorate" was, in a sense, promoted by the Reformed synod to a "Theological School," an institutional structure was instituted, and the faculty enlarged. In time, on the foundation laid by the synod of the Dutch Reformed Churches in 1784, the institution now known as New Brunswick Theological Seminary was established. The university and the seminary of New Brunswick were sisters by birth, though the younger (the seminary) had played the role of the rich and liberal aunt to the older (Rutgers) in the early decades of their alliance.[32] In more recent history, of course, that relationship has changed. Rutgers does not depend upon the seminary to fill its classrooms or to funnel charitable donations into its treasury. The seminary is dwarfed by the massive population and infrastructure of Rutgers, now a state university. Indeed, the seminary has recently become a yet smaller physical presence in New Brunswick, having sold a good bit of the "holy hill" in New Brunswick to the expanding university, in order to raise funds to improve infrastructure on the campus and to ensure the future financial stability of the institution. Rutgers, too, has changed. It is now a large and growing state university. As an educational institution it remains faithful to its founders, at least insofar as it resists domination by the Church of England or any Calvinist faction among the descendants of the inhabitants of New Netherland and still instructs young "men" in "useful" disciplines. Its leadership no longer, however, sees preparing graduates for service in churches as one of its core roles.

New Brunswick Theological Seminary, on the other hand, has a grand tradition of theological education and scholarship. For more than

---

[31]   The name, judging from the early records of the denomination, was not yet fixed.

[32]   John W. Coakley, *New Brunswick Theological Seminary: An Illustrated History, 1784-2014,* The Historical Series of the Reformed Church in America, ed. Donald J. Bruggink, no. 83 (Grand Rapids: Eerdmans, 2014), 1-26.

three decades, John Coakley has been a member of the seminary faculty. In conjunction with his long-enduring efforts to prepare women and men for the ministry, Coakley has devoted his considerable energies and acumen to scholarly research and writing as well. Committed, as he has been, to researching and teaching history, it seems altogether likely that those who founded both New Brunswick educational institutions would have admired of his work: there is no evidence that he has ever expressed loyalty to the Church of England and he has practiced and taught an arguably "useful" discipline. His contributions to the Reformed Church in America, as one who has trained countless people for its offices, his contributions to his community and region, as an agent of the Reformed Church reaching out to and serving churches and individuals around them, and his contributions as a scholar who has served his denomination, his seminary, and fellow scholars through his insightful research on an impressive variety of subjects—all of these deserve tribute and celebration.

CHAPTER 9

Student Life at NBTS
The Diary of Samuel M. Zwemer

Matthew Gasero and Russell L. Gasero

Introduction

It is an honor to have an opportunity to participate in a festschrift for John Coakley. He has been a wonderful colleague and friend. His knowledge, insight, and wisdom has been valuable for the RCA Archives and helped to ease its passage through a number of obstacles.

One of the hallmarks of John's teaching and work with students has been his desire for students to have access to original source material as part of their experience of Christian history. That is evident by his co-editing of *Readings in World Christian History*[1]. For many years, John has taught Reformed church history at New Brunswick Theological Seminary and has selected a variety of source material from the RCA Archives for students to study and to which they can relate.

The purpose was never just to read some old documents and papers to fill in a student's understanding of the past, but rather to engage the documents. He always urged them to examine what he selected and

---

[1] John W. Coakley and Andrea Sterk, *Readings in World Christian History* (Maryknoll, NY: Orbis Books, 2004).

Samuel Zwemer (*left*) with fellow student
James Cantine and John G. Lansing (*center*)

suggested they see what questions are raised. They were encouraged to push further, gain a more intimate and deeper relationship with that past and then understand how it has affected the present. To that end, the selection presented here fits a main focus of John's teaching.

This is the diary of Samuel Marinus Zwemer during his second term as a student at New Brunswick Theological Seminary. It is one of the only extant diaries of a student at the end of the nineteenth century at the seminary. The diary is transcribed as it was written with underlining intact, misspellings, and abbreviations.[2] Fellow students of Zwemer are indicated in the footnotes.[3]

Samuel M. Zwemer and his diary

Samuel Marinus Zwemer is best known as "The Apostle to Islam." He helped to establish what was to become the RCA's Arabian Mission.

---

[2] For more information about New Brunswick Seminary and student life see John W, Coakley, *New Brunswick Theological Seminary: An Illustrated History, 1784-2014* (Grand Rapids, MI: Wm. B. Eerdmans Publishing Co., 2014).

[3] More information about individual ministers in the diary may be found in Russell L. Gasero, *Historical Directory of the Reformed Church in America, 1628-2000* (Grand Rapids, MI: Wm. B. Eerdmans Publishing Company, 2000). More information on the faculty may be found in John Howard Raven, *Biographical Record*, New Brunswick, NJ: New Brunswick Theological Seminary, 1934.

James Cantine was a year ahead of him and went out to the field firs, but Zwemer promoted the mission and became known more widely than Cantine. He became the face of the mission and, in a large part, the face of Christian mission to Islam to many in the United States.[4]

Zwemer was born in Vriesland, Michgan, on April 12, 1867. He attended Hope College and graduated in 1887 and then attended New Brunswick Theological Seminary. He graduated from New Brunswick in 1890. During his student years he also undertook a study of medicine on his own. More needs to be researched and written about Zwemer,[5]and these diaries will open up new source material for scholars. At this writing, the diaries are being digitized and decisions will be made in regard to the best manner in which to make them available.

This early desire for mission is seen clearly in his diary. His love for mission, both domestic and foreign, was already at work during his first year at seminary. His ability to promote and raise funds is clearly demonstrated as early as his second semester as a student. By the end of his first year, he was addressing the General Synod and conversant with the leadership of the mission boards.

Zwemer's diary indicates a young man with a strong drive and a sharp focus. He seeks to extend that focus and drive to others that he encounters, as well. The selections transcribed here represent three separate months during his second and third semesters as a student at New Brunswick seminary. The entry for June includes his attendance at the General Synod of the Reformed Church in America.

The Diary

January, Sunday 1. 1888.

Arose at 8.30. Attended Prayer Meeting at Med. Miss Training Institute. 118 E 45th St. New York. Breakfast with the boys & ladies. Went to Dr. J. Hall's church & heard a fine sermon on missions text. Ps. 96:10 Congregational Singing. Took dinner. Went to Mission for Xtian Jews conducted by Rev. Freshman. Had an interesting class of Jewish boys — regular heathen! Went from there to the Roosevelt St. Mission. One of the worst places in N.Y. Was insulted & thrown with dirt by one

---

[4]   For more about Zwemer and the mission see Lewis R. Scudder, III, *The Arabian Mission's Story: In Search of Abraham's Other Son* (Grand Rapids, MI: Wm. B. Eerdmans Publishing Co., 1998).

[5]   See J. Christy Wilson, *Apostle to Islam. A biography of Samuel M. Zwemer* (Grand Rapids, MI: Baker Book House, 1952).

First page of Samuel Zwemer's student diary.

of the boys in my class. Took lunch at the Dispensary. Went to Bleecker St. Mission. Very pleasant meeting about 12 <u>inquirers</u>. Many promised to Reform. A Happy New Year's day!

January, Monday 2. 1888.

Left Dr. Doucomt [sp?] at 9.30 Took 3rd Ave elevated car for Bowery. Walked to Ferry Took train for New Brunswick Spent P.M. in reading & writing.

Was invited to take supper at Dr. Lansing[6].

Spent a very pleasant evening seeing Egyptian curiosities etc.

Saw Photographs (taken from mummy) of Rameses I & II & of Seti I. Also coins & other things.

Went home at 10. & Retired at eleven.

My vacation days have been very pleasant.

Recd. A fine New Years Card from A. B. Reed & also from my sisters.

---

[6]   John Gulian Lansing (1851-1906), Professor of Old Testament Languages and Exegesis, 1884-1898.

January, Tuesday 3. 1888.

Spent A.M. In reading & writing letters to Father & Sisters & Brother F.J.Z[7].

Went up town & purchased a book- case & some other things for my room.

Spent P.M. In reading & studying.

Read Part of Revelation.

What a glorious book full of promises.

Wrote to Miss A.B. Reed in Evening. Told her of the New York Mission'y society.

Read the Harpers for January. "Virginia of Virginia" is a fine story.

Retired at 12 M.

Enjoyed a season of prayer for day. "Ah for a closer walk with God." It is only near Him that one is safe.

January, Wednesday 4. 1888.

Arose at 7.30 Attended all Recitations. Dr Woodbridge[8] spoke on the benefit of Symbols in preaching. Went up town & received a Registered package — a New Years present from home. A penwiper $2. & a long letter from Sister Rika.

Spent afternoon in study. Recd. money in full from Rev. Nies & sent same to J.F.Z[9].

Attended Prayer Meeting — Week of prayer — in 3rd Ref. Church. Subject, Personal Work. A very good meeting. Spent a pleasant season. of prayer in Mr. Andrew's[10] Room. Read Bible & Retired.

Weather today warm for January. No snow as yet.

January, Thursday 5. 1888.

Arose at 7. Attended Recitations. Dr. De Witt[11] discussed John's Logos [Λογοσ] vs. Philo's. We came to the conclusion that John may

---

[7] Frederick James Zwemer (1858-1903). More information about RCA clergy may be found in Russell L. Gasero, *Historical Directory of the Reformed Church in America, 1628-2000* (Grand Rapids, MI: Wm. B. Eerdmans Publlishing Co., 2000).

[8] Samuel Merrill Woodbridge (1819-1905), Professor of Pastoral Theology, Ecclesiastical History and Church Government, 1857-1901

[9] James Frederick Zwemer (1850-1921)

[10] Lewis Curry Andrew (1852-1938)

[11] John DeWitt (1821-1906), Professor of Biblical Literature, 1863-84 and Professor of Hellenistic Greek and New Testament Exegesis, 1884-92

have borrowed the word from Philo the idea was new & transcendent. Received a letter from Brother P.J.Z[12]. Wrote to Passaic to get an agent for Father's book of poems.

Studied lessons. Read Greek according to custom with Rev. Willis[13] from 5:30-6. Exercised in Gymnasium Attended Evening Prayers. "[ditto - Attended] New Brunswick Choral Society. Read Bible & Retired.

Very pleasant day. Sorry I could not attend Prayer Meeting this evening.

January, Friday 6. 1888.

Arose at 7.00 Read Bible Attended Recitations, Handed Essay on Apostles Creed to Dr. Mabon[14].

Studied lessons & wrote to Brother Peter. Wrote article for "De Hope" on Missions. Expect to write an article for above paper every week. Spent evening in study & conversation.

January, Saturday 7. 1888.

Spent day in Study & writing. Read Book of Numbers.

Wrote essay on "The Connection of The Old & New Testaments" for Dr. Woodbridge.

Showed their connection by Design, Symbolism, Prophecy Quotations. Hist. Of Jews & the subject of both — Christ. Attended meeting of choir. Read & studied in evening. Enjoyed a season of prayer today.

God is always nearer than we think if we will only call upon Him.

January, Sunday 8. 1888.

Arose at 7.00 Attended service in 4th Ref. Church. Dr. Mabon on words "Ye are not your own." Consecration service. Good. Attended S.S. Meeting. Seven in my class. Lesson on Feeding The Multitude.

Went to Union Communion Service (after week of prayer) of all the denominations of the city — held in 2nd Ref. Church. Very impressive service "One Lord, One Faith One Baptism."

Went to Throop Ave. Mission after tea.

---

12   Peter John Zwemer (1868-98)
13   Ralph Willis (1815-95), Rector of Herzog Hall, 1880-88
14   William Augustus Van Vrankon Mabon (1822-92), Professor of Didactic and Polemic Theology, 1881-92.

Led the Meeting. Subject: The Good Shepherd. About 60 were present. No Inquirers. Walked home with Hieber[15]. Had a talk with Andrew about mission-work in the West. Retired.

A Very pleasant Sabbath.

January, Monday 9. 1888.

Attended Recitations in A.M. & read <u>commentaries</u> for my sermon. Received a <u>postal</u> from Fred[16] – <u>J.Z.</u> – very cold in Dakota 20 below zero. Here it is 30 above.

Exercised in the Gymnasium. Attended Preaching in Chapel. Mr. <u>Tilton</u> text "Search the Scriptures" Very good delivery but commonplace sermon. Went to Rehearsal of musical association in <u>Y.M.C.A.</u> Hall. Read Bible – <u>Timothy</u> until 12 M. Retired. Weather fine & warm.

January, Tuesday 10. 1888.

Arose at 8.00 & missed my breakfast. Attended Recitations
Hebrew Dr. Lansing
Methodology Dr. Mabon.
Preaching Dr. Demarest[17].

Mr. Andrews preached on "Resurrection" – a good argumentative sermon but not practical enough. No thought for the sinner. Delivery good.

Spent P.M. in study. Prepared essay for the Mission-Band on Life of John Williams – what a glorious life – a martyr death – a golden crown. Read his book on Polynesia. Mr. Wykhoff was present. Commenced to write sermon on John. 4:10 – My first effort. I hope it may be a first-fruits acceptable to my Master.

Retired at 11.30 P.M. Weather fine & warm.

January, Wednesday 11. 1888.

Attended Recitations.
Read & Studied.
Attended Preaching by Mr. Phelps[18] in the evening. Very good sermon on Xtian Benevolence. Text: the history of the widow's mite. Very earnest in language but not strong in delivery.

---

15   Louis Hieber (1863-1908)
16   Frederick James Zwemer (1858-1903).
17   David D. Demarest (1819-98), Professor of Pastoral Theology and Sacred Rhetoric, 1865-98
18   Philip Tertius Phelps (1862-1944)

Attended meeting of Soc. of Inquiry. Heard papers on Church Music & on the Episcopal Church. Acted as Sect'y.

Went to final rehearsal of Musical association. Very crowded stage. Retired at 11.30 after reading <u>Bible</u>.

January, Thursday 12. 1888.

Arose at 7. Attended Recit- at 9 A. M. Studied. Attended Instruction in Elocution by Prof. Peabody[19] in A.M. Gave a Prayer Meety [Meeting] talk on John 10. Exercised in Gymnasium. Attended 1st Concert given by the "N.B. Musical Association.

Program very good. Sang 1st Bass in the Chorus. Received letter notifying me of my appointment as one of the visitors of the Alliance formed by the churches for a Christian canvass of all the families of the town. I hope this movement will do much good. But I fear it is too much machinery for such work.

Retired at 12.00.

January, Friday 13. 1888.

Attended Recitations.

Dr. Mabon spoke on the different lives of Christ & recommended Edersheims as one of the best.

Spent P.M. in study. Attended a meeting of the New Brunswick Christian Alliance in the 4th Ref. Ch.

Dr. Mabon addressed us. Called on Miss. Willis & notified her of her appointment as one of the visitors. Went to Bethel Mission in evening with Frank Scudder.[20] Small audience but a pleasant time. Recd. letter from Sister Mary.

Studied & Read.

Retired at 12.30 A.M.

January, Saturday 14. 1888.

Arose at 7.30. Breakfast. Oh how sin draws us away from His presence. Came back in prayer. Wrote at sermon. Finished it before dinner. Went to Library & got several books on Missions.

The Gardener A. Sage Library has 49,500 volumes.

Exercised in Gymnasium. Read Greek with Rev. Willis Matthew's Gospel.

[19] Stephen George Peabody (1830-98), Instructor in Elocution, 1865-67, later at Princeton Seminary

[20] Frank Seymour Scudder (1862-1956)

Attended Choir Meeting. Read Bible & Retired. Oh that our prayer might always be "Oh for a closer walk with God"

Discussed to-day at the dinner table whether the need for workers was greater in the home than in the foreign field.

When will the boys see that a soul in Afrika = one in America! But they fail to see it.

January, Sunday 15. 1888.

Rainy & Muddy. Attended church in the A.M. Dr. Campbell[21] "Let Brotherly Love continue" Very eloquent. Home strikes. "Old how those Xtians love one another". Would that we might have more Xtian unity. Took dinner at Dr. Mabons. Pleasant time. Mrs. Mabon is a fine motherly sort of woman. Dr. Campbell in P.M. "Be not slothful to follow.....who through faith have inherited the promises." Good sermon on "Example". He spoke of Jerry Mc auley. SS class 8. Pleasant time. Lesson on Peter's Faith.

Attended Prayer meeting: "Trust" Remained at home in evening read Deuteronomy. & Mission Papers by Lowrie. Very good. Retired at 10 P.M. Very tired. Spent a blessed Sabbath day.

January, Monday 16. 1888.

Attended Recitations as usual.

Wrote a letter to H.V.S Peeke[22].

January, Tuesday 17. 1888.

Arose at 6.30 Studied. Attended Recitations.

Dr. Mabon commended my essay. Read & Studied in A.M. Wrote a letter to sister Mary. Exercised in the Gymnasium. Chest measure to-day 38 1/8 in. weight 154# & height 5:11 1/8 ft.

Attended Meeting of Mission Band. Very Interesting. Mr. Scudder led the meeting. Was appointed Secty. & Treasurer.

Spent evening in reading & writing. Weather cold. 15°.

Rain & warmer towards evening.

January, Wednesday 18. 1888.

Attended Recitations as usual.

Led Prayer Meeting. "Ye are my witnesses".

[21] William Henry Campbell (1808-1890). He served several professorships at the seminary from 1851 to 1886 as well as the presidency of Rutgers College from 1863 to 1882 (see Raven, *Biographical Directory*, p. 29).

[22] Harmon Van Slyke Peeke (1866-1929)

Studied. Gymnasium.

Recited Greek: Math 24. Commenced to study Hartshornes Conspectus v [of] Med. Science.

Read Joshua & part of Judges to-day.

Wrote letter to Prof. Lorsett & to Mr. Wilder of Princeton.

Spoke with Phelps on the practicability of holding a Miss'y Conference here of Union, Princeton & Lancaster Seminaries. Expect to carry it out if possible.

January, Thursday 19. 1888.

Attended Recitations.

Attended Lectures on Elocution by Prof. Peabody of Princeton. Read Rom. 8.

Studied & wrote letters to the boys at Lancaster Seminary & Crozer Seminary to see about the practicability of holding a Missionary Alliance at N.B. Wrote to Philip Sanlen, about our College Paper.

Exercised in the Gymnasium. Recited Greek. Studied Sermon. Read Medicine & Read book of Judges & part of I Samuel. Did not study my Bible enough last year but hope to do better this year.

The book of Judges is full of illustrations & curious texts. Recd. Letter from M. Assewande (?) in relation to the American Bible Society.

January, Friday 20. 1888.

[No Entry]

January, Saturday 21. 1888.

Called on Dr. Campbell today. Had a pleasant talk with him on Missions. Recd. Postal from Jas F. telling of the terrible Blizzard in Dakota & Iowa — hundreds of lives lost! by exposure to the cold.

Coal famine in Kansas.

9°+ in New Brunswick & very little snow.

January, Sunday 22. 1888.

Arose at 7.00 Dressed. Breakfast. Read Bible until Church time. Heard good sermon by the Old Doctor. on Xtian Fellowship. Very cold day thermometer..-3°.

Attended S.S. in P.M. & church Heard Sermon by Campbell on Xtian Endeavor. Prayer Meeting led by Sharpley[23] Recd. Letter from

---

[23]   Giles Herbert Sharpley (1864-?) student in the class after Zwemer.

F.J.Z. telling of his narrow escape from freezing to death on Jan 13th 88.
Read it to the boys.

Recd. several letters from R.P. Wilder on Missions. Attended
Domestic Mission Meeting in 2nd Ref. Ch. & heard a ridiculous account
of domestic missions in Iowa by Dr. Hutton[24]. How ignorant "The East"
is of the Western Church.

January, Monday 23. 1888.

Read Bible. Wrote letters. studied sermon. Recd. letter from Nellie
with $6 inclosed and also the first no. v 1 Missy. Review v 1 [of the]
world. Attended Recitations. Read letter from F.J.Z. To Dr. Woodbridge
& Dr. Mabon.

Studied in evening & wrote letters.

Read Bible I Samuel & II Samuel. Davids history is very instructive.
Retired at 11.30 P.M.

January, Tuesday 24. 1888.

Arose at 7.00 A.M. Studied & Preached <u>my first</u> sermon. John 4:10
Was criticised on some grammatical faults & because I omitted one
petition from the Lords Prayer.

For the rest I was happily calm in my delivery & Dr. Demarest said
it was "a good first effort"!

I expect to change it as soon as I have time & opportunity.

Attended Meeting of the Mission Band. Acted as secty. Got an
idea into my head that our Seminary ought to send its own Missy to the
foreign field at 7.30 P.M. Spoke to Phelps. Raised 150$ before 11 P.M.
among 1 [the] faculty & boys v 1 [of the] Seminary. God has blessed also
this effort of mine.

January, Wednesday 25. 1888.

Attended Recitations.

Did some more collecting now nearly $200. I hope we can raise
$1700 by Thursday evening & send out our man in May. Attended
Prayer Meety [Meeting].

Wrote letters to all the Seminaries in New York New Jersey &
Penn. To invite them to a District Miss'y Alliance at New Brunswick on
Feb 24th next.

---

[24]   Mancius H. Hutton (1837-1909), at that time he was pastor at Second Reformed
Church in New Brunswick.

Went out collect[ing] money with Philip Phelps. Raised about $75 more.

Society of Inquiry in evening. Good Meeting. Read & Retired early.

January, Thursday 26. 1888.

Day of Prayer for Colleges. Remained at home with F.S. Scudder who was sick. Attended Meeting in P.M. led by Jno. Allen[25] of the Senior class at the Seminary. Lively meeting.

At an after meeting the sum for our own Missionary was raised to $550. I subscribed $10 yearly. Studied & read in evening. Wrote to "De Hope" & to the boys at Holland

Very pleasant day. A little warmer outside & in my heart.

Oh that the boys at all the different Seminaries would awake & consecrate themselves unreservedly to God's Service.

Paul calls himself a "doulos [δουλοσ] of Jesus Xt. & can we not <u>be</u> the same.

January, Friday 27. 1888.

Attended Recitations.

Dr. Mabon spoke against form & endless liturgy in church service. A simple service attracts the sinner more than cloth & gilt. Whitfield said: "When I first came to America they had wooden churches & golden preachers but now they have golden churches & wooden preachers".

Heard Rev. G. Taylor[26] in the P. M. a very earnest speaker & city Missionary, at work in Hartford Connecticut. He addressed the Sem. boys for an hour this P.M. He recommends active laymen organization & more earnestness to win souls & less desire for Denominational glory. Read. Wrote to Maud & retired at 11.00 P.M.

January, Saturday 28. 1888.

Studied all A.M. Wrote for "De Hope" on Missions Read & Studied in P.M.

Had a call from Mr. Merril of Union Seminary. Received a Mission Chart as a present from Mr. Wilder of Union. Bought some ink & mucilage today. Sent catalogue of Seminary to Mils A.B.R.

Went to choir-meeting; Saw moon-eclipse— nearly total at 7:15 P.M. Had a pleasant time at Dr. Mabon's.

---

[25]   John Mitchell Allen (1861-1892).
[26]   Graham Taylor (1851-1938), NBTS, 1873.

Spent evening in writing to P.J.Z. & studying.

——

Commenced to read the Epistle of James in the original.

January, Sunday 29. 1888.

Arose at 7 A.M. Read & held prayer-meeting in my room with some of the Grammar-School boys. Attended Service in 4th Ref. Ch. with-Mr. Phelps. Sang in choir. Subject "Anchor of the Soul" — Dr. Campbell Attended S.S. in P.M. Translated Dutch letter for Dr. Drury.

Heard Sermon in P.M. by Dr. Campbell on "The Pharisee & Publican." Very eloquent effort. No Prayer Meeting. Read Bible & Mullers life v [of] Trust in Evening. F.S. Scudder made me a call.

January, Monday 30. 1888.

Attended Recitations in A.M. Dr. Woodbridge gave a lecture on Proverbs. & its relations to the rest of the Bible. Very Valuable book to learn by heart. Read & studied in P.M. Wrote letters. Exercised in the Gymnasium. Read Greek with Rev. Willis (Jas 2.)

Spent evening in my room.

Received a letter from my sister Maud.

January, Tuesday 31. 1888.

Arose at 7.00 A.M. Read & Studied. Attended Recitations. Sermon by Mr. Furbeck[27]. Very good language but not practical; too much oratory & not enough "home-thrust" Studied in the P.M.

Read Medicine one hour. Exercised in the Gymnasium. Led Meeting of the Mission Band.

Subject "the South Sea Islands." Very pleasant meeting. Attended 4th Ref. Ch. Prayer Meeting. Dr. Mabon led. Was invited to take a sleigh-ride to-morrow night, with a party of young people.

Walked home with Mr. Phelps. Read Bible. Wrote letter to Miss. Kollen Retired at 12 P.M.

♦ ♦ ♦

June, Friday 1. 1888.

Spent day in sightseeing in and around New York. Visited statue of liberty on Bedloe's Island.

Very imposing sight. Brother Fred came in town from Dakota to-day. Attended evening lecture in Collegiate Church in Evening.

---

[27] George Warren Furbeck (1864-1926), NBTS, 1890.

June, Saturday 2. 1888.

Spent day in New York

Went to Port Richmond Staten Island and took dinner at Mrs. E.B. Horton's. Pleasant time. Spoke with Mrs. E.B. on Home Missions. Left at 10.30 & arrived at New York at 12.00.

June, Sunday 3. 1888.

Attended church services to-day. A.M. Dr. H. Crosby & Parkhurst. P.M. heard Secty. Warburton on Social Purity. & visited R.R. Y.M.C.A.
Attended service at Brooklyn Tabernacle in evening. Text: "Sufficent to the day is the evil thereof".
Talmadge was not at his best.

June, Monday 4. 1888.

Left New York at 10 A.M. for New Brunswick. Packed trunk & made some farewell calls. Had a pleasant time on the train with Bros. F.J.Z. Went to Weehawken P.R. (?) & spent night at Rev. I.W. Gowen Very social time.
Fire in evening at Guttenberg near bye.

June, Tuesday 5. 1888.

Left Grove Parsonage at 10 A.M. train for New York. Called at Synod Rooms Received $10 from Rev. H.N. Cobb (?) on account. Called at Mrs. Sandham on 45th street
Took Elevated R.R. For port of Jay St. where we took "Kaaterskill" Steamer for Catskill. Arrived there at 5 A.M.

June, Wednesday 6. 1888.

Am staying at the Prospect Park Hotel. Many delegates to Genl. Synod have already arrived.
The hotel is first-class in all respects.
Attended meeting of Synod in A.M. Rev. M.H. Hutton was elected President. & P. Moerdyke vice president.

No business was transacted.
Rev. Shepherd preached the sermon in the evening from Acts 1:3.
Quite good but very long & tedious.
Heavy thunder-shower in evening.

June, Thursday 7. 1888.

Attended sessions of Synod. Heard discussion on Liturgy-question quite animated. Synod sent greetings to Holland with Rev. Dosker. & also cablegram to London Miss'y Conference. Wrote at Translation in evening. Very pleasant time.

Met Mr. & Mrs. Van Cleef. She is a nice social lady & enjoys hearing about the "West" etc. Brother F.J.Z. _ "the Missionary from Dakota is quite lionized here. Retired in Room 19 at 12 M.

June, Friday 8. 1888.

Attended sessions of Synod. Evening meeting was on Sabbath Schools & on Catechisms & instruction. Revs. Williamson & Peter Moerdyke made stirring speeches especially the latter. He emphasized the importance of Catechetical Instruction above the S.S. & its machinery.

Was asked by Dr. H.E. Cobb to speak next Monday night before Synod on the Student Volunteer question. Declined with thanks. Would like to have had the opportunity but I fear I shall hurt myself by making people think I seek prominence.

Retired with Bros. F.J.Z. At 11.30 P.M.

June, Saturday 9. 1888.

Attended Session of Synod. No special business.
Paid Bill at Hotel & went after dinner with Rev. E.A. Collier & Rev. Cox to Kinderhook N.Y. to speak on children's day. Spoke with Mr. Boyd Supt. Am. Bible Soc & found work for P.J.Z. for summer. Ferry to Hudson Station Train to Stuyvesant & thence by stage-line to Kinderhook. Pleasant little village; population largely retired merchants etc. Two banks & printing establishment. Spent evening in conversation & music.

Took walk, to Cemetery & saw Van Buren Monument. President Van Buren's residence is near Kinderhook.
Retired at 11:30.

June, Sunday 10. 1888.

Arose at 7 A.M. Attended service in Kinderhook Church. Rev. H.M. Cox. addressed the children in the A.M. Church is very old (1727.) Address good. Rehearsed after service for evening (!)

Spent P.M. in reading etc.

Addressed S.S. in evening Subject "Let your light shine" [candle talk illustration]

Children seemed to enjoy it very much.

Examined old church records of Kinderhook & received an old sermon for a present dated 1797 in the holland language — (manuscript.)

June, Monday 11. 1888.

Arose at 7.00. Received $5 from Rev. Collier for my work. Took stage-line to Stuyvezant & then train for Catskill station. Met Miss. Anderson- a real pleasant old maid. Attended Synod in P.M. no special business.

Evening session of Synod was in behalf of Foreign Missions. Good. Rev. Ballagh, Rev. Scudder, L.R. Scudder, & Rev. Sawyer spoke on the subject.

Rev. Cobb had asked me to speak, but I declined.

June, Tuesday 12. 1888.

Attended sessions of Synod. Synod voted $110000.00 at least for Foreign Missions! Good, but not enough for the ability of our church. At the afternoon session a ballot was taken for a Professor at Holland Theol. Seminary. Rev. J.W. Beardslee D.D. received at second ballot 102 votes & was therefore declared elected. How strange things form out. Who would have dreamed 8 years ago that theology would be restored at Hope & that Rev. Steffens & Beardslee would be its instructors!!!

This evening addresses were made on behalf of Domestic Missions by Rev. Gamble, F.J. Zwemer and Beardslee

Brother F.J. did himself credit. and was applauded heartily.

June, Wednesday 13. 1888.

Attended Synod-sessions. No important business. After dinner I packed my satchel & took omnibus for Steamboat Station.

The scenery along the Hudson & about Prospect Park is grand. I am sorry however that I could not take a trip up the mountains.

Arrived at Albany at 6 P.M. Took State Street car to Hamilton St.

Tea at Mrs. Dykstra

Met many old friends. Albany of 12 years ago is nearly the same!

Spoke on For. Missions in Holland language before a moderate audience in evening. Found some, but not much trouble with finding words to express myself. Retired at 12 M.

June, Thursday 14. 1888.

Spent A.M. In a visit to the Albany Capitol.

Very beautiful building — especially the Assembly Room — but also a sample of American Architecture — not durable.

Spoke before the women of the church at Jay St. & recommended the support of a native teacher. Distributed Missy. literature & took some subscriptions for Mission Field.

Supper at Mrs. De Rouville. (Le Daai)

Called on Mr. Phelps in evening & was very kindly received. Annie is an invalid. Retired after writing letters etc.

June, Friday 15. 1888.

Took train at 8:25 for Rochester. Mr. Van Drielle for company. Made a pleasant acquaintance on the road Miss. Porter of Farmersville, N.Y.

Took stop-over at Syracuse. Visited Y.M.C.A. & saw town.

Train at 4:55 for Rochester. Found quarters at the Temperance Hotel 212 E. Main St.

Very good, clear. Xtian place. to stay. Retired after writing some letters.

June, Saturday 16. 1888.

Arose early; took bath & shave. Breakfast. Surface-car for 49 Concord Ave Rev. P. De. Bruins. Saw City in company with Revs. Van Doren & Broek in P.M. Powers art Gallery.

Took train at 3.07 P.M. for Palmyra. Stage for Marion. Received very kindly by S. Hoogeboom. Mrs. H is very pleasant.

Spent evening in conversation & in rehearsing "Auld Lang Syne" & College days.

Rev. H. asked me to conduct both services tomorrow. Accepted.

June, Sunday 17. 1888.

Breakfast. S.S. service at 10.30. Church at 12 M.

Spoke in Holland Language on Acts 16:9.

Large attendance — full house. Was greatly helped in speaking.

Succeeded in interesting both Shepherd & Flock. Last year this church gave average .05 per per member to For. Missions!!

Hope to see a change next year. Rested in P.M. & read Van Oostezee's Practical Theology.

Meeting in evening. Missy lecture — maps, photographs etc. Interested audience & speaker. I am beginning to feel more free in public.

Met consistory after service & after a cup of tea at the parsonage retired.

June, Monday 18. 1888.

Rev. S. Hoogeboom drove me to depot at 7 A.M. Wrote letters while waiting for train. Train at 9.30 for Rochester. Arrived at R. at 10.45. Went to Rev. P. De Bruin who took me to Mr. A.W. Hopeman where I am now staying. He is a contractor, quite wealthy & very pleasant & social. The family had a severe loss in the death of their son John last fall.

Took a drive with their coach-man in the evening. Pleasant drive & good company. Retired late.

June, Tuesday 19. 1888.

Spent A.M. In driving through Rochester in company with Mr. Hopeman.

Saw new 2nd Ref. Church etc.

Visited Power's Art Gallery in P.M. Very fine in its collection & arrangement. "The Temptation of "St. Anthony." & the "Vespers in Kindergarten" were especially fine.

Spent evening in calling on Friends & secured a few subscribers to the Xtian Intelligencer. Van de Korde's are very kind people & remember Father & Mother when they were at Rochester.

June, Wednesday 20. 1888.

Spent A.M. in a drive along East Avenue.

Dinner at Rev. Van der Hart's. He seemed to find fault with my studying Theol. In the East instead of at Holland Mich.

Secured one subscriber to the Xtian Intelligencer. After tea at Hopeman's called for Rev. P. De B. & went with him to Union Meeting at 1st Ref. Chapel in behalf of For. Missions. Spoke 20 min. in Dutch & 15 in English on The Subject of the hour. Was not as fluent as I wished & did not seem as confident as I was at Marion or Albany.

I did not pray enough — that solves the difficulty.

Distributed Missy. Literature.

June, Thursday 21. 1888.

Took train at 8.15 for Buffalo. Purchased 1ˢᵗ Class Ticket on Mich. Central & Lake Shore to Grand Rapids from Rochester for $12.25

Stopped at Buffalo for 3 hrs. Saw Soldier's Monument & St. Paul's Cathederal with its grand organ (Centennial 1876). Train at 2 P.M. for Brockton Jc. & thence to Clymer.

One of Rev. Van Doren's Sons met me at Clymer St. & we went by buggy to parsonage. Mrs. V. D. is very pleasant. Thunder-Shower kept some people from church. Union Meeting with Abbe Church. Large attendance. Was helped in speaking & found pleasure in seeing my audience interested.

Met Dr. Reinsberger!
Where will he go next?

June, Friday 22. 1888.

Visited Rev. Hoffman & family. Clymer has 3 churches & only 400 population. Brockton has 650 population & only 5 churches! All Evangelical with one exception.

Went from Clymer to Brockton & am now at the Best hotel at the place – a bar-room concern. Waiting for trains is disagreeable work.

June, Saturday 23. 1888.

From Brockton to Cleveland. Remained at home of Mr. Nahuis-very pleasant family.

Saw city in P.M. & evening.
Garfield Monument etc.

June, Sunday 24. 1888.

Preached in A.M. At East Side church & in P.M. on West Side Good audiences on both occasions. Spoke in Dutch both times.

Heard a young Presb. student in evening. poor thought & delivery.

June, Monday 25. 1888.

From Cleveland at 5.45 A.M. To Holland via Allegan where arrived at 6 P.M. Attended lilfilas Club meeting etc. Very good.

Met P.J.Z. & the sisters.

June, Thursday 26. 1888.

Spent day in Holland & visited Mary at the Park. Ben & she are still enjoying life.

Attended Alumni exercises in evening & found them very enjoyable. The Chronicles were especially good.

June, Wednesday 27. 1888.

Spent A.M. in calling on Friends. P.M. ditto Commencement exercises in Evening were good
Peter's Valedictory capped the climax.
Was appointed this A.M. by Alumni association to prepare a college song. Accepted.
Rainy & disagreeable day.

June, Thursday 28. 1888.

Spent day in calling on friends etc.

Called on Dr. Chas. Scott in evening. Met Rev. Beardslee Prof. elect of the Seminary.

June, Friday 29. 1888.

Attended Picnic of Hope Church S.S. Pleasant time & met many acquaintances.

Took train at 6 P.M. for Gd. Rapids. Arrived there in company with Kate & James & their children. Pleasant family Reunion.

June, Saturday 30. 1888.

Called on Rev. P. Moerdyk & was asked to preach for him in the evening.

He wished to see me on the Western Seminary Question!!
He did. No results. Called on Friends in P.M. John Tronsfen [?] owns a clothing Store on Grandville Ave.

◆ ◆ ◆

December, Saturday 1. 1888.

Spent A.M. in writing an article on Missions for "De Hope" & in finishing the Translation of "Sketch of our Mission in China" into Dutch.

Went to town in afternoon. Made some purchases.

Spent evening in writing & reading.
Dr. Lansing called on me.
Took bath & retired.

December, Sunday 2. 1888.

Morning fine. Had prayer-meeting in my room. 7 present. Attended church in A.M. Communion Season. One of my S.S. scholars joined church. (Maggie Debolt); poor girl had one of her fainting attacks again. Helped her home. Walked home from church with Mrs. Corwin & had a pleasant talk.

S.S. in P.M. all my class except Maggie present.

Went to cottage-prayer-meeting in P.M. & was greatly blessed. Life among the lowly is often near to Christ.

Led evening prayers at the Hall.

Attended 1st Ref. Ch in evening & heard Mr. Sev. Cotton on Home Missions.

December, Monday 3. 1888.

Recitations & Study-

December, Tuesday 4. 1888.

Recitations as usual.

Rev. J. F. Ritts failed to meet the mission circle at 4 P.M. but came later.

Addressed the students in the chapel.

Pleasant talker. He is a pioneer in Medical Missy of the Baptist Church in Northern China.

Spent a social hour in the Parlor with him.

Retired late.

December, Wednesday 5. 1888.

Attended Recitations - Prayer Meeting at noon.

Attended meeting of the Society of Inquiry in evening & took part in debate.

Read & wrote letters.

December, Thursday 6. 1888.

Attended all the Recitations.
Spent P.M. in reading & writing for "De Hope" etc.

Called on Dr. Woodbridge with Mr. Phelps in evening. Pleasant time.
Wrote article for the Mission Field on "What do our Church Standards say on Missions?"
Retired late.

December, Friday 7. 1888.

Went to all lectures except Dr. Lansing who was un-well.

Took train at 2:20 P.M. for New York. Called at Synod's Rooms & went to Medical Institute Supper. Pleasant chat with Briggs, Wanless, & Kitts.
Took elevated R.R. for Union Theol. Seminary.

Met Stoops & Wilder—went with Stoops to "American Industrial Institute" Pleasant—
Profitable visit.
Prayer-meeting & Council in Wilder's Room. Good-day & Good night. 12.40 A.M.

December, Saturday 8. 1888.

Arose at 7.30. Breakfast with Stoops.
Went to several bookstores etc for shopping—
Called at M.E. & Poes. For. Missy Board Rooms for literature etc.
Train at 4.00 P.M. for Linden was met at depot by Mr. D. Demot & entertained at his home.
Pleasant people.
Little Besaie is a peculiar girl.

All are social & kind.

Attended Xmas Rehearsal in evening—

December, Sunday 9. 1888.

Preached at Linden N.J. A.M. I Cor.15:58 — Small attendance but very attentive. I was greatly helped in my speaking!

S School in P.M. taught the Bible-Class.

Preached on Missions in evening. Was helpd & blessed "exceedingly abundantly" —
Good collection.
Spent evening in conversation with Mr. Demot etc.

December, Monday 10. 1888.

Train for New Brunswick at 7.30. Studied & letters Attended Recitations.
Weather wet & disagreeable—
Spent evening in reading & writing letters, after Dr. Meyer's lecture on the Fall.
(see Lectures 1888-89)
The Lawn-Tennis club have their oyster-supper this evening.
Retired late, after reading my Bible.

December, Tuesday 11. 1888.

<No Entry>

December, Wednesday 12. 1888.

Dr. Baldwin of the M.E. Church addressed / Mission Circle to-day —
Very interesting

Met Secty of Y.M.C.A. & agreed to do "Slum" work among the Saloons this winter.

December, Thursday 13. 1888.

<No Entry>

December, Friday 14. 1888.

Supply pulpit for classmate Andrew. Took train for New York. Thence to West Farms where I led prayer-meeting—
Spoke with an inquirer.
Am staying with Mr. Squires.

December, Saturday 15. 1888.

Spent day in New York etc.
Called at Synod Rooms
Purchased some "Xmas Gifts—
Studied & wrote letters—

Called on Mr. Fitch—elder in evening.
Retired late—

December, Sunday 16. 1888.

Arose at 7 A.M.
Breakfast. S.School.
Took Bible Class. Lesson on Sampson.
Preached Missy. Sermon in A.M. on Prov. 24:12.

Went to Peabody Home for aged women & spoke there in P.M.
Called on Mr. Schrverki. Spoke on Missions in the Presbyterean
Ch in evening at 7.
Preached in Ref. Ch at 7.30 on Math 27: "Sitting down they
watched Him there".
Was greatly helped all day.

God's mercies are wonderful & his power marvellous.

December, Monday 17, 1888.

Train at 6 A.M. for New York—

Gave Missy Collection $8.50 to Rev. Cobb D.D. Train for New
Brunswick. Studied & Recited.

Read & Studied in P.M.
1st Lecture of Missy course in Seminary this evening by Rev. Stout
of Japan.
Quite Good.

December, Tuesday 18. 1888.

Attended Recitations as usual.

December, Wednesday 19. 1888.

Attended all Recitations Meet v [of] Soc v [of] Inq. In even[in]g —
Resigned posi- as treasurer.
Attended Cottage-Prayer-Meet[ing] with Mr. Keeling—
Was greatly blessed.
Spoke on Prodigal Son.

December, Thursday 20. 1888.

Attended Recitations as usual—
Spent P.M. in study—

Children of Rev. Edward
Tanjore Corwin, Euphemia
and Charles, ca. 1875

Called on Dr. Drury & received several small whunes (?) as pay for work as Correspondent to the Xtian Intelligencer.

Commenced work in Saloons of city on invitation v [of] Y.M.C.A. Secty Hines accompanied me.

Had a cordial reception in most places — surprised! One saloon had the motto: "In God we trust—all others must pay"!

Met 89 young men & distributed tracks & Y.M.C.A. Invitations— Retired late—

December, Friday 21. 1888.

Attended final Recita's Prof. De Witt was very pleasant.

Decided not to go with Phelps to Blenheim N.Y.

Studied & wrote article for the Press.

Spent P.M. in calling & correspondence.

Attended Y. P. Union in company with Miss. Corwin - pleasant time & the business meeting.

Pleasant walk home in the moonlight.

Retired after a game of Checkers - Miss. C. is champion—

December, Saturday 22. 1888.

Called on Addie Sebolt this A.M. Maggie is still sick — poor child — she gave me a bunch of wax flowers for Xmas.

Settled Bank account & took train at 12:55 for New York.

Purchased New overcoat at Hacket & Co - $10 Not stylish nor beautiful but very serviceable.

Boat for Ft. Lee.

Pleasant time with Miss. Person at the old homestead on the Palisades—

Called on Rev. Buckelew in evening—

Was asked to preach. Accepted—

Read Bible & retired

December, Sunday 23. 1888.

Arose late — Very cold. Attended Church & heard sermon by Rev. Buckelew on "The Magi". Dinner at Persons. S.S. in P.M. Taught Bible Class—

Read Genesis 1-6 with Miss. Person for study.

Supper Attended Church & preached on the Death of Christ "Sitting down they watched him there". Was helped in speaking. Read Bible, Conversa - & retired.

December, Monday 24. 1888.

Arose early. Boat for New York. Spent day in sight-seeing.

Visited Wall-Street & Trinity — attended Meet v [of] Pastor's Association & heard paper by Rev. Searle's on subject "Egypt in August".

Heard Dr. Dix in P.M. at Trinity—

Episcopalians v [of] that type are more than half Romish. Deliver me from such "Divine Service"!

Walked down Broadway & up to to 14th Street.

Train for New Brunswick. Called on Corwins'.

December, Tuesday 25. 1888.

Xmas day! Received $5.00 by mail from Father & other presents—

Letters from home—

Received Xmas Card at Breakfast from the Corwins.

Attended Catholic Church with Charlie Corwin.

Dinner Candy-pull — very interesting & extensive in character, games etc.

Called in the Parlor in the evening.

Played Mr. Schwartz a game of Chess.

Song & Candy.

A Merry Xmas indeed.

December, Wednesday 26. 1888.

Spent day in writing & reading.

Wrote article for "De Hope" on Missions & for the Mission Field.

Evening at the "Y Mission" for Drunkards—

Led meeting — played the organ — subject "Giving & Receiving at Xmas". John 3:16 – Math 2:1-14

Gave Candy & Oranges to the children at the Mission.

Long talk in Kesling's Room. He is a fine fellow & does hard service in the vineyard

December, Thursday 27. 1888.

Arose late. Read some in Augustine's Confessions this morning—

A strangely interesting book. How he addresses God as a child his father & conceals nothing from him.

Read & Studied a little. Prepared an address for Throop Ave. Mission.

Went to Suydam St. Ch Rehearsal with Miss. Corwin & from there to Throop Avenue.

Spoke at the meeting — she sang a Solo.

Rode home in tears

Pleasant company & good evening in every respect.

Had some candy-taffy in the parlor. /——

December, Friday 28. 1888.

Arose at 6.30. Spent A.M. in answering correspondence & other work—

Walk down town—

Call on Dr. Woodbridge.

Attended S.S. Entertainment at Suydam St. Church—

Large attendance—

Received 6 hand chiefs—

a Xmas present from James Mabon—

Walked home with Miss. Corwin. — Pleasant conversation—

Maggie Sebolt — my S.S. scholar had a falling fit again this evening—

helped her home—

Retired late.

December, Saturday 29. 1888.

Studied in A.M. —
took bath etc—
Train at 3:52 for Jersey City—
Am to preach at the Free Reformed in reply to a despatch from Rev. A.A. Zabriskie to supply pulpit
Was warmly welcomed at Mrs. Zabriskie—

Game of chess in evening. Interesting children—
Jennie & Harry.

Retired after reading Scripture & prayer for success on the morrow.

December, Sunday 30. 1888.

Arose late. Attended service in A.M. & spoke on John 8:12—
Was quite free in my delivery — but dislike to <u>read</u> sermons—

Dinner at Zabriskies—
Called on Alfred Duncombe in P.M. & found him some better — He has had severe spell of sickness.
Also on Dr. Van Cleef & Mrs. Pleasant talk with her on Missions & Raising funds—
Preached in evening before large number of young people — Math 27: "Sitting down they watched Him there"
Was helped but did not feel as free as last sabbath—

December, Monday 31. 1888.

Last day in the year!_
Arose early — Read a review of the year's <u>news</u> in "the Congrega'alis" [?]

Train for New Brunswick at 11 A.M. after some shopping & receiving $5.00 & expenses for my services—

P.M. at the Hall—
Called on Dr. Corwin's in the evening & remained with them to watch out the Old year. Chimes —Song — Candy — Thoughts

Read Diary for 1888 at 12:30 — & retired—

Welcome <u>1889</u>!

CHAPTER 10

A Copernican Re-evaluation of the Appenzeller-Underwood Mission in Korea

James Jinhong Kim

Introduction

In May of 2015 there was a commemorative conference in Seoul, Korea—an event significant in the history of Korean Christianity in that it became an occasion for the coming together of the two earliest Korean Protestant churches, founded by Henry Gerhard Appenzeller (1858-1902) and Horace Grant Underwood (1859-1916), respectively, in the spirit of inter-denominational evangelism by which these missionaries had so fruitfully planted the gospel in Choson, Korea, 130 years ago. Indeed, the extent of their cooperation and coordination marked a new phase in the history of Protestant missions, what one might call a new stage of maturity in the development of missiological evangelism. In the case of Roman Catholicism, there is relatively little conflict between its various orders because they all operate under the central authority of the papacy and the Vatican. Protestantism, however, is by nature given to divisiveness, which affects its evangelism, as well. Indeed, Protestant missions have sometimes been criticized for their so-called "Lone Ranger complex," with problems of peremptory mission policies, non-cooperation between mission teams, and conflicts with indigenous communities.[1]

What makes the work of Appenzeller and Underwood so significant in this context is that they demonstrated the possibility of inter-denominational cooperation and coordination for the best interests of mission site communities. That Korea was the first—and perhaps the only—beneficiary of this new missiological potential to date is important for us to consider in understanding the unprecedented success of Christianity in Korea. Even more importantly, the idea of evangelism founded on inter-denominational cooperation warrants further study from both missiological and theological perspectives for the future of Protestantism, especially as applicable to today's global contexts.

In speaking of western Christian missions, the nineteenth century was, without a doubt, the age of overseas missions, extending from India, Burma, Amoy, Africa, and South America, to China and Japan, with Choson, Korea, marking its end.[2] And whatever the problems facing Korean Christianity today, it cannot be denied that, of all the Third World countries, it was in Korea that the gospel brought by the Protestant missions took the deepest root and saw the most fruit—so much so that it has now become impossible to imagine a future of Korea devoid of Protestant presence and influence. The fact that, in a little over a century, this Christian faith has taken such a deep hold on the minds and hearts of the Korean people alongside Confucianism and Buddhism is, in itself, a remarkable achievement. The question is what future to build on this foundation.

Academia has, from time to time, pointed to an "absence of theology" in the Korean Church. My own diagnosis is that Christianity in Korea was founded on strong cornerstones of countless sacrifices for the sake of the gospel, both Catholic and Protestant, foreign and indigenous, but that it's going through a kind of malady associated with the process of seeking direction, identity, and purpose for the future.

---

[1]   Rob Moll, "Missions Incredible" *Christianity Today*, March, 2006, 28-34. See also Timothy Kiho Park, "Korean Christian World Mission: The Missionary Movement of the Korean Church" a paper presented at the Fifth Annual Underwood Conference held at the Center for Reformed Studies, NBTS, 2006.

[2]   William Carey (1761-1834) arrived in India in 1793, Adoniram Judson (1788-1850) to Burma in 1813, David Abeel (1802-46) to Kwangtong, Java, Siam, Singapore in 1830, then to Amoy in 1842, Francis T. McDougall (1817-86) to Borneo in 1847, Robert Morrison (1782-1834) to China in 1807, followed by Hudson Taylor (1832-94) in 1853, and Channing Williams to Japan in 1866.

The recent trend of Protestant conversions to Catholicism, for example, may be understood in part as popular appreciation for and response to the decades of courageous Catholic engagement with social issues and efforts toward Korean inculturation of the gospel. It is in this vein that we need to examine the inter-denominational cooperation demonstrated by Underwood, Appenzeller, and many other missionaries to Korea—not simply to establish and extol the *facts* of their accomplishments, as to understand the historical contexts on *both* sides of the Pacific that made the very motivation for inter-denominational coordination possible. Was it simply the personalities of the individual missionaries involved, some character of socio-religious "energy" emanating from deep within the Korean culture itself, the momentous synergy of Protestant sectarianism with the dynamics of explosive immigration to America in the nineteenth century, or perhaps all three? Whatever the answer, the assignment given to Korean Protestantism—perhaps from the very moments of its birth 130 years ago—must be to illuminate and rekindle that spirit both affirming and transcending denominational differences, to be adapted for the newly global contexts of Christianity emerging today. In my forthcoming book, I examine the relevant issues in much more detail; given the limits of this paper, I will touch on only a few main points, with my focus narrowed to Appenzeller and Underwood.

Two Characteristics of Protestantism

When we compare Protestantism to Roman Catholicism, the former has two distinct traits innate to its very nature. The first is that Protestantism is given to sectarianism and/or denominationalism; the second is that Protestantism, by principle, holds the Bible in higher authority than the church order. These two principles are in fact closely related. Let us now see briefly from the history of the Church why this should be so.

Protestant DE-Nominationalism

The United States, made up of immigrants from all countries of the earth, at one time called itself the "melting pot." The term implied the blending of many different ingredients to ultimately produce a dish of a single unified taste rather like a stew or metal alloy. In the 1960s, with the experience of the three Rights Movements (Women's Rights, Civil Rights, Anti-War), the metaphor was changed to that of a "salad bowl," where each ingredient retains its distinct flavor and texture while still presenting a composite taste for the palate. In the 1980s "multi-cultural" became the new catchphrase, with less emphasis on a single composite culture and more on respect and consideration for the many distinct and diverse Others within America. With the onset of the internet age in the twenty-first century, even that ideal has been supplanted by the idea of "global"—less focused on celebrating the diversity of peoples within the United States, and more on understanding the role of the United States as a member of the yet more diverse, decentralized global village.

Interestingly, the history of Protestantism cannot be understood apart from this history of America. Church historians have often commented that Martin Luther (1483-1546) accomplished only half the Reformation, breaking away from papal authority on strength of Biblical authority only to regroup as large state churches whose authority replaced that of the pope in determining the color of people's faith. Divided along regional lines and reinforced by political alliances, those residing in German states became Lutheran more or less by state decree, Switzerland Reformed or/and Calvinist, England Episcopalian (better known as Church of England), Scotland Presbyterian, etc. Those who sought further or different specificities in their understanding of the Bible beyond determinations of the state (or state-sanctioned) church faced continual persecution and/or death, and many chose the dangers of sea voyage across the Atlantic and a life away from all they knew of civilization for the promise of religious freedom (more properly Christian sectarian freedom) in the newly discovered Americas. In short, Protestantism was allowed to flower freely to its natural development only upon exodus to the new continent, subsequent to the War for US Independence (1776-1783) and Civil War (1861-1865), as well as the new and explosive influx of immigration from both Western and Eastern European countries between 1880 and 1920. I say the "natural development" of what Luther began nearly 500 years ago, and not its "completion." With the fire of Pentecostalism that had begun in the US in the early years of the twentieth century only now sweeping its way across much of the Third World, who is to say what new spark of the Spirit will reveal yet another facet of Protestantism?

So then, what does it mean to say Protestantism arrived at its natural development? While it is possible to answer from many different perspectives, for purposes of this paper it is that it became free to develop into and live as many denominations (from Latin *de* + *nominatus*, i.e., to name). According to data from 2010, Protestantism today encompasses over 30,000 different denominations and sects among its 500 to 800 million believers—in dramatic contrast to the mere 239 among the Catholic population of 1.2 billion.[3] Luther's Reformation had opened the door, in principle, to personal and independent relations between God and the individual mediated firstly by the Bible and only secondarily by the Church; indeed some scholars have pointed to the Reformation as providing the final cap to Western "individualism" begun in the Renaissance. For the many who sought to worship the God they encountered in the way they believed proper, it was only natural to seek to do so free from the prejudice, persecution, and interference of others. In the end, many found their way to America for that freedom—so much so that large numbers of Protestant denominations today claim America as either their birthplace or the place where they came into their own.

Protestant Biblicalism

But what drives Protestantism's tendency to difference and division in the first place? After all, Martin Luther had posted his 95 theses on the All Saints' Church in Wittenberg (1517) intending only to protest what he felt were certain corrupt practices within the Church and not to break away from it. The "protest" was pushed over the brink to "break" by mutual irreconcilability—Luther unable to reconcile practices of the Church with what he read in the Bible, and the Church unwilling to reconcile its authority over Biblical interpretation and Christian tradition with that of an "upstart" critic. The protest had worked to bring to light an irreconcilable difference within the Catholic Church, ultimately leading to a full-scale reform and re-formation of Christianity itself with the birth of a new Christian "denomination" called Protestant. Significantly, Luther's claim to legitimacy of his protest rested on the supremacy of the Bible's authority on all matters of God, superseding that of the papacy, the Church, or tradition: "*sola Scriptura*" or "only Scripture!" The problem was the standard of its interpretation. Who can claim to have the one true interpretation of such a complex, composite text?

In time, Luther, Zwingli, Calvin, and other leaders of the Protestant movement each had no recourse but to uphold in their turn the authority of the established Church—this time their own—to interpret the Bible, if only because some sort of interpretive unity was necessary to give defined shape and structure to the community that is a Church. Those to whom these new authoritative interpretations

---

[3]   David B. Barrett, *World Christian Encyclopedia*, 2001, "Table 1-1: World Religions," 5; "Table 1-3 Organized Christianity," 12.

and practices were unacceptable protested in turn, armed with their different understandings of the Bible, to be either driven out of the established community or to leave for places where protest was no longer necessary. The cycle has subsequently continued to this day, and will, necessarily, continue into the future for as long as anyone denies the authority of any teaching, tradition, or dogma of the Church over the text of the Bible itself. In short, in Protestantism, reformation is ever in the present and ongoing by nature of its focus on text. Indeed this is an essential life force of Protestantism itself.

With the growing popularity of Protestantism, voices within the Roman Catholic Church began to call for serious self-examination, resulting in the so-called Counter-Reformation, with the Council of Trent (1545-1563) at its core. The Council's conclusion at the end of eighteen years of discussion, however, was to affirm that the seven sacraments as practiced by the Roman Catholic Church were theologically sound. The Council moreover put forward policies strengthening the authority of the papacy and the Church so as to prevent similar outbreaks in the future.[4]

With the papacy taking this trenchant position, European states were forced to take a stand, either to remain Catholic and under the authority of the pope, or to turn Protestant. In important ways, it was a choice directed at rulers of states rather than individuals, but, with the protracted period of war and violence that followed, many individuals turned to the New World in the Americas. It follows then that, in America, Christianity was founded on principles of religious or denominational freedom. When the Civil War (1861-1865) divided America into North and South, many denominations also split; Southern Baptist and Southern Methodist denominations are some byproducts of that period. The United Methodist Church (UMC) and the Presbyterian Church in the United States of America (PCUSA), on the other hand, are results of efforts to reunite after the War.

To conclude, Protestant faith carries two innate characteristics of denominationalism and Biblical authority above all, each of which is conditioned by the other. In giving the Bible greater authority than the Church, inevitable interpretive differences will lead to differences of faith, and the need for freedom to exercise that faith will lead to denominational divide. The tendency toward division, therefore, cannot

---

[4]   See H. J. Schroeder, ed. & trans. *The Canons and Decrees of the Council of Trent* (Rockford, IL: TAN Books, 1978). See also, John W. O'Malley, *Trent: What Happened at the Council* (Cambridge, MA: Harvard Univ. Press, 2013).

be considered only in negative terms. Rather, the more important point is for the divide to *not* be turned into walls. In a sense, for Protestants, learning to come together as an inter-denominational community is as integral to its being as the multi-ethnic, multi-cultural United States sustaining itself by building mutual respect, cooperation, and pride as a diverse yet united community. As a Protestant saying coined in early seventeenth century and taken up as a popular motto in early nineteenth-century America posits:

"In Essentials, Unity;
In Non-Essentials, Liberty;
But In Everything, Charity."

A Re-evaluation of the Denominational Divide in Korean Protestantism

Because of the nature and history of Protestantism playing itself out in America, as it were, there were great differences in the approaches and beliefs of missionaries from America throughout the nineteenth century. Unlike the missions to India, Burma, Japan, Amoy, or China initiated long before the US Civil War (1861-1865), for example, missions to Korea had their start only in the fourth quarter of the ninteenth century—which is to say, *after* the North-South lines drawn by the Civil War but *before* those lines had time to heal and moved toward reunification. This meant that relatively more denominations poured into Korea in a very short time. Many point to this as the source of the contentious divisiveness within the Korean Protestant Church today, in which permanent walls seem to have been erected between denominations. But whatever the surface truths of such a criticism, I would on the contrary hold that the early denominational diversity in Korea was and will prove to be one of the major reasons for the unparalleled success of Protestant missions here and the secret of its hardy roots for longevity. Indeed this is precisely the point of Copernican revolution in perspective from which to reconsider the phenomenon of Protestant denominationalism in Korea today.

Had the Protestant missions to Choson Korea been dominated by a single denomination, as was the case in many Third World countries, it is likely that Korea, too, would have become a "religious colony" of that state church or denomination, inconducive to freedom of thought and action, or desensitized to its legitimate necessity. This may be only so much speculative hypothesis to some. But consider for a moment that much of the so-called sectarian contentiousness in Korea today is less between the different sects of Protestantism and more between the 100-plus splinter groups within the Presbyterian Church that over the decades has become by far the single largest and most dominant denomination in Korea. As discussed earlier, division according to differences of faith is an inherent character of Protestantism universally and not unique to Korea; that such a large denomination as the Korean Presbyterian Church should undergo division is in many ways only natural and should not, in and of itself, be viewed as a negative phenomenon only. Indeed one could argue it's even preferable to Europe where, with the Protestant Reformation only "half achieved", attendance at church is on average barely three percent of the population. There is little denominational conflict, but also little motivation toward denominational harmony.

Yet the original motivation of Protestantism's call to faith founded on the Bible was not thick walls of acrimony or mutual ignorance and indifference, but rather the harmony created by and through those differences, "that all things work together for good" (Romans 8:28). In that sense, the goal for Korean Christians is not the superficial coming together of different faith groups under forced slogans of unity; it is rather mutual affirmation and respect for the real differences of the other, supported by a spirit of sincere cooperation in working together toward a shared kingdom of God. Whatever the Church, it is, after all, only a means for the gospel, never its end.

Extended to missiology, if either the Korean Presbyterian Church or the Korean Methodist Church were to insist that their missions to Africa or South America repudiate everything but their own denominational principles, how could the missionaries work for the good of the local communities or be sensitive to the context and needs of the indigenous peoples? Multiply that by missionaries from other denominations also insisting on their understandings of faith: what would be the effect on the local believers (and non-believers)? The more diverse the denominational missions sent to a region, the more urgently crucial their inter-denominational cooperation for the successful enculturation of the gospel in that region. This is even more true when envisioning enculturation of the Christian gospel for the long term. When the object of mission is to lay the ground for a people to meet, love, and serve God in full cognizance of the particular historical context in which they have been placed, with the knowledge, foresight, and humanity required to become instruments of God in shaping their own future into a kingdom of God, rather than to increase the number of churches or church attendance in the shortest amount of time, missiology inevitably encompasses the education of the whole person—whether of children, women, youths, the laboring, or the underprivileged classes—and not of religious doctrine only. And, in this endeavor, Appenzeller and Underwood recognized the necessity of inter-denominational alliance founded on mutual cooperation. By his first sabbatical leave from Korea, Underwood was traveling to recruit prospective fellow missionaries from throughout North America and Canada irrespective of denominational affiliation, so that, on his return, he was accompanied by four Southern Presbyterian missionaries and one Canadian Methodist. This led to the founding of the first Korean Southern Presbyterian mission in November, 1892,[5] which continued to work closely with Underwood and his Northern Presbyterian Church to the end. Oliver R. Avison (1860-1956), the Canadian Methodist medical missionary recruited by Underwood, not only allowed himself to be underwritten by the Northern Presbyterian mission but carried on the founding of Yonsei University after Underwood's untimely death.

It is interesting to note that such inter-denominational cooperation seems *not* to have been the case or the plan from the beginning. According to recently-discovered letters of George C. Foulk (1856-1893), an officer in the naval diplomatic corps responsible for the safety of missionaries stationed in Korea, petty rivalry between denominations was a common source of his administrative frustration in the early days of the mission.[6] This should not come as a surprise. These people we now know simply as great missionaries were at one time also young men and women in their twenties, fresh and inexperienced to their task and to life in such new surroundings. But they had crossed the Pacific out of passion to sow the Christian gospel among the last known corners of the earth.[7] Moreover, most of them had grown up between 1860 and 1880, as themselves first or first-and-a-half-point-five generation immigrants to the United States and Canada, viscerally absorbing what it takes to hold together a united ethnic group from the multi-denominational, multi-cultural, multi-ethnic civilization that America

---

[5] Harry A. Rhodes, *History of the Korea Mission Presbyterian Church U.S.A: Vol.1 (1884-1934)*; In Korean, Jai-Keun Choi, trans., <미국 북장로교 한국 선교회사> (Yonsei University Press, 2008), 558.

[6] George C. Foulk, "Letter [to the Family] of August 18, 1885" in James S. Field, Jr., *History of the United States Naval Operations: Korea* (Washington DC: US Naval Historical Center, 2001), Ch.2.

[7] "We had been told before we went out to work in other lands that Korea was a land into which it was almost death to go. It was the last country to break the seal." H. G. Underwood, "Address" in *Report of the Twelfth Annual Convention of the American Inter-Seminary Missionary Alliance* (Pittsburgh: Murdoch, Kerr & Co., 1892), 53-54.

was fast becoming, especially during the mass immigrations in the wake of the Industrial Revolution.[8] So, what of the certain perception that they had been less than sincere sowers of the gospel in Korea, that they transplanted a certain white superiority together with their imposition of a Westernized Christ, that their denominational "district system" not only helped create thick walls of denominational division but exacerbated regional conflicts within Korea as well? It is easy enough to see, for example, that Northern Kyongsang and Pyong'an provinces are predominantly American Northern Presbyterian, Hamkyong province Canadian Presbyterian, Hwanghae province Methodist, Ch'ungch'ong province Baptist, Cholla province American Southern Presbyterian, Southern Kyongsang province Australian Presbyterian, etc. How can we understand these two very contradictory views of early missionary impact? To do that, let us first turn to examine the famous Nevius Plan, which was to have such enormous influence in Korea.

Rethinking the Impact and Influence of Nevius Plan in Korea

In June, 1890, the group of mostly young Presbyterian missionaries led by Underwood invited to Korea John Livingstone Nevius (1829-1893), a veteran Northern Presbyterian missionary who had been serving in Shanghai, Hangzhou, Shandong, and other regions of China since 1854, to give a series of seminars. Over the course of the next two weeks, Nevius gave lectures based on works he had previously published in the *Chinese Recorder*, such as the "Planting and Development of Missionary Churches" and "Methods of Mission Work," the basic principles of which Underwood and his cohort of Presbyterian missionaries then used to articulate their own mission policies. In other words, what they drafted in 1891 was a Policy of the *Presbyterian* Mission in Choson Korea, meant only to guide the Presbyterian missionaries among them, but which, out of convenience, later came to be called simply the Nevius Plan, and came to have tremendous influence on the work of other missions in Korea, as well.

Sources clearly show that the primary motivation for adopting the Nevius Plan was to "prevent the possibility of denominational conflict among missions as well as wastefulness of resources, time, and effort by avoiding missiological overlap wherever possible."[9] Accordingly, as

---

[8]   For example, Chicago, a town of just 17 houses in 1833, was by 1900 a metropolis of 1.7 million people. In the case of New York City, its population of one million in 1860 had more than tripled to three and a half million by 1900, creating major urbanization problems.

[9]   Man-Yeol Yi, *History of Korean Christianity*, from a semester-long series of lectures delivered at Princeton Theological Seminary, 1992, Session 3.

early as June 11, 1892, Underwood—together with Appenzeller—sought the following agreement on mission policy between the Northern Presbyterian and the Choson Mission of the American Methodist Church:

1. Shared mission activities in cities of over 5000 people.
2. In cities of less than 5000, recognize the first come first occupy policy; but in cases of more than 6 months of inactive mission work, allow another denomination to launch their work.
3. Recognize the right of Christian converts to change denominations.

The draft agreement ultimately was not officially recognized, but it may well have influenced the missions in Korea to a degree nevertheless. The essence of the Presbyterian Mission Policy, a.k.a. the Nevius Plan, was as follows:[10]

1. Prioritize evangelizing to the working classes more than the upper class.
2. Make special effort toward evangelism of women and the education of young girls, as they will have the most influence over the education of future generations.
3. Churches should be self-supporting. Lessen the number of native Christians dependent on help from missionaries, and increase the number of self-supporting individuals capable of contributing to society.
4. Encourage self-evangelism of Koreans by Koreans. Accordingly, focus more on producing educated Korean evangelists rather than going to the frontlines ourselves.
5. Emphasize medical missions. Medical professionals have more opportunities and time to get to know and teach patients, and these should include issues pertaining to the mind.

The influence of Nevius' Three-Self Policy—i.e., self-supporting, self-governing, and self-evangelizing—is clearly evident, together with emphasis on the evangelism of women and working classes, and the education of children, the effects of which can still be easily seen in Korean Christian demographics today. Nowhere in the document is there any suggestion of Presbyterian superiority over other denominations, or

---

[10]   C.C. Vinton, "Presbyterian Mission Work in Korea" in *The Missionary Review of the World*, Vol. XI, No. 9, 1893. Also translated and included in Kyung-bae Min, <한국기독교회사> *History of Korean Christianity*, 1892, 194-196 (Rearranged by James Jinhong Kim).

of a non-cooperative, isolationist policy. Methodist missionaries soon followed suit by adopting similar mission policies of their own. Indeed, for some Presbyterian missionaries like Horace Newton Allan (1858-1932) who had a strong bureaucratic as well as medical background, such a grassroots approach to mission and evangelism was difficult to understand and accept, even calling Underwood a "Methodist missionary within Presbyterian Church." If we look at Appenzeller, the first Methodist missionary to Korea opened a school within four months of his arrival with just two students.[11] If the Presbyterian mission focused their education program on nurturing young men and women who would then be sent back to their hometowns and churches as capable evangelists, the Methodist mission sought to provide general education for the people and use that as a pathway to the gospel.[12] Also, having comparatively more women missionaries among them and holding to the idea that "The wellbeing of a home, prosperity of a nation, and strength of a people depend on the education of its women,"[13] the Methodist mission was able to contribute greatly to the education and evangelism of women. For Underwood, who believed equally if not even more in the importance of education as a foundation for long-term enculturation of the gospel, it became an ideal point of mutual cooperation between the denominations.

The spirit of inter-denominational cooperation exemplified by Underwood and Appenzeller in the early days of Korean mission soon spread to include Fenwick (Malcolm C. Fenwick 1863-1935; initially a non-denominational missionary who arrived in Korea in 1891 and who later became the founder of the forerunner to the Baptist Church of Korea), Hardie (Robert A. Hardie, 1865-1949, a Southern Methodist who arrived in Korea in 1890), Avison (Oliver R. Avison, 1860-1956, a Canadian Methodist who arrived in Korea as a Northern Presbyterian medical missionary in 1893), and other missionaries of various denominations, and Protestantism was able to spread quickly well beyond Korea's urban centers and elite educated classes to all regions and demographics.

If early Korean Protestant missions thus began with an unprecedented, multi-denominational, coordinated effort, nevertheless at its center were Underwood and Appenzeller. For the duration of their life and active service, they were able to maintain a balanced missiological

---

[11]   *Historical Sketch of the Korean Methodist Church*, 75th Anniversary, Seoul, 1969, 17.
[12]   Kyung-bae Min, <한국기독교회사> *History of Korean Christianity*, 1892, 196-7.
[13]   <대한 그리스도인 회보> *Korean Christian Revue*, Vol. 1-48, Dec. 20, 1898.

program shared by the Northern and Southern Presbyterian, Northern and Southern Methodist, Australian Presbyterian, Canadian Presbyterian, Canadian Methodist, and Baptist (Great Korean Christian) missions. Since the two men traveled to Korea on the same ship crossing the Pacific, it is easy to imagine that they already shared their ideas and ideals for the Korean mission while on board. However, it remains unclear exactly when they became committed to working together on such close terms. As discussed in the earlier lecture by Professor John Coakley, Appenzeller and Underwood both had been attendees at the fourth meeting of the Inter-Seminary Mission Alliance (ISMA) at Hartford Theological Seminary in Connecticut in October of 1883, but there is no evidence from that meeting of their knowing one another or of planning to travel to Korea together.[14] At the next meeting of ISMA at Princeton in October, 1884, Underwood was introduced to the congregants as a missionary soon leaving for Choson; since this was about the time it was known that Appenzeller would be going to Choson instead of Japan, as well, we might assume the two engaged in some discussion of their upcoming missions at that point.[15]

Appenzeller was a fifth generation immigrant from his father's side, his great-great grandfather having come to America after France's Louis XIV abolished, in 1685, the earlier Edict of Nantes (signed by England's Henry IV in 1598, safeguarding the civil rights of Calvinist Protestants in what was essentially Catholic France). His mother, on the other hand, was a Swiss Mennonite and a recent immigrant, who imparted to her children her pietistic tradition of faith. Not only did Appenzeller's father and their neighbors speak mostly in German, his mother was far from fluent in English, so that the young Appenzeller grew up speaking "Pennsylvania German" almost exclusively until he was twelve.[16] His secondary education continued in the German/Swiss

---

[14]   Griffis believes the two met at Hartford; "Underwood and Appenzeller first met at the Inter-Seminary Alliance Conference at Hartford, Connecticut, and within two years went to Korea together." W. E. Griffis, *A Modern Pioneer in Korea, the Life Story of Henry G. Appenzeller* (New York: Fleming H. Revell, 1912), 71; Also quoted in Kyungbae Min, <한국기독교회사> *History of Korean Christianity*, 1982, 154.

[15]   Kroehler, a Methodist historian, believes the two met only on the ship to Inchon from Japan in 1885. Kent E. Kroehler, "A Century After: The Legacy of the Appenzellers, Pioneer Missionaries to Korea" in the *Journal of the Historical Society of the EPA Conference*, 2008, 20, writes, "At Kobe, [to set sail to Korea in March 1885] they were joined by Underwood from the Presbyterian Mission. Underwood did not know the Appenzellers and had been told . . . ."

[16]   Kent E. Kroehler, "A Century After: The Legacy of the Appenzellers, Pioneer Missionaries to Korea" in the *Journal of the Historical Society of the EPA Conference*, 2008, 16,

Reformed tradition at the Franklin and Marshall College located in Lancaster, Pennsylvania, but, at age twenty-one, he began to attend a Methodist Episcopal church,[17] and—having come to a conclusion about the efficacy of the Methodist approach to evangelism—decided to receive his seminary education at the Methodist Drew Theological Seminary. It should be noted that Pennsylvania, where Appenzeller was born and raised, was home to more religious/sectarian diversity than anywhere in America at the time, while the Lancaster region, where much of his education took place, was sometimes called the "mecca of Reformation immigrants." Indeed, for Appenzeller, "Protestant faith" must have seemed truly a colorful rainbow, running the gamut of Quakers, Shakers, the Amish, Mennonites, Moravian Brethren, and many others who filled the "Pennsylvania German" community. Perhaps it was from this that Appenzeller was able to look beyond the German/Swiss Reformed theology and tradition he had inherited from his family and disengage, too, from controversy begun by the retro-conservative and liturgical Mercersberg Movement at the Franklin and Marshall College, choosing instead Methodist theology and education, with its emphasis on social diversity and grassroots approach toward education of the working and under-privileged classes. His call and evangelical passion was ever for the poor and ignorant, and even his last moments on earth were spent trying to save a little girl from a sinking boat.

His work in Choson, Korea, greatly exhausted his health, so that in September, 1900, only fifteen years after his arrival and still in his early forties, Appenzeller was ordered by the Methodist Mission to return to America on sabbatical. Shrunk from his former 82kg (180 lbs.) down to a mere 63kg (139 lbs.), it is said that his friends and colleagues back in America could not recognize him. But throughout his leave he continued to concern himself with the work left behind in Korea, and made the decision to return there after only nine months. His close friend and classmate from Drew, the Rev. Robert Watts, proposed that Appenzeller remain in America, that the "Korea climate was too severe for him. I urged him to take work in his Conference, Philadelphia." But Appenzeller's reply was only that, "I have given myself to Korea and a few years more or less do not so much matter. I am more needed there than at home. I shall probably go to heaven from the Hermit Kingdom. It is no less near there than in America."[18] Perhaps foreseeing his death

---

17   i.e., First Methodist Episcopal (currently First United Methodist) Church of Lancaster, Pennsylvania.

18   William Elliot Griffis, *A Modern Pioneer in Korea: The Life Story of Henry G. Appenzeller* (New York: Fleming H. Revell, 1912), 258.

in Korea, he returned to Korea alone, leaving his wife Ella and their four children back in Lancaster, and died without seeing them again. And the children, though put severely to test by the untimely death of their father, ultimately continued his legacy by living out their days in dedication to Korea themselves. As just one—quite well-known— example, the Ehwa University of today could not exist without the work of Alice Appenzeller (1885-1950), Henry's eldest daughter.

He had begun his mission with the prayer, repeated every year on Easter Sundays in churches everywhere in Korea: "May He who [this] day burst asunder the bars of death . . . bring light and liberty [to Korea] . . ."[19] He had prayed, "If God permits, to preach the gospel in every corner of Korea, from its tiger hunters in the north to its rice farmers of the south." Today, the prayer continues in the hearts of the 25,000-strong Korean missionaries taking the gospel to all corners of the global community.

Underwood, on the other hand, was born to somewhat different circumstances, in British London to a family of Scottish Presbyterians. After losing his mother at the tender age of ten, the young Horace and his brother Fred were sent to a Catholic boarding school in Boulogne-sur-Mer, northern France, and only rejoined the rest of his family after some two years, by which time they had emigrated to America. A so-called one-point-five generation immigrant at almost thirteen years old, he and his family joined a Dutch Reformed congregation in New Jersey called the Grove Reformed Church, and went on to major in education at New York University, receiving both his Bachelors and Masters degrees in six years (1877-1883). The year he finished his undergraduate studies, he also enrolled in the Dutch Reformed Theological Seminary (today's New Brunswick Theological Seminary) for simultaneous theological training, and applied for a year's medical training just prior to his graduation as well. Having dreamed of becoming a missionary since he was four years old, Underwood did not hesitate to take active part in community services such as the Salvation Army that had little to do with his seminary education or to share his passion and ideas for overseas mission at student gatherings.[20] Coincidentally, Dr. William A. Mabon (1822-1892), formerly the Head Pastor at Underwood's own

---

19   The exact words from the *Methodist Correspondences* (1885) is: "We came here on Easter. May He who on that day burst asunder the bars of death, break the bands that bind this people, and bring them to the light and liberty of God's children."

20   i.e., the Society of Inquiry on Missions. See John W. Coakley, *New Brunswick Theological Seminary: An Illustrated History, 1784-2014* (Grand Rapids, MI: Eerdmans, 2014), 19, 111, 46-48.

Grove Reformed Church, joined the Dutch Reformed Theological Seminary (aka New Brunswick Theological Seminary) as faculty about the same time that Underwood enrolled in the program there. We have yet to find conclusive evidence as to whether Mabon influenced Underwood's choice of seminary or not, but, given that the former was known for founding no less than thirteen new churches in the spirit of social activism and evangelism, it would not be surprising if Underwood indeed looked up to him as a role model.[21]

The enormous influence Arthur Tappan Pierson (1837-1911) had on Underwood since the time of his seminary education has been recently discovered by Coakley and others. Pierson is considered by many to be the father of inter-denominational mission as well as the world mission movement of the nineteenth century. Underwood, through sustained contact with Pierson since the early days of his mission in Korea, learned much from Pierson's inter-denominational, social activist movement for the gospel, and benefitted as well from Pierson's worldwide network of missionaries; Pierson, on the other hand, found in Underwood someone who faithfully and intelligently applied his evangelical vision from the frontlines. Their mutual respect inspired Pierson, in December, 1910, at the advanced age of 73, to make faraway and politically destitute Korea the destination of his last tour of inspection. And having seen for himself the dynamic Christian revival taking place there, he made it his will that a Normal Bible School be erected after his death—not in any of the mission sites already prepared by his own children in India, or in China or Japan—but in Choson, Korea. Consequently, his son, Delavan Leonard Pierson (1867-1952), worked closely with Underwood to found the Arthur T. Pierson Memorial Bible School (today's P'yongt'aek University), to be managed jointly by the Northern Presbyterian, Southern Methodist, and Northern Methodist Churches. Although Underwood became the Academy's first Principal, when he passed away, leaving his son, Horton (1890-1951), still finishing his studies, it was Robert A. Hardie (1865-1949), a Southern Methodist medical missionary who fulfilled the responsibilities in the interim.[22] Coincidentally, Hardie had, years earlier, followed Underwood's advice to leave Seoul for the underdeveloped mission in Wonsan, there sparking off the Wonsan Revival Movement that later spread its fervor to P'yongyang and beyond.

---

[21]   Ibid., 46-48.

[22]   Sang-Yol Jo, *Authur T. Pierson Memorial Bible School*, Seoul: Daehan Kidok-kyoseohoe, 2011, esp. Ch.1, "Cooperation of Horace G. Underwood and Pierson"(언더우드: 피어선과의 만남과 협력), 33-59; See also, Dana L. Robert, *Occupy until I Come: A. T. Pierson and the Evangelization of the World* (Grand Rapids, MI: Eerdmans, 2003), 294-298.

The passions of two Christian young men in their twenties were the brainchild of late nineteenth century overseas mission movement, uniting the spirit of inter-denominational cooperation, social activism, and conservative evangelism to help Koreans overcome their poverty and ignorance and give them the Christian dream of living the kingdom of God in *and through* harmony with others. The gospel they shared had been shaped, in turn, by the education and hopes their parents and spiritual forebears had shared with them. It carried within it an appreciation for the denominational and Bible-oriented character of Protestantism, as well as awareness of their potential for divisiveness, persecution, and violence as played out most clearly in the history of Europe. It carried, too, compassion for the wretched plight of millions who, newly devalued and abused in the wake of the Industrial Revolution, sought to start new lives in the New World via explosive mass immigrations to America. As children of immigrants, Underwood and Appenzeller developed a visceral understanding of how to live with different Others in multi-cultural, multi-denominational America—an understanding that was applied toward fully respecting denominational independence and differences, while at the same time balancing it with the willingness and the ability to work in concert, for the implicitly greater, more comprehensive vision of Christ than any single denomination can hope to provide. This gift, given almost uniquely to Korea, must be recognized as a legacy to be now rekindled by Korea's own Christian missions as they look outward to share the gift of the gospel with the global community.

Conclusion

With the regrettably early deaths of Appenzeller at the age of forty-four (in 1902) and Underwood at 57 (1916), the Presbyterian Church, which had grown much more rapidly than any of her sister denominations, increasingly began to show signs of intra- if not yet inter-denominational discord. But such seeds within the Presbyterian Church were initially overshadowed by the controversy over Japanese imposition of worship at their shrines to the emperor, which had the effect of dividing the denominations according to their position on the edict. Another important issue to think about at this point is that, in Korea, Western missionaries—mostly from radically multi-cultural, multi-denominational North America—came face to face with a country that was racially and linguistically more homogenous than arguably any other on earth. Is it possible that this radical, even insistent unity of the Korean people inspired and became the basis for those missionaries to envision a unified alliance or union of Christian denominations?[23] The question warrants further research. Even so, what the missionaries failed to take sufficiently into account was that, as a racially and linguistically homogenous culture, Choson society was inexperienced and unschooled in what it is to accept and share lives with people of different languages and cultures. What little motivation they did have to try to befriend and understand different Others was the trickle of new ideas and goods brought in from the outside world by the enlightenment party, increasing infiltration by foreign powers, contact with new continents like North America, and—at a time when the very fate of the nation was at peril with the Sino-Japanese War (1894-1895) and the Japan-Korea Treaty (a.k.a. the Eulsa Treaty, 1905)—the efforts of those who frequented Manchuria and China in the hopes of staving off the loss of country. It was the case for Suh Sangryun (1848-1926), who founded the very first Protestant church in Korea (i.e., Sorae Church in or before 1882 as an "Ersatz Clergy" congregation) after becoming Christian in Manchuria; it may also help explain why the great Christian revival movements in this early period arose in northern provinces like Wonsan, P'yongyang, and Euiju rather than Seoul.

Although the early North American missionaries to Choson had learned from their missiological predecessors such as William Carey (1761-1834, pioneering Protestant missionary to India), Adoniram Judson (1788-1850, first missionary to be sent overseas—to Burma—by the American Board of Commissioners for Foreign Missions, founded in 1810), Robert Morrison (1782-1834; missionary to China), and Hudson Taylor (1832-1894; missionary to China) about the need to listen to the indigenous community one is sent to evangelize and to understand their context, they did not come to Korea with actual prior experience of it. It has been said that, during the first decade or so of their mission (1884-1893,) this first generation of missionaries

---

[23] Starting with joint prayer meetings begun on January 1, 1888, under the leadership of Appenzeller and Underwood and their two respective Jeong-dong churches (i.e., Jeong-dong First Methodist Church and Jeong-dong Presbyterian Church later known as Samunan Church), missionaries engaged actively in inter-denominational meetings and projects. The Korean Tract Society was created as inter-denominational in 1890; in 1893 the four Presbyterian missions, i.e., American Northern and Southern, Australian, and Canadian, united to create the Presbyterian United Council; in 1905, 150 Presbyterian and Methodist missionaries gathered together to found the General Council of Evangelical Mission in Korea. In June, 1910, Underwood with Yun, Chi-ho (186501945) and Samuel A. Moffett (1864-1939) participated the Edinburgh World Missionary Conference where Pierson presented a paper on the theme of "Cooperation and Unity".

to Korea were concerned mainly to apply to Choson what they knew and had been taught of evangelism; in the second decade (1894-1903), they tried to better understand the cultural context of Choson; and only in their third and final decade were they able to evangelize in a manner adapted or fitted to Choson.[24] This pattern can be easily seen in Underwood himself, if we examine the changes to appellations for God: for example, Underwood had at first insisted on using "Shangdi" ("Lord on High," from Chinese) or "Ch'onju" ("Lord of Heaven"). It was only as late as 1903 that he understood the purely Korean term "Hananim" as an acceptable translation for Christian God and agreed to its exclusive use in the 1906 authoritative translation of the New Testament. Hardie's repentance of his pride in front of a large crowd of native Choson Christians likewise took place in 1903, signaling a new phase of intimacy and sense of unity between Western missionaries and the Korean people. It was this spirit that fed the burgeoning of the great revival movement in P'yongyang.

We can see certain similarities of pattern, then, between the condition of Christianity in North America of the late nineteenth century that produced missionaries such as Appenzeller and Underwood and current tendencies in Korean Protestant missions. If we overlook the relatively minor difference of detail in the various data sources available, Korea currently maintains between 10,000 and 25,000 missionaries overseas. This is in addition to the countless self-sponsoring lay missionaries who regularly travel to Asia, South America, Africa, and all corners of the world on short-term mission trips. As we move forward, the example of inter-denominational mission spirit shown by Appenzeller and Underwood gives us several concrete principles or guiding points to consider. First, there needs to be much more effort to become fluent in the language(s) of the local peoples. Second, Korean missionaries do well to follow the pattern of building from small Bible Study groups to establishing schools, arranging for medical facilities, and constructing churches. But more important than the fact of founding schools and facilities is what kind of schools, and, in this matter as in many others, there must be recognition of how much more efficient and effective it will be to have as input the experience and cooperation of all missionaries, regardless of race, denomination, or language, than to make decisions based on the limits of what one has learned alone. Third, missionaries should be encouraged to

---

[24] Sung-Deuk Oak, *The Making of Korean Christianity: Protestant Encounters with Korean Religions, 1876-1915* (Waco, TX: Baylor Univ. Press, 2013), 25-32.

become missionary *families*. This means planning for mission legacies to continue with the second, third, fourth generations to enable long-term vision and commitment. Fourth, training in inter-denominational cooperation is necessary not only for the field missionaries but equally for the church leaders and lay congregation members at home. Fifth, those "sending" missionaries to the field—i.e., church leaders and lay congregation members at home—need to understand and be prepared to accept that field missionaries will often face situations necessitating ecumenical approaches. Finally, there needs to be much more education and prior training for missionaries on how to cope with and respond fruitfully to conditions of living in community with other cultures and religions.

It may well be, in the end, that these missionaries from Korea and their descendants, sent out to the world to experience and learn from the multi-ethnic, multi-cultural, multi-religious communities of the world, will grow and change the future of Korea and its Christianity—just as, a century ago, the missionaries and their descendants from nineteenth-century North America changed the cultural leadership of America from within. In that sense, the goal set by Korean World Mission Association (KWMA)—to sponsor 100,000 Korean full-time vocational overseas missionaries by year 2030, and 1 million short-term, self-supporting missionaries by year 2020—stands as a dynamic challenge—not so much for whether those numbers will be actualized or not, but for its potential to transform Korea and especially its Christians into true leaders in the global community.[25] More than ever, global leadership will belong to those who are recognized by the heart of other peoples—as Appenzeller and Underwood had been—as both well-informed and motivated by generosity in serving the wellbeing of those others.

If today's Korean missionaries can inspire in others such recognition and respect for Korea and Korean Christianity, they will have succeeded to the legacy left by Appenzeller and Underwood. Community based on tolerance of other cultures, religions, and denominations assumes a two-way street. It is important for every member to have a healthy and aspirational sense of identity, but at the same time it also requires special consideration and understanding of different Others. Without such consideration and understanding, that community cannot have a future, but instead will be burdened with conflict, division, and contention over interests. Besides Underwood,

[25] Rob Moll, "Missions Incredible" *Christianity Today*, March 2006, p. 34.

Appenzeller, and their fellow early missionaries already mentioned, there were many other Protestant missionaries who contributed to the enculturation of the gospel through inter-denominational efforts. And it should be emphasized that "inter"-denominational here refers to close cooperation *between* denominations, *not* to dis-denominational or non-denominational attitudes that disregard denominational differences.

Those who aspire to a better future do not accept what is now as the best that can be. And the gap between what is and what should be leads them to feelings of hope rather than despair—a hope that lets us experience what is now with gratitude despite not having yet reached what is hoped for. When those who want for nothing desire more, it becomes greed. The gift of the gospel is to allow us to live in constancy of hope despite want, but, when that want is focused on material things, hope becomes debased to blessings-based dealing with God. Underwood and Appenzeller saw the magnitude of Korea's want, but it was people's spiritual rather than material impoverishment that motivated the greater part of their anxiety. With the optimism to believe that the gospel would be "spread to all corners of the earth and the whole world Christianized by year 2000,"[26] Underwood envisioned and sought to prepare a Korea that was ready to take a proactive, leading role in the global community to come, even one where Korea would extend one hand to China and the other to Japan for a Christian alliance spanning the three nations. Planning for every aspect of the mission with respect to his long-term vision, he refused to limit his energies to resolving immediate urgent problems or focusing on short-term gains. This is why the deeper effects of his mission are only beginning to be understood and better appreciated now, more than a century after they were sown, and why—despite the tremendous opposition and criticism from even his fellow missionaries in the Presbyterian Church—he stubbornly insisted on founding the YMCA and secular universities such as Yonsei.[27] Indeed his vision as a missionary was nothing less than a "Christian Korea" (as distinct from Christians in Korea) founded on judicious enculturation of the gospel—a vision that would not be possible unless founded on inter-denominational cooperation. It goes without saying that neither unchecked discord nor theological and missiological confusion created

[26]   H. G. Underwood, "Address" *Report of the Twelfth Annual Convention of the American Inter-Seminary Missionary Alliance* (Pittsburgh: Murdoch, Kerr & Co., 1892), 53-54. "It is possible that the world may be evangelized before the year 2000 rolls around. Let us be up and doing here at home and in the foreign field."

[27]   The Educational Committee, *The Minutes of Korean Mission Presbyterian Church in the U.S.A.* (1915), 11.

by rampant proliferation of hairsplitting denominations would be healthy influences for enculturation, but so would the domination of a single denomination that can all too easily turn a community into its administrative, intellectual, and religious colony. Ultimately, the only true way to becoming one is by maturing *through* the process of diversity, toward the oneness that embraces the many.

Unlike Appenzeller, who could "head to Heaven" directly from Korea, it took Underwood much longer to realize his dream of being buried in Korea. Exhausted from constant opposition and pressures, he was in Atlantic City, New Jersey, trying to recuperate enough to get back to Korea, when he passed away. His last words were, "I think, I think, I could travel that far." When his wife whispered to him, "Where, dear, to Korea?", his face is supposed to have lit up as he nodded.[28] His last wish, to be buried in Korea, was made true in 1999, nearly a century after his death, when Underwood was finally moved from his family plot in Grove Reformed Church, New Jersey, to Yang'hwajin, Korea, where his wife, son, daughter-in-law, and granddaughter-in-law all had preceded him.[29] Today, Yang'hwajin continues to call out to the hearts of every Christian who passes by it, "Where are you from? What denomination are you? But let us all be one for the dream of a Christian Korea . . ."

On March 16, 2015, the Yonsei University, founded by Underwood, held the opening ceremony for a branch theological institution called GIT in Inch'on's new Songdo urban development area. GIT is acronym for Global Institute of Theology. Sister to the United Graduate School of Theology at Yonsei, it plans to matriculate 30 international students annually for the next four years, offering both post-master (Th.M.) and doctoral (Ph.D.) programs in theology, to an eventual full capacity of 100-120 graduates every year. Amazingly, tuition, room and board, and even matriculation expenses are all to be paid by the school. Given the school's very name, the program will be open to anyone in the world, but its organizers hope especially to provide students from the Third World with the opportunity to study the gospel and the Bible in close depth, free from both social/political persecution and financial hardship. The

---

[28]   Lillias H. Underwood, *Underwood of Korea* (New York: Fleming H. Revell, 1918), 332.

[29]   His wife, Lilias Horton Underwood (1851-1921) in 1921; son, Horace Horton Underwood (1890-1951) in 1951; daughter-in-law, Ethel von Wagoner (1888-1949), who was killed by a group of young Communists in 1949; and granddaughter-in-law, Joan Vida Davidson (1915-76) in 1976, were buried at Yanghwajin foreign missionary cemetery in Seoul. After him, in 2004, his grandson, Horace Grant Underwood, III, (1917-2004), and, in 2000, great-granddaughter-in-law, Gale Clarke (1955-2000) were buried there.

project obviously requires enormous resources; happily, a great portion of the financial commitment is said to come from efforts of many denominations joined in inter-denominational alliance. Dr. Sok-Hwan Jeong, former Dean of the United Graduate School of Theology and a driving force behind the project, has said with conviction,

> "From here will come the next, and the next, Underwood and Appenzeller."

> May it be so in God.

CHAPTER 11

More Loss than Loyalty?
The Reformed Church in America, 1994–2015

Lynn Japinga

John Coakley has been a mentor and friend for almost thirty years. I did not have the privilege of being his student, but I benefitted from his insight and wisdom when I wrote my dissertation and my book.[1] He encouraged me to test my ideas in lectures at New Brunswick Theological Seminary (NBTS) and in his summer Ministerial Formation Certification Agency (MFCA) courses.

John loves history, teaching, and the Reformed Church in America (RCA). He was not born into the RCA, but it became his adopted home, and he devoted much of his career to helping RCA members understand the ways in which denominational identity has been shaped by the past. In honor of John's retirement, this essay will explore some of the events of the last two decades. It is not intended to be a thorough analysis, but rather an opinion piece that I hope will spark some discussion about the current state of the RCA, and its future.

What is the value of studying history? Some people think that history is irrelevant. The past is past, after all, and we need to focus on

---

[1] *Loyalty and Loss: The Reformed Church in America, 1945-1994* (Grand Rapids, MI: Eerdmans, 2013).

235

the future, the goal, the mission, the vision. We need to be transformed and transforming; we cannot be bogged down in the past. The world in which we live now is so completely different that the values which guided the past are no longer relevant to the present or the future.

Others argue with equal passion that we cannot move into the future if we do not know what has shaped us in the past. In 1970, American religious historian Sydney Ahlstrom wrote, "I believe that an historical understanding of one's self and one's situation constitutes a kind of essential wisdom. It orients the disoriented. It helps people—individually and collectively—to know who they are. Those who are at sea are given some idea of their location and the direction of their drift."[2] I believe that the RCA has been adrift in the last couple of decades. The denomination may have its goals and plans, but in the midst of a great deal of conflict and loss, one of the casualties has been the loss of a clear sense of identity.

Despite being a relatively homogeneous denomination, the RCA has experienced a significant amount of conflict. In the eighteenth century, RCA members disagreed about whether to continue a close connection with the church in Amsterdam or become independent. They disagreed about revivalism and the role of emotion in worship. The conflicts increased in 1847 when new immigrants from the Netherlands arrived, full of passionate intensity but skeptical of established religious bodies.[3]

There has been a long history of conflict, but, most of the time, the RCA managed to survive as a denomination even when its members did not all think alike. RCA members were held together by Dutch ethnicity and a strong web of relationships. After World War II, conflict intensified, in part because of disputes about two merger proposals and about membership in ecumenical councils. In the late 1940s, late 1960s, and late 1970s, the RCA was seriously divided and some members believed that schism was inevitable. Each time, the tension was partly dissipated when RCA leaders tried to unite the church around mission and outreach. The common goal helped transcend disagreement and defuse anger. Each time, however, the relative peace and cooperation

---

[2]   Sydney Ahlstrom, "The Problem of the History of Religion in America," *Church History* 39 (1970), 224-235.

[3]   One discontented group in West Michigan left and formed the Christian Reformed Church in 1857. In the 1880s, another group left the RCA for the CRC, because they did not think Freemasons should be members of the church. "Passionate intensity" is used by William Butler Yeats in his poem, "The Second Coming."

lasted only about a decade before conflict reappeared, sometimes in an even more virulent form.[4]

If we were to look at the history of the RCA over the past four centuries, and the way it navigated its conflicts, what kind of understanding might we gain about our identity? What kind of essential wisdom might we find from the past? That is a subjective question that might be answered in many different ways, but one possible answer sounds like this. The RCA is a small denomination with Dutch roots. It valued the theological system of John Calvin and insisted on an educated clergy. The RCA maintained strong connections with other mainline churches and engaged in many cooperative efforts.

The RCA achieved its greatest renown and respect in the realm of foreign missions. In Japan, China, India, and the Middle East, RCA missionaries made significant contributions in health care, education, and evangelism. Many missionaries were household names in RCA homes because their work was so well publicized and widely supported by congregations.

The RCA treasured its polity, liturgy, and theology. It has been particularly shaped by the Heidelberg Catechism, especially the first question and answer about belonging to God. These values at times meant that RCA resisted change, new forms of ministry, and challenging ideas. The RCA saw itself as a family, but it has not always welcomed other people. The RCA definitely had its flaws, but it was built on a foundation which balanced head and heart, tradition and reformation, divine and human, purity and unity.

If we were to narrow the focus and look only at the history of the RCA in the past two decades, what would it tell us about our identity as a denomination? Who are we and what is important to us? On one hand, we would see that the denomination is encouraging congregations to be a life-giving presence in their communities. The RCA has emphasized starting new churches and revitalizing existing congregations.

Underlying this focus on mission and outreach, however, is a powerful strain of anxiety and fear. Despite the effort to start new churches, RCA membership numbers continue to decline. Anxiety about the future heightens the long-simmering conflicts over ecumenism,

---

[4] See my *Loyalty and Loss* for a detailed discussion of conflict and mission during these years. RCA members had sharply different views on ecumenism, the Bible, and the nature of the church. After coming to the precipice of schism, people were nicer to each other for a while, but then the unresolved differences reappeared, along with the passionate intensity.

sexuality, and biblical interpretation. A cursory review of our "drift" in the last two decades suggests that the RCA is obsessed with the issue of homosexuality.[5] Overtures, dialogues, heated debates, mean-spirited letters to the editor, pleas for tolerance, and a heresy trial have shaped denominational life. Despite all this activity, the denomination is not only polarized but paralyzed. The RCA's position on homosexuality has barely moved beyond what was written in 1978 and 1979. Meanwhile, cultural, psychological, and legal attitudes have radically changed.

This essay will explore some of the decisions made in the RCA during the last two decades, especially regarding homosexuality and denominational communication. How have these choices shaped our current identity? Do these decisions accurately reflect who we are as a denomination? Do we want to be defined by these choices?

It is not only the decisions themselves that are significant, but how the denomination makes them. Is decision-making based on thoughtful, critical engagement with Scripture, tradition, and culture? Are we driven by anxiety and panic? Do we take actions out of fear that we will lose members? Are debates driven by the desire for power? The need to be right? The fear of being wrong?

The issues I've chosen to describe do not show the RCA at its best. Instead they illustrate the loss of the center or the mainstream identity of the RCA. We are moving away from our polity and instead making decisions via task forces or special councils. We are less inclined to study and reflection. We are reluctant to take seriously the insights of psychology and recent biblical studies if they seem to threaten our stated position. We do not want to deal with the fact that not only cultural attitudes but the law of the land has changed, as demonstrated in the recent Supreme Court ruling which allowed marriage equality. Instead, we are making significant decisions out of fear rather than faith. We act as adversaries, we engage in power struggles, we want to win. We react quickly to a perceived problem, we make a decision, and then we realize there should be some dialogue. Unfortunately, dialogue is not very meaningful when the decision has already been made.

Perhaps the most destructive aspect of our decision-making processes has been the loss of commitment to the denomination. In *Loyalty and Loss*, I noted that the RCA had been held together by the stubborn loyalty of many of its members to one another and to the

---

5   The phrase "the issue of homosexuality" is a particularly unfortunate and abstract term that loses sight of the personhood of gay and lesbian (and bisexual, transgendered, and queer) people. This is not simply an "issue" that the church can resolve by debate. We are talking about human lives and real people who have experienced harsh treatment from both church and society.

denomination. In the last few years, many of our debates have been clouded by the threat that somebody will leave if they don't get their way. Some churches and pastors have already done so.

This account is necessarily selective, and others might choose to tell the story differently, but I hope these examples will help the RCA consider how we make decisions, handle controversial topics, and treat those with whom we disagree.

The RCA's long painful conflict over homosexuality began in the 1970s.[6] The Theological Commission published a two-part paper in 1978 and 1979.[7] The RCA discussed the topic again in the midst of the AIDS crisis in the late 1980s. In 1989, the RCA adopted a statement that people should be accepted in the church and treated as God's children regardless of sexual orientation. That kind of grace made some people nervous. After heated discussion during the following year, in 1990 synod voted "to adopt as the position of the RCA that the practicing homosexual lifestyle is contrary to scripture, while at the same time encouraging love and sensitivity toward such persons as fellow human beings."[8] A motion to refer this statement to the Theological Commission for study before voting was defeated. One pastor insisted that if the synod delayed a decision, "people will say we are wishy-washy on sin." Jonathan Gerstner, executive secretary of the Council of the Reformed Church in Canada, claimed that if the RCA stated clearly that homosexuality was sinful, disaffected congregations from the United Church of Canada might want to join the RCA.[9] After the vote, the synod decided that perhaps theological reflection *was* warranted, and asked the Commission on Theology to write a new paper.

The Commission on Theology formed a task force to study the issues and write the paper. In an initial attempt to gather information in 1993, the task force offered a workshop at General Synod where they invited participants to reflect on their perceptions about homosexuality. Over a hundred people attended, and, because they were not debating a policy, they actually listened to one another. The task force concluded that the RCA would be more helped by conversation than another

---

[6]   For a discussion of RCA actions regarding homosexuality, see *Loyalty and Loss*, 207-10, 273-75, 277-80, 295-97.

[7]   The papers were relatively forward thinking for their time, but are marred by the use of problematic language ("pervert" and "invert"). They acknowledge that homosexuality may not be a choice and that it was very difficult to change. The most radical (and currently most ignored) observation was that homosexual people should not be denied their civil rights. That was a bold statement for the late 1970s.

[8]   *Acts and Proceedings*, 1990, 459-460.

[9]   Jeffrey Japinga, "Policy: Reject Lifestyle, But Not Gay Persons," *Church Herald*, July 1990, 10-11.

position paper, and, in 1994, asked synod to approve a process of dialogue throughout the denomination. Some synod delegates resisted. People feared that dialogue meant the RCA could change its position.[10] After heated debate, and late night caucusing by members of the task force and the Commission on Theology, synod approved a recommendation to prepare a study guide to help people engage in dialogue. The guide should be based on the 1978-79 papers and not encourage policy change. The anxiety persisted, however, and, in 1995, several classes tried to direct the content of the study guide, but synod chose to trust the process and the task force.

During the next five years, the debate over homosexuality shifted from the RCA's position toward scrutiny of an ecumenical partner, the United Church of Christ (UCC). The RCA, the UCC, and the Presbyterian Church (USA) had spent ten years in dialogue with the Evangelical Lutheran Church in America and produced The Formula of Agreement, which outlined a new relationship between the Reformed and Lutheran churches. Few RCA members objected to the ELCA, but many disapproved of the fact that the UCC ordained gay and lesbian pastors. In 1996, several overtures demanded that the RCA delay approval of the Formula of Agreement until the UCC repented of its sins. Edwin Mulder, former General Secretary, begged the synod not to become a one-issue church. The delegates listened and denied the overtures.

The synod of 1996 dealt with two controversial issues, and yet the meeting was relatively congenial. Terry DeYoung, managing editor of the *Church Herald*, attributed the good will to the quality of preaching and worship services.[11] The planning team and worship leader used world music, which was something of a compromise between hymns and praise music.[12]

---

[10]   In 1990 a critical letter to the editor responded to a Platform by a gay man describing the fact that he had not chosen his orientation. This author wrote: "When we start saying that homosexuals are born that way, we take away the sinfulness of their actions." Exactly. Opponents of dialogue did not welcome hearing stories about gay and lesbian people that might challenge their stereotypes about choice and sin. Abe Vander Vwide, "Flak and Flattery," *Church Herald*, March 1990, 7.

[11]   Terry DeYoung, "Worship Unites Delegates," *Church Herald*, July/August 1996, 19. The other controversial issue was the uniqueness of Christ as Savior, sparked by a conflict between the Classis of Muskegon and Richard Rhem, the pastor of Christ Community Church in Spring Lake, Michigan. Both Rhem and the church left the RCA. The church was allowed to keep its property (and large mortgage) and this set a precedent for future departures.

[12]   As worship preferences grow more diverse in the RCA, it has become increasingly difficult to plan worship at synod that is unifying rather than divisive. Does worship use the organ or the praise band? Hymnbooks or praise choruses on the screen? One preacher for the week, or a different preacher every day? What is the impact

The RCA was the first of the four denominations to vote on the Formula of Agreement in the summer of 1997. Supporters of the Agreement feared that the RCA would vote no and derail a decade of ecumenical work. A powerful worship experience occurred in an unscripted moment on the morning of the debate, when delegates continued to sing the final hymn ("the Holy Spirit must come down and set God's people free") as they walked from the worship space to the meeting space. That day, Synod debated the Formula at length, but finally voted to approve it. Delegates recognized the significance of the Formula in helping to heal the division between Lutheran and Reformed churches that had existed for four centuries. They recognized the need for cooperation and connection among these churches that shared the heritage of the Reformation.

Opposition to the UCC continued, however, and, in 1998, nine overtures asked synod to break ties or clearly limit the relationship. Although most came from the Classis of Canadian Prairies, and did not necessarily represent the view of the majority of the RCA, the overtures required considerable time and energy. In an effort to encourage the synod to attend to other topics, General Secretary Wesley Granberg-Michaelson recommended that the RCA refrain from debate about homosexuality at the Synods of 1998, 1999, and 2000.[13] He advocated instead a period of reflection and discernment by pastors, elders, and congregations. Synod agreed, although some people resented the recommendation because it seemed to silence their concerns rather than take a firm stand against homosexuality.

The *Church Herald* occasionally published personal essays in which an author asked for tolerance and compassion for gay and lesbian people. One pastor wrote about his brother and another friend who died of AIDS. Both felt certain they were not welcome in the church. Another pastor noted that some RCA members had children who were gay or lesbian, and he encouraged the church to be more accepting of them. Each essay sparked a flurry of letters to the editor. Most of the critical letters demonstrated absolute certainty that homosexuality was a choice and therefore a sin. God might be loving, but, more importantly, God is righteous, and will not tolerate human sinfulness. Gay and lesbian people must repent and leave their sinful past behind, and, if they do, God will save them from homosexuality and straighten

---

of the venue? Synod has often tried to save time by having morning worship in the meeting space. When synod meets at Hope College, for example, Dimnent Chapel offers a far more worshipful space than the arena where athletic contests are held!

13 N.a., "Shaping the Future," *Church Herald*, July/August, 1998, 8.

out their orientation.[14] It is no wonder gay and lesbian people did not feel welcome in many RCA churches.

Granberg-Michaelson recognized the impasse, and encouraged the denomination to think more about ministry and less about sex. In part, this was a matter of survival. The RCA was increasingly anxious about the loss of members.[15] Christina Van Eyl, editor of the *Church Herald*, articulated the persistent question: "Can the Reformed Church survive as a denomination?" Her strategy was both simple and difficult: "Let's stop obsessing about ourselves and get on with the work of the Kingdom."[16]

In 1997, Granberg-Michaelson proposed a new Mission and Vision Statement that encouraged congregations to try new forms of ministry to their communities. He also changed synod meetings to emphasize outreach and worship more than policy debates. To that end, the General Synod meeting in 2000 included a weekend celebration of Pentecost and invited all members to attend. Delegates and others spent the weekend in worship, discernment, reflection, and envisioning what the RCA might become.

During the business session, however, synod had to address the continuing criticism of the UCC. Despite the moratorium on debate, several classes submitted overtures in 1999 and 2000 protesting the continuing relationship.[17] In 2000, synod approved a statement that defined the RCA's relationship with the UCC and promised that it would not be increased or developed beyond common membership in ecumenical councils.[18] That placated the critics. Unfortunately, the RCA had spent more time and energy fighting about the UCC than it did finding creative ways to live out the Formula of Agreement with its new partners. Passionate intensity about purity did not permit much cooperation.

---

14   David Jones, "A Place for Broken People," *Church Herald*, Feb. 1997, 6. "Flak and Flattery, " April, 1997, 4-5. Jack Branford, "Leave These People to God," Feb. 1998, 7. "Flak and Flattery," March, 1998, 5-7. Louis Lotz, "Just As I Am," *Church Herald*, May, 2001, 45.

15   During the 1990s, the RCA dropped from over 200,000 members to 182,000. Wesley Granberg-Michaelson, "Resolved to Grow," *Church Herald*, Jan. 2001, 11.

16   Christina Van Eyl, "Embracing Life," *Church Herald*, Jan. 1999, 4.

17   A dozen overtures were sent in 2000. Classis of Southwest Michigan wanted to admonish the UCC's unrepentant acceptance of practicing homosexuals in its membership. The rest asked to break the relationship. *Church Herald*, June 2000, 10. The overtures about the UCC during these years often carried a rather self-righteous tone. Needless to say, many UCC members found this offensive, and yet it is also true that some UCC members disapproved of their denomination's position on homosexuality. And of course, some RCA members agreed with the UCC.

18   N.a., "Resting Place Found on UCC Issue," Church Herald, July/Aug. 2000, 12-13.

In 2001, Granberg-Michaelson again tried to steer the RCA into a more missional direction. He reported that the General Synod Council planned to develop concrete and measurable goals for denominational health and numerical growth.[19] Congregations should no longer simply function as social and spiritual clubs for Christians but engage in ministry to those outside the church. In 2003, the RCA adopted Our Call, a ten-year goal which included multiplication of new churches and revitalization of established churches.

Implementing the goal was more challenging than approving it. Some congregations were rapidly losing members but had few ideas about how to be a positive presence in the community and attract new people to the church. Some congregations were in areas where the population was declining. Some people had a very traditional sense of what church ought to be (evening service, prayer meetings, women's service groups) and found it difficult to think about other ways of defining church.[20] In the same issue as Granberg-Michaelson's call for change, the *Church Herald* published an article entitled "A Clean Sweep" which listed a number of things the RCA should eliminate. Some were tongue-in-cheek, such as ham buns, but others were more controversial: Sunday evening services, racism, "heresy" labels, and Dutchness. Two months later, a number of angry letters vigorously defended the old orthodoxies and old ways of doing things. One writer suggested that a clean sweep should begin with the *Church Herald* staff.[21]

Some of the anger and fervor about homosexuality waned a bit once the UCC's relationship with the RCA was minimized. Denominational staff and congregations poured considerable energy into Our Call. The program needed money and publicity. The *Church Herald* received about a million dollars of assessment money every year in a time when every dollar of increased assessment was fought and resented. Some people wondered whether the magazine was the best use of scarce resources that the denomination did not control. The editors of the *Church Herald* answered to an Editorial Council rather than to the GSC. They fought to retain their independence so that they would not become simply a house organ for the denomination. Denominational staff, on the other

---

[19] Wesley Granberg-Michaelson, "Resolved to Grow," *Church Herald*, Jan. 2001, 11.

[20] There were also some occasions where small churches with elderly members who had a valuable building or piece of land felt somewhat bullied by the emphasis on outreach. They might be pressured to close so that the classis could use their resources for a new church. See Bob Wegter, "Celebrate: New Life," *Church Herald*, Apr. 2006, 8-13.

[21] N.a., "A Clean Sweep," *Church Herald*, Jan 2001, 8-10. "Flak and Flattery," Mar. 2001, 5.

hand, thought that a magazine receiving such generous funding should be completely supportive of denominational efforts. Staff members also resented the expectation that they pay to advertise programs or fund-raising efforts.

The *Church Herald* had always sparked some controversy because of its editorial decisions, but conflict intensified in 1992 after synod approved President Louis Lotz' proposal to send the *Church Herald* to every RCA family. This cost about five dollars per member, and some churches complained that they were forced to pay for a magazine they did not want. The magazine received numerous awards recognizing its high quality. It provided news about the whole denomination. It included articles about personal spirituality, social action, and congregational life. It included numerous articles about the various aspects of the Ten-Year Goal. The magazine kept the family informed about what was happening in the RCA, and gave them a sense that they belonged to something bigger than their own congregation.

The magazine commissioned several surveys of its readers and each survey showed that people read and appreciated it. In 1995, a Gallup survey found that 91% of responders said that someone in the household read the magazine; 77% thought it was important to receive the magazine; 67% said it helped them feel more connected to the denomination. A 1999 survey showed that only seven percent of recipients did not read it at all. On average, people spent an hour reading each issue.[22]

The magazine saw itself not as *the* voice of the RCA but as a forum where all its members could speak. It presented all the diverse voices in the denominations, even those that harshly criticized the magazine. It printed Platforms (opinion essays) and letters to the editor that sharply criticized other members of the denomination. This meant that almost everyone could find something offensive in the magazine. Some of the most progressive churches refused to have it sent to their members because the tone of the magazine seemed hopelessly conservative. Some conservative churches insisted that their members could not be exposed to such a liberal magazine. The diverse opinions in the denomination could be harsh and unappealing. This was the reality of a diverse church. The *Church Herald* did not create disagreement, but merely showcased it. The RCA was polarized and people did not always like each other. The magazine became a scapegoat for the frustration RCA members felt with each other and with the denomination as a whole. It was easier

[22]   Andrew DeBraber, "Wheel of (Good) Fortune," *Church Herald*, Feb. 2003, 8-12.

to blame the *Church Herald* for publishing inappropriate material than it was to deal with the sharp divisions in the denomination.[23]

Despite the criticism of the magazine, it was appreciated by many of the RCA members who were most knowledgeable about and loyal to the denomination. The magazine provided a way for them to be connected, just as Louis Lotz had suggested in 1992. They read about missionaries, General Synod, and their friends in other parts of the church. They read the obituaries. They might roll their eyes at the letters in Flak and Flattery, but they knew those letters did not represent the whole denomination.

In 2003, the GSC proposed a restructure which would create a communications council which would be accountable to the GSC. The *Church Herald* staff thought this would "allow GSC and denominational staff to control the magazine's content, staffing and budget."[24] The Christian Heritage and Communication Advisory Committee discussed this proposal at Synod, but recommended instead that "GSC officers and staff to work with Editorial Council and *Church Herald* staff to develop a strategy for coordinated communication." Synod approved this proposal by a wide margin. People did not always like everything that the magazine published, but they recognized the value of an independent magazine that was not merely a house organ.[25]

In 2004, denominational leadership made another attempt to deal with the *Church Herald*. Synod President David Schutt proposed that the magazine's funding be gradually cut in half over a period of three

---

[23] Several other examples of the scapegoating occurred. In Jan. 2004, the magazine published an article about the problems of the RCA's health insurance plan. In April, a letter to the editor accused the magazine of negativity. In Jan. 2006, Oliver Patterson wrote an article about the racism which was evident in the response to Hurricane Katrina. A letter to the editor blamed the magazine, not the author, for its political correctness and liberal agendas! Another letter then criticized the magazine for running the racist response. After the synod of 2006, critics said that the magazine only mentioned debates about homosexuality and failed to report all the good things being accomplished in the Ten-Year Goal. "Flak and Flattery," Oct. 2006, 5. Another letter urged the magazine to "shrug off attempts at intimidation and continue to cover our denomination, not merely do our public relations." Jeff Johnson, "Flak and Flattery," Dec. 2006, 6.

[24] N.a., "GSC Separates Office of Worship from Social Witness Responsibilities," *Church Herald*, May, 2003, 36-37.

[25] N.a., "Strategy, Yes; Structure, No." *Church Herald*, July/August, 2003, 15. It is not entirely clear why the staff and GSC were so eager to control the magazine. The first two editors of the *Church Herald*, Louis Benes and John Stapert, were far more critical of the denomination than Christina Van Eyl and Terry DeYoung. Anxiety over the future of both magazine and denomination led to a significant power struggle.

years. He graciously allowed them to maintain editorial independence! The Synod Advisory Committee did not support this and neither did Synod, in part because synod approved a coordinated communication plan in which a Communication, Vision, and Evaluation Group would develop a strategy which would be implemented by magazine and denomination staff, and coordinated by the editor of the *Church Herald* and the GSC's Director of Communication.[26]

Conflict over communication was less an issue at the next General Synod, in 2005, because the debate about homosexuality roared back into the RCA. The opportunity for dialogue during the three year moratorium on debate had not made people any less argumentative. At the synod of 2004, the Classis of Canadian Prairies asked synod to define marriage as the union of one man and one woman, to the exclusion of all others. Same-sex marriage had been approved in Canada, and some ministers claimed they could be prosecuted if they refused to perform such marriages. They insisted that a clear statement would protect them. Synod discussed tabling or referring, but eventually approved the recommendation and also asked for an amendment to the *Book of Church Order* (*BCO*). After the vote, synod asked the Commission on Theology to provide a study paper on human sexuality and marriage. Once again, synod acted first and studied later.[27]

Later in the summer of 2004, Norman Kansfield, General Synod Professor and President of New Brunswick Theological Seminary, officiated at the wedding of his daughter and her partner. A number of clergy throughout the denomination brought charges against Kansfield. As a General Synod Professor of Theology, he was accountable to the synod, rather than a classis, and he was brought to trial at the Synod of 2005. Synod found him guilty of three charges. Officiating at a same-sex marriage was contrary to RCA faith and beliefs. He violated his ordination vow to seek unity, purity and peace, and he violated his promise to submit to the counsel of the General Synod. He was deposed from the office of Professor and suspended from the office of Minister of Word and Sacrament.[28] This punishment was harsher than many

---

[26] *Acts and Proceedings*, 2004, 86-95.

[27] *Acts and Proceedings*, 2004, 332-3. In 2005, the Commission on Church Order declined to propose an amendment, in part because it had become clear that Canadian pastors would not be prosecuted. The Commission also noted that the Commission on Theology was studying the issue, and expressed its reluctance to use church order to make a statement about a controversial social issue. The most significant reason the Commission offered was that the statement made by the General Synod in 2004 did not in fact have the status of definitive church teaching. *Acts and Proceedings*, 2005, 90-91.

[28] *Acts and Proceedings*, 2005, 43-57. See also the essay by Mary Kansfield in this volume.

people had expected. As it had done before, synod made a stern and punitive decision, but then decided that the church needed to engage in dialogue. John Stapert was later appointed to develop a process for conversations within classes.[29]

The trial was a divisive and difficult moment for the RCA. Kansfield had a long history in theological education. Louis Lotz described Kansfield as a man of towering intellect and deep personal piety. He was not a heretic, Lotz said, and synod went too far in its punishment of him.[30] On the other side of the debate, two of the ministers who filed charges against Kansfield wrote Platform articles. Kevin DeYoung insisted that unity was impossible in the RCA unless everyone agreed with *his* understanding of doctrine.[31] Ron Sanford said that the RCA must be united in its view of the Bible, and that had to be *his* view of the Bible as divinely inspired and inerrant.[32]

2005 was a difficult, heavy, depressing year in the RCA. Much of the sadness and pain was evident in the *Church Herald*. Again, it was easy to scapegoat the magazine for reporting on the debate and printing all the ugly letters, but it was not their fault that people were rude to one another. The *Church Herald* offered a forum for members to speak, without critique or censure.

Synod again took up the discussion of communications and the *Church Herald* in 2007. The effort to develop a coordinated communication plan had not been fully successful and there was still considerable disagreement between the magazine's desire for independence and

[29] Kansfield's action and the trial sparked many letters to the editor. See the "Flak and Flattery" pages in February, April, June, and October of 2005. Further conversation occurred on an electronic discussion board sponsored by the magazine. The letters criticizing Kansfield repeated common themes. The Bible is clear and must be read literally. Homosexuality is a choice and therefore a sin. Sin cannot be tolerated but must be confronted. Truth is more important than grace. The letters supporting Kansfield argued for a more nuanced reading of Scripture, and insisted that homosexual orientation was not a choice and could not be changed.

[30] Louis Lotz, "Search for Common Ground," Church Herald, July/Aug. 2005, 46.

[31] Kevin DeYoung, "What Kind of Unity?" Platform, *Church Herald*, Feb. 2006, 7. Less than a decade later, DeYoung and his congregation left the RCA. It is interesting that several of the clergy who brought the complaint against Kansfield might be considered angry young men who were not educated at RCA seminaries and seemed to think that the RCA was not pure enough.

[32] Ron Sanford, "The Real Issue," Platform, *Church Herald*, May 2006, 7. See the responses in July/August. Sanford's view of Scripture is shaped more by fundamentalism than by classic Reformed and Calvinist theology. The RCA's Theological Commission wrote in 1963 that Scripture was infallible in all it intended to teach. Sanford was asking the RCA to conform to a view of Scripture that was not part of its Reformed identity.

the GSC and staff's desire for control. GSC proposed a budget that eliminated funding for the *Church Herald* with the expectation that the magazine would operate again on a subscription basis. Delegates to synod discussed this for about ninety minutes in advisory groups, but it was not a particularly effective process. Many delegates had little knowledge of the long history and the issues involved. Many assumed that if the magazine no longer received five dollars per member, that the churches would see their assessments decline by that amount. Instead, the denomination returned only about eighty cents, and retained the rest of the money to use for Our Call. This struck some people as disingenuous at best, and manipulative at worst.[33]

This decision was reached at about the same time as a serious downturn occurred in the American economy. The magazine had about 20,000 subscribers in 2008, but that number dwindled to about 15,000 in 2009. The denominational staff had started publishing *RCA Today* three times a year as a way to promote the work of Our Call. The magazine requested funding from the denomination in 2008, and another committee was formed to explore cooperation efforts between the magazine and the GSC. The committee made three recommendations to synod in 2009. The *Church Herald* and *RCA Today* could jointly publish eleven issues a year for an assessment of $5.30 per person. They could publish six issues for $2.85. If no assessment was approved, they could publish an electronic version.

Delegates were given about ninety minutes in their advisory groups to discuss the options and vote on their preference. Not surprisingly, few people wanted to increase the assessments, since they had seen no appreciable reduction when the magazine stopped going to every family. Delegates were also allowed to make comments and suggestions that were later processed by a small committee. There were numerous complaints about the magazine. The small committee gave its recommendations to the delegates late on Monday night and the issue was slated for discussion on Tuesday morning, the last day of Synod. Staff members of the *Church Herald* were asked to leave the room

---

[33]   *Acts and Proceedings*, 2007, 187-95. The report from the Communication, Vision, and Evaluation Group (CVEG) believed that GSC and denominational staff could do a better job at communicating than the *Church Herald* did. The magazine may have provided a forum for discussion, but the issues discussed were not what most of the denomination cared about. The magazine supposedly did not provide enough coverage of Our Call, and yet the magazine was filled with articles on the various aspects of the ten-year goal. The CVEG report suggested that the magazine may provide the sidewalks of connection that Louis Lotz had envisioned, but now the denomination needed a super-highway of high-tech communication.

and could not participate in the discussion. A great deal of confusion and parliamentary maneuvering ensued. One vote to approve an independent evaluation of all communication was initially approved, but then reversed after a delegate complained that his electronic voting device had not worked. The small committee was asked to discern the mind of the Synod using on a sheet of paper from each advisory committee that contained its vote and any other comments people wished to make. Based on this scant and subjective information, and a rather bizarre process, the small committee recommended that the denomination simply did not want to receive the magazine. Synod agreed, and thus ended 175 years of a denominational publication.[34] Christina Van Eyl later observed, "Perhaps we will see that the *Herald* has been something that has been holding back the RCA, and from here on out it will be clear sailing. I hope that's true. I would hate to think that the *Herald* was killed off for nothing."[35] The RCA lost something that was valued by its most loyal members. What did they receive in exchange?

In the last four years, the RCA made two more controversial decisions about homosexuality. As same-sex marriage became legal in more states, some RCA clergy officiated at weddings of their gay and lesbian parishioners. Opponents of same-sex marriage thought these pastors were flouting RCA policy, but a minister cannot bring disciplinary charges against a pastor in another classis. In 2012, four classes submitted lengthy overtures which asked that ministers who officiate at same sex marriages be disciplined, because such actions were sinful. Several overtures included a list of pastors and congregations which were violating the rules. After one of the most acrimonious debates in recent memory,[36] synod approved a statement which said that any person, congregation, or assembly that advocates homosexual behavior or provides leadership for a same-sex marriage has committed

---

[34] *Acts and Proceedings*, 2009, 211-226. I am clearly not objective about this issue! As a historian, I have made significant use of the *Church Herald* and its predecessors in my study of the RCA in the twentieth century. It was an invaluable resource for understanding the denomination and I grieve its loss. On the other hand, most denominational magazines are struggling and unable to continue in their old ways. It is ironic, though, that the various cooperative communication groups insisted that they wanted innovative and attractive communications worthy of a super highway, but I suspect that many RCA members now feel less connected and knowledgeable than they did before.

[35] Christina Van Eyl, "Talking Back to an Exclusive Process," *Church Herald*, July/Aug. 2009, 14-15.

[36] Some of the same angry young men who brought charges against Kansfield were particularly aggressive in this debate.

a disciplinable offense. Further, the statement recommended the formation of an eight person committee to find a way forward for the church.[37]

This unusual statement sparked a great deal of anger and criticism, along with multiple overtures. In 2013, synod stated that the synod of 2012 had demonstrated a lack of decorum and civility in its discussion of the topic, and usurped the disciplinary authority of the classes. The Way Forward Committee reported that they had conversed in a loving, respectful manner, and recommended the formation of another committee to provide resources to help other groups have similarly positive and productive conversations.[38]

For those filled with passionate intensity for purity and discipline, more conversation was not the solution they sought. In 2015, synod president Greg Alderman offered a very unusual recommendation. As he traveled around the RCA, he said, he repeatedly heard this question: "What is the church going to do about homosexuality?" He insisted that the church wanted the General Synod to provide leadership and a clear answer. He recommended that synod approve the formation of a special committee of about eighty people who would meet for four or five days and find a constitutional way forward. Delegates raised numerous questions about the wisdom and feasibility of this approach, but approved it. Once again, synod seemed to be operating out of fear. Alderman had said that some new congregations refused to join the RCA because it did not have a firm position. He failed to acknowledge the fact that other congregations might choose to leave if the RCA adopted a position that was punishing and ungracious.[39]

As of this writing, the special council meeting is about a month away. People on both sides of the issue are suspicious and skeptical about the process and the outcome. It is difficult to envision a workable compromise. Each side feels strongly. The RCA has avoided conducting a thorough study of homosexuality, in part because it might result in threatening ideas. There is precedence for that. The ELCA and PCUSA both had produced in-depth theological papers before the approved ordination and marriage for GLBTQ people. We might ask, though, what we are afraid of. If church life and polity and mission can all be

---

[37] *Acts and Proceedings*, 2012, 136-150.
[38] *Acts and Proceedings*, 2013, 111-16, 175-81.
[39] *Acts and Proceedings*, 2015, 20-25, 101-7. The language of the question "what is the church going to do about homosexuality?" makes it sound like an abstract policy statement that can simply be debated, rather than a painful and often bruising discussion of human lives

transformed and transforming, what about our deepest beliefs about humanity, sexuality, and relationships? Is it possible that the RCA might be wrong, as it has been wrong about slavery and a number of other issues?

Conversation has not provided the magic solution either. Some groups have the right kind of chemistry from the beginning and they have plenty of time to get to know each other in a relatively safe environment. That is not the norm. Most of the time having meaningful conversation is extremely difficult. We fear the judgment of others. We fear the judgment of God also, and we sometimes allow ourselves to wonder if God's judgment will be administered as we expect. Maybe we are all wrong. We do not want to hurt other people. Most of us know GLBTQ people, and we know they have been hurt, and we want them to thrive. We do not agree what that thriving will be like.

So much of this debate has to do with the reality that we read the Bible very differently. We talk about the biblical view of marriage, but a quick read of Genesis shows about a dozen views of marriage, most of which are dysfunctional! Reformed Christians have traditionally (with exceptions, of course) not read the Bible as an absolute rule book, but view the Bible as a record of the ways that people have tried to make sense of God's presence in their lives. Perhaps the Bible does not actually condemn committed same sex relationships.

A "constitutional way forward" seems like a way to warfare. Many people remember the constant battles and repeated votes about the ordination of women in the 1970s. It was not a happy time in the RCA. Almost any definitive change to the *BCO* would require approval by two-thirds of the classes, which might be difficult to obtain.

I wonder if the best way forward might be some form of the conscience clause that recognizes that people of good faith and deep commitment disagree about this. Congregations could decide who can be married or who can be members in their church.[40] Classes can decide who is ordained. Those in favor of same-sex marriage would have to give up their desire that the entire RCA is as open and affirming as they might want. But their congregation and classis can be a place where there is room for all. Those opposed to same sex marriage would have to give up the idea that the denomination can be pure, and they will have to compromise and learn to live with difference.

It has not been easy to be the church in the last century, and particularly the last couple of decades. So much has changed, and it is

---

[40]   The Commission on Church Order proposed this to General Synod in 2015, but consideration of it was postponed until 2016. *Acts and Proceedings*, 2015, 188-92.

not easy to discern whether change is positive or negative. At times we have been overwhelmed by fear, loss, and anxiety, and we have made decisions that do not always reflect the grace and mercy of God. Those choices do not have to define or limit us. For almost four centuries, the RCA has been a church that values the intellect, theology, community, loyalty, and above all, grace. I hope that in the future we will be able to make more of our decisions guided by those values, confident that we belong to God, and to each other.

CHAPTER 12

Making Room for All

Mary L. Kansfield

In June, 2005, the Reformed Church in America experienced a cataclysm. Its General Synod tried and convicted the Rev. Dr. Norman J. Kansfield, a General Synod Professor of Theology and President of its New Brunswick Theological Seminary, on three charges arising from his officiating at the wedding of his daughter Ann to Jennifer Aull in June, 2004.[1] During the trial, a small group of faithful and passionate

---

[1]   The charges include:
   1. The charge that Dr. Kansfield acted contrary to our faith and beliefs as affirmed by the Holy Scriptures and the decisions of the General Synod concerning the relationships of active homosexuality;"
   2. The charge that Dr. Kansfield contradicted his ordination declaration that stated: "I accept the Scriptures as the only rule of faith and life," as well as his affirmations stating "that I believe the Gospel of the Grace of God in Christ Jesus as revealed in the Holy Scriptures of the Old and New Testaments...;" that Dr. Kansfield contradicted his ordination promise to "walk in the Spirit of Christ, in love and fellowship with the church, seeking the things that make for unity, purity, and peace" and;
   3. The charge that he failed to keep his promise to "submit myself to the counsel and the admonition of the General Synod, always ready, with gentleness and reverence, to give account of my understanding of the Christian faith." *Acts and Proceedings of the General Synod of the Reformed Church in America* (hereafter *Acts and Proceedings*) , 2005, 43-44.

supporters of Dr. Kansfield knelt just beyond the mandated distance from the entrance to the building where the trial was proceeding and prayed for Dr. Kansfield and for a positive outcome to the trial. The verdicts were not positive. Dr. Kansfield was found guilty on all charges.

The penalty phase of the trial continued late into the night. When it was announced that Dr. Kansfield would be removed from the Office of Professor of Theology and suspended from the Office of Minister of Word and Sacrament, some who earlier prayed so passionately outside the building huddled together in a motel room and grieved with Dr. Kansfield's family. There they cried and held each other close. The removal of Norm Kansfield from the Office of the Professorate was understandable. After all, if members of the General Synod held in question any concern about his gifts for ministry or his theological positions beyond those outlined in the *Book of Church Order (BCO)*, this would be logical. But suspending his ordination from the Office of Minister of Word and Sacrament, thus classifying him as a heretic, made no sense to them at all.[2]

Important as the Kansfield trial was, this essay seeks to show that long before that trial there were opening salvos that should have alerted the General Synod to the fact that supporters of Lesbian, Gay, Bisexual, and Transgender (LGBTQ[3]) inclusion were not only present within the denomination, but indeed were prepared to care for and to advocate on behalf of LGBTQ persons. After referring to these persons and moments in the RCA's LGBTQ history, this essay will focus on the establishment and growth of the RCA advocacy group called Room for All (RfA), that was founded after Norman Kansfield's trial.

[2]   A judicial error had occurred. See "Case Dismissed", *Church Herald* (hereafter CH), July/August, 2006, 15, as to why it made no sense to those gathered in the motel room that night. In this issue of *The Church Herald*, the editor says, "Although deposed from the professorial office, Synod 2005 failed to dismiss Kansfield to a classis as required by the *Book of Church Order (BCO)*. Technically, this action was consistent with an unintended anomaly in the *BCO*, requiring that one suspended remain amenable to the judicatory that voted to suspend—in this case, General Synod. . . . The actions of General Synod 2005 left both Kansfield and the Synod in a quandary because General Synod has no constitutional authority to supervise ministers of Word and sacrament—only professors of theology, the office from which Kansfield was deposed." CH, July/August, 2006, 15.

[3]   Use of the "Q" designation generally refers to those "questioning" their sexual identity. For some others, the "Q" designation refers to "queer" or those who experience fluidity in their sexuality or gender identification.

Before the Trial #1: New Brunswick Seminary's Hiring of Judith Hoch Wray

In the Spring of 1998, President Kansfield learned that two tenured faculty members would be leaving New Brunswick Theological Seminary (NBTS). To fill these faculty positions, a year long search process for each position would have to take place. Acting on the prerogative of his office, President Kansfield appointed interim professors in Old Testament and New Testament for one-year terms, thus allowing time for thorough searches. He appointed Dr. Judith Hoch Wray to the one-year interim position in New Testament. Dr. Wray was not new to the New Brunswick faculty. She had been teaching as an adjunct professor for six years, and she had also served as stated supply pastor for an RCA congregation. Students spoke very highly of her teaching, and her pastoral skills were clearly evident. As a lesbian in a committed relationship, Dr. Wray was open although not assertive about her sexual orientation. This was known to the administration, the faculty, and the student community.

Within one day of signing the contract, word spread within the church and immediately brought about a fire storm of controversy. Pressure quickly mounted for President Kansfield to withdraw the contract. This he refused to do. The threat of introducing the matter at the upcoming General Synod in Holland, Michigan, brought Wesley Granberg-Michaelson, the denomination's General Secretary, to New Brunswick to meet with the Seminary's Board of Trustees. Granberg-Michaelson, an *ex officio* member of the Board, "effectively arm-wrestled the Board into most reluctantly rescinding the contract"[4]..."for the peace

---

[4]   Norman Kansfield in *Defending Same-Sex Marriage,Vol 2: Our Family Values: Same-Sex Marriage and Religion*, Edited by Traci C. West (Westport, CT, Praeger, 2006), 200. "The Board took its action to rescind the contract with Dr. Wray only after attaching four clauses to the action: 1) They were committed to paying Dr. Wray for the entire value of her contract, so that she was in every way financially whole, in spite of the rescinding; 2) they wanted their action to be seen as taken solely for the peace and unity of the church; 3) they called upon the General Secretary and all other responsible persons within the RCA immediately to facilitate the conversation on the role of homosexual persons within the church that the Synod of 1994 had called for and that had never happened; and 4) they call for the General Secretary and others to assume homosexual persons with the church a safe participation within that conversation. They also committed themselves and the Seminary to a program of self-education about the issues that have prevented homosexual persons from open participation within the life of the church." Minutes of the NBTS Board of Trustees, May 28-30, 1998, as noted in "The Reformed Church in America: One Denomination's Response to Same-Sex Marriage", *Defending Same-Sex Marriage,* Vol 2, edited by Traci C. West, (Westport, CT: Praeger, 2006).

and unity of the church."[5] While agreeing to rescind the contract with Dr. Wray, the Board stipulated that the full value of the contract would be paid to Dr. Wray. However, the pain and damage to her career was irreversible. This was painful for the Board and for President Kansfield, but especially for Dr. Hoch Wray and her partner, Donna Prince.

The matter was brought before the General Synod when the Classis of Passaic Valley (New Jersey) requested the Synod to take action and instruct NBTS "to neither hire nor continue to employ any person in its faculty or administration whose theological and moral commitments concerning homosexual practice are not in agreement with the teachings of Scripture, RCA doctrinal standards, and past General Synod actions, all of which clearly say that homosexual practice is sin."[6]

Before any action could be added to the Agenda as New Business, the General Secretary used his Synod Report to call the Synod "to refrain from deliberative debate and policy decisions relating to homosexuality...and to urge this same action upon the 1999 and 2000 General Synods..."[7] This the Synod agreed to do. Toward the end of the Synod, Dr. Kansfield was given an opportunity to speak. He seized this opportunity to say:

> ...You already know where my commitments lie. So, while I assure you of my and New Brunswick's full future compliance with that part of the recommendation which requests "all commissions, agencies, assemblies, and institutions related to the General Synod to refrain from taking any action that would be in obvious contradiction of our stated positions, as expressed especially in 1978, 1979, 1990, and 1994...I ask you also to count me among those who are committed carefully to listen to and, as necessary, to speak on behalf of homosexual persons, most of whom will not feel free enough to participate in the church's important conversations.[8]

This left no doubt about President Kansfield's commitment to the issue of LGBTQ inclusion.

---

[5]   *Acts and Proceedings*, 1998, 58.
[6]   *Acts and Proceedings*, 1998, 32.
[7]   Ibid, 60.
[8]   See Room for All Archives for the full text of this General Synod Address.

Before the Trial #2: The Buchanan Group and the Holy Relationships Conference

In January, 2002, President Kansfield received a telephone call from the Rev. C. David Buchanan. The Rev. Buchanan had graduated from NBTS in 1975 and was then serving the United Methodist Church in Manlius, New York. Having received an unexpected inheritance from his mother, he and his wife, Diane, who have a gay son, wished to advance the conversation within the RCA and the broader church regarding the place and ministry of homosexual persons within the life of the church. Members of a planning committee first met at the Seminary on October 27, 2003.[9] In subsequent meetings a group of ten participants plus the Rev. Buchanan; Sherrill Holland, Dean of the Seminary; Everett Zabriskie, Director of Development at the Seminary; and President Kansfield came together to pray, to study, and to plan a national conference that "comes to grips with the pain within the church..."[10]

This group of clergy and laity, diverse in gender and sexual orientation, as well as academic and denominational affiliation, soon became known as "The Buchanan Group". Dr. Judith Hoch Wray served as Moderator, and the Conference they planned took place October 16-18, 2005, in New Brunswick, New Jersey.[11] Titled "Holy Relationships: A Conference on Theology and Sexuality", this conference enlisted outstanding keynote speakers[12] and workshop leaders. It brought together persons from many denominations, and joined almost two hundred (almost fifty participants came from the RCA[13] alone) to worship, to embrace one another, and to grow in understanding the

[9]   Participants on that Planning Team included: Dr. Jane Dickie of Hope College; the Rev. Seth Kaper-Dale, Pastor of the Highland Park Reformed Church; Rich McCarty from Iowa City, Iowa; Rhonda Shipley from Indianapolis, Indiana; Dr. Judith Hoch Wray; the Rev. Everett Zabriskie, Director of Development at NBTS; and Dr. Norman Kansfield, NBTS President.

[10]   Rev. David C. Buchanan quoted in "One United Methodist Pastor Seeks Healing in the Church", *The Christian Century*, August 9, 2005.

[11]   The Holy Relations Conference Planning Team included: C. David Buchanan, Brad Clark, Sam Cruz, Jane Dickie, Howard Gaas, Ann Kansfield, Seth Kaper-Dale, Rich McCarty (Chair), Jill Russell, Rhonda Shipley, Rich Williams, and Judith Hoch Wray.

[12]   Keynote speakers included Rita Nakashima Brock, Virginia Ramey Mollenkott, David Myers, Letha Dawson Scanzoni, John Selders, Miguel De La Torre, Mel White, and Judith Hoch Wray.

[13]   Professor Jane Dickie of Hope College arranged for a bus to transport students and friends from the Holland, Michigan area to the conference.

issues that divide us.[14] The conference was "transformative"[15] and led to a movement that carried the Holy Relationships conversation forward at additional Holy Relationship Conferences.[16]

Before the Trial #3: The 2004 Women's Triennial

Additional events contributed to denominational awareness of the LGBTQ issue. Beginning in 1960, the women of the Reformed Church, jointly called Reformed Church Women's Ministries (RCWM), held a national conference every three years. "Triennials," as they were called, were held in different geographic locations, and, in July, 2004, a Triennial was held at the Crystal Cathedral in Garden Grove, California. Originally a workshop was offered titled "A Time of Togetherness for Silent Mothers" that focused on sharing stories and the common bond of having a gay or lesbian child.[17] It didn't take long before conservative voices rose up in protest, and the workshop was pulled from the registration. But, since some conference registrants had already signed up for the workshop, it was quietly decided to give those participants an opportunity to come together. Five women met at a covert location in the undercroft of the church.[18] There they shared their individual stories and their experiences as loving mothers. It was a time of embrace. This Triennial experience revealed the depth of the tension over LGBTQ inclusion among women within the denomination.

---

[14]   The sites of the conference included the First Reformed Church, Christ Episcopal Church, and the Hyatt Regency Hotel in New Brunswick. Sponsors of the event included: the Buchanan Group in association with New Brunswick Theological Seminary, the Collegiate Church of the City of New York, Union Theological Seminary in the City of New York, Metropolitan Community Church in North Brunswick and Park Avenue Christian Church (Disciples of Christ) New York City.

[15]   As described by Shari Brink, Room for All Archives, Email to RoomforAll@googlegroups.com, May 15, 2006.

[16]   Regional Conferences held included the first Holy Relationships Midwestern Conference, October 19-20, 2006, in Iowa City, Iowa. Another conference took place November 2-4, 2007, in Indianapolis, IN at the campus of the University of Indianapolis. Room for All Archives, *Holy Relationships,* "*Newsletter of the Holy Relationships Movement*", Vol. 1, Issue 1, Summer, 2007 and Vol. 1, Issue 2, Winter, 2007.

[17]   The title of the workshop was "A Time of Togetherness for Silent Mothers," and was to be taught by Mary Kansfield. The workshop description noted, "To increase a sense of confidentiality, the location of this workshop will only be disclosed to those who have pre-registered." Triennial, July 22-24, 2004, folder in possession of the author.

[18]   Those women included Carol Babinsky, Mary Kansfield, Carol Mutch, Barbara Neevel, and Marjorie Shimmin (names revealed with permission).

Before the Trial #4: Friends of Norm

The nervousness within the RCA increased dramatically following the wedding Dr. Kansfield performed on June 19, 2004. Word of the marriage spread quickly. Use of the Internet and chat groups was still fairly new, but their use served to fan the flames of controversy. An immense amount of mail delivered to the Kansfield home revealed both positive and negative responses to Dr. Kansfield's act. While some postings firmly supported the action Dr. Kansfield had taken, other postings steadfastly opposed. At this point, Dr. Kansfield's children and their friends decided to initiate a support group of their own. Founded in December, 2004, they created a Google Group website called "Friends of Norm."[19] It didn't take long before friends and those advocating for LGBTQ inclusion began signing their names to the list. As the number grew, the word spread.[20]

Before the Trial #5: Engage in Dialogue or Hold Us Accountable, Too

Among those whole-heartedly supporting Norm's act of marrying Ann and Jennifer was a young RCA pastor serving as co-pastor of the Reformed Church of Highland Park, New Jersey, named Seth Kaper-Dale. Feeling "bound in ropes of sinfulness" by failing to speak out on the issue, the Rev. Kaper-Dale prepared a statement to be read at the upcoming General Synod titled "Engage in Dialogue or Hold Us Accountable, Too". With the help of Friends of Norm and their website, signatories to the document affirmed that they agreed with what Dr. Kansfield had done and that they had or would have acted similarly. Signatories invited the denomination to further the dialogue on homosexuality or to hold the signatories accountable as well. [21] Introduced as New Business at General Synod, the document was read

---

[19] April Greenberg, a close college friend of Ann, set up the website friendsofnorm@ googlegroups.com. Ann was not without computer skills, and she aggressively solicited support using the website.

[20] It is recorded that by February 9, 2015, up to 267 names appeared on the Friends of Norm list. By May 11, the number exceeded 600. May 10, 2005, E-mail from Rob Williams to Mary DeJonge-Benishek, Room for All Archives, in possession of the author.

[21] As of the day before the beginning of General Synod, 167 signatories and one whole Consistory had signed the "Engage in Dialogue or Hold Us Accountable Too" document. In signing the document, signatories identified their respective offices in the RCA.

aloud. The names and offices of the signatories were written into the Minutes of the General Synod.

If the aborted hiring of Dr. Judith Hoch Wray in 1998 occurred within the context of NBTS and was viewed as "a Kansfield matter," a broader circle of supporters quickly extended beyond the Kansfield family. "Outsiders" as well as RCA members added their names to lists supporting LGBTQ inclusion. Those attending the Holy Relationships Conference represented not only RCA folks, but a diversity among participants who shared a variety of backgrounds and varying church traditions. When the names of those claiming accountability were read into the public record of the General Synod, another step was taken. A movement was under way.

Making Room for All[22]

Once the trial was over, the need for a proactively prophetic voice, yet one open to dialogue within the RCA, became clear.[23] The pain of the trial, the stress for so many from public revelations of what formerly had been deeply held secrets, and the horrendous letdown from feeling betrayed by our own denomination, all contributed to tremendous individual pain and a sense that the RCA didn't care. During the early founding days of Room for All, whoever could make it gathered around the back tables at Dano's Restaurant on Fifth Avenue in Manhattan before our meetings at Marble Collegiate Church,[24] not only to pray and dine together, but mostly to minister to the searing pain each one felt. The pain didn't abate much, but sharing stories, embracing one another and feeling the assurance that we were there for each other made a positive future seem more possible.

From its beginning,[25] the founders of Room for All recognized the need to identify and incorporate certain foundational tools. The

---

[22] Mary Kansfield serves as the Archivist for Room for All, and the Archives currently are housed in the Kansfield library, 126 Hideaway Lane, East Stroudsburg, PA 18301. Access to the Archives should be made in written form. Use of time-sensitive and confidential materials should be made in writing to the Archivist or to Marilyn Paarlberg, Executive Director of Room for All at P. O. Box 11495, Albany, NY 12211, or at www.roomforall.com.

[23] Meetings began within three weeks of the trial and regularly took place at Marble Collegiate Church in New York City.

[24] It was mostly ministers who came together. Never known to be highly paid, the cost of traveling into New York City, parking, and eating out limited some from participating in the RfA founding group. This was unfortunate. Participants in the early meetings were also limited to those living in the eastern Tri-state area.

[25] Records in the Room for All Archives identify a formational meeting that took place on July 7, 2005, at Marble Collegiate Church. No minutes survive of this meeting. The first recorded meeting for which minutes appear is November 2, 2005.

"Room for All" name was formally adopted[26] as well as a logo showing a ripple of water symbolizing Acts 10:47, "Can anyone withhold the water for baptizing these people who have received the Holy Spirit just as we have?"

A Board of Directors was immediately established.[27] Applications for Incorporation in New York State and for IRS tax exempt status were drawn up and submitted in September, 2005.[28] The Incorporation Certificate states the purpose of Room for All to be:

> The Corporation is organized to engage in charitable, educational, religious and community activities. The Corporation's purposes are to support, to educate and to advocate for the full participation of gay, lesbian, bi-sexual and transgender (GLBT) persons in all aspects of the life and ministry of the Reformed Church in America as compelled by the inclusive love of God revealed to us by our Lord and Savior Jesus Christ.[29]

At its November meeting, officers were elected and Committee Chairs identified.[30]

After taking inventory of the immediate financial needs of the organization, it was estimated that it would require $11,000. All members of the Board made a commitment to make Room for

---

[26] The name first appeared as the logo on tee shirts worn by those maintaining a prayer vigil at the trial of Dr. Kansfield. The full logo read "Reformed Church in America, Increasingly Inclusive since 1628".

[27] The By-Laws of the Articles of Incorporation state that "There shall be not less than nine (9) and no more than twenty-one (21) Directors." The original Board of Directors included fifteen: Jennifer Aull, Beverly J. Bell, J. Karel Boersma, Jack Branford, Ann M. Kansfield, Mary Kansfield, Norman Kansfield, Hank Lay, Marilyn Lay, Stacey Midge, William F. Rupp, Conrad J. Strauch, Ronald E. Vande Bunte, Ken Walsh, and Rob Williams.

[28] The names of Directors on the Articles of Incorporation were limited to persons living in New York State at that time. They include: Beverly J. Bell, Jan Karel Boersma, Shari Brink, Ann M. Kansfield, Harold W. Lay, Marilyn Mariani Lay, Stacey Midge, and Conrad J. Strauch. The Rev. Beverly J. Bell, Esq., along with William F. Rupp, Esq. and the Rev. J. Karel Boersma served as Kansfield's defense team during the trial. As a partner with Humes & Wagner, LLP, the Rev. Bell submitted the legal documents on behalf of the Board.

[29] Taken from the Certificate of Incorporation of Room for All, Inc. Under Section 402 of the Not-for-Profit Corporation Law.

[30] Officers included Shari Brink and Rob Williams, Co-Presidents; Stacey Midge, Vice-President; J. Karel Boersma, Secretary; and Conrad J. Strauch, Treasurer. Ann Kansfield became the Communications Director, and Norm Kansfield became the Fundraising Officer. Room for All Minutes (hereafter RfAMin), Nov. 2, 2005.

All their second or third cause for charitable giving.[31] On Monday, November 7, 2005, Norm and Mary Kansfield were invited to meet with the Collegiate Consistory of New York City, where Norm presented the case for supporting Room for All.[32] The Consistory's response was overwhelming. Instead of underwriting only the start up costs of $11,000, the Consistory voted to make $15,000 available for this purpose.[33]

Beyond these organizational steps, Board members recognized the need to move in several different directions simultaneously. One early step involved coming to know and learn from the vast experience of similar advocacy groups. Thanks to Harry Knox, then Director of the Religion and Faith Project of the Human Rights Campaign (HRC), and leaders from the Institute for Welcoming Resources (IWR), RfA Board members participated in a day-long directors' workshop on January 11, 2006. Over the years, membership in IWR has continued to allow representatives from Room for All to meet semi-annually with leaders from other Welcoming initiatives and to benefit from their collected wisdom and support.[34]

Communication and Use of the Internet

Once the domain names were secured,[35] a plan was developed for the website. The website would contain five navigation sections: 1) About RfA (its purpose, names of Board members and history), 2) Regional Gatherings, (3) Stories, 4) Resources, and 5) Means for taking action. A Google group was established that would allow for conversation, and links were established with IWR, HRC and other Welcoming groups. Over time, the website would morph as technology and web design improved, but, as of December, 2005, it functioned well.[36]

---

[31] This commitment has remained in place to the present time.

[32] See "Conversation with The Collegiate Consistory NY, NY, Nov. 7, 2005". RfA Archives.

[33] Over time, additional grants from a variety of sources, church mission shares, and contributions from an ever expanding donor base served to meet the budget needs of Room for All.

[34] Among Christian and Unitarian Universalist congregations, almost every denomination has a LGBTQ advocacy group. Most of these groups are yoked together in a federated or umbrella arrangement known as IWR. In 2005 Rebecca Voelkel served as IWR's Program Director.

[35] Both www.roomforall.com and www.roomforall.net were available for purchase.

[36] Once again Ann's college friend, April Greenberg, designed the website. GiftWorks software was purchased by the Board.

Early Strategies

1. With the Holy Relationships Conference scheduled for October 16-18, 2005, the Room for All Board scurried to use its resources, especially its network resources, to support and promote the Conference. Among those attending the Conference, word of the fledgling RfA organization spread quickly.

2. Seeking to publicize its identity and its commitment to participate in a denomination-wide dialog mandated by the 2005 General Synod, RfA requested to take out an advertisement for each of three months in the *Church Herald*, the denomination's monthly magazine.[37] The ad appeared in the May, 2006 issue, and immediately there was a firestorm. Pressured by the *Church Herald* Editorial Council, the Editor, Christina Van Eyl, announced that future ads would not be run.[38]

3. With the trial of Norm Kansfield forcing the actualization of an "honest and intentional denomination-wide dialogue on homosexuality", the RCA hired the Rev. Dr. John C. Stapert in December, 2005, to serve as dialog facilitator.[39] Seeking to have its voice heard, the RfA Board collected stories[40] from those who struggled with their gender identity and/or sexual orientation within the RCA and made them available to Dr. Stapert and the

---

[37] The quarter-page ad showed the ripple of a single drop of water with the quotation from Acts 10:47 "Can anyone withhold the water for baptizing these people who have received the Holy Spirit just as we have?" plus the bylines "Responding to the inclusive love of God through welcome and support for lesbian, gay, bisexual and transgender people and their allies, and authentic dialogue with those who think differently."

[38] Room for All was told by the Editor that the RfA ad conflicted with the *Church Herald* advertising policy—that "Ads that challenge or denigrate Reformed Church in America polities, programs, or personnel are not accepted." "*Church Herald* Advertising Policy, September, 2004 attached to email from Chris VanEyl to Ann Kansfield, May 24, 2006. RfAArchives.

At its June, 2009, meeting, the General Synod voted to suspend publication of *The Church Herald*.

In November, 2006, Mary Kansfield, a Room for All Board member, submitted to the *Church Herald* an article titled "To Love and Embrace All God's Children" for which she received a one-time publishing fee of $150. However, the article failed to appear—that is, until the very last issue of *The Church Herald* appeared in print. RfA Archives.

[39] Dr. Stapert was supported in his work by a steering committee of eight members representing the eight regional synods of the denomination.

[40] A total of seven vignettes were shared, four of which were signed, three listed as anonymous. Email from Mary Kansfield to Rob Williams, September 26, 2006. RfA Archives.

Rev. Mark Kellar[41] in preparation for their visit with the Board on September 17, 2006. Listening to one another was believed to be beneficial to the dialog process, although grave concern was expressed by Board members that no LGBTQ person had been invited to serve on the Steering Committee. Without a LGBTQ voice present in planning the three year dialog, it was difficult to imagine how LGBTQ voices would be heard within the initial "listening phase" of the conversation much less in the "dialog" phase of this important conversation.

4. Beginning in 2006 and at every succeeding General Synod, delegates and visitors have been invited to meet with RfA members "off site" following the end of one day's official business. Palm cards[42] were used surreptitiously to identify when and where these gatherings would be held. Any distribution to Synod members of flyers or RfA brochures was strictly forbidden and uniformly enforced by denominational administrators. Over time, these meetings have attracted anywhere from fifty to three hundred persons and proven to be an extremely useful way to dialog with persons within the denomination and to tell them who we are and what we stand for.[43]

5. In 2007, the last of the RCA Women's Triennials was held in Chicago.[44] Planning this event was a herculean task, and the growing presence of the homosexual issue within the church found its way to this event. Once again, RfA was forbidden from meeting on the conference site or handing out brochures and flyers. Although asked not to hand out palm cards, RfA supporters continued to do so. At the last minute, space in the basement of the hotel conference site became available, and 100 of the 550 women registered for the event crowded into a room designed

---

41   The Rev. John C. Stapert, Ph.D. previously served as Editor of the *Church Herald* (1975-1991). Since 1994 he worked as a psychologist in private practice in Scottsdale, Arizona. The Rev. Mark Kellar participated as one of the members of the Steering Committee. Mark served as pastor of the First Reformed Church of Jamaica, Queens.

42   Palm cards were the approximate size of business cards and would be slipped into the palm of a person's hand when introductions were made.

43   At the very first such Synod gathering, more than 50 delegates and RCA members attended, and during the meeting it was announced that a $1,000 challenge grant had been made. In response $5,600 was pledged that night.

44   No Triennial has been held since 2007, and none is presently planned. The first Triennial, which was called the "First National Women's Assembly" was held in 1957 in Buck Hill Falls, PA.

to hold 50 people. There these women listened to presentations about the work of RfA and an explanation of the acronym TULIP[45] that appeared on the tee shirts that were given out[46] Copies were provided of David Myers's workshop presentation on homosexuality. Originally planned for the conference, the workshop was cancelled due to a firestorm of response and threats of boycotting the conference. RfA commitment forms and contact data were gathered, and the conversation proved so engaging that twenty-seven women remained until one o'clock in the morning talking and sharing stories.[47]

Developing Regional Groups as Hubs of Influence

Of all the challenges facing the founders of Room for All, organizing a network of regional groups became a top priority. Using the boundary lines of regional synods that already existed within the denomination,[48] these groups would form the heart and soul of the organization. Of special concern to the founders were the many hurting persons whose stories came to light especially at the Holy Relationships Conference in October, 2005. Speaking to the Collegiate Consistory on November 7, 2005, Norm Kansfield spoke of "envisioning a denomination-wide network of committed persons who will stand with, counsel, and encourage persons facing issues/concerns about their sexuality. Among the ministers alone, at least 280 persons whom we know we can trust for this purpose.[49]

[45]   Taken from the Cannons of Dort, the TULIP letters refer to Total depravity, Unlimited election, Limited atonement, Irresistible grace and the Perseverance of the saints. But on the tee shirts was printed, "totally unconditional love includes all people."

[46]   In total 180 tee shirts were given out. One of the conference speakers appeared at the gathering. When asked if she would like to take along a tee shirt, she replied, "No"—and then, with additional thought, said, "Yes, maybe someday I'll be able to wear it." "Final Report to the RfA Board, Sept. 17, 2007, RfA Archives.

[47]   "Google Report Chicago Women's Conference July 20, 2007" RfA Archives.

[48]   These are mid-sized assemblies/judicatories composed of a number of classes within a geographic area. They were formerly referred to as Particular Synods.

When the women of the RCA organized on January 7, 1875 to form the Woman's Board of Foreign Missions, they likewise recognized the need to form "hubs of support". They utilized the existing classes boundary lines and by this means became an extremely powerful organization until 1946, when the denomination's mission boards were encouraged to merge in the interest of efficiency. See Mary L. Kansfield, *Letters to Hazel: Ministry within the Woman's Board of Foreign Missions of the Reformed Church in America*, Historical Series of the Reformed Church in America, no. 46 (Grand Rapids, William B. Eerdmans, 2004).

[49]   "Conversation with the Collegiate Consistory of New York, NY, November 7, 2005, RfA Archives.

Using the Friends of Norm list, the volume of mail received from supporters (and detractors alike!), and old and new supporters who reached out to the new RfA organization, a network plan was agreed upon at the May 4, 2006 Board meeting.[50] "Point persons" were identified in eight regional locations,[51] and Board members forwarded to these group leaders lists of potential group members who might like to come together to dialog and support one another.

On February 18-19, 2007, thirty persons, who included representatives of nine regional groups, joined Board members to share and support one another, to develop a plan of action, to improve communication among network groups, and to talk about size, structure, and diversity within the Board. It was an eye-opening meeting![52] This was the first such meeting, but it would not be the last. Regional group representatives returned to their homes traumatized by the stories of those in need, yet energized, full of new ideas and above all else, hopeful.

Coming out of this meeting, the Room for All Board prepared a letter that was sent to the RCA General Synod Council, the RCA's governing group that functioned in place of the General Synod when the Synod was not in session. The letter said:

> You know our organization. You know our purpose and our goals. We are faithful members of the Reformed Church in America. Most of us are officeholders within the church—elders or ministers of Word and Sacrament. In everything that we seek to do, we would do nothing to harm the Reformed Church in America. We seek only to offer pastoral care to persons within the denomination who have concerns about their sexuality; to provide accurate and helpful information to individuals and congregations who attempt to minister to such persons; and to encourage those who love gay, lesbian, bisexual, or transgender persons to keep the baptismal promises that they and the church have made.
>
> In every attempt we have made to carry out these intentions within the denomination we have been thwarted. When we sought

---

[50]   RfAMin, May 4, 2006, 3.

[51]   These regional groups included: upstate New York, New York City, central New Jersey, Holland, Michigan, Grand Rapids, Michigan, Chicago, Illinois, central Iowa, and Denver, Colorado. "A Report to the Consistory of the Collegiate Church ," October 10, 2006, 5.

[52]   "Room for All Gathering of Regional Representatives, February 18-19, 2007," RfA Archives.

to hold an open meeting during the General Synod of 2006, our signs were removed. When we tried to purchase advertizing space within the *Church Herald*, the Editor felt obligated to deny our request. When we attempted to have a display table at the Women's Gathering in Chicago this summer, again we were told that it is not possible. When we offered to serve the denomination's dialogue on inclusion, we were told that that would be too political.

We are totally frustrated in our efforts to make this special ministry known within the denomination. We therefore seek your advice. How do you propose we should proceed? What methods would you have us follow, as good and faithful members of the Reformed Church?

> Most sincerely,
> Shari Brink, Co-President
> Robert Williams, Co-President[53]

The letter is dated March, 2007. It wasn't until August, 2012, that executives and officers of the RCA met with the officers of Room for All.[54]

Becoming Room for All Rostered Church and Classes

Within the strategy for building regional hubs of influence, it was early recognized that leaders would have to be trained to enable congregations and classes to move ahead in their commitments to become welcoming. Stepping in to help meet this need were leaders and trainers from The Institute for Welcoming Resources (IWR), an umbrella organization and support group yoking together almost all Protestant church groups advocating for LGBTQ inclusion. IWR provided community organizing training sessions to regional groups and held workshops in 2011 at the RfA national conference.[55]

It was always the dream of the RfA Board to create a network of congregations and classes who both inwardly and outwardly commit

[53] Letter in RfAMin, March, 2007, RfA Archives

[54] "Five Pivotal Moments in the History of the Reformed Church in America's Commitment to Ministry for and with LGBTQ Persons," as referenced in Email from Marilyn Paarlberg to Gwen Ashby, October 2, 2012. RfA Archives.

[55] The Rev. Dr. Rebecca Voelkel and Rev. Vicki Wunsch from IWR served as trainers on numerous occasions, and the training process was called "Building an Inclusive Church". Rebecca served as the Speaker at the 10th Anniversary Banquet held as part of the RfA national conference, October 22-25, 2015 held in Grand Rapids, MI.

     Board members recognized the need for their own training. On April, 2007, six board members and three guests of the Board participated in an all-day media training workshop at Auburn Seminary's Media Division. RfAMin, April 23, 2007.

themselves to be genuinely LGBTQ-inclusive.[56] IWR was instrumental in helping RfA become part of the larger Welcoming and Affirming movement. IWR helped clarify the process for becoming Open and Affirming (O&A) and hence becoming "Rostered." [57]

Already in October, 2006, the RfA Board received a request from the Old First Reformed Church of Brooklyn to become an O&A RfA congregation. They were the first.[58] Since the Rostering of churches began in June, 2011, 29 churches are RfA Rostered congregations. To date no Classis has become Rostered.[59]

Celebrating Three National Conferences

The first of three national RfA conferences was held October, 27-29, 2009. At this and the following two national conferences, RfA was hosted by Central Reformed Church in Grand Rapids, MI.[60] Board members and their regional RfA allies planned the conference in hope and in faith—hope that people would come to bless and to be blessed by their presence, and faith that scholarship aid and the necessary means for financing the conference would somehow be found.[61] The conference was an overwhelming success!

---

[56] For further commentary in this regard see "A Report to the Consistory of the Collegiate Church" by Norman J. Kansfield, October 10, 2006, p. 7, RfA Archives.

[57] To become "Rostered", RfA congregations and classes undertake an intentional process in introspection and study. There are four steps in this process: 1) to discuss and discern, 2) to write a statement of inclusion, 3) to send the statement that has been approved by the Consistory to RfA requesting to be Rostered, and 4) to make the statement public and to celebrate. See http://www.roomforall.com/welcoming-and-affirming-congregations/.

[58] RfAMin, October 21, 2006

[59] "In February, a small group of LGBT people and their allies brought a proposal to incorporate LGBT inclusion into the bylaws of the Classis of New Brunswick. Changing the bylaws requires two votes. The first, in February, secured well over the 50% approval needed. After considerable efforts to organize allies, the second vote fell just two votes short of the required 2/3s majority. Though the bylaw change was defeated, we considered this a huge organizing success and the classis continues to engage in dialog around this topic," as stated in Carpenter Foundation grant application, September 14, 2006, p.4, RfA Archives.

[60] By hosting this conference in the heart of the conservative Midwest, Central Reformed Church was associating its name with LGBTQ inclusivity. This was a brave act. Members of the congregation cooked and served the meals for the conference to help keep the costs of board as low as possible. Delicious meals were served, and the Central Reformed spirit of hospitality pervaded this and future conferences.

[61] The title of the conference was "Making Room for All". Almost 140 people participated, including 39 Hope College students. Peggy Campolo was the Keynote Speaker, and six workshops were available. The Rev. Dr. Louis Lotz preached

For the second national conference, which took place October 22-25, 2011, the Rev. Sophie Mathonnet-VanderWell and the Rev. Thomas Goodhart served as worship leaders.[62] At the Conference's closing Communion service, a special note of celebration occurred when Ann Kansfield and her father, Norm Kansfield, served as Celebrants. In 2007, the Classis of New York, RCA, refused to ordain Ann because of her sexuality, and she was subsequently ordained in the United Church of Christ. Norm Kansfield's ordination in the RCA was suspended in 2005 for marrying his daughter to a woman, and his ordination was subsequently reinstated on October 18, 2011. Their joint presence in presiding at the Lord's Supper was extremely symbolic.

The third national conference occurred October 22-25, 2015, and marked the 10th anniversary of Room for All's founding.[63] In addition to the speaker, the workshops and worship services, conference participants and guests attended a new play about relationships, sexuality and the church. Titled *Listening for Grace: Variations on a Theme of Struggle and Hope,* the play was written by Ted Swartz and performed by Ted Swartz, Justin Yoder and Phillip Martin. The play seemed to capture fully the spirit of the conference.

Hiring an Executive Director and Community Organizer

As early as 2007, Board members began to voice the need for someone in a paid position to help carry out the expanded involvements resulting from the organization's growth. A staff person was needed "to help with movement building, resource development, communications coordination, administrative liaison work in the Welcoming Church Movement, and to assist the volunteer treasurer with financial responsibilities."[64] In the Fall of 2010, the RfA Board hired Marilyn

---

a sermon titled, "In My Father's House There Are Many Closets". A memorable concert by the Michigan Gay Men's Choir drew loud applause. The colorful IWR Shower of Stoles Project was on display. In this display, stories are told of LGBTQ persons of faith in leadership positions within IWR member denominations.

[62] Shari K. Brink served as the Keynote Speaker at this conference. She served as co-president on the founding RfA Board. At the time of the conference she served as the Executive Minister of Marble Collegiate Church in NYC.

[63] Jeff Chu served as the Keynote Speaker, and the Rev. Dr. Renee House, minister of Old Dutch Church (Kingston, New York) led worship. At the opening anniversary banquet, the Rev. Dr. Rebecca Voelkel spoke on "From Sorrow to Celebration: A Love Letter from the LGBTQ Movement to Room for All." See RfA National Conference Registration form, RfA Archives.

[64] As identified in Grant Request to the Collegiate Church, NYC, March 5, 2010, RfA Archives.

Paarlberg from Albany, New York.[65] Marilyn's work has been a gift to RfA. Her roots in the RCA, her speaking, writing, and computer skills, her ability to manage as well as her commitment to the cause of RfA, have all helped to move RfA into the future.

In January, 2015, a second full-time employee of the Board began his responsibilities. Mr. Cameron Van Kooten joined the RfA staff as a Community Coordinator. His roots in the RCA and background in non-profit management and community organizing wonderfully enable him to further the work of Room for All's growth.

Today, the Room for All mission remains the same:

> to support, to educate and to advocate for the full participation of lesbian, gay bi-sexual and transgender (LGBTQ) persons in all aspects of the life and ministry of the Reformed Church in America as compelled by the inclusive love of God revealed to us by our Lord and Savior Jesus Christ.

The call is clear.

[65]   Marilyn began her RfA responsibilities on September 13, 2010, RfAMin Sept. 17-18, 2010.

CHAPTER 13

A Fair Trial: The Separation of Church and State Expressed in a Reformed Church Order

Allan Janssen

The eventual establishment of what would become the Reformed Church in America necessitated a fundamental alteration in its church order. The emerging United States clearly and forthrightly shifted the relation between church and state. This is most clearly put in the first article of the Bill of Rights, where it states: "Congress shall make no law respecting the establishment of religion or prohibiting the free exercise thereof...." Thus was constructed the so-called "wall of separation" between church and state. In 1771, the Reformed Church[1] had established itself as separate from the Dutch church in its "Plan of Union." However, it continued to use the church order of Dort as constitutional. Conditions in the United States could not allow that to continue.

The Provisional Synod of the new church took the extraordinary position that it would not adopt a new church order but would produce a set of "Explanatory Articles" that made necessary alterations to the

---

[1] In fact the "Reformed Protestant Dutch Church" – shortened for the purposes of this paper to "Reformed Church – would be renamed the "Reformed Church in America" in 1866.

271

old order. The preface to the Explanatory Articles points out the major change that is being made to the church order of Dort is that "Whatever relates to the immediate authority and interposition of the Magistrate in the government of the church, and which is introduced more or less into all the national establishments in Europe, is entirely omitted in the Constitution now published."[2] This was necessitated because the "Church is a Society, wholly distinct in its principles, laws, and end, from any which men have ever instituted for civil purposes."[3] Hence,

> Whether the Church of Christ will not be more effectually patronized in a civil government where full freedom of conscience and worship is equally protected and insured to all men, and where truth is left to vindicate her own sovereign authority and influence, than where men in power promote their favorite denominations by temporal emoluments and partial discriminations, will now, in America, have a fair trial.[4]

The purported author of these words, and the primary author of the Explanatory Articles, is John Henry Livingston.[5] A brief glance at his involvement will illuminate our subject. In 1766, Livingston was sent to study at the University of Utrecht. There he came under the influence of John Locke. He would return to the colonies in 1770, where he would be instrumental in the construction of the aforementioned "Plan of Union." Later, in a letter to his cousin Robert Livingston, he would comment on the role of religious freedom in the new constitution for the state of New York, and in so doing make reference to Locke's *Letter on Toleration*, claiming that the draft constitution "'breathes the same spirit' in the sense of embodying the notion that all people have a right to 'believe for themselves and worship God according to the dictates of their conscience without depending upon fellow subjects, sister churches, or even the civil magistrates in religion,' and that this is in

---

2   Edward Tanjore Corwin, *A Digest of Constitutional and Synodical Legislation of the Reformed Church in America* (New York: Board of Publication, 1906), vi.
3   Corwin, v.
4   Corwin, vi.
5   For a recent sketch of Livingston, see John W. Coakley, "John Henry Livingston: Interpreter of the Dutch Reformed Tradition in the Early Republic," in Leon Van den Broeke, et. al., ed., *Transatlantic Pieties: Dutch Clergyh in Colonial America* (Grand Rapids: Eerdmans, 2012), 295-314. John Coakley is the Reformed Church's primary interpreter of Livingston. This author is indebted to him for many of the references to him in this essay. This author also extends his gratitude to Coakley for his encouragement of my own occasional forays into Reformed Church history.

fact a natural right, not a gift from the state."[6] In a July 4 sermon—an occasion for political celebration in the churches as well as in society—Livingston would exclaim that "here an undisturbed freedom in worship forms the first principle of government."[7]

The new relation between church and state would come to expression directly in the Explanatory Articles and indirectly in an extended struggle to legally incorporate both local consistories and the General Synod itself.

First, in establishing itself as an independent church in a new land, the Reformed church formally adopted the church order of Dort at the General Convention of the Reformed Church of New York and New Jersey in its session of October 15-18, 1771.[8] Article XXVIII of that church order, concerning the role of Christian magistrates, states

> As it is the duty of Christian Magistrates to countenance the worship of God, to recommend religion by their example, and to protect the members of the community in the full and regular exercise of religious liberty; so it is the duty of Ministers, Elders, and Deacons zealously and faithfully to inculcate upon all their congregations, that obedience, love, and homage, which they owe to the magistrate.[9]

This state of affairs was, of course, impossible, given the new American constitution.

But two other places in that same church order are significant. Article V, concerning the calling of ministers states that

> If any one has a valid right of presentation, or any other claim, by means of which he can be useful and edifying, without doing injury to the Church of God and good Church-Order, *may it please the Civil Authorities* and the Synod of the respective Provinces to give it their attention, and to make all necessary regulation in the interest of the Churches.[10]

Or, to take another example, this time concerning the calling of a General Synod, article L requires that the church that has been chosen

---

6   John W.Coakley, "John Henry Livingston and the Liberty of the Conscience," *Reformed Review*, Winter 1992, vole. 46, no. 2, 124.
7   Coakley, "John Henry Livingston and the Liberty of Conscience,"126.
8   Hugh Hastings, *Ecclesiastical Records of the State of New York*, Vol. VI (J.B. Lyon: Albany, NY, 1905), 4218.
9   The church order of Dort is found in Corwin, *Digest*,
10   Hastings, 4219.

to call a General Synod "shall also give timely notice thereof to the Civil Authorities, in order that, with their knowledge, and—in case it should please them to send also a certain number to the Classis—in their presence and with their advice, the Deputies may transact their business."[11]

As a matter of fact, the "magistrates" would no longer have any role in the life of the church. Article XXXV in the Explanatory Articles, in which the call of a minister to a congregation is laid before the relevant classis for approval, all civil presence disappears. A note appended to the article explains:

> In the United States of America, where civil and religious liberty are fully enjoyed, and where no ecclesiastical establishments can be formed by civil authority; the approbation of magistrates in the calling of Ministers is not required or permitted. It was therefore judged proper in the translation of the Church Orders to omit every paragraph which referred to any power of the magistrate, in ecclesiastical affairs, as a matter merely local, and peculiar to European establishments.[12]

The separation of the church from the state and the implications in and for the church order can be seen from an insistent struggle concerning the legal incorporation of churches. Beginning in 1784, it was possible, in New York State[13] for religious bodies to incorporate. The Dutch church would be included in 1788. The church can exist as an independent entity. This was to provoke consternation among the Reformed churches however, as a number of congregations moved to incorporate. To see why, we might refer again to Livingston. In a letter to the new mayor of the city of New York, James Duane, where Livingston remarks concerning what would appear to be an alteration in the old charter for the New York church (of which Livingston was the minister). The "stile" required for the new bill would refer to "The ministers, Elders and deacons of the Reformed Protestant Dutch Church of the City of New York... It is only wished that liberty may be granted to chuse [sic] now such new elders and deacons as the church may require, to make up the number of those who have died or who are

---

[11]   Hastings, 4223.

[12]   Corwin, *Digest*, xl.

[13]   While I will speak of New York State, similar dynamics would take place in other states. Incorporation is under the purview of the individual states, not the federal government, in the United States.

absent..."[14] Indeed, the issue for the Reformed church would be that the religious body is to have "trustees." This is not consistent with the Explanatory Articles where Ministers, Elders and Deacons constitute a consistory that has among its duties the trusteeship of the local church. This tension would continue through the nineteenth century.[15] The Reformed Church, in a new situation, still works to find its place of separation, or, might one say, "freedom of conscience"?

In his book on the Constitution of the Reformed Church in America, Daniel J. Meeter comments that the preface to the Explanatory Articles, and indeed the articles themselves, establish the Reformed church as a confessional church, in contradistinction from a national church, and that the church is "known and defined by its testimony and confession."[16] I think Meeter is correct. I wish to argue further, however, that, while the category appears not to be in the minds of those colonial "fathers" of the Reformed Church, it is the *holiness* of the church that finds expression in the church order. Whether the "fair trial" brings success remains an open question.

The civil arrangement that is the separation of church and state is, from a theological perspective, a manifestation of the *holiness* of the church. In Biblical terms, to be "holy" is to be separate; more specifically, the holy is separated from the profane. For the church, its holiness is in a sanctified *people*, but in a specific sense. It is as a people who have been set aside, who are made holy as the Holy Spirit is poured out on them. And it is as a *people*, a church. So that it is "the setting apart of the church *in* Christ and *for* newness of life."[17] Or, as Hans Küng puts it, the church is "without spot or wrinkle... insofar as Christ has already given himself up for it, has cleansed it in the word by the washing of water in baptism, and intends to sanctify it, so that it may be presented like a bride without spot or wrinkle, in all its splendor."[18] Küng goes on to claim that the "church has been set apart from the world in order to live and act in the world in a different way from those who do not believe. The holy Church exists wherever in the world of everyday life men hear the word of God's grace and love, believe it and only it by handing on the love given them in their acts for their fellow men."[19] The holiness of the church, then, is for the sake of the world.

---

[14] John H. Livingston, "Note from James Duane" Dated Wednesday, Feb. 11, 1784, #117, Duane papers, reel 2. I am indebted to John Coakley for this reference.

[15] On the long process of incorporating congregations, see Corwin, *Digest*, 328-335.

[16] Daniel J. Meeter, *Meeting Each Other In Doctrine, Liturgy & Government* (Grand Rapids: Eerdmans, 1993), 43.

[17] G.C. Berkhouwer, *The Church* (Grand Rapids: Eerdmans, 1976), 331.

[18] Hans Küng, *The Church* (New York: Sheed and Ward, 1967), 327.

[19] Küng, 330.

Because the holiness is conferred upon the church as the church abides in Christ through the Spirit, holiness is manifest in Christ's presence in Word and Sacrament. Leo Koffeman, in his discussion of the holiness of the church, which he designates as the *integrity* of the church, states that the "provisional and eschatological character of the church and its dependence on the Lord come to expression in the liturgy, and the non-identity of the church and the kingdom are disclosed and vouchsafed."[20] Or, as A. van de Beek puts it, the "holiness of the church primarily has its place in the liturgical celebration in which the communion with Christ is practiced."[21] The holiness of the church, then, finds expression in the Reformation marks of the church: Word and Sacrament. It is in this way that the church, as Christ's body and as the communion of the Spirit, is maintained in holiness, has been set aside for the honor of God and service to God's world. It is maintained by God as separate from the world for the sake of the world.

The church order exists to open the church to that space where God separates the church, free from voices that may wish to turn the church to other ends. It is put like this, e.g., in the *Book of Church Order* of the Reformed Church: "The church shall not exercise authority over the state, nor should the state usurp the authority of the church." [22] The church order does so as it manifests the *offices* of the church. It is the nature of office to stand over and against the church. The office-bearer, as representative of Christ, comes from *without* to exist *within* the church thereby to establish it in Christ, by means of Word and Sacrament. As such, office expresses the authority of Christ to rule the church. Moreover it does so as it maintains both the orthodoxy of the church's teaching as well as the orthopraxy of its life.[23] The church order centers around the offices of the church as they are gathered into the assemblies of the church. In this way, the holiness of the church is related to the apostolic nature of the church. The integrity of the church (Koffeman) is a function of the church's authenticity, as it remains faithful to the gospel that beats at the church's heart.

It is clear that a church order cannot, of itself, guarantee that the gospel will be preached with integrity and that the sacraments will

---

[20] Leo Koffeman, *Het goed recht van de kerk: Een theologische inleiding op het kerkrecht* (Kampen: Kok, 2009), 268.

[21] A. van de Beek, *Lichaam en Geest van Christus: De theologie van de kerk en de Heilige Geest* (Zoetermeer: Meninema, 2012), 59.

[22] *Book of Church Order of the Reformed Church in America* (New York: Reformed Church Press, 2013), 3.

[23] On this see A.A. van Ruler, *Ik geloof*, 7th ed. (Nijkerk: Callenbach, n.d.), 136.

be administered in purity. God alone maintains the church. Rather, the order is the church's response to God as the Spirit creates *gestalten* as the means by which God can act. It is for that reason that I claimed above that the church order creates a certain space. It does so through the offices as it provides the means by which those who proclaim the Word are called, examined, and ordained by an assembly of ministers and elders, as the classis retains oversight of ministers that they remain faithful in teaching and preaching, and as boards of elders are charged with maintaining the integrity of the pulpit. The sacraments are administered under the oversight of a board of elders.

More so, offices are gathered into the various assemblies for the governance of the church. They do so as offices, responsible not to the faithful—church governance is not a parliamentary system—but to Christ. Classes, for example, retain the ultimate right of ownership of the property of their member churches, with no interference from civil authorities, save a common oversight that the church not violate its own constitution.

It is at this point where the third Reformation mark, discipline, finds expression in the church order and functions as an expression of the church's holiness. Indeed, as Koffeman remarks, "holiness requests discipline."[24] It is not, as too often presumed, that discipline keeps members and office-bearers morally pure as it governs behavior. It is the case that bad behaviors can and do bring dishonor to the church. But it is important to see just why. A woman approached me one Sunday following the morning service at which I had presided. I knew her as a faithful member of a neighboring congregation. She explained to me in tears that her own pastor had been caught in a series of falsehoods as he denied having an extra-marital affair with a parishioner of that church. The woman, speaking with me sadly, remarked that if the minister lied about his life, how could she trust that what he said about God was true? Could she believe the pastor when he declared that her sins were forgiven for the sake of Christ? The issue is not simply the behavior of the minister, but how that behavior affects those who depend on the message he or she brings. The case would be similar *mutatis mutandis* when a minister preaches heresy, claiming, e.g., that a certain political system is a means of salvation. That the church has a system of discipline separate from that of civil courts is also an expression of its holiness.

In fact, discipline can be understood in two different ways: in a more general and in a more restricted sense. In the general sense,

---

[24] Koffeman, 261.

the entire church order may be considered a discipline. As the classis ascertains that the minister of the Word evidences faithfulness to the gospel as received from the apostles (for the Reformation churches, this is faithfulness to the apostolic message, scripture), the church is engaged in a discipline. A consistory or a synod considering a particular policy for the congregation or the broader church lives under the discipline of its Lord. This is, in fact, particularly the case when the church speaks *to* civil authority as it is compelled by its Lord, the Lord who stands over and against powers of this world as well as over and against the church itself. This would be the assemblies of the church themselves functioning as "offices" in the whole. And, as per the church order, all Christians are "under" one discipline or another.

And, of course, the more restricted sense of discipline would be as "disciplinary procedures" function, ranging from pastoral injunction to deposition from office and excommunication. In this sense as well the church attends to the holiness of the church. Again, this is not simply the purity of morals of the church's members or office-bearers, but has primarily to do with the fact that, established by Christ in the Spirit, the church lives separate from the world. In this instance it is particularly clear that the American church functions separately from the civil order. Governmental agencies have no part in ecclesiastical discipline[25] and the "means of correction" available to the church is, at most, excommunication.

As it turns out, discipline makes clear the failure of the "fair trial." However, to offer a fair evaluation, it is helpful to return to the historical context of the development of the church order of the Reformed Church. As Reinhold Seeberg points out in his magisterial history of Christian doctrine, the churches of a Calvinist heritage have from the outset displayed a clear independence from the political order.[26] For the Reformed, the order of the church is not a matter of indifference, but is established by God in Scripture. While Calvin and his immediate descendants did not advocate what we call the "separation of church and state," they were clear that in matters of faith, the church remains independent of political control. This was the beginning of a development that would stretch over several centuries. The church order on which the American Reformed church is based, that of Dort, was itself a matter of struggle over the nature of the involvement of the

---

[25]   And, in fact, civil courts are wary of intra-ecclesiastical disputes and will remit any such cases to the relevant church body.

[26]   *Lehrbuch der Dogmengeschichte*, vol. 4 (Basel: Benno Schwavbe & Co., 1954), 616ff.

magistrates in the life of the church. However, the European situation was such that a mutual relationship did exist between the church and the state in such a way that was intended to be mutually beneficial to both.[27] In the case of the American church's predecessor, the Dutch church, this would mean that the Reformed Church was *the* church, the official "public" church. That "privilege" was ceded, necessarily so, when the Reformed Church became independent in the United States.

And it is just here that the trial runs aground. The American church built its order in the context of the existence of multiple denominations.[28] The plurality of churches is accepted as a given. At the same time, the church order pretends to order the church as though it were one. This manifests the deeper understanding of the relationship between the church and the state. A view of the church, evident in Article 36 of the Belgic Confession, for example, sees governing authorities as protectors of the church. The state guarantees the unity of the church. This could be the case because the Biblical norms—laws—are recognized by the entire society.[29] Theocratic notions stand in the background. While this could not be the case in the new country, an assumption remained that while the churches would follow their own confessional commitments, the country would remain "Christian" in its norms. The church could be plural *and* one. This would be the basis of what Martin Marty called the "Righteous Empire," nineteenth century America with its many churches, but churches that would increasingly work together in a variety of agencies on common projects.[30] The "unity" of the church was maintained by a common understanding.

This would, however, run aground on discipline. It is nearly impossible to practice discipline with integrity in the context of what has become a radical individualism. If admonished by one church, one simply need go down the street or across town to a church that is more compatible. This reaches even into the ordained ministry. One needn't consider formal discipline in this matter. It is even difficult to engage in pastoral conversation that might in any way be uncomfortable, lest the conversation end abruptly, and nothing has been gained either for the souls of those involved or the gospel of Jesus Christ.

---

27 See the *Belgic Confession*, Article 36.
28 The current church order begins, "The purpose of the Reformed Church in America, together with all other churches of Christ . . ." *BCO*, 1. On the one hand, this is an ecumenical claim. The Reformed church doesn't claim to be the *only* church. On the other hand, it is only one among a plurality of churches.
29 See Seeberg, 643, on this tendency particularly in what he calls "Anglocalvinism."
30 Martin Marty, *The Righteous Empire* (New York: Harper Torchbook, 1977).

In fact, the church order has attempted to adjust to this "impossible possibility." The church order of necessity acts as though the church is one. At the same time it acknowledges the practical reality of the multiplicity of churches, and so necessarily adjusts to this reality. This is manifest, for example, in provisions for "receiving ministers from other denominations." "Other denominations" exist and they have ministers. The Reformed church can receive them, but only under condition that the minister in question adhere to the doctrinal standards of the Reformed church. Thus a nod is given to apostolic task; does this person preach the gospel in its purity? That this is awkward, however, was evident when a classis asked the church's General Synod to clarify what constituted a "duly organized body" of the Christian church. The church order allowed classes to examine ministers ordained by such bodies as ministers of the church.[31]

Thus, theologically, we have moved from holiness (and apostolicity) to the other Nicene attributes of the church, unity with attendant catholicity. The "trial" could be construed as such that the church did not need the civil government to maintain its unity. Its unity is in Christ through the Spirit. And that is correct. However, the American church lost as much as it gained. The "fault," perhaps is not to be laid at the feet of a church that could have done little else in the environment in which it found itself. Nonetheless, there is little confession of the sin of disunity.

The issue, finally, is not one of church order, but of the church itself. Just so, the matter may lay elsewhere than in a common subscription to confession. Thus, I end with a query. Do Reformed churches seek unity—and hence holiness—in a common confession of faith, or in their one Lord? This may put the matter a bit too strongly. The church's confession is in its one Lord. But discipline is often understood to circle around the confession. How differently would it look if discipline focused on the sacraments, on the Supper and on Baptism? What might the results of the "trial" be if the Reformed began to pay more attention to the sacramental core of the church? This need not devalue the centrality of the preached Word. But it might enable the church to find its center as it finds its way to the inherent unity of the church, of the Reformed churches with their sister and brother communions.

---

[31]   *The Acts and Proceedings of the 205th Regular Session of the General Synod*, 2011, 113-115.

CHAPTER 14

A Joyful Duty

Gregg A. Mast

In 1563, the Heidelberg Catechism was adopted for use in the Church in Palatinate and with it a liturgy that was still serving the Reformed Church in America more than 300 years later. Quite remarkably, the communion prayer in the Palatinate Liturgy was substantially unchanged during the three centuries in spite of the fact that it had been carried from Heidelberg to Frankenthal to London to the Netherlands and finally to the shores of the new world. Interestingly, when an increasingly English-speaking Collegiate Church in New York City demanded a communion liturgy in English, the Collegiate Church didn't compose a new prayer, but simply borrowed the old prayer from English-speaking congregations in the Netherlands. With the formation of the new American church in 1792, the same communion prayer, with its liturgy that had been written in Heidelberg more than two centuries before, was adopted. It was not until 1873, almost a century later, that we find a new Eucharistic Prayer offered as an alternative to the Palatinate prayer. In 1906, this same Eucharistic Prayer was divided and revised and adopted as the "official" communion prayer of the

Reformed Church in America. By then, almost 350 years had passed since the creation of the communion prayer in Heidelberg.[1]

In a worship world that often changes its prayers and practice almost weekly, to discover a prayer that remained at the heart of Reformed life for 350 years is a remarkable story. To be sure, we have no idea how often the prayer was used or ignored in those centuries, but we can observe that it survived and, at times, flourished.

This introductory section will provide the text of the communion prayer with such an amazing life span, describe the mystery that shrouded the sudden appearance of the Eucharistic Prayer in 1873 and provide the text of that prayer as well. While we explore the roots of the communion prayer, our eyes will finally come to rest on the prayer adopted by the RCA in 1966 which moved us substantially back into the main stream of Western liturgical practice. It will be the appearance of "joy" in that prayer which has begun to change centuries of somber and sober communion life for those who identify themselves as members of the Reformed Church in America.

The Palatinate prayer composed and adopted in 1563 reads:

> O most merciful God and Father, we beseech Thee that Thou wilt be pleased in this Supper in which we celebrate the glorious remembrance of the bitter death of Thy beloved Son, Jesus Christ, to work in our hearts through the Holy Ghost, that we may daily, more and more, with true confidence, give ourselves up unto Thy Son, Jesus Christ, so that our affected and contrite hearts through the power of the Holy Ghost, may be fed and comforted with His true body and blood; yea, with Him, true God and Man, that only heavenly bread: and that we may no longer live in our sins, but He in us and we in Him; and thus truly be made partakers of the new and everlasting covenant of grace: that we may not doubt that Thou wilt forever be our gracious Father, nevermore imputing our sins unto us, and providing us, as Thy beloved children and heirs, with all things necessary, as well for the body as the soul.
>
> Grant us also Thy grace that we may take upon us our cross, cheerfully deny ourselves, confess our Savior, and in all tribulations with uplifted heads expect our Lord Jesus Christ from heaven, where he will make our mortal bodies like unto His

---

[1]   See Howard G. Hageman's article "The Eucharistic Prayer in the Reformed Church in America," *Reformed Review* 30, no. 3 (Spring 1977), for a good summary of the early history of the Palatinate Communion Prayer.

most glorious body and take us unto Himself in eternity. OUR
FATHER Etc. . . .[2]

To be sure, the instructional portion of the communion liturgy
was far longer and carried the theological and liturgical "freight" that
commended the service for congregational use. Indeed, a significant
transition between the 1563 liturgy and the one adopted in 1966 is the
belief that the church's Eucharistic theology should be embedded in
the prayer rather than a pedagogical discourse.

The 1563 Palatinate communion prayer, adopted formally in
1792 by the newly organized Reformed Church, appeared each time
the liturgy was printed in nineteenth century. In the liturgy published
in 1873, there suddenly and mysteriously appeared a new alternative
prayer entitled "The Eucharist Prayer." It reads as follows:

> It is very meet and right, above all things, to give thanks to Thee,
> O Eternal God: who, by Thy word, didst create heaven and earth
> and all things therein. For all Thy bounties known to us, for all
> unknown, we give Thee thanks; but chiefly that when, through
> disobedience, we had fallen from Thee, Thou didst not suffer us
> to depart from Thee forever, but hast ransomed us from eternal
> death, and given us the joyful hope of everlasting life, through
> Jesus Christ Thy Son: Who, being Very and Eternal God, became
> Man for us men and for our salvation.
>
> Not as we ought, but as we are able, we bless Thee for His
> holy incarnation; for His life on earth; for His precious sufferings
> and death upon the cross; for His resurrection from the dead; and
> for His glorious ascension to Thy right hand.
>
> We bless Thee for the giving of the Holy Ghost; for the
> sacraments and ordinances of the Church; for the communion of
> Christ's Body and Blood; for the great hope of everlasting life and
> of an eternal weight of glory.
>
> Thee, Mighty God, Heavenly King, we magnify and praise,
> with angels and archangels, and all the host of heaven, we worship
> and adore Thy glorious Name, joining in the song of Cherubim
> and Seraphim and saying:-
> HOLY, HOLY, HOLY, LORD GOD OF SABAOTH,
> HEAVEN AND EARTH ARE FULL OF THY GLORY, HOSANNA
> IN THE HIGHEST. BLESSED IS HE THAT COMETH IN THE
> NAME OF THE LORD. HOSANNA IN THE HIGHEST.

[2]   Ibid., 167.

And we most humbly beseech Thee, O Merciful Father, to vouchsafe unto us Thy gracious presence, as we commemorate in this Supper the most blessed sacrifice of Thy Son; and to bless and sanctify with Thy word and Spirit these Thine own gifts of bread and wine which we set before Thee, that we, receiving them accordingly to our Saviour's institution, in thankful remembrance of His death and passion may, through the power of the Holy Ghost, be very partakers of His body and blood, with all His benefits, to our salvation and the glory of Thy Most Holy Name.

And here we offer and present to Thee, O Lord, ourselves, our souls and bodies, to be a reasonable, holy and living sacrifice unto Thee; humbly beseeching Thee that all who are partakers of this Holy Communion may be filled with Thy grace and heavenly benediction. And though we be unworthy, through our manifold sins, to offer unto Thee any sacrifice, yet we beseech Thee to accept this our bounden duty and service; not weighing our merits, but pardoning our offences, through Jesus Christ our Lord.

And rejoicing in the communion of Thy saints, we bless Thy holy Name for all Thy servants who have departed in the faith, and who, having accomplished their warfare, are at rest with Thee; beseeching Thee to enable us so to follow their faith and good example, that we with them may finally be partakers of Thy heavenly kingdom—when, made like unto Christ, we shall behold Him with unveiled face, rejoicing in His glory, and by Him we, with all Thy Church, holy and unspotted, shall be presented with exceeding joy before the presence of Thy glory. Hear us, O heavenly Father, for His sake; to Whom, with Thee and the Holy Ghost, be glory forever and ever. AMEN.[3]

This prayer, which was included as an alternative to the prayer in the communion liturgy, has a fascinating history. The Catholic and Apostolic Church was founded by Edward Irving, a Scottish Presbyterian pastor before his removal from the ministerial rolls for his involvement in miraculous healings and charismatic worship. The Catholic and Apostolic Church believed both in imminent return of Christ and the rich liturgical life of the church. To that end, it sent out into the world twelve apostles to gather the "best" liturgical material the church had to offer. The apostles borrowed material from the Roman, Orthodox and Anglican traditions to produce a remarkable book of liturgies.

---

[3]   Ibid., 173-174.

When the German Reformed Church in North America, through its Mercersburg movement in the 1850s, looked to renew its worship life, strangely, they looked to the Catholic and Apostolic Church for inspiration. Indeed, Philip Schaff, the great 19th church historian who was deeply involved in the production of new liturgy for the German Church in America, wrote movingly of his visit to a Catholic Apostolic Church in London and declared its worship to be the most perfect he had ever experienced. I believe I have made clear in my 1985 dissertation, through textual comparisons, that the Eucharistic prayer from the Irvingites became the model for the communion prayer in the German Reformed liturgy in 1857. From there it moved again across the Atlantic to the liturgical renewal spearheaded by the Church Service Society in the Church of Scotland in the 1860s, only to return to America in the Dutch Reformed Liturgy of 1873, where it was identified simply as "The Eucharistic Prayer."

It was this prayer that became the source and foundation of the 1906 communion prayer as the Palatinate prayer was finally relegated to a secondary status. While the Liturgical Commission in the 1950s and 1960s knew the history of the prayer of 1873, they rather looked to the work of the French Reformed Church and the Church of South India as the major source of a prayer that has now been at the heart of our worship life for fifty years.

The first sentence of the Eucharistic Prayer of the Reformed Church in America, adopted sixty years after the 1906 liturgy and fifty years ago, in 1966, reads:

> Holy and right it is and our *joyful duty* to give thanks to you at all times and all places, O Lord, our Creator, almighty and everlasting God![4]

We begin the communion prayer with a "joyful duty." I know that I when I was growing up, first in the Christian Reformed Church in North America and then in the Reformed Church in America, there was little joy in the duty of communion. Indeed, we would have never imagined that we could "celebrate" the sacrament, but rather we "kept" the Lord's Supper four times a year with the somber and sober mood of a funereal meal. The Supper was, first and foremost, a place and time when we confessed our manifold sins and looked to the cross of Christ as the place where God forgave us and sent us forward as dutiful and obedient servants.

---

[4]   Emphasis added by the author.

In 1960, Dr. Howard Hageman was invited to provide the Stone Lectures at Princeton Theological Seminary. It was a remarkable invitation, as Howard did not possess a terminal degree in theology and was, as he often observed, a simple parish pastor in Newark, New Jersey. There was nothing simple about Hageman, who was one of the most important liturgical American Reformed scholars of the latter half of the twentieth century. The premise of the lecture was that, while John Calvin could be identified as the theological father of the Reformed tradition, it was Zwingli who had become the liturgical master who had imprinted Reformed Churches with a sacramental theology that was spare, indeed almost anemic, and a worship life that was almost exclusively focused on the preaching and hearing of the Word. While Hageman would have preferred the far richer liturgical theology and practice of Calvin, he felt it imperative that, if we were to reform our worship life, we needed to know our roots before we could imagine new ways forward in a growing ecumenical age.

What this meant was that almost all Reformed churches followed Zwingli in his custom of appending the communion meal to the Sunday morning service. It was Hageman's contention that Zwingli built his Eucharistic practice on the medieval liturgical service of the prone, which provided a preaching service often separate from the mass. While Calvin argued for a biblical model of the unity of supper and sermon, Zwingli in Zurich invited his parishioners four times each year to return to the sanctuary for an afternoon Lord's Supper service. Zwingli had, in one fell swoop, ignored the biblical unity of sermon and supper, and understood communion to be, in Hageman's words, the celebration of the "real absence" of Christ. Hageman acknowledged this state of affairs in his lecture, and suggested that there were a number of little-known chapters in Reformed liturgical history that could inspire a more Calvinistic and thus more fulsome and catholic way forward.

In 1981, twenty years after Hageman's Stone Lectures, Nicholas Wolterstorff delivered the Kuyper Lectures at the Free University of Amsterdam. They were published a few years later in a book entitled *Until Justice and Peace Embrace*. While the central lectures of the book focus on the challenge of poverty and nationalism in the world order, he concludes with a chapter that suggests that a renewal of the worship life of Reformed Churches could have a salutary impact on our social ethics as well. Wolterstorff makes a distinction between the actions directed toward us from God, which he identifies as "proclamation," and the actions we direct toward God, which he calls "worship." In the midst of the Chapter VII—entitled "Justice and Worship: The Tragedy of Liturgy in Protestantism"—he writes:

I submit that there is a tragedy of liturgy in Protestantism, especially, but no means, exclusively, within the Reformed/ Presbyterian tradition. The tragedy consists in there being so little within the tradition of the very thing that we have been discussing: worship. The tragedy consists in the fact that within this tradition there is a suppression of the central Christian actions of celebrating the memorial.[5]

Wolterstorff, just a few pages later, observed:

What also results from the worship dimension of liturgy is the seriousness, the sobriety, the absence of joy so characteristic of traditional Reformed liturgy and so contrary to divine rest and people's liberation that we intend to mirror.[6]

When I served some thirty years ago as the Minister of Social Witness and Worship in the Reformed Church in America—an interesting and creative combination of the concerns before us—I observed that those who were driven toward a rich liturgical life were often oblivious to the pain of systemic evil around them, and those who spent their lives demonstrating for causes that were worthy of our passion, often believed that worship had little to do with the struggle for justice. It became apparent to me that justice-seekers all too often ran out of gas because they seemed totally dependent on their personal reserves of energy and vision, and liturgical folk ran out of relevance as they ignored a world that was collapsing. As Hageman often reminded his students, the liturgy begins on Sunday morning but continues into the week as the common work of the people in service of God's vision of shalom.

And so how do we move forward? It appears that we need to understand more deeply our "joyful duty" to worship the Lord. In some essential way we need to move toward a more sacramental and mysterious understanding of the Eucharist that provides for a sense of joy and anticipation in addition to our call to remember the sacrifice of Calvary.

In the 1966 Eucharistic Liturgy of the Reformed Church in America, which has remained almost untouched in the last fifty years, the Eucharistic Prayer is preceded with a pedagogical statement entitled

---

[5] Nicholas Wolterstorff, *Until Justice & Peace Embrace*, (Grand Rapids, Michigan: Wm. B. Eerdmans, 1983), 257.
[6] Ibid.,259.

the "Meaning of the Sacrament." I have little doubt that, as the worship commission completed its fifteen-year quest to reimagine communion as an essential part of every Sunday morning worship, the RCA was attempting to reattach itself to the Eucharistic tradition of the Western Church. At the same time, it was concerned that a more celebratory prayer would leave the traditional didactic nature of the Lord's Supper behind. The "Meaning of the Sacrament" was included to address this concern, and has become so embedded in the sacramental life of the RCA that I have actually witnessed pastors who have moved from its reading to the words of institution ignoring the central act of the communion prayer!

Hageman, who had served on the Worship Commission since the early 1950s, often shared the story that he was the primary author of the "Meaning of the Sacrament," allegedly writing it in one evening after another member of the commission declared that it was impossible to explain communion in a single page. The "Meaning of the Sacrament" reads:

> Beloved in the Lord Jesus Christ, the holy supper we are about to celebrate is a feast of remembrance, communion and of hope.
>
> We come in remembrance that our Lord Jesus Christ was sent of the Father into the world to assume our flesh and blood and to fulfill for us all obedience to the divine law, even to the bitter and shameful death of the cross. By his death, resurrection, and ascension he established a new and eternal covenant of grace and reconciliation that we might be accepted by God and never be forsaken by him.
>
> We come to have communion with this same Christ who promised to be with us always, even to the end of the world. In the breaking of the bread he makes himself known to us as the true heavenly Bread that strengthens us unto life eternal. In the cup of blessing he comes to us as the Vine, in whom we must abide if we are to bear fruit.
>
> We come in hope, believing this bread and this cup are a pledge and foretaste of the feast of love of which we shall partake when his kingdom has fully come, when with unveiled face we shall behold him, made like unto him in his glory.
>
> Since by this death, resurrection, and ascension Christ has obtained for us the life-giving Spirit who unites all in one body, so we are to receive this Supper, mindful of the communion of saints.[7]

---

[7]   *Worship the Lord: The Liturgy of the Reformed Church in America,* (New York: Reformed Church Press, 2005), 11.

The weaving together of the past, present, and future marks these words as a way to approach the Eucharistic Prayer with Zwingli in one pocket, Calvin in the other, and the eschatological hope of the table, seen so clearly in the Anabaptist tradition, in the third. Christopher Dorn, in his doctoral dissertation at Marquette University a few years ago, reviewed the 1966 liturgy, identifying the ways it connected and remained separate from the Western Eucharistic tradition. Dorn argues that the "Meaning of the Sacrament" appears to have been drafted independently.[8] I am not so sure. Listen to these words in the heart of the prayer:

> Most righteous God, we remember in the Supper the perfect sacrifice offered once on the cross by our Lord Jesus Christ for the sin of the whole world. In the joy of his resurrection and in expectation of his coming again, we offer ourselves to you as holy and living sacrifices.[9]

We hear the past, present and future themes of Communion as the congregation looks back with gratitude, celebrates the presence of Christ, and anticipates a future filled with hope. Note the presence of "joy" in this oblation portion of the Eucharistic prayer as well as in the first sentence which calls us to a "joyful duty." In a tradition that had kept its communion services as if one were attending a meal following a funeral, the injection of joy must have been surprising.

It is here that Dorn is most helpful in pointing to the fact that the Worship Commission of the RCA was very intentional in borrowing heavily from the Liturgy of the French Reformed Church, first published in 1950 and in its definitive edition in 1963[10]. The French liturgy also has within it the words, "the joy of his resurrection", as this point of the oblation. I believe that Dorn is particularly insightful in pointing to the work of Oscar Cullman, the ecumenical and biblical scholar, as influential in looking to the post resurrection meals as a source of the early church's life as well as the tradition of the Last Supper. Cullman and FJ Leenhardt in their *Essays on the Lord's Supper,* published in the 1950s, include an English translation of an essay Cullman wrote already in 1936. He begins the first chapter with these words:

> That joy which, according to Acts 2:46, filled the hearts of the first believers united for the breaking of bread could not have

---

8   Christopher Dorn, *The Lord's Supper in the Reformed Church in America*, (Peter Lang International Academic Publishers, 2007), 121.

9   *Worship the Lord,*13.

10   Dorn, 114.

been elicited by the recollection of the Last Supper or by the recollection of the daily meals taken with our Lord during his lifetime. . . . There is only one group of meals, the recollection of which could justify this overflowing joy: those which the first Christians took together immediately after the death of Jesus, meals during which Christ suddenly appeared to them. . . .[11]

Cullman and others have called us to reclaim the joyful and eschatological dimensions of the communion meal. In so doing, Cullman argues that our hearts include not only gratitude for the past, but joy in the present and a hopeful longing of that time when we join the heavenly banquet. He marks this understanding of communion by encouraging the church to join with the faithful of all ages in exclaiming "Maranatha." I believe it is not coincidental that the Eucharistic prayer approved by the RCA in 1966 concludes with the words "Even so, come, Lord Jesus."

It has been my attempt to suggest that joy, gratitude, and expectation are at the heart of the Lord's Supper for Reformed Christians. They are also at the heart of a Reformed Ethic. Our response to God's grace, which is one of joy, gratitude, and expectation, provides the foundation for our actions in the church and the world. The unique third use of the law, explicated by Calvin and seen clearly in the Heidelberg Catechism, calls the church to express our gratitude through obedience and joy in the law of God. In the RCA Liturgy of 1966, the Ten Commandments or the Summary of the Law is found following the Assurance of Pardon, after the Confession of Sin. Ethical behavior is inspired by our gratitude for grace, our joy at our justification, and our expectation of a kingdom that is fully not yet come.

While we are profoundly moved by this faithful and gracious participation in the life of the sacrament, John Calvin reminds us again and again that the presence of the risen Christ in our midst as we eat and drink together remains a profound mystery. He exclaims:

Now, if anyone should ask me how this takes place, I shall not be ashamed to confess that it is a secret too lofty for either my mind to comprehend or my words to declare. And to speak more plainly, I rather experience than understand it.[12]

11   Oscar Cullman and F. J. Leenhardt, *Essays on the Lord's Supper,* (Richmond, Virginia: John Knox Press, 1958), 8.
12   The Library of Christian Classics, Volume XXI: *Calvin: Institutes of the Christian Religion* (Philadelphia: The Westminster Press, 1973), IV, xvii.32, 1403f.

Calvin encourages us to participate in sacraments that are mysterious and in an ethical life that finds its inspiration in gratitude and joy. For Reformed Christians, the Sacrament of the Lord's Supper finds its locus in sacramental actions rather than sacramental objects. We are far more interested in what happens *at* the table rather than *on* the table. We are far more interested in a community "eating and drinking" together at the Lord's Table, rather than holding and reserving the sacramental objects of bread and cup. The idea of sacramental actions giving direction and inspiration to ethical actions is a natural way for us to reflect about liturgy and the public life. In addition, while the sacraments may feel to many as the "property" of the covenantal community, they are at their very heart meant to feed the world and wash it clean. The goal of the sacraments is to redeem public life through very personal, but public, rituals of justice.

It was Sara Miles, in her book *Take this Bread: A Radical Conversion,* who came to Christ through the Eucharistic table from a land far from the church and the presence of God. She writes:

> The first time I came to the Table at St. Gregory's, I was a hungry stranger. Each week since then, I've shown up—undeserving and needy—and each week, someone's hands have broken bread and brought me into communion.
>
> Because of how I've been welcomed and fed at the Eucharist, I see starting a food pantry at church not as an act of "outreach" but one of gratitude. To feed others means acknowledging our own hunger and at the same time acknowledging the amazing abundance we're fed with by God. At St. Gregory's, we do it now on Sundays, standing in a circle with saints dancing bright above us. I believe we can do it one more time each week- gathered around the Table under those same icons, handing plastic bags full of macaroni and peanut butter to strangers, in remembrance of him.[13]

One temptation that must be resisted in a theology that focuses on sacramental actions rather than objects is that it may demean and ultimately dismisses the material world in favor of the spiritual one. As an example of this concern, I have often asked seminarians to talk about what happens to the communion elements following the Supper. Almost inevitably they look somewhat embarrassed. Bread and wine are thrown away or left for the birds or carried home to be disposed of in

---

[13]   Sara Miles, *take this bread*, (New York: Ballantine Books, 2007), 110.

a more private place and time. Once the sacramental meal and actions are finished, the sacramental objects of bread and wine appear to lose all significance. This is a pastoral and liturgical quandary that should not be ignored.

The Genesis story declares the created, material world to be good, and so, from the very first moment, the material world is received as a gift from a gracious God. The incarnational story declares that Christ, flesh of our flesh and bone of our bone, has taken on the created, material world and sanctified it with his presence and ministry. And the Pentecost story declares that children of the covenant are adopted into the Body of Christ, the Spirit-formed physical community that lives out its ethical life in the world. At every juncture, the spiritual and material worlds are both expressions of God's goodness and grace. It is for that reason that I have always been taken back by Calvin's observation that God "stoops" to us in Christ and through the sacraments. No, I believe that, in God, these physical expressions of God's presence and peace have been created and sanctified for God's use. God has condescended once and for all in creation, incarnation, and church, and so the material world is part of God's world. And so we are able to follow another Calvinistic theme and be invited into the very presence of God through the work and witness of the Holy Spirit.

For my entire forty year career I have participated in teaching worship to Reformed students. I have witnessed a remarkable shift in the attitudes of seminary graduates toward worship. In the early years there was often a strong resistance to any liturgy that had been intentionally prepared and breathed the tradition of the church. In the last decade, there has been a slow but sure movement toward a greater appreciation for the mystery of worship, a higher commitment to more frequent celebration of the sacraments, and a deep concern that the liturgy lead to a very public theology and practice. Recent seminary graduates look for worship that is contextual, genuine, mysterious, and inspiring to public acts of charity and justice.

We come together in liturgy and life to perform a "joyful duty." It is a life inspired by gratitude, marked by joy, and hopeful for a time when the world will be washed and fed. *Maranatha—Even so, come, Lord Jesus.*

Published Works of John W. Coakley

Ondrea Murphy and Kathleen Hart Brumm

This is a selected list of the Reverend Doctor John Coakley's depth and breadth of intellectual inquiry, research, and scholarship.

Books

2014

Coakley, John W. *New Brunswick Theological Seminary, 1784-2014: An Illustrated History.* Grand Rapids: William B. Eerdmans, 2014.

2006

Coakley, John W. *Women, Men and Spiritual Power: Female Saints and Their Male Collaborators.* New York: Columbia University Press, 2006.

2004

Coakley, John W. and Sterk, Andrea (editors). *Readings in World Christian History: Earliest Christianity to 1453.* Maryknoll: Orbis Books, 2004.

2002

Coakley, John W. (editor) *Concord Makes Strength: Essays in Reformed Ecumenism.* Grand Rapids: Eerdmans, 2002.

1999

House, Renée S. and Coakley, John W. (editors). *Patterns and Portraits: Women in the History of the Reformed Church in America.* Grand Rapids: Eerdmans, 1999.

1994

Matter, E. Ann and Coakley, John W. (editors). *Creative Women in Medieval and Early Modern Italy: a Religious and Artistic Renaissance.* Philadelphia: University of Pennsylvania Press, 1994.

Essays in Peer-reviewed Journals and Collections

2014

Coakley, John W. *"The Conversion of St. Francis and the Writing of Christian Biography (1228-1263)".* In Franciscan Studies 72 (2014): 27-71.

Coakley, John W. *"Afterword: Ordinary Life and the Gendered Imagination,"* In Partners in Spirit: Women, Men, and Religious Life in Germany, 1100–1500, edited by Fiona J. Griffiths and Julie Hotchin, 401-21. Turnhout, Belgium: Brepols, 2014.

2012

Coakley, John W. "John Henry Livingston (1746-1825): Interpreter of the Dutch Reformed Tradition in the Early American Republic". In *New World Clergy: Continuities and Changes among Dutch Colonial Clergy* ed. Leon van den Broeke, Hans Krabbendam, and Dirk Mouw, 295-314. Grand Rapids: Eerdmans, 2012.

2010

Coakley, John W. "Women's Textual Authority and the Collaboration of Clerics". In *Medieval Holy Women in the Christian Tradition* ed. Rosalynn Voaden and A.J. Minnis, 83-104. Turnhout, Belgium: Brepols, 2010.

2009

Coakley, John W. "Christian Holy Women and the Exercise of Religious Authority in the Medieval West." *Religion Compass* 3, no. 5 (September, 2009): 847-56.

Coakley, John W. "John Henry Livingston as Professor of Theology". In *Tools for Understanding: Essays in Honor of Donald J. Bruggink,* ed. James Hart Brumm, 189-200. Grand Rapids: Eerdmans, 2009.

2007

Coakley, John W. "Thomas of Cantimpré and Female Sanctity," In *In the Comic Mode: Medieval Communities and the Matter of Person [essays presented to Caroline Bynum]*, ed. Rachel Fulton and Bruce Holsinger, 45-55. New York: Columbia University Press, 2007.

2005

Coakley, John W. *"The Reformed Church in America as a National Church,"* In Church, Identity, and Change: Denominational Structures in Unsettled Times, ed. David Roozen and James Nieman, 400-09. Grand Rapids: Eerdmans, 2005.

1999

Coakley, John W. *"A Marriage and Its Observer: Christine of Stommeln, the Heavenly Bridegroom, and Friar Peter of Dacia."* In Gendered Voices: Medieval Saints and Their Interpreters, ed. Catherine M. Mooney. Philadelphia: University of Pennsylvania Press, 1999.

Coakley, John W. *"Women in the History of the Reformed Church in America,"* In Patterns and Portraits: Women in the History of the Reformed Church in America, ed. Renee S. House and John Coakley (1999; see above), 1-16.

1994

Coakley, John W. "Introduction: Women's Self-Expression in Religious Context," In *Creative Women in Medieval and Early Modern Italy*, ed. E. Ann Matter and John Coakley (1994; see above),. 1-16.

Coakley, John W. *"Gender, Friars and Sanctity: Mendicant Encounters with Saints, 1250-1325,"* in *Medieval Masculinities*, ed. Clare Lees, 91-110. Minneapolis: University of Minnesota Press, 1994.

1992-1993

Coakley, John W. "John Henry Livingston and the Liberty of the Conscience." *Reformed Review* 45 (1992): 119-135. Reprinted in *Clarity, Conscience and Church Order* (New Brunswick: Archives of the Reformed Church in America [1993]), 4-17. http://images.rca.org/docs/archives/bcoreflections.pdf#page=4)

1991

Coakley, John W. "Gender and the Authority of Friars: The Significance of Holy Women for Thirteenth-Century Franciscans and Dominicans." *Church History* 60 (December, 1991): 445-460.

Coakley, John W. *"Friars as Confidants of Holy Women in Medieval Dominican Hagiography,"* In Images of Sainthood in Medieval Europe, ed. Renate Blumenfeld-Kosinski and Timea Szell, 226-46. Ithaca: Cornell University Press, 1991.

Articles in Non-Peer-Reviewed Periodicals and Collections

2015

Coakley, John W. "The New Brunswick Theological Seminary's Connection to Rutgers," *Rutgers Robert Wood Johnson Medical School Retired Faculty Association Newsletter* 8, no. 3 (September 2015): 1-7.

Coakley, John W. "The Seminary Years of the Missionaries Horace G. Underwood and Henry G. Appenzeller." *Korean Presbyterian Journal of Theology* 47 (2015): 59-82.

2009

Coakley, John W. "Church Review: The Reformed Church of Highland Park, New Jersey." *Perspectives: A Journal of Reformed Thought* 24, no. 10 (December 2009): 18-19.

2003

Coakley, John W., ed. "The Latin Hymn," in *O Sacred Head: A Passiontide Hymn*, 1-3. Oxford: Jericho Press, 2003.

2001

Coakley, John W. "Critical Christianity: Remembering John W. Beardslee III. A sermon preached at the Memorial Service for the Rev. Dr. John W. Beardslee III, April 29, 2001." *New Brunswick Theological Seminary Update*, Fall/Winter 2001: 6.

1999

Coakley, John W. "On the Unconditional." [1999 baccalaureate sermon, New Brunswick Seminary] *New Brunswick Theological Seminary Update*, Summer/Fall 1999: 1, 4, 9.

1989

Coakley, John W. "Women in Christian Tradition." In *The Church Herald* 46/6 (1989): 24-26.
1988

Coakley, John W. "The Meanings of 'Spirituality'." In *Perspectives: A Journal of Reformed Thought* 3, no. 10 (1988): 4-7.

1985

Coakley, John W. "Anniversary Reflections on the Repression of the Huguenots." In *New Brunswick Seminary Newsletter* 14, no. 8 (1985): 5-6.

Articles in Reference Works

2015

Coakley, John W. "John 17:14-19: Theological Perspective," and "John 17:20-26: Theological Perspective." In *Feasting on the Gospels—John, vol. 2*, ed. E. Elizabeth Johnson and Cynthia Jarvis. Louisville: Westminster/John Knox Press, 2015.

2013

Coakley, John W. "Matthew 8:18-22: Theological Perspective," "Matthew 8:23-27: Theological Perspective," and "Matthew 8:28-9:1: Theological Perspective." In *Feasting on the Gospels—Matthew, vol. 1*, ed. E. Elizabeth Johnson and Cynthia Jarvis, 200-04, 206-10, 212-16. Louisville: Westminster/John Knox Press, 2013.

2009

Coakley, John W. "Colossians 3:12-17: Theological Perspective"; "Ephesians 1:3-14: Theological Perspective"; and "Ephesians 3:1-12: Theological Perspective". In *Feasting on the Word: Preaching the Revised Common Lectionary, Year C, volume 1*, ed. David L. Bartlett and Barbara Brown Taylor, 158-62, 184-86, 206-210. Louisville: Westminster/John Knox Press, 2009.

2008

Coakley, John Wayland. "Advent through Transfiguration." In *Feasting on the Word : Preaching the Revised Common Lectionary*, edited by David L. Bartlett and Barbara Brown Taylor. Louisville, KY: Westminster John Knox Press, 2008.

2005

Coakley, John W. "Christendom;" "Investiture Controversy;" "Middle Ages;" and "Renaissance". In *Encyclopedia of Christianity*, ed. John Bowden, 209-11, 644-45, 740-43, 1026-29. New York: Oxford University Press, 2005.

2004

Coakley, John W. "New Brunswick Theological Seminary," in *The Encyclopedia of New Jersey*. New Brunswick: Rutgers University Press, 2004.

2000

Coakley, John W. "Dévotion, littérature de," and "Direction spirituelle," in *Dictionnaire encyclopédique du moyen âge chrétienne*, edited by André Vauchez, 1:458-59, 468. Paris: Éditions du Cerf, 1997. English version: *Encyclopedia of the Middle Ages*. Cambridge: Clark & Co., 2000.

Books Reviewed

2015

Coakley, John W., Review of *"Legenda Maior sive Legenda Admirabilis Virginis Catherine de Senis: Edizione critica,"* by Raimondo da Capua, ed. Silvia Nocentini. In *Speculum* 90 (2015)

2013

Coakley, John W., Review of *"The Poor and the Perfect: The Rise of Learning in the Franciscan Order, 1209-1310"*, by Neslihan Senocak. In *Church History* 82 (2013): 962-64.

Coakley, John W., Review of *"Contested Canonizations: The Last Medieval Saints"*, by Ronald Finucane. In *Journal of Ecclesiastical History* 64 (2013): 163.

2012

Coakley, John W., Review of *"Sensual Encounters: Monastic Women and Spirituality in Medieval Germany"*, by Erika Lauren Lindgren. In *Speculum* 87 (2012):251-52.

2011

Coakley, John W., Review of *"Hildegard of Bingen and her Gospel Homilies: Speaking New Mysteries"*, by Beverly Mayne Kienzle . In *Church History* 80 (2011): 151-53.

Coakley, John W., Review of *"Savonarola's Women: Visions and Reform in Renaissance Italy"*, by Tamar Herzig . In *Speculum* 86 (2011): 215-17.

2010

Coakley, John W., Review of *"The Female Mystic"*, by Andrea Janelle Dickens . In *Catholic Historical Review* 96 (2010): 776-77.

2007

Coakley, John W., Review of *"Discerning Spirits: Divine and Demonic Possession in the Middle Ages"*, by Nancy Caciola . In *Magic, Ritual and Witchcraft* 2 (2007): 79-81.

2006

Coakley, John W., Review of *"God and the Goddesses: Vision, Poetry, and Belief in the Middle Ages"*, by Barbara Newman. In *Journal of Religion* 86 (2006): 113-14.

2005

Coakley, John W., Review of *"Dominican Penitent Women"* edited by Maiju Lehmijoki-Gardner. In *Catholic Historical Review* 91 (2005): 793-94.

Coakley, John W., Review of Dyan Elliott, *"Proving Woman: Female Spirituality and Inquisitional Culture in the Later Middle Ages"*. In *American Historical Review* 110 (2005): 540-41.

2004

Coakley, John W., Review of *"The Poverty of Riches: St Francis of Assisi Reconsidered"* by Kenneth Baxter Wolf, In *Speculum* 79 (2004): 861-2.

2002

Coakley, John W., Review of *"From Mission to Church: the Reformed Church in America Mission to India"* by Eugene P. Heideman. In *Journal of Presbyterian History* 80 (2002): 118-19.

2001

Coakley, John W., Review of "Worldly Saints: Social Interaction of Dominican Penitent Women in Italy, 1200-1500". In *Church History* 70 (2001): 566-67.

2000

Coakley, John W., Review of *"In Remembrance and Hope: The Ministry and Vision of Howard G. Hageman."* by Gregg A. Mast. In *Journal of Presbyterian History* 78 (2000): 178-79.

1999

Coakley, John W., Review of *"The Mystics of Engelthal: Writings from a Medieval Monastery."* by Leonard P. Hindsley. In *Church History* 68 (1999): 987-88.

1998

Coakley, John W., Review of *"Prophets Abroad: The Reception of Continental Holy Women in Late-Medieval England."* edited by Rosalynn Voaden. In *Church History* 67 (1998): 143-44.

1997

Coakley, John W., Review of *"A Monk's Confessions: The Memoirs of Guibert of Nogent."* ed. and tr. by Paul J. Archambault. In *Church History* 66 (1997): 329-30.

Coakley, John W., Review of *"Violence and Miracle in the Fourteenth Century: Private Grief and Public Salvation"* by Michael E. Goodich. In *Church History* 66 (1997): 100-01.

1996

Coakley, John W., Review of « *L'âge d'or des écoles de Chartres* », by Édouard Jeauneau. In *Speculum* 71 (1996): 967-68.

1994

Coakley, John W., Review of *Revelaciones, Book IV,* by Birgitta of Sweden, ed. Hans Aili. In *Speculum* 69 (1994): 1117-19.

Coakley, John W., Review of *Angelic Monks and Earthly Men: Monasticism and Its Meaning to Medieval Society.* by Ludo J.R. Milis. In *Church History* 63 (1994): 269-270.

1993

Coakley, John W., Review of *Hildegardis Bingensis Epistolarium pars Prima I-XC,* ed. Lieven van Acker. In *Speculum* 68 (1993): 1132-3.

Coakley, John W., Review of *Encyclopedia of the Early Church,* ed. by Angelo di Berardino. In *Bible Review* 9/2 (April, 1993): 13.

1992

Coakley, John W., Review of *The Guitar of God: Gender, Power and Authority in the Visionary World of Mother Juana de la Cruz (1481-1534)* by Ronald E. Surtz. In *Church History* 61 (1992): 447-448.

Coakley, John W., Review of *Alfonso of Jaén. His Life and Works with Critical Editions of the Epistola Solitarii, the Informaciones and the Epistola Servi Christi* by Arne Jönsson. In *Church History* 61 (1992): 303-304.

1991

Coakley, John W., Review of *St. Nicholas of Myra, Bari and Manhattan* by Charles W. Jones, In *Church History* 60 (1991): 429-430.

Index

Scripture Index

Name and Subject Index

Publications in the Historical Series of the Reformed Church in America

The following Historical Series publications may be ordered easily through the Wm. B. Eerdmans web site at www.eerdmans.com/

The home page has a section titled "Categories" at the upper left, under which find "series" and click it. "Sets and Series" will appear. Alphabetically, well down the page under G, click on The Historical Series of the Reformed Church in America. Titles will appear with the option of adding to cart. Books may also be ordered by hard copy or at your local bookstore.

You may also enter the following URL into your browser: http://www.eerdmans.com/Products/CategoryCenter.aspx?CategoryId=SE!HSRCA

1. *Ecumenism in the Reformed Church in America*, by Herman Harmelink III (1968)
2. *The Americanization of a Congregation*, by Elton J. Bruins (1970)
3. *Pioneers in the Arab World*, by Dorothy F. Van Ess (1974)
4. *Piety and Patriotism*, edited by James W. Van Hoeven (1976)
5. *The Dutch Reformed Church in the American Colonies*, by Gerald F. De Jong (1978)
6. *Historical Directory of the Reformed Church in America, 1628-1978*, by Peter N. VandenBerge (1978)
7. *Digest and Index of the Minutes of General Synod, 1958-1977*, by Mildred W. Schuppert (1979)
8. *Digest and Index of the Minutes of General Synod, 1906-1957*, by Mildred W. Schuppert (1982)
9. *From Strength to Strength*, by Gerald F. De Jong (1982)
10. *"B. D."*, by D. Ivan Dykstra (1982)
11. *Sharifa*, by Cornelia Dalenburg (1983)
12. *Vision From the Hill*, edited by John W. Beardslee III (1984)
13. *Two Centuries Plus*, by Howard G. Hageman (1984)
14. *Structures for Mission*, by Marvin D. Hoff (1985)

15. *The Church Speaks*, edited by James I. Cook (1985)
16. *Word and World*, edited by James W. Van Hoeven (1986)
17. *Sources of Secession: The Netherlands Hervormde Kerk on the Eve of the Dutch Immigration to the Midwest*, by Gerrit J. tenZythoff (1987)
18. *Vision for a Christian College*, by Gordon J. Van Wylen (1988)
19. *Servant Gladly*, edited by Jack D. Klunder and Russell L. Gasero (1989)
20. *Grace in the Gulf*, by Jeanette Boersma (1991)
21. *Ecumenical Testimony*, by Arie R. Brouwer (1991)
22. *The Reformed Church in China, 1842-1951*, by Gerald F. De Jong (1992)
23. *Historical Directory of the Reformed Church in America, 1628-1992*, by Russell L. Gasero (1992)
24. *Meeting Each Other in Doctrine, Liturgy, and Government*, by Daniel J. Meeter (1993)
25. *Gathered at Albany*, by Allan J. Janssen (1995)
26. *The Americanization of a Congregation*, 2nd ed., by Elton J. Bruins (1995)
27. *In Remembrance and Hope: The Ministry and Vision of Howard G. Hageman*, by Gregg A. Mast (1998)
28. *Deacons' Accounts, 1652-1674, First Dutch Reformed Church of Beverwyck/Albany*, trans. & edited by Janny Venema (1998)
29. *The Call of Africa*, by Morrill F. Swart (1998)
30. *The Arabian Mission's Story: In Search of Abraham's Other Son*, by Lewis R. Scudder III (1998)
31. *Patterns and Portraits: Women in the History of the Reformed Church in America*, edited by Renée S. House and John W. Coakley (1999)
32. *Family Quarrels in the Dutch Reformed Churches in the Nineteenth Century*, by Elton J. Bruins & Robert P. Swierenga (1999)
33. *Constitutional Theology: Notes on the* Book of Church Order *of the Reformed Church In America*, by Allan J. Janssen (2000)
34. *Raising the Dead: Sermons of Howard G. Hageman*, edited by Gregg A. Mast (2000)
35. *Equipping the Saints: The Synod of New York, 1800-2000*, edited by James Hart Brumm (2000)
36. *Forerunner of the Great Awakening*, edited by Joel R. Beeke (2000)
37. *Historical Directory of the Reformed Church in America, 1628-2000*, by Russell L. Gasero (2001)
38. *From Mission to Church: The Reformed Church in America in India*, by Eugene Heideman (2001)
39. *Our School: Calvin College and the Christian Reformed Church*, by Harry Boonstra (2001)

"Beginning with Donald Bruggink's own notion that 'history is a tool for understanding,' the dozen essays in this volume are tools for understanding four areas of his life and his fifty-five years of ministry. While all the contributors to this volume have benefited from Bruggink's friendship, teaching, and ministry, the first and last essays are by the contributors he has known longest, who had a formative role in his life"

— Eugene Heideman and I. John Hesselink.

61. *Chinese Theological Education*, edited by Marvin D. Hoff (2009) 470 pp. ISBN: 978-0-8028-6480-2

This book offers insight into the emergence of the Christian church after Mao's Cultural Revolution. While reports of Communist oppression have dominated American perceptions of church and state in China, this is an increasingly dangerous view as China changes. Dr. Marvin D. Hoff, as executive director for the Foundation for Theological Education in Southeast Asia, traveled at least annually to China for the period covered by this book. The original reports of his encounters with Chinese Christians, especially those involved in theological education, are a historic record of the church's growth—and growing freedom. Interspersed with Hoff's accounts are reports of essays by Chinese and other Asian Christians. Introductory essays are provided by Charles W. Forman of Yale Divinity School, Daniel B. Hays of Calvin College, and Donald J. Bruggink of Western Theological Seminary.

62. *Liber A*, edited by Frank Sypher (2009) 442 pp. ISBN: 978-0-8028-6509-0

Liber A of the Collegiate Church archives contains detailed seventeenth-century records of the Reformed Dutch Church of the City of New York, including correspondence, texts of legal documents, and lists of names of consistory members. Especially significant are records pertaining to the granting in 1696 of the royal charter of incorporation of the Church, and records relating to donations for, and construction of the church building on Garden Street. The full Dutch texts have never before been published.

63. *Aunt Tena, Called to Serve: Journals and Letters of Tena A. Huizenga, Missionary Nurse to Nigeria*, edited by Jacob A. Nyenhuis, Robert P. Swierenga, and Lauren M. Berka (2009) 980 pp. ISBN: 978-0-8028-6515-1

When Tena Huizenga felt the call to serve as a missionary nurse to Africa, she followed that call and served seventeen years at Lupwe, Nigeria, during a pivotal era in world missions. As she ministered to the natives, she recorded her thoughts and feelings in a diary and in countless letters to family and friends--over 350 in her first year alone. Through her eyes, we see the Lupwe mission, Tena's colleagues, and the many native helpers. Aunt Tena (Nigerians called all female missionaries

"Aunt") tells this profoundly human story. Interesting in its own right, the book will also prove invaluable to historians, sociologists, and genealogists as they mine this rich resource.

The extensive letters from Tena's brother Pete offer marvelous insights into the Dutch Reformed subculture of Chicago's West Side. Because his scavenger company later evolved into Waste Management Inc., those letters are especially valuable. Pete's winsome descriptions and witty dialogue with his sister add a Chicago flavor to this book.

64. *The Practice of Piety: The Theology of the Midwestern Reformed Church in America, 1866-1966*, by Eugene P. Heideman (2009) 286 pp. ISBN: 978-0-8028-6551-9

"With the instincts of a historian and the affection of a child of the RCA, Gene Heideman has accessed both Dutch and English sources in order to introduce us to the unique theology and piety of the Midwestern section of our denomination from 1866 to 1966. Through the words of pastors, professors, and parishioners, he has fleshed out the Dutch pilgrims of the 19th century who found their roots in the Netherlands but their fruit in America. Accessing the Dutch language newspaper *De Hope*, and the writings and lectures of a century of Western Seminary professors, the history of the RCA in the Midwest has come alive. This book is a gracious and winsome invitation to its readers and other scholars to dig deeper and understand more fully the theological and ethnic heritage of those who have helped ground our past and thus form our future."

— Gregg A. Mast, president, New Brunswick Theological Seminary

65. *Freedom on the Horizon: Dutch Immigration to America, 1840 to 1940*, by Hans Krabbendam (2009) 432 pp. ISBN: 978-0-8028-6545-8

"It's been eighty years since the last comprehensive study of the Dutch immigrant experience by a Netherlands scholar—Jacob Van Hinte's magisterial *Netherlanders in America* (1928, English translation 1985). It was worth the wait! Krabbendam has a firmer grasp of American history and culture than his predecessor, who spent only seven weeks on a whirlwind tour of a half-dozen Dutch 'colonies' in 1921. Krabbendam earned an M.A. degree in the USA, is widely traveled, versed in American religious culture, and has written the definitive biography of Edward W. Box (2001). *Freedom on the Horizon* focuses on the ultimate meaning of immigration—the process by which one's inherited culture is reshaped into a new Dutch-American identity. 'Only the steeple was retained,'

Krabbendam notes in his tale of a congregation that tore down its historic church edifice in favor of a modern new one. This is a metaphor of the Dutch immigrant experience writ large, as told here in a masterful way."

— Robert D. Swierenga, Kent State University

66. *A Collegial Bishop? Classis and Presbytery at Issue*, edited by Allan Janssen and Leon Vanden Broek (2010) 176 pp. ISBN: 978-0-8028-6585-4

In *A Collegial Bishop?* classis and presbytery are considered from a cross-cultural, indeed cross-national, perspective of the inheritors of Geneva and Edinburgh in their contemporary contexts in the Netherlands, South Africa, and the United States.

"Dutch theologian A. A. van Ruler compares church order to the rafters of a church building. Church order sustains the space within which the church is met by God, where it engages in its plan with God (liturgy), and where it is used by God in its mission in and to God's world. Presbyterian church order intends to be faithful to its root in God's Word, as it is shaped around the office of elder and governed through a series of councils of the church."

Alan Janssen

— Pastor, Community Church of Glen Rock, NJ

67. *The Church Under the Cross*, by Wendell Karssen (2010) 454 pp. ISBN: 978-0-8028-6614-1

The Church Under the Cross: Mission in Asia in Times of Turmoil is the illustrated two-volume account of Wendell Paul Karsen's more than three decades of cross-cultural missionary work in East Asia.

In one sense a missionary memoir of Karsen's life and ministry in Taiwan, Hong Kong, China, and Indonesia, the work also chronicles the inspiring story of the Christian communities Karsen served—churches which struggled to grow and witness under adverse circumstances throughout years of political turbulence and social upheaval.

68. *Supporting Asian Christianity's Transition from Mission to Church: A History of the Foundation for Theological Education in Southeast Asia*, edited by Samuel C. Pearson (2010) 464 pp. ISBN: 978-0-8028-6622-6

"This volume, telling the story of how one North American ecumenical foundation learned to move from a 'missions' stance to one of 'partnership,' is at once informative, intriguing, and instructive for anyone curious about or interested in the development of contextual theological education and scholarship in China and Southeast Asia. It traces the efforts of Protestant churches and educational institutions emerging from World War II, revolution, and colonization to train an indigenous leadership and to nurture theological scholars for the political, cultural, and religious realities in which these ecclesial bodies find themselves."

— Greer Anne Wenh-In Ng, Professor Emerita, Victoria University in the University of Toronto

69. *The American Diary of Jacob Van Hinte*, edited by Peter Ester, Nella Kennedy, Earl Wm. Kennedy (2010) 210 pp. ISBN: 978-0-8028-6661-5

"This is a charming translation, scrupulously annotated, of the long-lost travel diary of Jacob Van Hinte (1889–1948), author of the monumental Netherlanders in America. Van Hinte's energetic five-week sprint in the summer of 1921 from "Dutch" Hoboken up the river by dayliner to Albany and on to the Dutch-settled towns and cities in the Midwest convinced him that the "migration to America had been a blessing" to the Dutch. But in his brief sojourn among the descendants of the immigrant generation, he also became aware of the "tales of misery" and the "noble struggles" of the settlers that will put readers of all ethnic backgrounds to wondering about their own poignant histories."

— Firth Fabend, author of Zion on the Hudson: Dutch new York and the New Jersey in the Age of Revivals

70. *A New Way of Belonging: Covenant Theology, China and the Christian Reformed Church, 1921-1951*, by Kurt Selles (2011) 288 pp. ISBN: 978-0-8028-6662-2

"As someone who spent much of my childhood on the mission field described in this book, I anticipated having my early memories refreshed by reading it. I did indeed find the book to be an accurate and thorough account of the work of the CRC China Mission as I remember it, but—more surprising—I also learned a good deal of new information. Kurt Selles has performed an important service for the history of missions by uncovering so much new information and doing such impressive research under difficult circumstances. Although the events took place more than a half-century ago, Selles has been able to retrieve a vast amount of detail. His analysis of the cross-cultural dynamics of this work is insightful. Anyone interested in the successes and failures of Christian mission should find this study interesting and informative."

— J. William Smit, professor of sociology, Calvin College, child of CRC China missionary Albert Smit

71. *Envisioning Hope College: Letters Written by Albertus C. Van Raalte to Philip Phelps, Jr., 1857-1875*, edited by Elton J. Bruins and Karen G. Schakel (2011) 556 pp. ISBN: 978-0-8028-6688-2

These letters between the colony's leader and the first president of Hope College in Holland, Michigan, are sequentially placed in historical context and richly footnoted. They offer an intimate view of Van Raalte as he seeks funding for his college from the Dutch Reformed Church in the east, as well as insights into his pioneer community in the midst of conflagration and war.

72. *Ministry Among the Maya*, by Dorothy Dickens Meyerink (Dec. 2011) 434 pp. ISBN: 978-0-8028-6744-5

Dorothy Meyerink entered her ministry among the Maya of Chiapas, Mexico, in 1956, and spent her entire service there. *Ministry Among the Maya* is an exciting account of persecution and success, relating the story of how, through the faithful witness of the laity and the early ordination of Mayan ministers, a strong, large, indigenous church was established and continues to flourish. Meyerink interweaves her personal experiences and the history of the church with reflections on the effective application of church growth principles.

73. *The Church Under the Cross, Vol. 2*, by Wendell Karsen (Dec. 2011) 802 pp. ISBN: 978-0-8028-6760-5

See volume 67.

74. *Sing to the Lord a New Song: Choirs in the Worship and Culture of the Dutch Reformed Church in America, 1785-1860*, by David M.Tripold (2012) 304 pp. ISBN: 978-0-8028-6874-9

As their privileged status evaporated in America's melting pot, the Dutch Reformed Church was forced to compete with a host of rising Protestant denominations in the New World. Survival became linked to assimilating within a new American way of life, with its own distinct language, culture, and religious practices. Gradually, organs, hymns and institutional church choirs were added to the traditional singing of the Psalter—innovations that altered the very fabric of Dutch Reformed religious life in America.

Sing to the Lord a New Song examines how choirs in particular revolutionized the Dutch Reformed Church in the nineteenth century, transforming the church's very nature in terms of worship, ecclesiastical life, institutional structures, and even social, fiscal, and moral practices. Moreover, the book examines how choirs helped break social barriers, particularly those regarding the status and role of women in the church.

Includes audio CD.

75. *Pioneers to Partners, The Reformed Church in America and Christian Mission to the Japanese,* by Gordon Laman (2012) ISBN: 978-0-8028-6965-4

Beginning with Japan's early exposure to Christianity by the very successful Roman Catholic mission to Japan in the sixteenth and seventeenth centuries, and the resultant persecution and prohibition of Christianity, Laman lays the groundwork for understanding the experience of nineteenth-century Protestant missionaries, among whom those of the Reformed Church in America were in the forefront. The early efforts of the Browns, Verbecks, Ballaghs, and Stouts, their failures and successes, are recounted within the cultural and political context of the anti-Western, anti-Christian Japan of the time.

Verbeck's service to the government helped bring about gradual change. The first Protestant church was organized with a vision for ecumenical mission, and during several promising years, churches and mission schools were organized. Reformed Church missionaries encouraged and trained Japanese leaders from the beginning, the first Japanese ministers were ordained in 1877, and the Japanese church soon exhibited a spirit of independence, ushering in an era of growing missionary/Japanese partnership.

The rise of the Japanese empire, a reinvigorated nationalism, and its progression to militarist ultranationalism brought on a renewed anti-Western, anti-Christian reaction and new challenges to both mission and church. With the outbreak of World War II, the Japanese government consolidated all Protestant churches into the Kyodan to facilitate control.

Laman continues the account of Reformed Church partners in mission in Japan in the midst of post-war devastation and subsequent social and political tensions. The ecumenical involvement and continued clarification of mutual mission finds the Reformed Church a full participant with a mature Japanese church.

76. *Transatlantic Pieties,* ed by Hans Krabbendam, Leon van den Broeke, and Dirk Mouw (2012) 359 pp. ISBN: 978-0-8028-6972-2

Transatlantic Pieties: Dutch Clergy in Colonial America explores the ways in which the lives and careers of fourteen Dutch Reformed ministers illuminate important aspects of European and American colonial society of their times. Based on primary sources, this collection reexamines some of the movers and shakers over the course of 250 years. The essays shed light on the high and low tides, the promises and disappointments, and the factors within and beyond the control of a new society in the making. The portraits humanize and contextualize the lives of these men who served not only as religious leaders and cultural mediators in colonial communities, but also as important connective tissue in the Dutch Atlantic world.

77. *Loyalty and Loss, the Reformed Church in America, 1945-1994,* by Lynn Japinga (2013) ISBN: 978-0-8028-7068-1

Offering a meticulously researched yet also deeply personal history of the Reformed Church in America throughout much of the twentieth century, Lynn Japinga's *Loyalty and Loss* will be of intense interest to the members of the RCA, reminding them of where they have come from, of the bonds that have held them together, and of the many conflicts and challenges that they have together faced and ultimately surmounted.

For those outside the RCA the questions of identity raised by this book will often sound very familiar, especially, perhaps, in its account of the church's struggle throughout recent decades to reconcile the persistently ecumenical spirit of many of its members with the desire of others within the denomination to preserve a real or imagined conservative exclusivity. Others may find the conflicts within the RCA reflective of their own experiences, especially as they relate to such issues as denominational mergers, abortion, the Viet Nam war, and women's ordination.

78. *Oepke Noordmans: Theologian of the Holy Spirit,* Karel Blei (tran. By Allan Janssen) (2013) ISBN: 978-0-8028-7085-8

Oepke Noordmans was one of the major Dutch theologians of

the twentieth century, whose recovery of a vital doctrine of the Holy Spirit placed him at the center of thought on the nature of the church and its ministry.

In this volume Karel Blei, himself a theological voice of note, has provided a lucid introduction to and summary of Noordmans's thought and contextual impact. The book also includes substantial excerpts of Noordmans's writing in translation, offering a compact representation of his work to an English-speaking audience.

79. *The Not-So-Promised Land, The Dutch in Amelia County, Virginia, 1868-1880,* by Janet Sjaarda Sheeres (2013) 248 pp. ISBN: 978-0-8028-7156-5

The sad story of a little-known, short-lived Dutch immigrant settlement.

After establishing a successful Dutch colony in Holland, Michigan, in 1847, Albertus Van Raalte turned his attention to the warmer climes of Amelia County, Virginia, where he attempted to establish a second colony. This volume by Janet Sheeres presents a carefully researched account of that colonization attempt with a thorough analysis of why it failed. Providing insights into the risks of new settlements that books on successful colonies overlook, this is the first major study of the Amelia settlement.

A well-told tale of high hopes but eventual failure, *The Not-So-Promised Land* concludes with a 73-page genealogy of everyone involved in the settlement, including their origins, marriages, births, deaths, denominations, occupations, and post-Amelia destinations.

80. *Holland Michigan, From Dutch Colony to Dynamic City* (3 volumes), by Robert P. Swierenga (2013) ISBN: 978-0-8028-7137-4

Holland Michigan: From Dutch Colony to Dynamic City is a fresh and comprehensive history of the city of Holland from its beginnings to the increasingly diverse community it is today.

The three volumes that comprise this monumental work discuss such topics as the coming of the Dutch, the Americans who chose to live among them, schools, grassroots politics, the effects of the world wars and the Great Depression, city institutions, downtown renewal, and social and cultural life in Holland. Robert Swierenga also draws attention to founder Albertus Van Raalte's particular role in forming the city—everything from planning streets to establishing churches and schools, nurturing industry, and encouraging entrepreneurs.

Lavishly illustrated with nine hundred photographs and based on meticulous research, this book offers the most detailed history of Holland, Michigan, in print.

The volume received the Historical Society of Michigan 2014 State History Award in the Books, University and Commercial Press category

81. *The Enduring Legacy of Albertus C. Van Raalte as Leader and Liaison,* edited by Jacob E. Nyenhuis and George Harinck (2013) 560 pp. ISBN: 978-0-8028-7215-9

The celebration of the bicentennial of the birth of Albertus C. Van Raalte in October 2011 provided a distinct opportunity to evaluate the enduring legacy of one of the best-known Dutch immigrants of the nineteenth century. This book of essays demonstrates his unique role not only in the narrative of the migration to America but also in the foundation of theological education for Seceders (Afgescheidenen) prior to his emigration. These essays were all presented at an international conference held in Holland, Michigan, and Ommen, Overijssel, the Netherlands, with the conference theme of "Albertus C. Van Raalte: Leader and Liaison." Three broad categories serve as the organizing principle for this book: biographical essays, thematic essays, and reception studies.

Van Raalte began to emerge as a leader within the Seceder Church (Christelijk Afgescheidene Gereformeerde Kerk) in the Netherlands, but his leadership abilities were both tested and strengthened through leading a group of Dutch citizens to the United States in 1846. In his role as leader, moreover, he served as liaison to the Reformed Protestant Dutch Church in America in the eastern United States (renamed the Reformed Church in America in 1867) to the Seceder Church in the Netherlands, and to the civil authorities in the United States, as well as between business and their employees.

These fifteen essays illuminate the many facets of this energetic, multi-talented founder of the Holland kolonie. This collection further enhances and strengthens our knowledge of both Van Raalte and his Separatist compatriots.

82. *Minutes of the Christian Reformed Church, Classical Assembly, 1857-1870, General Assembly, 1867-79, and Synodical Assembly, 1880,* edited and annotated by Janet Sjaarda Sheeres (2014) 668 pp. ISBN: 978-0-8028-7253-1

"Janet Sheeres, noted scholar of the Dutch in North America, here turns her skill to the early years of the Christian Reformed Church in North America. She has painstakingly researched all the individuals who attended denominational leadership gatherings and the issues discussed and debated at these meetings. Her extensive annotations to a new translation of the minutes provides unprecedented and cogent insight into the early years of the denomination and the larger Dutch trans-Appalachian immigration of the nineteenth century. The annotations reflect Sheeres's characteristically detailed research in both Dutch and English. Scholars of immigration, religion, Dutch-American immigrants, and the Christian Reformed Church will benefit from data in this book, and the appendix of biographical data will be invaluable to those interested in family research."

— Richard Harms, archivist of the Christian Reformed Church

83 *New Brunswick Theological Seminary: an Illustrated History, 1784-2014.* John W. Coakley (2014) ISBN: 978-0-8028-7296-8

This volume marks the 230th anniversary of New Brunswick Theological Seminary and the reconfiguring of its campus by retelling the school's history in text and pictures. John Coakley, teacher of church history at the seminary for thirty years, examines how the mission of the school has evolved over the course of the seminary's history, focusing on its changing relationship to the community of faith it has served in preparing men and women for ministry.

In four chapters representing four significant eras in the seminary's history, Coakley traces the relationship between the seminary in New Brunswick and the Reformed Church in America, showing that both the seminary and the RCA have changed dramatically over the years but have never lost each other along the way.

84. *Hendrik P. Scholte: His Legacy in the Netherlands and in America.* Eugene P. Heideman (2015) 314 pp. ISBN: 978-0-8028-7352-1

This book offers a careful contextual theological analysis of a nineteenth-century schismatic with twenty-first-century ecumenical intent.

Hendrik P. Scholte (1803-1868) was the intellectual leader and catalyst of a separation from the Nederlandse Hervormde Kerk. Leaving the state church meant being separated from its deacon's funds, conflict with the laws of the state, and social ostracism. Due to poverty, Scholte emigrated with a group that settled Pella, Iowa. Schismatic tendencies continued in this and other nineteenth-century Dutch settlements with the most notable division being between those who joined the

Reformed Church in America and those who became the Christian Reformed Church in North America.

As Heideman says: "Although this book concentrates on what happened in the past, it is written with the hope that knowledge of the past will contribute to the faithfulness and unity of the church in the future."

85. *Liber A:1628-1700 of the Collegiate Churches of New York, Part 2,* translated, annotated, and edited by Frank J. Sypher, Jr. (2015) 911 pp. ISBN: 978-0-8028-7341-5

See volume 62.

86. *KEMP: The Story of John R. and Mabel Kempers, Founders of the Reformed Church in America Mission in Chiapas, Mexico,* by Pablo A. Deiros. 558 pp. ISBN 978-0-8028-7354-5

"This faithful story reveals God's power to transform thousands of people's lives through a couple committed to spreading God's message of love and devotion. The Kempers' commitment to their slogan "Chiapas para Cristo" was evidenced in all that they did. They were our surrogate parents, mission colleagues, and mentors."

— Sam and Helen Hofman, career RCA missionaries in Chiapas, Mexico.

"Employing a creative narrative style, Pablo Deiros has fashioned a fully documented biography into a compelling story of the lives and witness of John and Mabel Kempers. *Kemp* is a must read for those who are interested in the intersection of the Christian Church and the social revolution in Mexico during the twentieth century, the struggles of Maya cultures in Chiapas, and the transformative impact of the gospel of Jesus Christ among the people of Chiapas. *Kemp* is an inspiring and engaging history."

— Dennis N. Voskuil, Director, Van Raalte Institute